STUDENT'S SOLUTIONS MANUAL

TO ACCOMPANY
JAMES T. McCLAVE AND P. GEORGE BENSON'S

A FIRST COURSE IN BUSINESS STATISTICS

FIFTH
EDITION

NANCY S. BOUDREAU
Bowling Green State University

DELLEN PUBLISHING COMPANY
an imprint of
MACMILLAN PUBLISHING COMPANY
NEW YORK

MAXWELL MACMILLAN CANADA
TORONTO

Copyright © 1992 by Dellen Publishing company,
an imprint of Macmillan Publishing Company

Printed in the United States of America

Macmillan Publishing Company
866 Third Avenue, New York, New York 10022

Macmillan Publishing Company is
part of the Maxwell Communication
Group of Companies.

Maxwell Macmillan Canada, Inc.
1200 Eglinton Avenue East
Suite 200
Don Mills, Ontario M3C 3N1

Permissions: Dellen Publishing Company
                400 Pacific Avenue
                San Francisco, California 94133

Orders: Dellen Publishing Company
                c/o Macmillan Publishing Company
                Front and Brown Streets
                Riverside, New Jersey 08075

ISBN: 0-02-312713-9

Printing: 1 2 3 4 5 6   Year: 2 3 4 5 6

Preface

This solutions manual is designed to accompany the text *A First Course in Business Statistics*, Fifth Edition, by James T. McClave and P. George Benson (Dellen Publishing Company, 1992). It provides answers to most odd-numbered exercises for each chapter in the text. Other methods of solution may also be appropriate; however, the author has presented one that she believes to be most instructive to the beginning statistics student. The student should first attempt to solve the assigned exercises without help from this manual. Then, if unsuccessful, the solution in the manual will clarify points necessary to the solution. The student who successfully solves an exercise should still refer to the manual's solution. Many points are clarified and expanded upon to provide maximum insight into and benefit from each exercise.

Instructors will also benefit from the use of this manual. It will save time in preparing presentations of the solutions and possibly provide another point of view regarding their meaning.

Some of the exercises are subjective in nature and thus omitted from the Answer Key at the end of *A First Course In Business Statistics*, Fifth Edition. The subjective decisions regarding these exercises have been made and are explained by the author. Solutions based on these decisions are presented; the solution to this type of exercise is often most instructive. When an alternative interpretation of an exercise may occur, the author has often addressed it and given justification for the approach taken.

I would like to thank Brenda Dobson for her assistance and for typing this work.

Nancy S. Boudreau
Bowling Green State University
Bowling Green, Ohio

Contents

WHAT IS STATISTICS?

1.1 Descriptive statistics utilizes numerical and graphical methods to look for patterns, to summarize, and to present the information in a set of data. Inferential statistics utilizes sample data to make estimates, decisions, predictions, or other generalizations about a larger set of data.

1.3 A population is a set of existing units such as people, objects, transactions, or events. A variable is a characteristic or property of an individual population unit such as height of a person, time of a reflex, amount of a transaction, etc.

1.5 An inference without a measure of reliability is nothing more than a guess. A measure of reliability separates statistical inference from fortune telling or guessing. Reliability gives a measure of how confident one is that the inference is correct.

1.7 a. The population of interest is all the students in the class. The variable of interest is the GPA of a student in the class.

b. Since the population of interest is all the students in the class and you obtained the GPA of every member of the class, this set of data would be a census.

c. Assuming the class had more than 10 students in it, the set of 10 GPAs would represent a sample. The set of ten students is only a subset of the entire class.

d. This average would have 100% reliability as an "estimate" of the class average, since it is the average of interest.

e. The average GPA of 10 members of the class will not necessarily be the same as the average GPA of the entire class. The reliability of the estimate will depend on how large the class is and how representative the sample is of the entire population.

1.9 a. The population of interest is all citizens of the United States.

b. The variable of interest is the view of each citizen as to whether the President is doing a good or bad job. It is nonnumerical.

c. The sample is the 2000 individuals selected for the poll.

d. The inference of interest is to estimate the proportion of all citizens who believe the President is doing a good job.

1.11 a. There are two populations of interest to House. The first is the set of all trainees who have or will receive in the future the revised program. The second is the set of all trainees who have or will receive in the future the old program.

b. The variable he measured was the number of absences for each trainee in the course.

c. The first sample was the collection of 51 trainees who received the revised program. The second sample was the collection of 49 trainees who received the old program.

d. House concluded that the number of absences per person in the trainee group receiving the revised program was significantly less than that for the group trained under the old policies.

1.13 a. The population of interest is the set of 497 corporations listed on the New York Stock Exchange who acquired control of the assets of another firm that resulted in the listing of the acquired firms' stock during the period from 1958 - 1980.

b. The variable of interest is the change in the value of the holdings of the bidder firm's bondholders.

c. The sample is the set of 38 corporations selected.

d. Based on the information obtained from the 38 firms, one might want to estimate the proportion of all firms whose value of the holdings increased as a result of the merger. One might also want to estimate the average change in the value of the holdings as a result of the merger.

1.15 a. The population of interest is the collection of all department store executives.

b. Two variables are measured. The first is the job satisfaction of the executives and the second is the "Machiavellian" rating of each executive.

c. The sample is the collection of the 218 department store executives selected for the study.

d. The authors concluded that those executives with higher job satisfaction scores are likely to have a lower "Mach" rating.

1.17 a. The population of interest is all RV owners in the United States. The variables of interest are the preferences with respect to the features of a portable generator (e.g., size, manual or electric start, etc.). The sample is the collection of 1052 RV owners who returned the questionnaire. The inference of interest is to generalize the preferences of the 1052 sampled RV owners to the population of all RV owner preferences on the features of a portable generator. Specifically, the sample results will be used to decide what features should be included on a portable generator by estimating the proportion that like each feature suggested on the questionnaires.

b. One factor that may affect the reliability of inferences is the group of RV owners who return the questionnaire. Often, the people who return questionnaires have very strong opinions about the items on the questionnaire and may not be representative of the population in general. Another factor may be those receiving the questionnaire may no longer be RV owners.

1.19 a. The process of interest is the monitoring well for a coal-fired power plant in Miami, Florida. This is a process because it "generates" water quality over time.

b. The variables of interest are the levels of certain water quality parameters.

c. The sample is the collection of water samples taken from the monitoring well each quarter.

d. Based on the water quality parameters from the sample, the DER determines whether the water quality meets the State's guidelines.

e. When the water samples are taken may influence the reliability of the inference. If the water sample is taken when the plant is shut down or when the plant is running on low capacity the results may be quite different than when the plant is running at full capacity. The time of day the water samples are taken may also influence the results. Different operations may take place in the plant at different times during the day that may influence the quality of the water.

CHAPTER 2

GRAPHICAL DESCRIPTIONS OF DATA

2.1   a.   Nominal data are measurements that simply classify the units of the
           sample or population into categories. These categories cannot be
           ranked. Ordinal data are measurements that enable the units of the
           sample or population to be ordered or ranked with respect to the
           variable of interest.

      b.   Interval data are measurements that enable the determination of the
           differential (how much more or less) of the characteristic being
           measured between one unit of the sample or population and another.
           Interval data will always be numerical, and the numbers assigned to
           the two units can be subtracted to determine the difference between
           the units. However, the zero point is not meaningful for these
           data. Thus, these data cannot be multiplied or divided. Ratio
           data are measurements that enable the determination of the multiple
           (how many times as much) of the characteristic being measured
           between one unit of the sample or population and another. All the
           characteristics of interval data are included in ratio data. In
           addition, the zero point for ratio data is meaningful

      c.   Qualitative data have no meaningful numbers associated with them.
           Qualitative data include nominal and ordinal data. Quantitative
           data have meaningful numbers associated with them. Quantitative
           data include interval and ratio data.

2.3   The data consisting of the classifications A, B, C, and D are qualita-
      tive. These data are nominal and thus are qualitative. After the data
      are input as 1, 2, 3, and 4, they are still nominal and thus qualita-
      tive. The only difference between the two data sets are the names of
      the categories. The numbers associated with the four groups are
      meaningless.

2.5   a.   Nominal; possible brands are "Guess," "Levis," "Lee," etc., each of
           which represents a nonranked category.

      b.   Ratio; the number of hours of sports programming carried in a
           typical week is measured on a numerical scale where the zero point
           has meaning. Ten hours of sports programming is five times as much
           as two hours of sports programming.

c. Ratio; the percentage of their workdays spent in meetings is measured on a numerical scale where the zero point has meaning. Forty percent of workdays spent in meetings is twice as much as twenty percent.

d. Ratio; the number of long distance telephone calls is measured on a numerical scale where the zero point has meaning. Twenty phone calls is four times as many as five phone calls.

e. Interval; SAT scores are measured on a numerical scale where the zero point has no meaning. A score of 500 is not twice as good as a score of 250.

2.7 a. Nominal; brand of stereo speaker would be measured using nonranked categories.

b. Ratio; loss (in dollars) is measured on a numerical scale where the zero point has meaning. A loss of $600 is three times as much as a loss of $200.

c. Nominal; color is measured using nonranked categories.

d. Ordinal; ranking of football teams orders the teams, but does not indicate how much better one team is than another.

2.9 The frequency for a category is the total number of measurements that fall in the category. The relative frequency for a category is the proportion of the total number of measurements that fall in the category. The relative frequency is found by dividing the number of measurements in a category by the total number of measurements.

2.11 a. The defects are classified into four categories. Thus, the data are nominal.

b. The frequency of Type C defectives is the total number of Type C defectives, which is 6. The relative frequency is the frequency divided by the total number of chips, which is 6/1000 = .006.

c.

CATEGORY	FREQUENCY	RELATIVE FREQUENCY	
A	3	3/1000 =	.003
B	21	21/1000 =	.021
C	6	6/1000 =	.006
D	34	34/1000 =	.034
No Defect	936	936/1000 =	.936
Total	1000		1.000

The relative frequencies add to 1.0.

The frequency bar chart is constructed by placing the type of defect on the horizontal axis and the frequency on the vertical axis.

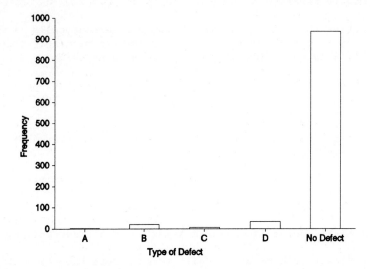

The relative frequency bar chart is constructed by placing the type of defect on the horizontal axis and the relative frequency on the vertical axis.

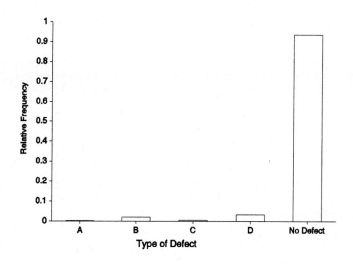

CHAPTER 2

d. The frequency of Type C defectives among the defective chips is the total number of chips with the Type C defect, which is 6. The relative frequency of the Type C defectives among the defective chips is the frequency divided by the total number of defectives and is 6/64 = .094.

e.

CATEGORY	FREQUENCY	RELATIVE FREQUENCY
A	3	3/64 = .047
B	21	21/64 = .328
C	6	6/64 = .094
D	34	34/64 = .531
Total	64	1.000

The relative frequencies add to 1.0.

The frequency bar chart is constructed by placing the type of defect on the horizontal axis and the frequency on the vertical axis.

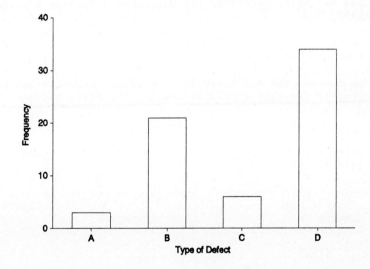

The relative frequency bar chart is constructed by placing the type of defect on the horizontal axis and the relative frequency on the vertical axis.

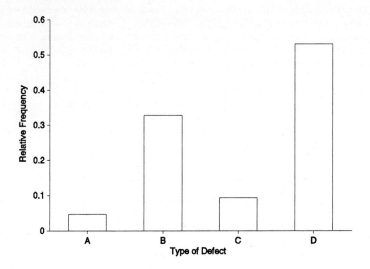

2.13 a. The bar chart describes the cigarette sales for six companies in 1985.

b. The Philip Morris Company sold the most cigarettes; approximately 211.8 billion.

c. To convert the bar chart to a relative frequency bar chart, we must compute the sample size by summing the sales for each company.

$$n = 211.8 + 189.7 + 69.1 + 48.6 + 43.9 + 29.8 = 592.9$$

Calculate the relative frequencies for each company by dividing the sales by n, f_i/n.

COMPANY	FREQUENCY	RELATIVE FREQUENCY f_i/n
Philip Morris	211.8	.36
Reynolds	189.7	.32
Brown & Williamson	69.1	.12
Lorillard	48.6	.08
American	43.9	.07
Liggett	29.8	.05
	592.9	1.00

The relative frequency bar chart is constructed by placing the company on the vertical axis and the relative frequency on the horizontal axis.

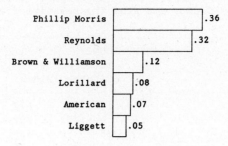

Phillip Morris .36
Reynolds .32
Brown & Williamson .12
Lorillard .08
American .07
Liggett .05

2.15 a. A frequency bar chart is constructed by placing the cities in
         Ramsey County on the horizontal axis and the frequencies on the
         vertical axis. The frequencies represent the number of apartments
         converted to condominiums.

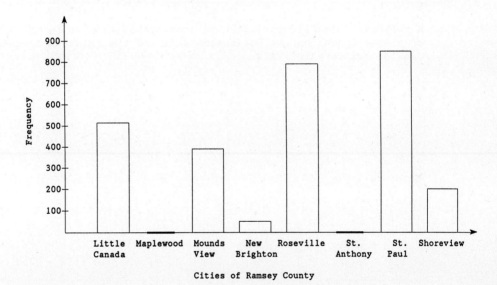

b. First we need to compute the total number of condominiums in each
    city of Ramsey County and find the relative frequencies.

City	RAMSEY COUNTY Total Number of Condominiums	Relative Frequency f_i/n
Little Canada	511 + 101 = 612	612/3723 = .164
Maplewood	0 + 252 = 252	.068
Mounds View	385 + 0 = 385	.103
New Brighton	54 + 0 = 54	.015
Roseville	767 + 30 = 797	.214
St. Anthony	0 + 148 = 148	.040
St. Paul	832 + 443 = 1275	.342
Shoreview	192 + 8 = 200	.054
	n = 3723	1.000

A relative frequency bar chart is constructed by placing the cities
of Ramsey County on the horizontal axis and the relative frequencies on the vertical axis.

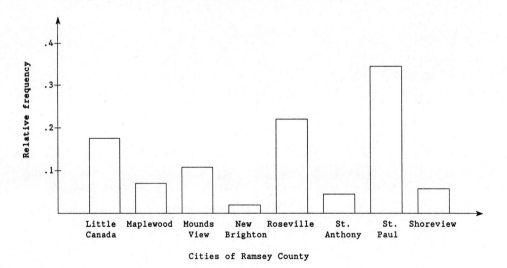

Cities of Ramsey County

Now we need to compute the total number of condominiums in each
city of Dakota County and find the relative frequencies.

City	DAKOTA COUNTY Total Number of Condominiums	Relative Frequency f_i/n
Burnsville	409 + 135 = 544	544/1213 = .4485
Eagan	8 + 128 = 136	.1121
Farmington	0 + 36 = 36	.0297
Inver Grove Heights	0 + 84 = 84	.0692
Lilydale	0 + 139 = 139	.1146
Mendota Heights	0 + 200 = 200	.1649
West St. Paul	66 + 8 = 74	.0610
	n = 1213	1.0000

A relative frequency bar chart is constructed by placing the cities
of Dakota County on the horizontal axis and the relative frequencies on the vertical axis.

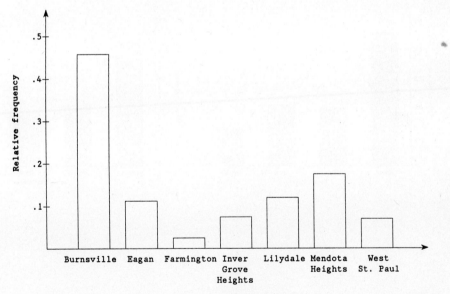

Cities of Dakota County

c. By referring the bar charts in part (b):

In Ramsey County, St. Paul had the largest share of the county's
condominiums (1275 out of 3723).

In Dakota County, Burnsville had the largest share of the county's condominiums (544 out of 1213).

2.17 a. To construct the relative frequency bar charts, we must first calculate the relative frequencies for barrels added and barrels withdrawn.

	BARRELS ADDED		BARRELS WITHDRAWN	
COMPANY	Frequency f_i	Relative Frequency f_i/n	Frequency f_i	Relative Frequency f_i/n
Exxon	124	124/270 = .46	270	270/621 = .43
Texaco	55	55/270 = .20	127	127/621 = .21
Socal	57	57/270 = .21	121	121/621 = .19
Mobil	34	34/270 = .13	103	103/621 = .17
	n = 270	270/270 = 1.00	n = 621	621/621 = 1.00

A relative frequency bar chart is constructed by placing categories along the horizontal axis and relative frequency on the vertical axis.

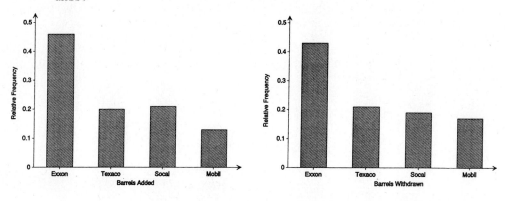

b.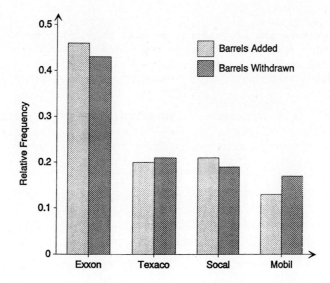

c. The bar charts show you that each company used and found oil with the same relative frequency. However, by looking at the data, you can see that each company withdrew more than double what they found.

2.19 First, find the angle corresponding to each category by multiplying the relative frequency by 360°.

CATEGORY	RELATIVE FREQUENCY	ANGLE
1	.10	.10 × 360 = 36
2	.15	.15 × 360 = 54
3	.40	.40 × 360 = 144
4	.35	.35 × 360 = 126
		Total 360

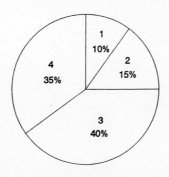

2.21 a. To construct the pie charts, we must calculate the relative
frequency and the size of the pie slice for each year.

1960

LIVING AREA	(Millions) FREQUENCY f_i	RELATIVE FREQUENCY f_i/n	SIZE OF PIE SLICE $(f_i/n) \times 360°$
Suburbs	54.9	.3062	110.232°
Cities	58.0	.3235	116.46°
Other	66.4	.3703	133.308°
	n = 179.3	1.0000	360°

1970

LIVING AREA	(Millions) FREQUENCY f_i	RELATIVE FREQUENCY f_i/n	SIZE OF PIE SLICE $(f_i/n) \times 360°$
Suburbs	75.6	.372	133.92°
Cities	63.8	.314	113.04°
Other	63.8	.314	113.04°
	n = 203.2	1.000	360°

1980

LIVING AREA	(Millions) FREQUENCY f_i	RELATIVE FREQUENCY f_i/n	SIZE OF PIE SLICE $(f_i/n) \times 360°$
Suburbs	101.5	.448	161.28°
Cities	67.9	.300	108.00°
Other	57.1	.252	90.72°
	n = 226.5	1.000	360°

The pie charts are given below.

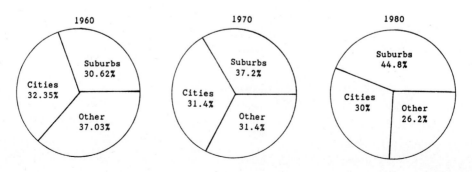

b. The percentage of people living in the cities decreased slightly from 1960 to 1980. The percentage of people living in the suburbs grew considerably (from 30.62% to 44.8%) and the percentage living in other areas decreased considerably over this period.

2.23 a. Employment in private services increased considerably from 1950 to 1983. Employment also increased in the state and local governments. Considerably large decreases were found from 1950 to 1983 in agriculture and nonagricultural goods.

b. In 1950, .86 of the jobs in the United States were nonagricultural (.14 were agricultural).

In 1983, .96 of the jobs in the United States were nonagricultural (.04 were agricultural).

c. In 1950, 1,928,000 + 4,098,000 = 6,026,000 people worked for either the federal or state government.

In 1983, 2,752,000 + 13,099,000 = 15,851,000 people worked for either the federal or state government.

2.25 a. The original data set has 1 + 3 + 5 + 7 + 4 + 3 = 23 observations.

b. For the bottom row of the stem and leaf display:

The stem is 0.
The leaves are 0, 1, and 2.
The numbers in the original data set are 0.0 × 10 = 0, 0.1 × 10 = 1, and 0.2 × 10 = 2.

2.27 Since the leaves consist of two digits, drop the second digit.

Stem	Leaf
10	5
11	0
12	1 5
13	0 1 3 4 7
14	0 9
15	3
16	1 3 6
17	0 6 6 7 8 8 8 9
18	1 3 9
19	0
20	
21	1

Key: Leaf units are tens

2.29 a. The leaf will consist of the last digit of the number and the stem
          is the first one or two digits. The stem will range from 3 to 27
          in order to include all the numbers in the data set.

Stem	Leaf
3	5
4	5 5
5	5 7
6	2 4 4 4 5
7	3 4 4 6 8
8	0 2 4 6
9	2 2 2 3 4 7
10	
11	2 6 6
12	3 3 4 8
13	
14	0 3
15	
16	
17	3
18	
19	
20	
21	4
22	
23	
24	
25	5
26	
27	7

Key: Leaf units are ones

     b. For this sample, the stem and leaf display shows that the number of
         trading days between announcement and the effective merger date is
         usually between 35 and 143. The other four data points (173, 214,
         255, and 277) look like outliers in this data set.

2.31 a. To construct the stem and leaf displays, the stem will be the tens
          digit and the leaf will be the ones digit.

Auto Parts

Stem	Leaf
0	7 8 8 9 9 9 9
1	0 0 0 1 2 2 3 3 3 4 4 5 5

Key: Leaf units are ones

Electronics

Stem	Leaf
0	8
1	0 1 2 2 2 4 4 4 5 6 9 9
2	0 2 4 7 7
3	9
4	
5	
6	
7	
8	5

Key: Leaf units are ones

b. From the stem and leaf displays, the P/E ratios are always less than 16 for the auto parts industry, while for electronics, most of the numbers are less than 27 with two numbers even larger. Therefore, the P/E ratios of firms in the electronics industry tend to be larger than the P/E ratios for the auto parts industry.

2.33 a. This is a frequency histogram because the number of observations is graphed for each interval rather than the relative frequency.

b. There are 14 measurement classes.

c. There are 49 measurements in the data set.

2.35 Since there are only 25 observations, 6 measurement classes would be sufficient.

$$\text{The class interval width} = \frac{\text{Largest measurement} - \text{Smallest measurement}}{\text{Number of intervals}}$$

$$= \frac{15.6 - .5}{6} = 2.52 \approx 3$$

The lower boundary for the first class is .5 − .05 = .45. The measurement classes and class frequencies for the data are shown in the following table.

CLASS	MEASUREMENT CLASS	FREQUENCY
1	.45 − 3.45	8
2	3.45 − 6.45	5
3	6.45 − 9.45	6
4	9.45 − 12.45	5
5	12.45 − 15.45	0
6	15.45 − 18.45	1
		n = 25

The frequency histogram for these data is shown below:

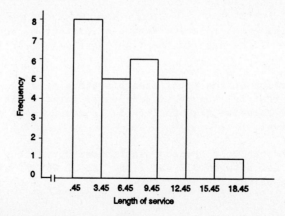

2.37 a. The measurement classes, class frequencies, and class relative
          frequencies for the data are shown in the following table.

CLASS	MEASUREMENT CLASS	CLASS FREQUENCY	CLASS RELATIVE FREQUENCY
1	46.5 – 49.5	2	2/25 = .08
2	49.5 – 52.5	2	2/25 = .08
3	52.5 – 55.5	5	5/25 = .20
4	55.5 – 58.5	8	8/25 = .32
5	58.5 – 61.5	5	5/25 = .20
6	61.5 – 64.5	3	3/25 = .12
		n = 25	1.00

The relative frequency histogram for this data is shown below.

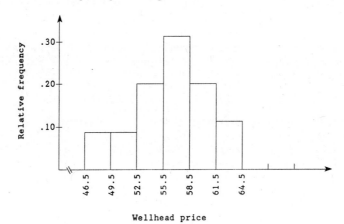

Wellhead price

b. There are 16 numbers in the data set of wellhead prices that exceed
    55¢. Therefore, the proportion of wellhead prices that exceed 55¢
    is 16/25 = .64.

    From examining the relative frequency histogram, we see that the
    proportion of the area to the right of 55¢ is (.32 + .20 + .12) =
    .64.

c. The proportion of the total area beneath a relative frequency
    histogram that falls above a particular interval is equal to the
    sum of the relative frequencies of the measurement classes above
    that interval.

2.39 a. Most of the publicly traded bonds issued by utility companies had
          asking prices between $72 and $108. About 90% of all bonds issued
          had asking prices in this range.

b. The data set contains 23 bonds with an asking price higher than
    $84. Therefore, the proportion of bonds in the sample with an
    asking price higher than $84 is 23/30 = .767.

2.41 a. In order to compare the 3 histograms, we will use the same
          measurement classes. Suppose we select 10 measurement classes to
          span the entire set of observations. The class interval width

$$= \frac{\text{Largest measurement} - \text{Smallest measurement}}{\text{Number of intervals}}$$

$$= \frac{41 - 4}{10} = 3.7 \approx 4.$$

The lower boundary for the first class is 3.5 (.5 below the
smallest measurement). The measurement classes and frequencies for
the data sets are shown below:

CLASS	MEASUREMENT CLASS	TENTH PERFORMANCE FREQUENCY	THIRTIETH PERFORMANCE FREQUENCY	FIFTIETH PERFORMANCE FREQUENCY
1	3.5 – 7.5	0	4	10
2	7.5 – 11.5	1	15	11
3	11.5 – 15.5	2	4	3
4	15.5 – 19.5	9	1	0
5	19.5 – 23.5	8	1	1
6	23.5 – 27.5	2	0	0
7	27.5 – 31.5	1	0	0
8	31.5 – 35.5	1	0	0
9	35.5 – 39.5	0	0	0
10	39.5 – 43.5	1	0	0

The frequency histogram for the tenth performance is:

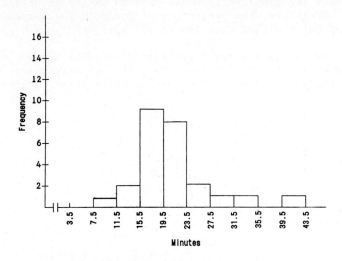

The frequency histogram for the thirtieth performance is:

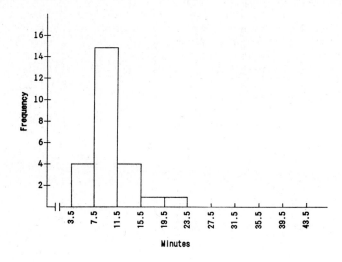

The frequency histogram for the fiftieth performance is:

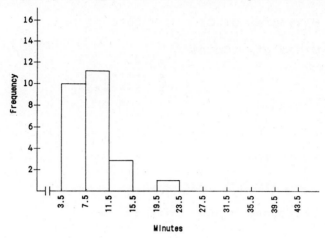

b. The histogram for the 10th performance shows a much greater spread of observations than do the other two histograms. The histogram for the 30th performance shows a shift to the left--implying shorter completion times than for the 10th performance. In addition, the histogram for the 50th performance shows an additional shift to the left compared to the histogram for the 30th performance. However, the last shift is not as great as the first shift. This agrees with statements made in the problem.

c. Using MINITAB, the histograms are:

Tenth Performance

Histogram of C1   N = 25

Midpoint	Count	
10	1	*
15	5	*****
20	13	*************
25	3	***
30	1	*
35	1	*
40	1	*

```
                 Thirtieth Performance

           Histogram of C1    N = 25

           Midpoint    Count
                6          2   **
                8          4   ****
               10          9   *********
               12          6   ******
               14          1   *
               16          2   **
               18          0
               20          1   *


                 Fiftieth Performance

           Histogram of C1    N = 25

           Midpoint    Count
                4          1   *
                6          5   *****
                8          9   *********
               10          5   *****
               12          2   **
               14          1   *
               16          1   *
               18          0
               20          1   *
```

2.43 a. The frequency is the same as the number of observations. The
          relative frequency is found by dividing the frequency by the total
          number of observations n, where n = 12 + 7 + 22 + 15 + 4 = 60. The
          cumulative frequency is found by adding the frequency of a category
          with all the frequencies in categories above it. The relative
          cumulative frequency is found by dividing the cumulative frequency
          by n = 60. All are summarized in the following table:

MEASUREMENT CLASS	FREQUENCY	RELATIVE FREQUENCY	CUMULATIVE FREQUENCY	CUMULATIVE REL. FREQ.
1.00 - 1.99	12	.200	12	.200
2.00 - 2.99	7	.117	19	.317
3.00 - 3.99	22	.367	41	.683
4.00 - 4.99	15	.250	56	.933
5.00 - 5.99	4	.067	50	1.000
TOTAL	60	1.001*		

*Failure to equal 1.00 due to rounding

b. The frequency histogram is:

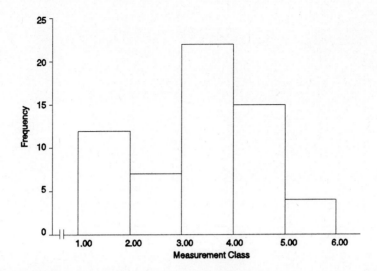

The cumulative frequency histogram is:

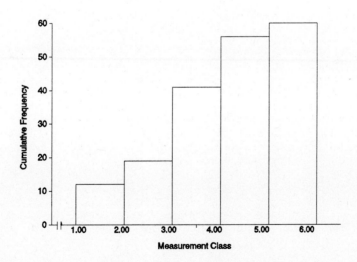

c. The relative frequency histogram is:

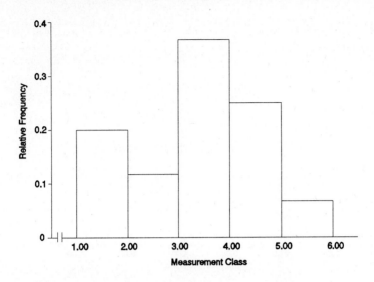

The cumulative relative frequency histogram is:

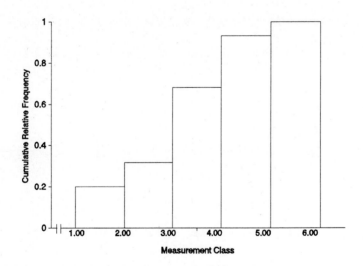

2.45 a. Since each rectangle is at least as high as the rectangle to the left and the right most rectangle is equal to 1.00, this is a cumulative relative frequency distribution.

b. There are 5 measurement classes.

c. No. Since we do not know n, we cannot determine the actual number of measurements in each class.

d. By the time the last measurement class has been reached, all (n) observations have been accounted for. Thus, the cumulative frequency for the last measurement class is n and the cumulative relative frequency is n/n = 1.

e. The relative frequency for each measurement class will be equal to the cumulative relative frequency minus the cumulative relative frequency for the measurement class just less than it. The relative frequency distribution is:

CLASS	MEASUREMENT CLASS	CUMULATIVE RELATIVE FREQUENCY	RELATIVE FREQUENCY
1	0 – 1	.08	.08
2	1 – 2	.26	.18
3	2 – 3	.72	.46
4	3 – 4	.90	.18
5	4 – 5	1.00	.10
			1.00

The relative frequency histogram is:

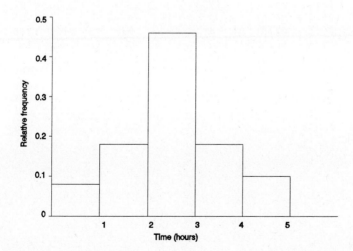

2.47   a.   To construct a cumulative relative frequency histogram for the ages
            of the buildings, we need to decide on the number of measurement
            classes. For this example, we will use 10 classes.

$$\text{The class interval width} = \frac{\text{Largest measurement} - \text{Smallest measurement}}{\text{Number of intervals}}$$

$$= \frac{82 - 3}{10} = \frac{79}{10} = 7.9$$

Rounding upward, the class width is 8.

The lower boundary for the first class is 2.5 (.5 below the
smallest measurement).

The measurement classes, class frequencies, class cumulative
frequencies, and class cumulative relative frequencies for the data
are shown in the following table.

CLASS	(in thousands) MEASUREMENT CLASS	CLASS FREQUENCY	CLASS RELATIVE FREQUENCY	CLASS CUMULATIVE RELATIVE FREQUENCY
1	2.5 – 10.5	1	1	1/79 = .013
2	10.5 – 18.5	10	11	11/79 = .139
3	18.5 – 26.5	12	23	.291
4	26.5 – 34.5	1	24	.304
5	34.5 – 42.5	1	25	.316
6	42.5 – 50.5	2	27	.342
7	50.5 – 58.5	10	37	.468
8	58.5 – 66.5	9	46	.582
9	66.5 – 74.5	18	64	.810
10	74.5 – 82.5	15	79	1.000

The cumulative relative frequency histogram for this data is shown as follows.

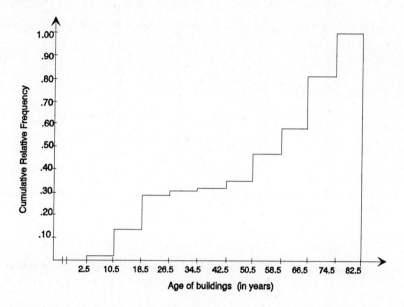

b. From the graph in part (a), approximately 34.2% of the apartment buildings are less than 50 years old. Therefore, 65.8% of the buildings are more than 50 years old.

   Also from the graph in part (a), 29.1% of the apartment buildings are less than 27 years old. Thus, at least 29.1% are less than 28 years old.

c. From the graph in part (a), 46.8% are less than 59 years old and 58.2% are less than 67 years old. Thus, approximately 50% are less than 63 years old and approximately 50% are more than 63 years old.

d. From the graph in part (a), 81% of the buildings are less than 75 years old. Since n = 79, 79 x .81 = 64 of the buildings are less than 75 years old.

2.49 Find the cumulative frequency for each of the three data sets by adding the frequency of a category to all the frequencies in categories above it. The cumulative frequencies are:

MEASUREMENT CLASS	10th PER. FREQ.	10th PER. CUM. FREQ.	30th PER. FREQ.	30th PER. CUM. FREQ.	50th PER. FREQ.	50th PER. CUM. FREQ.
3.5 – 7.5	0	0	4	4	10	10
7.5 – 11.5	1	1	15	19	11	21
11.5 – 15.5	2	3	4	23	3	24
15.5 – 19.5	9	12	1	24	0	24
19.5 – 23.5	8	20	1	25	1	25
23.5 – 27.5	2	22	0	25	0	25
27.5 – 31.5	1	23	0	25	0	25
31.5 – 35.5	1	24	0	25	0	25
35.5 – 39.5	0	24	0	25	0	25
39.5 – 43.5	1	25	0	25	0	25

The cumulative frequency histogram for the tenth performance is:

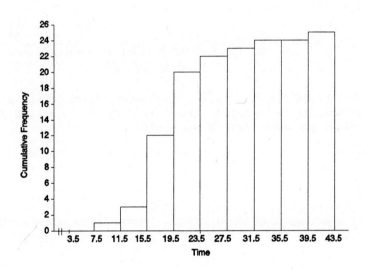

The cumulative frequency histogram for the thirtieth performance is:

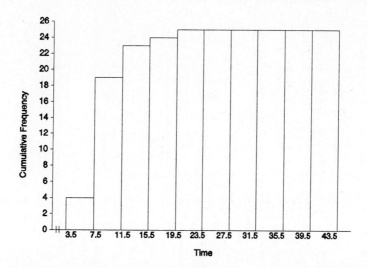

The cumulative frequency histogram for the fiftieth performance is:

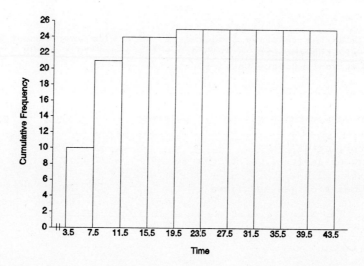

The histogram for the 10th performance shows a greater spread of observations than do the other two histograms because the graph reaches 25 further to the right than the other two. The histogram for the thirtieth performance reaches 25 again further to the right than does the graph for the fiftieth performance. This agrees with the results in Exercise 2.41.

2.51 To find relative frequencies, divide the market share by 100%. The relative frequency bar chart is:

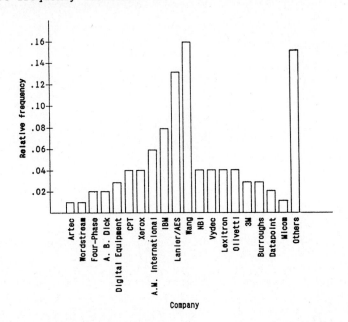

2.53 a. To find the relative frequencies, we divide each amount by the sum of all the amounts, n = 10.6 + 5.1 + 4.8 + 79.5 = 100. The relative frequency table is:

HOW YOUR NATURAL GAS DOLLAR IS SPENT	AMOUNT	RELATIVE FREQUENCY
Labor, et al.	10.6	.106
Cost of capital	5.1	.051
Taxes	4.8	.048
Payments of gas suppliers	79.5	.795
	100.0	1.000

The relative frequency bar chart is:

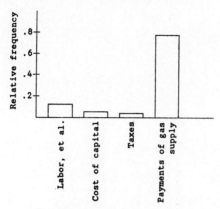

How Natural Gas Dollar Is Spent

b. Our data are actually parts of a whole, not frequencies.

c. For every dollar the customer pays for gas, NSP pays the gas
    suppliers $.795.

d. The relative frequency for taxes is .048. Thus, when a customer
    pays $80, .048 x $80 = $3.84 goes to the government in the form of
    taxes.

2.55 a. To construct relative frequencies, we divide the populations in
          each category by the total population in that year.

LOCATION	POPULATION 1984	RELATIVE FREQUENCY	POPULATION 2000	RELATIVE FREQUENCY
Africa	513	.110	851	.139
Asia	2,730	.584	3,564	.581
Europe	489	.105	511	.083
Latin America	390	.083	564	.092
North America	259	.055	302	.049
Oceania	24	.005	29	.005
USSR	272	.058	309	.050
	4,677	1.000	6,130	.999

The relative frequency bar chart for 1984 is:

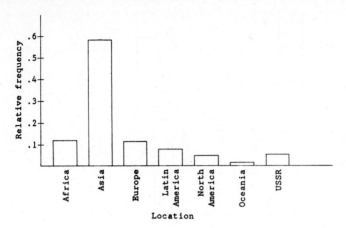

The relative frequency bar chart for 2000 is:

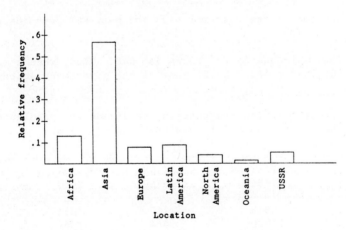

b. Proportionally, the biggest shift in population is in Africa--from
    .110 to .139 or an increase of .029. The next largest shift in
    population is in Europe--from .105 to .083 or a decrease of .022.
    All the rest of the shifts are .01 or less.

2.57 a. The 50th percentile or median is the observation that has 50% of
          the observations above it. Since 79 is odd, the median is the
          middle number or the 40th number which is 63. Thus, 50% of the
          ages exceed 63 years.

      b. There are 14 buildings more than 75 years old and there is only one
          building less than 10 years old.

2.59 First, change the percents to proportions or relative frequencies by
dividing the percents by 100%. The relative frequency bar chart is:

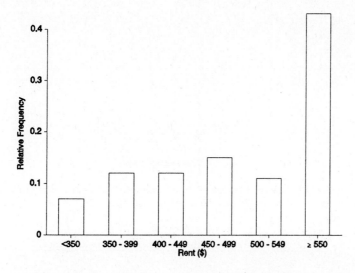

2.61 a. (1) We will use a relative frequency histogram to describe the
processing time of the marketing department. We will select 7
measurement classes. The class interval width

$$= \frac{\text{Largest measurement} - \text{Smallest measurement}}{7}$$

$$= \frac{11.0 - .1}{7} = \frac{10.9}{7} = 1.557 \approx 1.6$$

The lower boundary for the first class is .05 (.05 below the
smallest measurement). The measurement classes, frequencies
and relative frequencies are shown in the table below:

CLASS	MEASUREMENT CLASS	FREQUENCY	RELATIVE FREQUENCY
1	.05 – 1.65	7	7/50 = .14
2	1.65 – 3.25	8	.16
3	3.25 – 4.85	7	.14
4	4.85 – 6.45	17	.34
5	6.45 – 8.05	8	.16
6	8.05 – 9.65	1	.02
7	9.65 – 11.25	2	.04
		n = 50	1.00

The relative frequency histogram is:

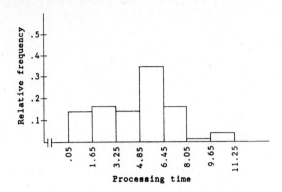

(2) We will again choose 7 measurement classes for the processing
     time of the engineering department. The class interval width
     is

$$\frac{\text{Largest measurement} - \text{Smallest measurement}}{7}$$

$$= \frac{14.4 - .4}{7} = 2 \approx 2.1$$

The lower boundary for the first class is .35 (.05 below the
smallest measurement). The measurement classes, frequencies
and relative frequencies are shown in the following table:

CLASS	MEASUREMENT CLASS	FREQUENCY	RELATIVE FREQUENCY
1	.35 - 2.45	18	18/50 = .36
2	2.45 - 4.55	7	7/50 = .14
3	4.55 - 6.65	10	.20
4	6.65 - 8.75	6	.12
5	8.75 - 10.85	2	.04
6	10.85 - 12.95	5	.10
7	12.95 - 15.05	2	.04
		n = 50	1.00

The relative frequency histogram is:

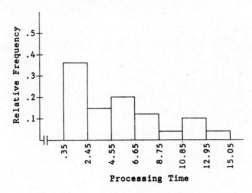

(3) We will again choose 7 measurement classes for the processing time of the accounting department. The class interval width is

$$\frac{\text{Largest measurement} - \text{Smallest measurement}}{7}$$

$$= \frac{30.0 - .1}{7} = 4.27 \approx 4.3$$

The lower boundary for the first class is .05 (.05 below the smallest measurement). The measurement classes, frequencies, and relative frequencies are shown in the following table:

CLASS	MEASUREMENT CLASS	FREQUENCY	RELATIVE FREQUENCY
1	.05 - 4.35	39	39/50 = .78
2	4.35 - 8.65	4	.08
3	8.65 - 12.95	2	.04
4	12.95 - 17.25	2	.04
5	17.25 - 21.55	1	.02
6	21.55 - 25.85	1	.02
7	25.85 - 30.15	1	.02
		n = 50	1.00

The relative frequency histogram is:

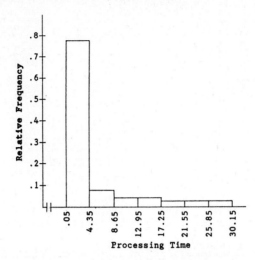

(4) First, we must sum the processing times for the 3 departments for each request number. The sums are shown in the following table:

REQUEST	TOTAL PROCESSING TIME	REQUEST	TOTAL PROCESSING TIME	REQUEST	TOTAL PROCESSING TIME	REQUEST	TOTAL PROCESSING TIME
1	13.3	13	3.4	25	10.4	37	6.1
2	5.7	14	13.6	26	3.3	38	7.4
3	7.6	15	14.6	27	8.0	39	17.7
4	20.0	16	14.4	28	6.9	40	15.4
5	6.1	17	19.4	29	17.2	41	16.4
6	1.8	18	4.7	30	10.2	42	9.5
7	13.5	19	9.4	31	16.0	43	8.1
8	13.0	20	30.2	32	11.5	44	18.2
9	15.6	21	14.9	33	23.4	45	15.3
10	10.9	22	10.7	34	14.2	46	13.9
11	8.7	23	36.2	35	14.3	47	19.9
12	14.9	24	6.5	36	24.0	48	15.4
						49	14.3
						50	19.0

We will choose 7 measurement classes for the total processing time. The class interval width is

$$\frac{\text{Largest measurement } - \text{ Smallest measurement}}{7}$$

$$= \frac{36.2 - 1.8}{7} = 4.914 \approx 5$$

The lower boundary for the first class is 1.75 (.05 below the smallest measurement). The measurement classes, frequency, and relative frequencies are shown below:

CLASS	CLASS MEASUREMENT	FREQUENCY	RELATIVE FREQUENCY
1	1.75 - 6.75	8	8/50 = .16
2	6.75 - 11.75	13	.26
3	11.75 - 16.75	18	.36
4	16.75 - 21.75	7	.14
5	21.75 - 26.75	2	.04
6	26.75 - 31.75	1	.02
7	31.75 - 36.75	1	.02
		n = 50	1.00

The relative frequency histogram is:

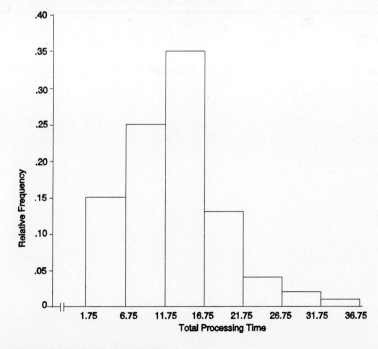

b. Of the 50 requests, 10 were lost. For each of the three
    departments, the processing times for the lost requests are
    scattered throughout the distributions. The processing time does
    not appear to be related to whether the request was lost or not.
    Arbitrarily, for the marketing department, if we set the maximum
    processing time at 6.45, we would reduce by a little less than
    half the number of lost requests while still including 78% of the
    request times. For the engineering department, if we set the
    maximum processing time at 10.85, we would reduce the number of
    lost requests by 3 while still including 86% of the data. For the
    accounting department, if we set the maximum processing time at
    12.95, we would reduce the number of lost requests by 3, while
    still including 90% of the data.

c. Using MINITAB, the stem and leaf display for the processing time
    of the engineering department is:

$$\text{Stem-and-leaf of C1} \qquad N = 50$$
$$\text{Leaf Unit} = 0.10$$

```
    7       0  4466699
   14       1  3333788
   19       2  12246
   23       3  1568
   (5)      4  24688
   22       5  233
   19       6  01239
   14       7  22379
    9       8
    9       9  66
    7      10  0
    6      11  3
    5      12  023
    2      13  0
    1      14  4
```

2.63   a.   First, we construct a cumulative frequency and cumulative relative frequency distribution for each year:

			1960			1985	
CLASS	AGE GROUP	FREQUENCY	CUM. FREQUENCY	CUM. RELATIVE FREQUENCY	FREQUENCY	CUM. FREQUENCY	CUM. RELATIVE FREQUENCY
1	Under 5	20,431	20,431	.113	18,004	18,004	.074
2	5 - 9	18,810	39,151	.217	16,822	34,826	.146
3	10 - 14	16,925	56,076	.310	17,101	51,927	.217
4	15 - 19	13,442	69,518	.385	18,587	70,514	.295
5	20 - 24	11,134	80,652	.446	21,214	91,728	.383
6	25 - 29	10,936	91,588	.507	21,892	113,620	.475
7	30 - 34	11,983	103,571	.573	20,346	133,966	.560
8	35 - 39	12,542	116,113	.643	17,762	151,728	.634
9	40 - 44	11,679	127,792	.707	14,077	165,805	.693
10	45 - 49	10,914	138,706	.768	11,652	177,457	.742
11	50 - 54	9,664	148,370	.821	10,945	188,402	.787
12	55 - 59	8,471	156,841	.868	11,342	199,744	.835
13	60 - 64	7,154	163,995	.907	10,995	210,739	.881
14	65 & Over	16,675	180,670	1.000	28,540	239,279	1.000

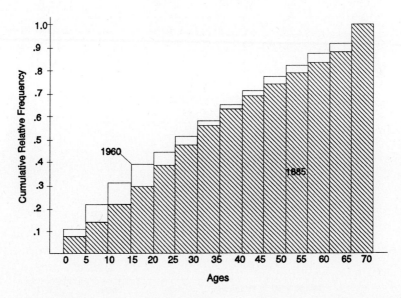

(The shaded area corresponds to the 1985 data while the nonshaded area corresponds to the 1960 data.)

b. In 1985 there is a smaller proportion of younger ages than in
    1960. The cumulative distributions are very similar in the 30-49
    age range. Thus, there is a greater proportion of 30-49 year-olds
    in 1985 than in 1960. From ages 50 to 65, again the 1960
    proportions are higher than 1985. However, there is a higher
    proportion of ages over 65 in 1985 than in 1960.

c. In 1960, those born since World War II would be 15 years old or
    less. Thus, .310 of the population consisted of baby-boomers. In
    1985, baby-boomers would be between 20 and 40 years old. The
    proportion of the population between 20 and 40 is .634 - .295
    = .339.

2.65 a. First, construct a relative frequency distribution for the
          departments.

CLASS	DEPARTMENT	FREQUENCY	RELATIVE FREQUENCY
1	Production	13	.241
2	Maintenance	31	.574
3	Sales	3	.056
4	R & D	2	.037
5	Administration	5	.093
	TOTAL	54	1.001

The Pareto diagram is:

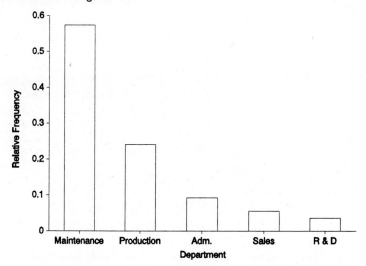

From the diagram, it is evident that the departments with the
worst safety record are Maintenance and Production.

b. First, construct a relative frequency distribution for the type of injury in the maintenance department.

CLASS	INJURY	FREQUENCY	RELATIVE FREQUENCY
1	Burn	6	.194
2	Back strain	5	.161
3	Eye damage	2	.065
4	Cuts	10	.323
5	Broken arm	2	.065
6	Broken leg	1	.032
7	Concussion	3	.097
8	Hearing loss	2	.065
	TOTAL	31	1.002

The Pareto diagram is:

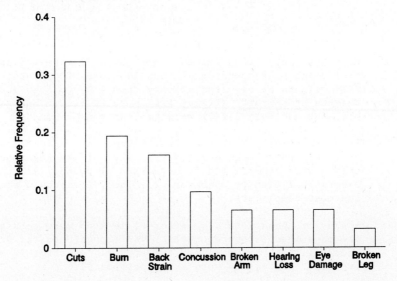

From the Pareto diagram, it is evident that cuts is the most prevalent type of injury. Burns and back strain are the next most prevalent types of injuries.

2.67   a.   The time series plot is:

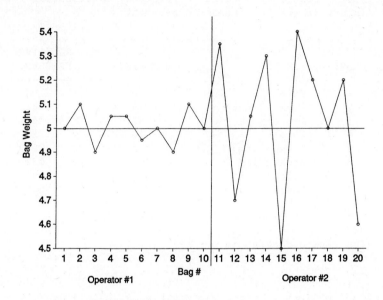

b.   From the plot, it is evident that there is more variability in the
     fill weights of operator #2 than in those of operator #1. The
     fill weights of operator #2 vary from 4.50 to 5.40 while the fill
     weights of operator #1 vary from 4.90 to 5.10. However, each
     operator had only 3 fill weights less than 5 pounds.

c.   From the plot, 30% or 6 of the 20 bags were underfilled, while 50%
     or 10 of the 20 bags were overfilled. Of the bags underfilled,
     only 3 were underfilled by more than .1 pound. All three of these
     bags were filled by operator #2. Thus, this could account for the
     customer complaints.

d.   Again, it appears that operator #1 is much more consistent filling
     the bags than is operator #2. Even though operator #2 tends to
     underfill bags by more than operator #1, operator #2 also tends to
     overfill the bags by more than operator #1.

CHAPTER
3

NUMERICAL DESCRIPTIVE MEASURES

3.1   Assume the data are a sample. The mode is the observation that occurs most frequently. For this sample, the mode is 15, which occurs 3 times.

The sample mean is:

$$\bar{x} = \frac{\sum\limits_{i=1} x_i}{n} = \frac{18 + 10 + 15 + 13 + 17 + 15 + 12 + 15 + 18 + 16 + 11}{11}$$

$$= \frac{160}{11} = 14.545$$

The median is the middle number when the data are arranged in order. The data arranged in order are: 10, 11, 12, 13, 15, 15, 15, 16, 17, 18, 18. The middle number is the 6th number, which is 15.

3.3   The median is the middle number once the data have been arranged in order. If n is even, there is not a single middle number. Thus, to compute the median, we take the average of the middle two numbers. If n is odd, there is a single middle number. The median is this middle number.

A data set with 5 measurements arranged in order is 1, 3, 5, 6, 8. The median is the middle number, which is 5.

A data set with 6 measurements arranged in order is 1, 3, 5, 5, 6, 8. the median is the average of the middle two numbers which is

$$\frac{5 + 5}{2} = \frac{10}{2} = 5$$

3.5   Quite often when dealing with opinions, guesses, and estimates, there tend to be some very high or very low answers. Since the mean is more sensitive to extreme values, the median would represent a more accurate description of the responses.

3.7   a.   We can identify the sample observations using the notation:

$$x_1 = 110, \ x_2 = 90, \ \ldots \ , \ x_{19} = 162$$

Then, the sample mean is

$$\bar{x} = \frac{\sum\limits_{i=1}^{n} x_i}{n} = \frac{110 + 90 + \ldots + 162}{19} = \frac{3420}{19} = 180$$

Since n = 19 is odd, the median will be the middle observation (x_{10}) when the data are arranged from smallest to largest.

The data arranged from smallest to largest are:

90	162
110	176
110	181
114	187
125	200
129	200
158	230
159	274
162	290
	363

The median is 162.

b.   Since the median is less than the mean, the data set is skewed to the right.

c.   No, the median will not always be an actual value in the data set. When n is odd, it will always be an actual value; but when n is even, we average the two middle values in the data set. If these two values are not the same value, the median will not be an actual value of the data set.

3.9   a.   The sample mean is

$$\bar{x} = \frac{\sum\limits_{i=1}^{n} x_i}{n} = \frac{92.5 + 63.3 + \ldots + 69.7}{20} = \frac{1400.2}{20} = 70.01$$

Since n = 20 is even, the median is the average of the middle two numbers when the data are arranged from smallest to largest.

The data arranged from smallest to largest are:

63.3	64.9	69.0	74.9
63.4	65.5	69.7	74.9
63.9	65.7	70.6	76.8
64.6	67.6	70.8	76.8
64.6	68.5	72.4	92.5

The median is $\dfrac{x_{(10)} + x_{(11)}}{2} = \dfrac{68.5 + 69.0}{2} = \dfrac{137.5}{2} = 68.75$

The mode is the measurement that occurs with the greatest frequency. In this data set, 64.6 and 76.8 are both modes. (They both occur twice.)

b. The highest price in the data set is 92.5. By eliminating this price from the data set,

the sample mean $= \bar{x} = \dfrac{\sum x}{n} = \dfrac{1307.7}{19} = 68.83$

Since $n = 19$ is odd, the median is the middle number $\left(x_{(10)}\right)$ when the data are arranged from smallest to largest.

The median $= x_{(10)} = 69.0$

The modes are 64.6 and 76.8.

By dropping the highest value in the data set, the mean and median decreased while the mode did not change.

c. By eliminating the highest two prices (92.5 and 76.8) and the lowest two prices (63.3 and 63.4), the 80% trimmed mean is

$$\bar{x} = \dfrac{\displaystyle\sum_{i=1}^{n} x_i}{n} = \dfrac{1104.2}{16} = 69.0125$$

3.11 The mean value per coupon is the total value of the coupons $\left(\displaystyle\sum_{i=1}^{n} x\right)$ divided by the number of coupons redeemed (n).

$$\bar{x} = \dfrac{\displaystyle\sum_{i=1}^{n} x_i}{n} = \dfrac{2.24 \text{ billion}}{6.49 \text{ billion}} = 0.35$$

3.13 a. The sample mean is

$$\bar{x} = \dfrac{\displaystyle\sum_{i=1}^{n} x_i}{n} = \dfrac{3342}{100} = 33.42$$

Since n = 100 is even, the median is the average of the middle two numbers when the data are arranged from smallest to largest.

The data arranged from smallest to largest are:

1	2	5	6	7	8	8	9	10	10	10
11	11	12	12	13	15	15	17	18	19	19
19	19	20	20	20	20	21	21	22	22	23
24	24	24	24	25	25	25	26	27	27	27
28	28	28	28	29	29	29	29	30	30	30
30	30	31	32	32	33	33	33	33	34	34
35	35	36	36	37	38	39	40	41	42	43
43	44	44	45	45	48	48	49	52	55	55
58	58	63	66	70	75	80	88	90	92	110
126										

The median is $\dfrac{x_{(50)} + x_{(51)}}{2} = \dfrac{29 + 29}{2} = \dfrac{58}{2} = 29$

Since the median (29) is less than the mean (33.42), the data are skewed to the right.

b. To construct a frequency histogram, we can use 10 measurement classes.

The class interval width $= \dfrac{\text{Largest measurement} - \text{Smallest measurement}}{\text{Number of intervals}}$

$$= \frac{126 - 1}{10} = \frac{125}{10} = 12.5$$

Rounding upward, the class width is 13.

The lower boundary of the first measurement class is .5 below the smallest number, or 1 - .5 = .5.

The measurement classes and class frequencies are shown in the following table.

CLASS	MEASUREMENT CLASS	CLASS FREQUENCY
1	.5 - 13.5	16
2	13.5 - 26.5	25
3	26.5 - 39.5	32
4	39.5 - 52.5	13
5	52.5 - 65.5	5
6	65.5 - 78.5	3
7	78.5 - 91.5	3
8	91.5 - 104.5	1
9	104.5 - 117.5	1
10	117.5 - 130.5	1
		n = 100

The frequency histogram for the data set is illustrated below.

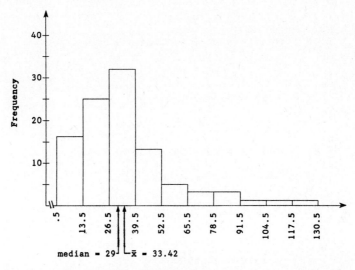

Total sales

c. If the two total sales figures ($20 and $250) were included in the data set, the median would not be affected since one of the values is below the original median and one is above it. Therefore, the median is still 29. The new mean would be

$$\bar{x} = \frac{\sum\limits_{i=1}^{n} x_i}{n} = \frac{3342 + 20 + 250}{102} = \frac{3612}{102} = 35.41$$

The new mean is higher than the original mean since the value $250 is quite a bit larger than the other sales figures in the data set.

3.15 a. $\sum\limits_{i=1}^{n} x_i = 5 + 9 + 6 + 3 + 7 = 30$

$\sum\limits_{i=1}^{n} x_i^2 = 5^2 + 9^2 + 6^2 + 3^2 + 7^2 = 200$

$\left(\sum\limits_{i=1}^{n} x_i\right)^2 = 30^2 = 900$

b. $\displaystyle\sum_{i=1}^{n} x_i = 3 + 1 + 4 + 3 + 0 + (-2) = 9$

$\displaystyle\sum_{i=1}^{n} x_i^2 = 3^2 + 1^2 + 4^2 + 3^2 + 0^2 + (-2)^2 = 39$

$\displaystyle\left(\sum_{i=1}^{n} x_i\right)^2 = 9^2 = 81$

c. $\displaystyle\sum_{i=1}^{n} x_i = 90 + 12 + 40 + 15 = 157$

$\displaystyle\sum_{i=1}^{n} x_i^2 = 90^2 + 12^2 + 40^2 + 15^2 = 10,069$

$\displaystyle\left(\sum_{i=1}^{n} x_i\right)^2 = 157^2 = 24,649$

d. $\displaystyle\sum_{i=1}^{n} x_i = -1 + 4 + 1 + 0 + 5 = 9$

$\displaystyle\sum_{i=1}^{n} x_i^2 = (-1)^2 + 4^2 + 1^2 + 0^2 + 5^2 = 43$

$\displaystyle\left(\sum_{i=1}^{n} x_i\right)^2 = 9^2 = 81$

e. $\displaystyle\sum_{i=1}^{n} x_i = 1 + 0 + 0 + 1 + 0 + 10 = 12$

$\displaystyle\sum_{i=1}^{n} x_i^2 = 1^2 + 0^2 + 0^2 + 1^2 + 0^2 + 10^2 = 102$

$\displaystyle\left(\sum_{i=1}^{n} x_i\right)^2 = 12^2 = 144$

3.17 a. $\displaystyle\sum_{i=1}^{n} x_i = 10 + 1 + 0 + 0 + 20 = 31$

$\displaystyle\sum_{i=1}^{n} x_i^2 = 10^2 + 1^2 + 0^2 + 0^2 + 20^2 = 501$

$\displaystyle\bar{x} = \frac{\sum_{i=1}^{n} x_i}{n} = \frac{31}{5} = 6.2$

$\displaystyle s^2 = \frac{\sum_{i=1}^{n} x_i^2 - \frac{\left(\sum_{i=1}^{n} x_i\right)^2}{n}}{n-1} = \frac{501 - \frac{31^2}{5}}{5-1} = \frac{308.8}{4} = 77.2$

$s = \sqrt{77.2} = 8.786$

b. $\displaystyle\sum_{i=1}^{n} x_i = 5 + 9 + (-1) + 100 = 113$

$\displaystyle\sum_{i=1}^{n} x_i^2 = 5^2 + 9^2 + (-1)^2 + 100^2 = 10,107$

$\displaystyle\bar{x} = \frac{\sum_{i=1}^{n} x_i}{n} = \frac{113}{4} = 28.25$

$\displaystyle s^2 = \frac{\sum_{i=1}^{n} x_i^2 - \frac{\left(\sum_{i=1}^{n} x_i\right)^2}{n}}{n-1} = \frac{10107 - \frac{113^2}{4}}{4-1} = \frac{6914.75}{3} = 2304.92$

$s = \sqrt{2304.92} = 48.010$

3.19 a. The range, variance, and standard deviation measure the variability of the data set. They give a measure of the spread of the data. The larger the value, the more spread out the data. The range gives you an idea how wide the data set is, the standard deviation tells you approximately how far the values are from the mean, and the variance gives the sum of the squared distances form the mean divided by the number of observations.

b. An advantage of using the range is that it is so easy to compute. A disadvantage is that it only uses the smallest and largest values of the data set. No information is used from the other observations of the data set.

An advantage of the variance is that it does take all of the values of the data set into account. It gives the sum of the squared distances from the mean divided by the number of observations. A disadvantage is that it is expressed in square units. This makes it hard to interpret. It is also harder to calculate than the range.

An advantage of the standard deviation is that it also takes all of the observations into account. It is also expressed in the original units of the problem so that it is easier to interpret than the variance. It gives a measure of the distance the observations are from the mean. A disadvantage is that it is hard to calculate.

3.21 This is one possibility for the two data sets.

Data Set 1: 0, 1, 2, 3, 4, 5, 6, 7, 8, 9

Data Set 2: 0, 0, 1, 1, 2, 2, 3, 3, 9, 9

The two sets of data above have the same range = largest measurement - smallest measurement = 9 - 0 = 9.

The means for the two data sets are:

$$\bar{x}_1 = \frac{\sum_{i=1}^{n} x_i}{n} = \frac{0 + 1 + 2 + 3 + 4 + 5 + 6 + 7 + 8 + 9}{10} = \frac{45}{10} = 4.5$$

$$\bar{x}_2 = \frac{\sum_{i=1}^{n} x_i}{n} = \frac{0 + 0 + 1 + 1 + 2 + 2 + 3 + 3 + 9 + 9}{10} = \frac{30}{10} = 3$$

The dot diagrams for the two data sets are shown below.

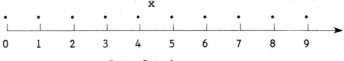

Data Set 1

Data Set 2

3.23 a. The mean value for the U.S. City Average Index for the data in the table is

$$\bar{x} = \frac{\displaystyle\sum_{i=1}^{n} x_i}{n} = \frac{2654.6}{21} = 126.4095$$

The mean value for the Chicago Index for the data in the table is

$$\bar{x} = \frac{\displaystyle\sum_{i=1}^{n} x_i}{n} = \frac{2678.4}{21} = 127.5429$$

b. For the U.S. City Average Index, the range = largest measurement - smallest measurement = 132.7 - 121.1 = 11.6.

For the Chicago Index, the range = largest measurement - smallest measurement = 133.8 - 121.5 = 12.3.

c. The standard deviation for the Chicago Index for the data in the table is

$$s = \sqrt{\frac{\displaystyle\sum_{i=1}^{n} x_i^2 - \frac{\left(\displaystyle\sum_{i=1}^{n} x_i\right)^2}{n}}{n - 1}} = \sqrt{\frac{341867.18 - \frac{2678.4^2}{21}}{21 - 1}}$$

$$= \sqrt{12.81957} = 3.5804$$

d. The Chicago Index displays the greater variation about its mean for this time period. This is evident by the larger standard deviation and range for the Chicago Index.

3.25 a. Germany - The range is 7.9 - 6.5 = 1.4
Italy - The range is 26.5 - 21.8 = 4.7
France - The range is 23.2 - 19.1 = 4.1
United Kingdom - The range is 20.1 - 11.3 = 8.8
Belgium - The range is 12.3 - 10.8 = 1.5

b. <u>Germany</u>

$$s^2 = \frac{\displaystyle\sum_{i=1}^{n} x_i^2 - \frac{\left(\displaystyle\sum_{i=1}^{n} x_i\right)^2}{n}}{n - 1} = \frac{157.95 - \frac{21.7^2}{3}}{3 - 1} = .4933$$

$$s = \sqrt{.4933} = .7024$$

Italy

$$s^2 = \frac{\sum\limits_{i=1}^{n} x_i^2 - \dfrac{\left(\sum\limits_{i=1}^{n} x_i\right)^2}{n}}{n-1} = \frac{1748.7 - \dfrac{72.2^2}{3}}{3-1} = 5.5433$$

$$s = \sqrt{5.5433} = 2.3544$$

France

$$s^2 = \frac{\sum\limits_{i=1}^{n} x_i^2 - \dfrac{\left(\sum\limits_{i=1}^{n} x_i\right)^2}{n}}{n-1} = \frac{1365.8 - \dfrac{63.8^2}{3}}{3-1} = 4.2433$$

$$s = \sqrt{4.2433} = 2.0599$$

United Kingdom

$$s^2 = \frac{\sum\limits_{i=1}^{n} x_i^2 - \dfrac{\left(\sum\limits_{i=1}^{n} x_i\right)^2}{n}}{n-1} = \frac{778.19 - \dfrac{47.1^2}{3}}{3-1} = 19.36$$

$$s = \sqrt{19.36} = 4.4$$

Belgium

$$s^2 = \frac{\sum\limits_{i=1}^{n} x_i^2 - \dfrac{\left(\sum\limits_{i=1}^{n} x_i\right)^2}{n}}{n-1} = \frac{402.49 - \dfrac{34.7^2}{3}}{3-1} = .5633$$

$$s = \sqrt{.5633} = .7506$$

c. Using the ranges from part (a), the ranks of the countries are:

1. Germany (range = 1.4)
2. Belgium (range = 1.5)
3. France (range = 4.1)
4. Italy (range = 4.7)
5. United Kingdom (range = 8.8)

Using the standard deviations from part (b), the ranks of the countries are:

1. Germany (s = .7024)
2. Belgium (s = .7506)
3. France (s = 2.0599)
4. Italy (s = 2.3544)
5. United Kingdom (s = 4.4)

d. Yes, the two sets of rankings in part (c) are in agreement. But no, the range and standard deviation will not always yield the same rankings. A data set could have a large range due to one extreme value. Another data set could have a slightly smaller range but more values near the extremes, thus having a larger standard deviation.

3.27 Chebyshev's theorem can be applied to any data set. The Empirical Rule applies only to data sets that are mound shaped--that are approximately symmetric, with a clustering of measurements about the midpoint of the distribution and that tail off as one moves away from the center of the distribution.

3.29 a. $\bar{x} = \dfrac{\sum\limits_{i=1}^{n} x_i}{n} = \dfrac{1442}{36} = 40.0556$

$s^2 = \dfrac{\sum\limits_{i=1}^{n} x_i^2 - \dfrac{\left(\sum\limits_{i=1}^{n} x_i\right)^2}{n}}{n-1} = \dfrac{57926 - \dfrac{1442^2}{36}}{36-1} = 4.7397$

$s = \sqrt{4.7397} = 2.1771$

b. A visual inspection of the data indicates that more than half of the measurements are 40 or over. The manufacturer would react favorably to this observation. Also, the mean is 40.0556 which is greater than 40.

c. Using Chebyshev's theorem, at least 8/9 of the measurements will fall within 3 standard deviations of the mean. Thus, the range of the data would be around 6 standard deviations. Using the Empirical Rule, approximately 95% of the observations are within 2 standard deviations of the mean. Thus, the range of the data would be around 4 standard deviations. We would expect the standard deviation to be somewhere between Range/6 and Range/4. For our data, Range/6 = (45 - 35)/6 = 1.667 and Range/4 = 10/4 = 2.5. Our computed value of s is 2.1771 which does fall between 1.667 and 2.5.

d. To construct a relative frequency histogram of the data set, we can
    use 6 measurement classes.

The class interval width = $\dfrac{\text{Largest measurement} - \text{Smallest measurement}}{\text{Number of intervals}}$

$$= \frac{45 - 35}{6} = 1.667$$

Rounding upward, the class width is 2.

The lower class boundary of the first measurement class is .5 below
the smallest number or 35 - .5 = 34.5

The measurement classes, class frequencies, and class relative
frequencies are shown in the following table.

CLASS	MEASUREMENT CLASS	CLASS FREQUENCY	CLASS RELATIVE FREQUENCY
1	34.5 - 36.5	2	.056
2	36.5 - 38.5	6	.167
3	38.5 - 40.5	13	.361
4	40.5 - 42.5	11	.306
5	42.5 - 44.5	3	.083
6	44.5 - 46.5	1	.028
		n = 36	36/36 = 1.000

The relative frequency histogram for this data set is illustrated
below.

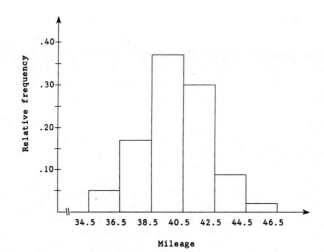

Mileage

Yes, the data set does look mound-shaped.

e. Since the data set does look mound-shaped, by the Empirical Rule we would expect approximately 68% of the measurements to fall within $\bar{x} \pm s$, 95% within $\bar{x} \pm 2s$, and essentially all or 100% within $\bar{x} \pm 3s$.

f. $\bar{x} \pm s \Rightarrow 40.0556 \pm 2.1771 \Rightarrow (37.8785, 42.2327)$

In this data set, $27/36 \times 100 = 75\%$ of the measurements fall within $\bar{x} \pm s$.

$\bar{x} \pm 2s \Rightarrow 40.0556 - 2(2.1771) \Rightarrow 40.0556 \pm 4.3542$
$\Rightarrow (35.7014, 44.4098)$

In this data set, $34/36 \times 100 = 94.4\%$ of the measurements fall within $\bar{x} \pm 2s$.

$\bar{x} \pm 3x \Rightarrow 40.0556 \pm 3(2.1771) \Rightarrow 40.0556 \pm 6.5313$
$\Rightarrow (33.5243, 46.5869)$

All of the measurements, 100% of them, fall within $\bar{x} \pm 3s$.

These results compare very well with the Empirical Rule used in part (e).

3.31 a. $\bar{x} = \dfrac{\sum\limits_{i=1}^{n} x_i}{n} = \dfrac{2078}{20} = 103.9$

b. $s^2 = \dfrac{\sum\limits_{i=1}^{n} x_i^2 - \dfrac{\left(\sum\limits_{i=1}^{n} x_i\right)^2}{n}}{n-1} = \dfrac{451432 - \dfrac{2078^2}{20}}{20-1} = \dfrac{235527.8}{19} = 12{,}396.2$

$s = \sqrt{12396.2} = 111.3$

c. Using Chebyshev's theorem, at least 8/9 of the measurements will fall within 3 standard deviations of the mean. Thus, the range of the data would be around 6 standard deviations. Using the Empirical Rule, approximately 95% of the observations are within 2 standard deviations of the mean. Thus, the range of the data would be around 4 standard deviations. We would expect the standard deviation to be somewhere between Range/6 and Range/4. For our data, Range/6 = (400 - 0)/6 = 66.67 and Range/4 = 400/4 = 100. Our computed value of s is 111.3. This is close to the above estimates. It is not in between them as would be expected since the data are not mound-shaped.

d. According to Chebyshev's theorem:

It is possible that none of the measurements will fall within the interval $\bar{x} \pm s$. Therefore, at most 100% will fall outside the interval $\bar{x} \pm s$.

At least 3/4 of the measurements will fall within $\bar{x} \pm 2s$. Therefore, at most 1/4 × 100% = 25% will fall outside the interval $\bar{x} \pm 2s$.

At least 8/9 of the measurements will fall within $\bar{x} \pm 3s$. Therefore, at most 1/9 × 100% = 11.1% will fall outside the interval $\bar{x} \pm 3s$.

e. $\bar{x} \pm s$ => 103.9 ± 111.3 => (-7.4, 215.2)

In this data set, 3/20 × 100% = 15% of the measurements fall outside $\bar{x} \pm s$.

$\bar{x} \pm 2s$ => 103.9 ± 2(111.3) => 103.9 ± 222.6
$\qquad\qquad\qquad\qquad\qquad\quad$ => (-118.7, 326.5)

In this data set, 1/20 × 100% = 5% of the measurements fall outside $\bar{x} \pm 2s$.

$\bar{x} \pm 3s$ => 103.9 ± 3(111.3) => 103.9 ± 333.9
$\qquad\qquad\qquad\qquad\qquad\quad$ => (-230, 437.8)

In this data set, none of the measurements (0%) fall outside $\bar{x} \pm 3s$.

These results seem to be comparable with the results of part (d).

3.33 a. To decide if Chebyshev's theorem or the Empirical Rule is more appropriate, we need to know if the sample has a mound-shaped distribution.

To construct a relative frequency histogram for the data set, we will use 7 measurement classes.

$$\text{The class interval width} = \frac{\text{Largest measurement} - \text{Smallest measurement}}{\text{Number of intervals}}$$

$$= \frac{290,000 - 65,000}{7} = 32142.857$$

Rounding upward, the class width is 32150.

The measurement classes, class frequencies, and class relative frequencies are shown in the following table.

CLASS	MEASUREMENT CLASS	CLASS FREQUENCY	CLASS RELATIVE FREQUENCY
1	64,999 - 97,149	26	.722
2	97,149 - 129,299	5	.139
3	129,299 - 161,449	1	.028
4	161,449 - 193,599	3	.083
5	193,599 - 225,749	0	.000
6	225,749 - 257,899	0	.000
7	257,899 - 290,049	1	.028
		n = 36	1.000

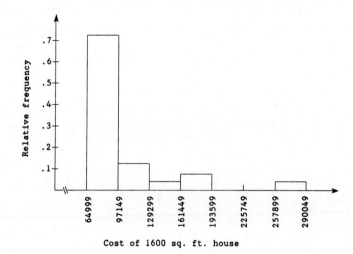

Cost of 1600 sq. ft. house

The relative frequency histogram above is not mound-shaped. Therefore, Chebyshev's theorem would be more appropriate.

b. The average price of a 1600 square-foot home in a desirable neighborhood is $96,732. The standard deviation is $45,322. At least 3/4 of all 1600 square-foot homes in desirable neighborhoods will be priced between $96,732 ± 2(45.322) or $6,088 and $187,376.

c. $\bar{x} \pm 2s \Rightarrow 96,731.94 \pm 2(45,322.18) \Rightarrow (6,087.58, 187,376.30)$

Using Chebyshev's theorem, we would expect at least $1 - \frac{1}{2^2} = .75$ of the sale prices to fall within this interval. For this data set, $\frac{34}{36} = .944$ of the sales prices actually fall in the interval. This is at least .75.

$$\bar{x} \pm 3s \Rightarrow 96,731.94 \pm 3(45,322.18) \Rightarrow (-39,234.60, 232,698.48)$$

Using Chebyshev's theorem, we would expect at least $1 - \frac{1}{3^2} = .889$ of the sale prices to fall within this interval. Thus, at most $1 - .889 = .111$ of the sale prices will fall outside this interval. For this data set, $\frac{1}{36} = .028$ of the sale prices actually fall outside the interval. This is at most .111.

d. The sale price of a home in Darien, Connecticut, is $290,000. The number of standard deviations $290,000 is from the mean is

$$\frac{\$290,000 - 96731.94}{45322.18} = 4.26$$

3.35 Since the distribution is approximately mound-shaped, we can use the Empirical Rule.

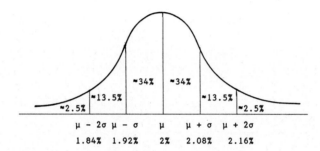

Percentage of zinc phosphide

As illustrated in the figure above, approximately 2.5% will contain less than 1.84% zinc phosphide. Therefore, the approximate probability is .025.

3.37 Since $\bar{x} = 385$ and $s = 15$,

$$\bar{x} \pm 3s \Rightarrow 385 \pm 3(15) \Rightarrow 385 \pm 45 \Rightarrow (340,430)$$

According to Chebyshev's theorem, at least $1 - \frac{1}{3^2} = \frac{8}{9}$ or .889 of the days the number of vehicles on the road falls within this interval.

3.39 $\bar{x} = 125$, $s = 15$

a. $\bar{x} \pm 3s \Rightarrow 125 \pm 3(15) \Rightarrow 125 \pm 45 \Rightarrow (80, 170)$

Since nothing is known about the distribution of utility bills, we need to apply Chebyshev's Theorem. According to Chebyshev's theorem, the fraction of all three-bedroom homes with gas or electric energy that have bills within this interval is at least

$$1 - \frac{1}{3^2} = \frac{8}{9}$$

b.   If it is reasonable to assume the distribution of utility bills is mound-shaped, we can apply the Empirical Rule.

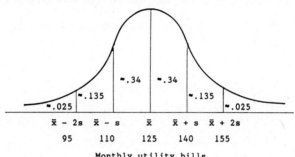

Monthly utility bills

As illustrated in the figure above, approximately .135 + .025 = .16 of three-bedroom homes would have monthly bills less than $110.

c.   Yes, these three values do suggest that solar energy units might result in lower utility bills. This is evident since if the solar energy units do not decrease the utility bills, only approximately .025 of the utility bills would be under $95. But all three of the sampled bills from houses with solar energy units were under $95.

3.41   Since we do not know if the distribution of the heights of the trees is mound-shaped, we need to apply Chebyshev's theorem. We know $\mu = 30$ and $\sigma = 3$. Therefore,

$$\mu \pm 3\sigma \Rightarrow 30 \pm 3(3) \Rightarrow 30 \pm 9$$
$$\Rightarrow (21, 39)$$

According to Chebyshev's theorem, at least $1 - \frac{1}{3^2} = \frac{8}{9}$ or .89 of the tree heights on this piece of land fall within this interval. However, the buyer will only purchase the land if at least $\frac{1000}{5000}$ or .20 of the tree heights are at least 40 feet tall. Therefore, the buyer should not buy the piece of land.

3.43 a. Since we know $\bar{x}$ and s, the sample z-score is

$$z = \frac{x - \bar{x}}{s} = \frac{31 - 24}{7} = \frac{7}{7} = 1$$

b. Since we know $\bar{x}$ and s, the sample z-score is

$$z = \frac{x - \bar{x}}{s} = \frac{95 - 101}{4} = \frac{-6}{4} = -1.5$$

c. Since we know μ and σ, the population z-score is

$$z = \frac{x - \mu}{\sigma} = \frac{5 - 2}{1.7} = \frac{3}{1.7} = 1.765$$

d. Since we know μ and σ, the population z-score is

$$z = \frac{x - \mu}{\sigma} = \frac{14 - 17}{5} = \frac{-3}{5} = -.6$$

3.45 a. From the problem, $\mu = 2.7$ and $\sigma = .5$

$$z = \frac{x - \mu}{\sigma} \Rightarrow z\sigma = x - \mu \Rightarrow x = \mu + z\sigma$$

For $z = 2.0$, $x = 2.7 + 2.0(.5) = 3.7$

For $z = -1.0$, $x = 2.7 - 1.0(.5) = 2.2$

For $z = .5$, $x = 2.7 + .5(.5) = 2.95$

For $z = -2.5$, $x = 2.7 - 2.5(.5) = 1.45$

b. For $z = -1.6$, $x = 2.7 - 1.6(.5) = 1.9$

c. If we assume the distribution of GPAs is approximately mound shaped, we can use the Empirical Rule.

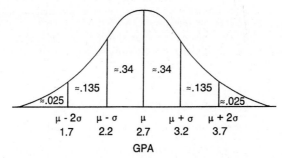

From the Empirical Rule, we know that ≈.025 or ≈2.5% of the students will have GPAs above 3.7 (with $z = 2$). Thus, the GPA corresponding to summa cum laude (top 2.5%) will be greater than 3.7 ($z > 2$).

We know that ≈.16 or 16% of the students will have GPAs above 3.2 (z = 1). Thus, the limit on GPAs for cum laude (top 16%) will be greater than 3.2 (z > 1).

We must assume the distribution is mound shaped.

3.47 a. To calculate the U.S. merchandise trade balance for each of the ten countries, take the exports minus imports.

COUNTRY	U.S. MERCHANDISE TRADE BALANCE (in billions)
Brazil	-3.825
Egypt	1.745
France	-2.787
Italy	-5.510
Japan	-56.326
Mexico	-5.689
Panama	0.387
Soviet Union	1.055
Sweden	-2.864
Turkey	0.622

b. To find the z-scores, we must first calculate the sample mean and standard deviation.

$$\bar{x} = \frac{\sum_{i=1}^{n} x_i}{n} = \frac{-73.152}{10} = -7.3152$$

$$s^2 = \frac{\sum_{i=1}^{n} x_i^2 - \frac{\left(\sum_{i=1}^{n} x_i\right)^2}{n}}{n - 1} = \frac{3270.68965 - \frac{(-73.152)^2}{10}}{10 - 1} = \frac{2735.56814}{9}$$

$$= 303.952$$

$$s = \sqrt{303.952} = 17.4342$$

Japan: $z = \frac{x - \bar{x}}{s} = \frac{-56.326 - (-7.3152)}{17.4342} = -2.81$

The relative position of the U.S. trade balance with Japan is 2.81 standard deviations below the mean. This indicates that this measurement is small compared to the other U.S. trade balances.

$$\underline{\text{Soviet Union:}} \quad z = \frac{x - \bar{x}}{s} = \frac{1.055 - (-7.3152)}{17.4342} = .48$$

The relative position of the U.S. trade balance with the Soviet Union is .48 standard deviation above the mean. This indicates that this measurement is larger than the average of the U.S. trade balances.

3.49   In 1989, Control Data Corporation ranked 153 out of 500. Therefore, $(500 - 153)/500 \times 100\% = 69.4\%$ of the corporations were ranked below Control Data Corporation. Control Data Corporation was at the 69.4th percentile. In 1984, Control Data Corporation ranked 71 out of 500. Thus, $(500 - 71)/500 \times 100\% = 85.8\%$ of the corporations were ranked below Control Data Corporation. Control Data Corporation was at the 85.8th percentile.

3.51   a.   From the Empirical Rule, we know that approximately 68% of the measurements will fall within $\bar{x} \pm s$, 95% within $\bar{x} \pm 2s$, and almost all within $\bar{x} \pm 3s$.

Since $\bar{x} = 35$ and $s = \sqrt{9} = 3$,

$$\bar{x} \pm s \Rightarrow 35 \pm 3 \Rightarrow (32, 38)$$

Therefore, approximately 68% of the measurements should fall between 32 and 38.

$$\bar{x} \pm 3s \Rightarrow 35 \pm 3(3) \Rightarrow 35 \pm 9 \Rightarrow (26, 34)$$

Therefore, almost all (100%) of the measurements should fall between 26 and 44.

b. $z = \dfrac{x - \bar{x}}{s}$

$$-1.33 = \frac{x - 35}{3}$$
$$-3.99 = x - 35$$
$$31.01 = x \text{ due to rounding}$$

The store sold 31 VCRs.

c.   We will calculate the z-score for $x = 41$ for both stores.

<u>Large department store:</u>

$$z = \frac{x - \bar{x}}{s} = \frac{41 - 35}{3} = \frac{6}{3} = 2$$

Rival department store:

$$z = \frac{x - \bar{x}}{s} = \frac{41 - 35}{2} = \frac{6}{2} = 3$$

The store with the lowest z-score is more likely to sell more than 41 VCRs. Thus, the first store is more likely to sell 41 or more VCRs.

3.53   a.   When the income x is $190,

$$z = \frac{x - \mu}{\sigma} = \frac{190 - 170}{10} = 2$$

Using Chebyshev's theorem, at least 3/4 of the incomes fall within 2 standard deviations of the mean. Therefore, at most 1/4 x 100% = 25% of the employees should expect an income over $190 per week.

When x = 160,

$$z = \frac{x - \mu}{\sigma} = \frac{160 - 170}{10} = -1$$

Using Chebyshev's theorem, it is possible that none of the incomes will fall within 1 standard deviation of the mean. Therefore, we cannot determine the percentage of employees that should expect an income under $160 per week.

When x = 200,

$$z = \frac{x - \mu}{\sigma} = \frac{200 - 170}{10} = 3$$

At least 8/9 of the incomes fall within 3 standard deviations of the mean. Therefore, at most, 1/9 x 100% = 11.1% of the employees should expect an income over $200 per week.

b.   When your income x is $185,

$$z = \frac{x - \mu}{\sigma} = \frac{185 - 170}{10} = 1.5$$

My salary would be 1.5 standard deviations above the mean salary.

3.55   The 25th percentile, or lower quartile, is the measurement that has 25% of the measurements below it and 75% of the measurements above it. The 50th percentile, or median, is the measurement that has 50% of the measurements below it and 50% of the measurements above it. The 75th percentile, or upper quartile, is the measurements that has 75% of the measurements below it and 25% of the measurements above it.

3.57　a.　Median is approximately 39.

　　　b.　Q_L is approximately 31.5 (Lower Quartile)

　　　　　Q_U is approximately 45 (Upper Quartile)

　　　c.　IQR = Q_U - Q_L ≈ 45 - 31.5 ≈ 13.5

　　　d.　The data set is skewed to the left since the left whisker is longer.

　　　e.　50% of the measurements are to the right of the median and 75% are to the left of the upper quartile.

*3.59　Using Minitab, the box plot for the sample is given below.

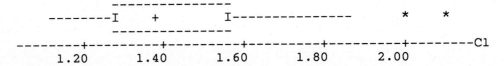

3.61　Owens-Illinois sales are at the upper quartile or the 75th percentile. This means that 75% of the nation's largest companies' 1989 sales were below $3,692 million and 25% were above $3,692 million.

*3.63　a.　Using Minitab, the box plot for the earnings per share for the 30 firms is given below.

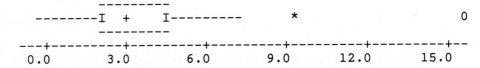

　　　　In the sample of 30 firms, the E/S for Washington Post (15.50) is an outlier. This measurement falls outside the outer fence.

　　　　In addition, the E/S for Reynolds Metals (9.20) may be an outlier. It lies outside the inner fence.

　　　b.　To determine the number of standard deviations a measurement is from the mean (the z-score), we must first calculate the sample mean and standard deviation.

$$\bar{x} = \frac{\sum\limits_{i=1}^{n} x_i}{n} = \frac{110.84}{30} = 3.695$$

$$s^2 = \frac{\sum\limits_{i=1}^{n} x_i^2 - \frac{\left(\sum\limits_{i=1}^{n} x_i\right)^2}{n}}{n - 1} = \frac{697.4438 - \frac{110.84^2}{30}}{30 - 1} = 9.9285$$

$$s = \sqrt{9.9285} = 3.151$$

For the E/S for Washington Post, $x = 15.50$, the z-score is:

$$z = \frac{x - \bar{x}}{s} = \frac{15.50 - 3.695}{3.151} = 3.75$$

For the E/S for Reynolds Metals, $x = 9.20$, the z-score is:

$$z = \frac{x - \bar{x}}{s} = \frac{9.20 - 3.695}{3.151} = 1.74$$

3.65　a. For Ford the median is approximately 23.5, while Honda's median is approximately 27.3. Therefore, Honda has the higher median mileage estimate.

　　　b. For Ford the range is approximately $41 - 17 = 24$, while Honda's range is approximately $51.1 - 22.4 = 28.7$. Therefore, Honda has the greater range.

　　　c. For Ford,

$$IQR = Q_U - Q_L \approx 27 - 19 \approx 8$$

For Honda,

$$IQR = Q_U - Q_L \approx 29.4 - 23.8 \approx 5.6$$

Therefore, Ford's mileage estimates have the greater interquartile range.

　　　d. For Ford the highest mileage estimate is approximately 41, while Honda's highest mileage estimate is approximately 51.1. Therefore, Honda has the model with the highest mileage estimate.

3.67　a. $\sum\limits_{i=1}^{n} x_i^2 = 11^2 + 1^2 + 2^2 + 8^2 + 7^2 = 239$

$\sum\limits_{i=1}^{n} x_i = 11 + 1 + 2 + 8 + 7 = 29$

$\left(\sum\limits_{i=1}^{n} x_i\right)^2 = 29^2 = 841$

b. $\displaystyle\sum_{i=1}^{n} x_i^2 = 15^2 + 15^2 + 2^2 + 6^2 + 12^2 = 634$

$\displaystyle\sum_{i=1}^{n} x_i = 15 + 15 + 2 + 6 + 12 = 50$

$\displaystyle\left(\sum_{i=1}^{n} x_i\right)^2 = 50^2 = 2500$

c. $\displaystyle\sum_{i=1}^{n} x_i^2 = (-1)^2 + 2^2 + 0^2 + (-4)^2 + (-8)^2 + 13^2 = 254$

$\displaystyle\sum_{i=1}^{n} x_i = -1 + 2 + 0 + (-4) + (-8) + 13 = 2$

$\displaystyle\left(\sum_{i=1}^{n} x_i\right)^2 = 2^2 = 4$

d. $\displaystyle\sum_{i=1}^{n} x_i^2 = 100^2 + 0^2 + 0^2 + 2^2 = 10{,}004$

$\displaystyle\sum_{i=1}^{n} x_i = 100 + 0 + 0 + 2 = 102$

$\displaystyle\left(\sum_{i=1}^{n} x_i\right)^2 = 102^2 = 10{,}404$

3.69 a. $\displaystyle s^2 = \frac{\displaystyle\sum_{i=1}^{n} x_i^2 - \frac{\left(\sum_{i=1}^{n} x_i\right)^2}{n}}{n-1} = \frac{246 - \dfrac{63^2}{22}}{22 - 1} = 3.1234$

b. $\displaystyle s^2 = \frac{\displaystyle\sum_{i=1}^{n} x_i^2 - \frac{\left(\sum_{i=1}^{n} x_i\right)^2}{n}}{n-1} = \frac{666 - \dfrac{106^2}{25}}{25 - 1} = 9.0233$

c. $\displaystyle s^2 = \frac{\displaystyle\sum_{i=1}^{n} x_i^2 - \frac{\left(\sum_{i=1}^{n} x_i\right)^2}{n}}{n-1} = \frac{76 - \dfrac{11^2}{7}}{7 - 1} = 9.7857$

3.71 a. $\sum\limits_{i=1}^{n} x_i = 4 + 6 + 6 + 5 + 6 + 7 = 34$

$\sum\limits_{i=1}^{n} x_i^2 = 4^2 + 6^2 + 6^2 + 5^2 + 6^2 + 7^2 = 198$

$\bar{x} = \dfrac{\sum\limits_{i=1}^{n} x_i}{n} = \dfrac{34}{6} = 5.67$

$s^2 = \dfrac{\sum\limits_{i=1}^{n} x_i^2 - \dfrac{\left(\sum\limits_{i=1}^{n} x_i\right)^2}{n}}{n - 1} = \dfrac{198 - \dfrac{34^2}{6}}{6 - 1} = \dfrac{5.3333}{5} = 1.067$

$s = \sqrt{1.067} = 1.03$

b. $\sum\limits_{i=1}^{n} x_i = -1 + 4 + (-3) + 0 + (-3) + (-6) = -9$

$\sum\limits_{i=1}^{n} x_i^2 = (-1)^2 + 4^2 + (-3)^2 + 0^2 + (-3)^2 + (-6)^2 = 71$

$\bar{x} = \dfrac{\sum\limits_{i=1}^{n} x_i}{n} = \dfrac{-9}{6} = -\$1.5$

$s^2 = \dfrac{\sum\limits_{i=1}^{n} x_i^2 - \dfrac{\left(\sum\limits_{i=1}^{n} x_i\right)^2}{n}}{n - 1} = \dfrac{71 - \dfrac{(-9)^2}{6}}{6 - 1} = \dfrac{57.5}{5} = 11.5 \text{ dollars squared}$

$s = \sqrt{11.5} = \$3.39$

c. $\sum\limits_{i=1}^{n} x_i = \dfrac{3}{5} + \dfrac{4}{5} + \dfrac{2}{5} + \dfrac{1}{5} + \dfrac{1}{16} = 2.0625$

$\sum\limits_{i=1}^{n} x_i^2 = \left(\dfrac{3}{5}\right)^2 + \left(\dfrac{4}{5}\right)^2 + \left(\dfrac{2}{5}\right)^2 + \left(\dfrac{1}{5}\right)^2 + \left(\dfrac{1}{16}\right)^2 = 1.2039$

$\bar{x} = \dfrac{\sum\limits_{i=1}^{n} x_i}{n} = \dfrac{2.0625}{5} = .4125 \text{ pounds}$

$$s^2 = \frac{\sum\limits_{i=1}^{n} x_i^2 - \frac{\left(\sum\limits_{i=1}^{n} x_i\right)^2}{n}}{n - 1} = \frac{1.2039 - \frac{2.0625^2}{5}}{5 - 1} = \frac{.3531}{4}$$

$$= .088 \text{ pounds squared}$$

$$s = \sqrt{.088} = .30 \text{ pounds}$$

d.　(a) Range = 7 - 4 = 3

(b) Range = \$4 - (\$-6) = \$10

(c) Range = $\frac{4}{5}$ pound - $\frac{1}{16}$ pound = $\frac{64}{80}$ pound - $\frac{5}{80}$ pound = $\frac{59}{80}$ pound

$$= .7375 \text{ pound}$$

3.73　a.　The population of interest is the set of all gasoline stations in the United States.

b.　The sample of interest is the set of 200 stations selected.

c.　The variable of interest is the price of regular unleaded gasoline at each station.

d.　μ = the mean price of regular unleaded gasoline at all stations in the United States.

σ = the standard deviation of the price of regular unleaded gasoline at all stations in the United States.

$\bar{x}$ = the mean price of regular unleaded gasoline at the 200 selected stations.

s = the standard deviation of the price of regular unleaded gasoline at the 200 selected stations.

e.　The mean price of a gallon of regular unleaded gasoline at the 200 selected stations is \$1.39, and the standard deviation is \$0.12. The distribution of the prices is probably approximately mound shaped. About half of the stations probably have prices above \$1.39 and about half have prices below \$1.39.

f.　For x = \$1.09, $z = \dfrac{x - \bar{x}}{s} = \dfrac{1.09 - 1.39}{.12} = \dfrac{-.30}{.12} = -2.5$

A price of \$1.09 per gallon is 2.5 standard deviations below the mean. Not many stations will have prices below this value.

3.75　A measure of relative standing is a descriptive measure which shows the relationship of a measurement to the rest of the data in the data set.

3.77   The mode is often not an acceptable measure of central tendency. If
       the data set has few observations, no value may occur more than one
       time. If the data set is of moderate size, several different values
       may occur the same number of times, giving little information about the
       center of the distribution.

3.79 $\bar{x}$ = 75, s^2 = 36, s = 6

   a. $\bar{x} \pm s \Rightarrow 75 \pm 6 \Rightarrow (69, 81)$

        Since we do not know the shape of the distribution, using
        Chebyshev's theorem we can say that at least $1 - \frac{1}{1^2} = 0$ will
        fall within this interval.

   b. $\bar{x} \pm 2s \Rightarrow 75 \pm 2(6) \Rightarrow 75 \pm 12 \Rightarrow (63, 87)$

        By Chebyshev's theorem, at least $1 - \frac{1}{2^2} = .75$ of the
        measurements should fall within this interval. So at most,
        $.25 \times 100\% = 25\%$ of the trainees would be expected to fail.

*3.81 a.   Using MINITAB, the box plot is:

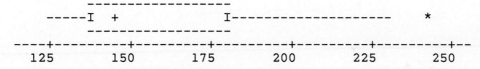

   b.   The frequency distribution of the data set is skewed right, since
        the right whisker is longer than the left whisker in the box plot.

   c.   There is one potential outlier in the data set. The observation
        242 corresponding to UTL lies outside the inner fence.

   d.   The mean of the data is $\bar{x} = \dfrac{\sum\limits_{i=1}^{n} x_i}{n} = \dfrac{3217}{20} = 160.85$

        For x = 242, $z = \dfrac{x - \bar{x}}{s} = \dfrac{242 - 160.85}{34.3} = \dfrac{81.15}{34.3} = 2.37$

   e.   No. Since we know from part (b) that the data are skewed, we must
        use Chebyshev's theorem. We know at least
        $1 - \frac{1}{k^2} = 1 - \frac{1}{2.37^2} = .82$ of the observations will fall within 2.37
        standard deviations of the mean. It is not real likely one would
        observe a value larger than 242.

NUMERICAL DESCRIPTIVE MEASURES

*3.83 a. $s \approx \dfrac{\text{Range}}{4} \approx \dfrac{30000}{4} \approx \$7500$

b. It is more likely that division B's sales next month will be over
$120,000 since it is fewer standard deviations from the mean of
$110,000.

$$(z = \frac{120,000 - 110,000}{7500} = 1.33 \text{ is smaller in magnitude than}$$

$$z = \frac{90,000 - 220,000}{7500} = -2.67)$$

c. Yes, it is possible for division B's sales next month to be
over $160,000. But it very unlikely since

$$z = \frac{x - \bar{x}}{s} = \frac{160,000 - 110,000}{7500} = 6.67$$

This is a very large z-score.

3.85 a. Account number 5021:

$$z = \frac{x - \bar{x}}{s} = \frac{38 - 23.4}{26.2} = .56$$

Account number 5872:

$$z = \frac{x - \bar{x}}{s} = \frac{110 - 23.4}{26.2} = 3.31$$

b. Using Minitab, the box plot is:

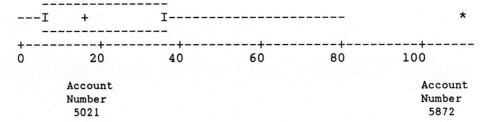

c. Account number 5021 is not an outlier since its age is inside the
inner fences.

Account number 5872 may be an outlier since its age is outside the
inner fences.

3.87   We know $\mu = 80$ and $\sigma = 5$.   Since the distribution of scores is mound-shaped, we can use the Empirical Rule.

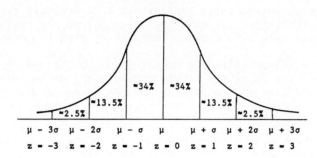

a. $z = \dfrac{x - \mu}{\sigma} = \dfrac{65 - 80}{5} = -3$

b.   As illustrated in the figure above, approximately 0% of the trainees will have z-scores less than or equal to -3.

c.   When the score x is 90,

$z = \dfrac{x - \mu}{\sigma} = \dfrac{90 - 80}{5} = 2.$

As illustrated in the figure above, approximately 2.5% of the trainees scored 90 or above.

When x = 65,

$z = \dfrac{x - \mu}{\sigma} = \dfrac{65 - 80}{5} = -3.$

Approximately 0% of the trainees scored 65 or below.

Therefore, if we arbitrarily selected a trainee from those who had taken the final test, it is more likely the trainee scored 90 or above than 65 or below.

3.89   a.   Using Chebyshev's theorem with k = 2, we would expect at least $1 - \dfrac{1}{2^2} = .75$ of the measurements to lie within 2 standard deviations of the mean.

b.   Using Chebyshev's theorem with k = 3, we would expect at least $1 - \dfrac{1}{3^2} = .89$ of the measurements to lie within 3 standard deviations of the mean.

c.   When k = 1.5, we would expect at least $1 - \dfrac{1}{1.5^2} = .56$ of the measurements to lie within 1.5 standard deviations of the mean.

d. When k = 2.75, we would expect at least $1 - \frac{1}{2.75^2} = .87$
of the measurements to fall within 2.75 standard deviations of the
mean. Therefore, at most $1 - .87 = .13$ of the measurements would
lie more than 2.75 standard deviations from the mean.

3.91 a. We will characterize the magnitude using the sample mean and the
variability using the sample variance of the 12 market
concentration ratios for each of the 6 countries.

United States:

$$\bar{x} = \frac{\sum\limits_{i=1}^{n} x_i}{n} = \frac{493}{12} = 41.08\%$$

$$s^2 = \frac{\sum\limits_{i=1}^{n} x_i^2 - \frac{\left(\sum\limits_{i=1}^{n} x_i\right)^2}{n}}{n - 1} = \frac{23885 - \frac{493^2}{12}}{12 - 1} = 330.08$$

Canada:

$$\bar{x} = \frac{\sum\limits_{i=1}^{n} x_i}{n} = \frac{850}{12} = 70.83\%$$

$$s^2 = \frac{\sum\limits_{i=1}^{n} x_i^2 - \frac{\left(\sum\limits_{i=1}^{n} x_i\right)^2}{n}}{n - 1} = \frac{66030 - \frac{850^2}{12}}{12 - 1} = 529.24$$

United Kingdom:

$$\bar{x} = \frac{\sum\limits_{i=1}^{n} x_i}{n} = \frac{725}{12} = 60.42\%$$

$$s^2 = \frac{\sum\limits_{i=1}^{n} x_i^2 - \frac{\left(\sum\limits_{i=1}^{n} x_i\right)^2}{n}}{n - 1} = \frac{50779 - \frac{725^2}{12}}{12 - 1} = 634.27$$

<u>Sweden:</u>

$$\bar{x} = \frac{\sum\limits_{i=1}^{n} x_i}{n} = \frac{1001}{12} = 83.42\%$$

$$s^2 = \frac{\sum\limits_{i=1}^{n} x_i^2 - \frac{\left(\sum\limits_{i=1}^{n} x_i\right)^2}{n}}{n-1} = \frac{89123 - \frac{1001^2}{12}}{12-1} = 511.17$$

<u>France:</u>

$$\bar{x} = \frac{\sum\limits_{i=1}^{n} x_i}{n} = \frac{796}{12} = 66.33\%$$

$$s^2 = \frac{\sum\limits_{i=1}^{n} x_i^2 - \frac{\left(\sum\limits_{i=1}^{n} x_i\right)^2}{n}}{n-1} = \frac{64372 - \frac{796^2}{12}}{12-1} = 1051.88$$

<u>West Germany:</u>

$$\bar{x} = \frac{\sum\limits_{i=1}^{n} x_i}{n} = \frac{673}{12} = 56.08\%$$

$$s^2 = \frac{\sum\limits_{i=1}^{n} x_i^2 - \frac{\left(\sum\limits_{i=1}^{n} x_i\right)^2}{n}}{n-1} = \frac{47723 - \frac{673^2}{12}}{12-1} = 907.17$$

b. We will characterize the magnitude using the sample mean and the variability using the sample variance of the 6 market concentration ratios for each of the 12 industries.

<u>Brewing:</u>

$$\bar{x} = \frac{\sum\limits_{i=1}^{n} x_i}{n} = \frac{325}{6} = 54.17$$

$$s^2 = \frac{\sum\limits_{i=1}^{n} x_i^2 - \frac{\left(\sum\limits_{i=1}^{n} x_i\right)^2}{n}}{n-1} = \frac{20809 - \frac{325^2}{6}}{6-1} = 640.97$$

Cigarettes:

$$\bar{x} = \frac{\sum\limits_{i=1}^{n} x_i}{n} = \frac{546}{6} = 91.00$$

$$s^2 = \frac{\sum\limits_{i=1}^{n} x_i^2 - \frac{\left(\sum\limits_{i=1}^{n} x_i\right)^2}{n}}{n - 1} = \frac{50396 - \frac{546^2}{6}}{6 - 1} = 142.00$$

Fabric weaving:

$$\bar{x} = \frac{\sum\limits_{i=1}^{n} x_i}{n} = \frac{214}{6} = 35.67$$

$$s^2 = \frac{\sum\limits_{i=1}^{n} x_i^2 - \frac{\left(\sum\limits_{i=1}^{n} x_i\right)^2}{n}}{n - 1} = \frac{9458 - \frac{214^2}{6}}{6 - 1} = 365.07$$

Paints:

$$\bar{x} = \frac{\sum\limits_{i=1}^{n} x_i}{n} = \frac{244}{6} = 40.67$$

$$s^2 = \frac{\sum\limits_{i=1}^{n} x_i^2 - \frac{\left(\sum\limits_{i=1}^{n} x_i\right)^2}{n}}{n - 1} = \frac{13560 - \frac{244^2}{6}}{6 - 1} = 727.47$$

Petroleum refining:

$$\bar{x} = \frac{\sum\limits_{i=1}^{n} x_i}{n} = \frac{375}{6} = 62.5$$

$$s^2 = \frac{\sum\limits_{i=1}^{n} x_i^2 - \frac{\left(\sum\limits_{i=1}^{n} x_i\right)^2}{n}}{n - 1} = \frac{26771 - \frac{375^2}{6}}{6 - 1} = 666.70$$

Shoes (except rubber):

$$\bar{x} = \frac{\sum\limits_{i=1}^{n} x_i}{n} = \frac{122}{6} = 20.33$$

$$s^2 = \frac{\sum\limits_{i=1}^{n} x_i^2 - \frac{\left(\sum\limits_{i=1}^{n} x_i\right)^2}{n}}{n-1} = \frac{2840 - \frac{122^2}{6}}{6-1} = 71.87$$

Glass Bottles:

$$\bar{x} = \frac{\sum\limits_{i=1}^{n} x_i}{n} = \frac{515}{6} = 85.83$$

$$s^2 = \frac{\sum\limits_{i=1}^{n} x_i^2 - \frac{\left(\sum\limits_{i=1}^{n} x_i\right)^2}{n}}{n-1} = \frac{45259 - \frac{515^2}{6}}{6-1} = 210.97$$

Cement:

$$\bar{x} = \frac{\sum\limits_{i=1}^{n} x_i}{n} = \frac{406}{6} = 67.67$$

$$s^2 = \frac{\sum\limits_{i=1}^{n} x_i^2 - \frac{\left(\sum\limits_{i=1}^{n} x_i\right)^2}{n}}{n-1} = \frac{31498 - \frac{406^2}{6}}{6-1} = 805.07$$

Ordinary steel:

$$\bar{x} = \frac{\sum\limits_{i=1}^{n} x_i}{n} = \frac{364}{6} = 60.67$$

$$s^2 = \frac{\sum\limits_{i=1}^{n} x_i^2 - \frac{\left(\sum\limits_{i=1}^{n} x_i\right)^2}{n}}{n-1} = \frac{23846 - \frac{364^2}{6}}{6-1} = 352.67$$

Antifriction bearings:

$$\bar{x} = \frac{\sum\limits_{i=1}^{n} x_i}{n} = \frac{484}{6} = 80.67$$

$$s^2 = \frac{\sum\limits_{i=1}^{n} x_i^2 - \dfrac{\left(\sum\limits_{i=1}^{n} x_i\right)^2}{n}}{n - 1} = \frac{40994 - \dfrac{484^2}{6}}{6 - 1} = 390.27$$

Refrigerators:

$$\bar{x} = \frac{\sum\limits_{i=1}^{n} x_i}{n} = \frac{465}{6} = 77.50$$

$$s^2 = \frac{\sum\limits_{i=1}^{n} x_i^2 - \dfrac{\left(\sum\limits_{i=1}^{n} x_i\right)^2}{n}}{n - 1} = \frac{37051 - \dfrac{465^2}{6}}{6 - 1} = 202.70$$

Storage batteries:

$$\bar{x} = \frac{\sum\limits_{i=1}^{n} x_i}{n} = \frac{478}{6} = 79.67$$

$$s^2 = \frac{\sum\limits_{i=1}^{n} x_i^2 - \dfrac{\left(\sum\limits_{i=1}^{n} x_i\right)^2}{n}}{n - 1} = \frac{39430 - \dfrac{478^2}{6}}{6 - 1} = 269.87$$

c. On the average, the most competition within its industries is in
    the United States since the average market concentration ratio is
    smallest in the U.S.

    On the average, the least competition within its industries is in
    Sweden since the average market concentration ratio is largest in
    Sweden.

d. The three most competitive industries are shoes, fabric weaving,
    and paints since they have the smallest averages; and the three
    least competitive industries are cigarettes, glass bottles, and
    antifriction bearings since they have the largest average market
    concentration ratios.

CHAPTER
4

PROBABILITY

4.1   A simple event is an outcome of an experiment that cannot be decomposed into a simpler outcome. An event is a collection of one or more simple events.

4.3   a.

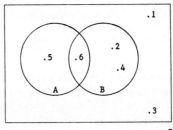

   b.   If a die is "fair," then there is an equal chance that any of the six numbers will be observed when the die is rolled.

   If the die is "fair," then you have an equal chance of observing any of the six numbers on the die. Therefore, the probability of observing a three is 1/6 since there is one three out of the six numbers.

   c. $P(A) = P(5) + P(6) = \frac{1}{6} + \frac{1}{6} = \frac{2}{6} = \frac{1}{3}$

   $P(B) = P(2) + P(4) + P(6) = \frac{1}{6} + \frac{1}{6} + \frac{1}{6} = \frac{3}{6} = \frac{1}{2}$

   d.   You could determine the probability of a 3 occurring by tossing the die a large number of times and counting the number of 3's that appear. Divide the number of 3's by the total number of tosses and this would be an estimate of the probability of observing a 3.

4.5   a. $\binom{10}{3} = \frac{10!}{3!(10-3)!} = \frac{10!}{3!7!} = \frac{10 \cdot 9 \cdot 8 \cdot 7 \cdot 6 \cdot 5 \cdot 4 \cdot 3 \cdot 2 \cdot 1}{(3 \cdot 2 \cdot 1)(7 \cdot 6 \cdot 5 \cdot 4 \cdot 3 \cdot 2 \cdot 1)}$

   $= 120$

   b. $\binom{6}{2} = \frac{6!}{2!(6-2)!} = \frac{6!}{2!4!} = \frac{6 \cdot 5 \cdot 4 \cdot 3 \cdot 2 \cdot 1}{(2 \cdot 1)(4 \cdot 3 \cdot 2 \cdot 1)} = 15$

c. $\dbinom{8}{3} = \dfrac{8!}{3!(8-3)!} = \dfrac{8!}{3!5!} = \dfrac{8 \cdot 7 \cdot 6 \cdot 5 \cdot 4 \cdot 3 \cdot 2 \cdot 1}{(3 \cdot 2 \cdot 1)(5 \cdot 4 \cdot 3 \cdot 2 \cdot 1)} = 56$

d. $\dbinom{5}{5} = \dfrac{5!}{5!(5-5)!} = \dfrac{5!}{5!0!} = \dfrac{5 \cdot 4 \cdot 3 \cdot 2 \cdot 1}{(5 \cdot 4 \cdot 3 \cdot 2 \cdot 1)(1)} = 1$

e. $\dbinom{4}{0} = \dfrac{4!}{0!(4-0)!} = \dfrac{4!}{0!4!} = \dfrac{4 \cdot 3 \cdot 2 \cdot 1}{(1)(4 \cdot 3 \cdot 2 \cdot 1)} = 1$

4.7 $P(A) = P(S_1, S_2) = .16$

$P(B) = P(S_1, S_2) + P(S_1, F_2) + P(F_1, S_2) = .16 + .24 + .24 = .64$

4.9 $P(A) = P(G_1, G_2) = \dfrac{1}{6}$

$P(B) = P(G_1, P_1) + P(G_1, P_2) + P(G_2, P_1) + P(G_2, P_2) + P(P_1, P_1)$

$= \dfrac{1}{6} + \dfrac{1}{6} + \dfrac{1}{6} + \dfrac{1}{6} + \dfrac{1}{6} = \dfrac{5}{6}$

4.11 We will denote the five successful utility companies as S_1, S_2, S_3, S_4, and S_5 and the two failing companies as F_1 and F_2. There are

$$\dbinom{7}{3} = \dfrac{7!}{3!4!} = 35$$

possible ways to choose three companies from the seven, as shown below:

(S_1, S_2, S_3)	(S_1, S_3, S_4)	(S_1, S_4, S_5)	(S_1, S_5, F_1)
(S_1, S_2, S_4)	(S_1, S_3, S_5)	(S_1, S_4, F_1)	(S_1, S_5, F_2)
(S_1, S_2, S_5)	(S_1, S_3, F_1)	(S_1, S_4, S_2)	
(S_1, S_2, F_1)	(S_1, S_3, F_2)		(S_1, F_1, F_2)
(S_1, S_2, F_2)			
(S_2, S_3, S_4)	(S_2, S_4, S_5)	(S_2, S_5, F_1)	(S_2, F_1, F_2)
(S_2, S_3, S_5)	(S_2, S_4, F_1)	(S_2, S_5, F_2)	
(S_2, S_3, F_1)	(S_2, S_4, F_2)		
(S_2, S_3, F_2)			
(S_3, S_4, S_5)	(S_3, S_5, F_1)	(S_3, F_1, F_2)	
(S_3, S_4, F_1)	(S_3, S_5, F_2)		
(S_3, S_4, F_2)			
(S_4, S_5, F_1)	(S_5, F_1, F_2)		
(S_4, S_5, F_2)			
(S_4, F_1, F_2)			

a. From the 35 events listed, 10 do not contain F_1 or F_2. Therefore, P(selecting none) = 10/35.

b. From the 35 events listed, 20 contain either F_1 or F_2, but not both. Therefore, P(selecting one) = 20/35.

c. From the 35 events listed, 5 contain both F_1 and F_2. Therefore, P(selecting both) = 5/35.

4.13   Define L: {Draw a Lenient Judge}

   a. Since Judge A (a strict judge) is leaving to go home, there are 3 strict judges (S_1, S_2, and S_3) and 3 lenient judges (L_1, L_2, and L_3) left. If you have an equally-likely chance of getting any of the 6 judges,

$$P(L) = P(L_1) + P(L_2) + P(L_3)$$

$$= \frac{1}{6} + \frac{1}{6} + \frac{1}{6}$$

$$= \frac{3}{6}$$

$$= \frac{1}{2}$$

   b. $P(\text{Judge B}) = P(S_1) = .3$ and $P(\text{Judge C}) = P(S_2) = .4$

Thus, $P(S_3) + P(L_1) + P(L_2) + P(L_3) = 1 - P(S_1) - P(S_2)$

Since $P(S_3) = P(L_1) = P(L_2) = P(L_3)$,

   $4P(S_3) = 1 - .3 - .4 = .3$

=> $P(S_3) = \frac{.3}{4} = .075$

=> $P(L_1) = P(L_2) = P(L_3) = .075$

$P(L) = P(L_1) + P(L_2) + P(L_3) = .075 + .075 + .075 = .225$

   c. Since Judge D (a lenient judge, L_1) never follows Judge A,

   $P(\text{Judge D}) = P(L_1) = 0$

   $P(\text{Judge B}) = P(S_1) = .3$

   $P(\text{Judge C}) = P(S_2) = .4$

Since the other three judges are equally likely,

   $P(S_3) + P(L_2) + P(L_3) = 1 - .3 - .4 = .3$

=> $3P(S_3) = .3$

=> $P(S_3) = \frac{.3}{3} = .1$

=> $P(L_2) = P(L_3) = .1$

Thus, $P(L) = P(L_2) + P(L_3) = .1 + .1 = .2$

4.15 a. Since each of the 15 states has an equal probability of being selected,

   P(Pennsylvania will be selected) = P(Florida will be selected)
     = P(Virginia will be selected) = 1/15.

   b. Since all of the states had a change in their unemployment rate, the probability of selecting a state that had no change is 0/15 = 0.

c. By looking at the change in the unemployment rates in the table for each of the 15 Atlantic coast states, 10 states had an increase in the unemployment rate from 1983 to 1984.

Therefore, the probability of selecting a state with an increase = 10/15 = 2/3, while the probability of selecting a state with a decrease = 5/15 = 1/3.

d. Three of the states had an increase of 1% or more. The probability of selecting a state with an increase $\geq$ 1% = 3/15 = .2.

One of the states had a decrease of 1% or more. The probability of selecting a state with a decrease $\geq$ 1% = 1/15.

4.17 a. The odds in favor of a Snow Chief win are $\frac{1}{3}$ to $1 - \frac{1}{3} = \frac{2}{3}$ or 1 to 2.

b. If the odds in favor of Snow Chief are 1 to 1, then the probability the Snow Chief wins is $\frac{1}{1 + 1} = \frac{1}{2}$.

c. If the odds against Snow Chief are 3 to 2, then the odds in favor of Snow Chief are 2 to 3. Therefore, the probability the Snow Chief wins is $\frac{2}{2 + 3} = \frac{2}{5}$.

4.19 a. A = {(1, 4), (4, 1), (2, 3), (3, 2)}

B = {(2, 3), (3, 2), (1, 3), (3, 1), (3, 3), (4, 3), (3, 4), (5, 3), (3, 5), (6, 3), (3, 6)}

A $\cap$ B = {(2, 3), (3, 2)}

A $\cup$ B = {(1, 4), (4, 1), (2, 3), (3, 2), (1, 3), (3, 1), (3, 3), (4, 3), (3, 4), (5, 3), (3, 5), (6, 3), (3, 6)}

b. There are 36 possible combinations from tossing two dice, so the probability of each simple event is 1/36. Thus,

$$P(A) = \frac{4}{36} \qquad P(B) = \frac{11}{36}$$

c. $P(A \cap B) = \frac{2}{36} \qquad P(A \cup B) = \frac{13}{36}$

4.21 The relative frequencies found by dividing the frequencies by n = 8000, are given in table form.

		INCOME		
		(D)	(E)	(F)
		Under $20,000	$20,000-$50,000	Over $50,000
	(A) Under 25	$\frac{950}{8000}$	$\frac{1000}{8000}$	$\frac{50}{8000}$
AGE	(B) 25-45	$\frac{450}{8000}$	$\frac{2050}{8000}$	$\frac{1500}{8000}$
	(C) Over 45	$\frac{50}{8000}$	$\frac{950}{8000}$	$\frac{1000}{8000}$

a. $P(B) = \frac{450}{8000} + \frac{2050}{8000} + \frac{1500}{8000} = \frac{4000}{8000}$

b. $P(F) = \frac{50}{8000} + \frac{1500}{8000} + \frac{1000}{8000} = \frac{2550}{8000}$

c. $P(C \cap F) = \frac{1000}{8000}$

d. $P(B \cup C) = \frac{450}{8000} + \frac{2050}{8000} + \frac{1500}{8000} + \frac{50}{8000} + \frac{950}{8000} + \frac{1000}{8000} = \frac{6000}{8000}$

e. $P(A^C) = 1 - P(A) = 1 - \left(\frac{950}{8000} + \frac{1000}{8000} + \frac{50}{8000}\right)$

$$= 1 - \frac{2000}{8000}$$

$$= \frac{6000}{8000}$$

f. $P(A^C \cap F) = \frac{1500}{8000} + \frac{1000}{8000} = \frac{2500}{8000}$

4.23 a. $B \cap C$ b. A^C c. $C \cup B$ d. $A \cap C^C$

4.25 a. A simple event is an event that cannot be decomposed into two or more other events. In this example, there are nine simple events. Let 1 be Warehouse 1, 2 be Warehouse 2, 3 be Warehouse 3, and let R be Regular, S be Stiff, and E be Extra stiff. The simple events are:

       (1, R)   (1, S)   (1, E)
       (2, R)   (2, S)   (2, E)
       (3, R)   (3, S)   (3, E)

b. The *sample space* of an experiment is the collection of all its simple events.

c. P(C) = P(3, R) + P(3, S) + P(3, E)
   =   .28   +   .18   +   0
   = .46

d. P(F) = P(1, E) + P(2, E) + P(3, E)
   =   .03   +   .02   +   0
   = .05

e. P(A) = P(1, R) + P(1, S) + P(1, E)
   =   .19   +   .08   +   .03
   = .30

f. P(D) = P(1, R) + P(2, R) + P(3, R)
   =   .19   +   .14   .28
   = .61

g. P(E) = P(1, S) + P(2, S) + P(3, S)
   =   .08   +   .08   +   .18
   = .34

4.27 a. The 20 simple events may be listed as follows:

E_1: (Under 1000, 12)	E_{11}: (4000-5999, 12)
E_2: (Under 1000, 24)	E_{12}: (4000-5999, 24)
E_3: (Under 1000, 36)	E_{13}: (4000-5999, 36)
E_4: (Under 1000, 42)	E_{14}: (4000-5999, 42)
E_5: (Under 1000, 48)	E_{15}: (4000-5999, 48)
E_6: (1000-3999, 12)	E_{16}: (6000 or more, 12)
E_7: (1000-3999, 24)	E_{17}: (6000 or more, 24)
E_8: (1000-3999, 36)	E_{18}: (6000 or more, 36)
E_9: (1000-3999, 42)	E_{19}: (6000 or more, 42)
E_{10}: (1000-3999, 48)	E_{20}: (6000 or more, 48)

where the first entry within the parentheses indicates the amount of the loan (in dollars), and the second entry indicates the length of the loan (in months).

b. P(Selected loan will be for $6000 or more)

= $P(E_{16})$ + $P(P(E_{17})$ + $P(E_{18})$ + $P(E_{19})$ + $P(E_{20})$

= $0 + 0 + \dfrac{2}{500} + \dfrac{50}{500} + \dfrac{24}{500} = \dfrac{76}{500} = .152$

Yes, this is the same answer obtained in part (b) of Exercise 4.6.

c. $P(E_{18}) = \dfrac{2}{500} = .004$

d. P(Selected loan is for three or four years)

= P(Selected loan is for 36 or 48 months)

= $P(E_3) + P(E_5) + P(E_8) + P(E_{10}) + P(E_{13}) + P(E_{15}) + P(E_{18})$
$+ P(E_{20})$

= $0 + 0 + \frac{27}{500} + 0 + \frac{92}{500} + \frac{112}{500} + \frac{2}{500} + \frac{24}{500} = \frac{257}{500} = .514$

e. P(Selected loan is a 42-month loan for $1000 or more)

= $P(E_9) + P(E_{14}) + P(E_{19})$

= $\frac{53}{500} + \frac{93}{500} + \frac{50}{500} = \frac{196}{500} = .392$

4.29 a. The employee is a male, or the highest degree obtained by the employee is a Ph.D.

b. The employee is a female, or the highest degree obtained by the employee is a high school diploma.

c. The employee is a male, and the highest degree obtained by the employee is a Master's Degree.

d. The employee is a female, and the highest degree obtained by the employee is a Bachelor's Degree.

4.31 a. The sale was paid by credit card, or the merchandise purchased was women's wear.

$P(A \cup B)$ = .04 + .37 + .11 + .04 + .18 = .74

b. The merchandise purchased was women's wear or men's wear.

$P(B \cup C)$ = .04 + .37 + .07 + .11 = .59

c. The merchandise purchased was women's wear, and it was paid by credit card.

$P(B \cap A)$ = .37

d. The merchandise purchased was men's wear, and it was paid by credit card.

$P(C \cap A)$ = .11

4.33 The following events are defined:

A: {male worker}
B: {female worker}
C: {service worker}
D: {managerial/professional worker}
E: {operator/fabricator worker}
F: {technical/sales/administrative worker}

a. $P(A \cap C) = .053$

b. $P(D) = P(A \cap D) + P(B \cap D)$
$= .137 + .109$
$= .246$

c. $P[(B \cap D) \cup (B \cap E)] = .109 + .040$
$= .149$

d. $P(F^C) = 1 - P(F) = 1 - [P(A \cap F) + P(A \cap F)]$
$= 1 - (.110 + .202)$
$= 1 - .312$
$= .688$

4.35 a. $P(A) = P(E_1) + P(E_2) + P(E_3)$
$= \quad .1 + \quad .1 + \quad .3$
$= .5$

$P(B) = P(E_2) + P(E_3) + P(E_5)$
$= \quad .1 + \quad .3 + \quad .1$
$= .5$

$P(A \cap B) = P(E_2) + P(E_3)$
$= \quad .1 + \quad .3$
$= .4$

b. $P(E_1 | A) = \dfrac{P(E_1 \cap A)}{P(A)} = \dfrac{P(E_1)}{P(A)} = \dfrac{.1}{.5} = .2$

$P(E_2 | A) = \dfrac{(P(E_2 \cap A)}{P(A)} = \dfrac{P(E_2)}{P(A)} = \dfrac{.1}{.5} = .2$

$P(E_3 | A) = \dfrac{P(E_3 \cap A)}{P(A)} = \dfrac{P(E_3)}{P(A)} = \dfrac{.3}{.5} = .6$

The original simple event probabilities are in the proportion .1 to .1 to .3 or 1 to 1 to 3.

The conditional probabilities for these simple events are in the proportion .2 to .2 to .6 or 1 to 1 to 3.

c. (1) $P(B | A) = P(E_2 | A) + P(E_3 | A)$
$= \quad .2 + \quad .6 \quad$ (from part (b))
$= .8$

(2) $P(B | A) = \dfrac{P(A \cap B)}{P(A)} = \dfrac{.4}{.5} = .8$ (from part (a))

The two methods do yield the same result.

d. If A and B are independent events, $P(B|A) = P(B)$.

From part (c), $P(B|A) = .8$. From part (a), $P(B) = .5$.

Since $.8 \neq .5$, A and B are not independent events.

4.37 a. If A and B are independent, then $P(A|B) = P(A)$.

$$P(A|B) = \frac{P(A \cap B)}{P(B)} = \frac{P(E_3)}{P(E_2, E_3, E_4)} = \frac{.15}{.31 + .15 + .22} = \frac{.15}{.68} = .221$$

$P(A) = P(E_1) + P(E_3) = .22 + .15 = .37$

$.221 \neq .37$; therefore, A and B are not independent.

b. If A and C are independent, then $P(A|C) = P(A)$.

$$P(A|C) = \frac{P(A \cap C)}{P(C)} = \frac{P(E_1)}{P(E_1) + P(E_5)} = \frac{.22}{.22 + .10} = .688$$

$P(A) = P(E_1) + P(E_3) = .22 + .15 = .37$

$.37 \neq .688$; therefore, A and C are not independent.

c. If B and C are independent, then $P(B|C) = P(B)$.

$$P(B|C) = \frac{P(B \cap C)}{P(C)} = \frac{0}{.32} = 0$$

$P(B) = P(E_2) + P(E_7) + P(E_4) = .31 + .15 + .22 = .680$

$0 \neq .680$; therefore, B and C are not independent.

4.39 $P(R) = \frac{1}{3}$, $P(S) = \frac{1}{3}$

Since R and S are mutually exclusive, $P(R \cap S) = 0$

$$P(R|S) = \frac{P(R \cap S)}{P(S)} = \frac{0}{\frac{1}{3}} = 0$$

$$P(S|R) = \frac{P(R \cap S)}{P(R)} = \frac{0}{\frac{1}{3}} = 0$$

4.41 We define the following events:

A: {saw ad}
B: {shopped at X}

a. $P(A) = \frac{100}{200} + \frac{25}{200} = \frac{125}{200} = \frac{5}{8}$

b. $P(A \cap B) = \frac{100}{200} = \frac{1}{2}$

c. $P(B|A) = \dfrac{P(B \cap A)}{P(A)} = \dfrac{\frac{100}{200}}{\frac{125}{200}} = \dfrac{100}{125} = \dfrac{4}{5}$

d. $P(B) = \dfrac{100}{200} + \dfrac{25}{200} = \dfrac{125}{200} = \dfrac{5}{8}$

e. If A and B are independent events, $P(A \cap B) = P(A)P(B)$

From part (a), $P(A) = \dfrac{5}{8}$ From part (b), $P(A \cap B) = \dfrac{1}{2}$

From part (d), $P(B) = \dfrac{5}{8}$

$$P(A)P(B) = \dfrac{5}{8} \times \dfrac{5}{8} = \dfrac{25}{64}$$

$$\dfrac{1}{2} \neq \dfrac{25}{64}$$

Therefore, the events A and B are dependent events.

f. If the events "Did not see the ad" and "Did not shop at X" are mutually exclusive,

$$P(A^c \cap B^c) = 0$$

But $P(A^c \cap B^c) = \dfrac{50}{200} = \dfrac{1}{4} \neq 0$

Therefore, the 2 events are not mutually exclusive.

4.43 a. We will define the following events:

A: {The first activation device works properly; i.e., activates the sprinkler when it should}

B: {The second activation device works properly}

From the statement of the problem, we know

$P(A) = .91$ and $P(B) = .87$.

Furthermore, since the activation devices work independently, we conclude that

$P(A \cap B) = P(A)P(B) = (.91)(.87) = .7917$.

Now, if a fire starts near a sprinkler head, the sprinkler will be activated if either the first activation device or the second activation device, or both, operates properly. Thus,

$$P(\text{Sprinkler head will be activated}) = P(A \cup B)$$
$$= P(A) + P(B) - P(A \cap B)$$
$$= .91 + .87 - .7917$$
$$= .9883$$

b. The event that the sprinkler head will not be activated is the complement of the event that the sprinkler will be activated. Thus,

$$P(\text{Sprinkler head will not be activated})$$
$$= 1 - P(\text{Sprinkler head will be activated})$$
$$= 1 - .9883$$
$$= .0117$$

c. From part (a), $P(A \cap B) = .7917$

d. In terms of the events we have defined, we wish to determine

$$P(A \cap B^C) = P(A)P(B^C) \text{ (by independence)}$$
$$= .91(1 - .87)$$
$$= .91(.13)$$
$$= .1183$$

4.45 Define the following events.

A: {A defective case gets by inspector 1}
B: {A defective case gets by inspector 2}

We want to know

A ∩ B: {A defective case gets by inspector 1 and inspector 2}.

We know that the two inspectors check the cases independently. Therefore,

$$P(A \cap B) = P(A)P(B) = (.05)(.10) = .005$$

4.47 Define the following events:

A: {Population under 10,000}
B: {Population 10,000-100,000}
C: {Population over 100,000}
D: {NE Region}
E: {SE Region}
F: {SW Region}
G: {NW Region}

a. $P(D|C) = \dfrac{P(C \cap D)}{P(C)} = \dfrac{.25}{.25 + .04 + .05 + .1} = \dfrac{.25}{.44} = .568$

b. $P(A|E) = \dfrac{P(A \cap E)}{P(E)} = \dfrac{.06}{.06 + .15 + .04} = \dfrac{.06}{.25} = .24$

c. $P[(A \cup B)|F] = \dfrac{P[(A \cup B) \cap F]}{P(F)} = \dfrac{.03 + .12}{.03 + .12 + .05} = \dfrac{.15}{.2} = .75$

d. $P[(B \cup C)|G] = \dfrac{P[(B \cup C) \cap G]}{P(G)} = \dfrac{.05 + .10}{0 + .05 + .1} = \dfrac{.15}{.15} = 1$

4.49   Define the following events:

        A: {Product A is profitable}
        B: {Product B is profitable}

We know that

        P(Individual product profitable) = .18,
and
        P(Two products profitable) = .05.

a. $P(A) = .18$

b. $P(B^C) = 1 - P(B) = 1 - .18 = .82$

c. $P(A \cup B) = P(A) + P(B) - P(A \cap B)$
            $= .18 + .18 - .05$
            $= .31$

d. $P((A \cup B)^C) = 1 - P(A \cup B)$
                $= 1 - .31$
                $= .69$

e. $P(A \cup B) - P(A \cap B)$
        $= .31 - .05$
        $= .26$

4.51   Define the following events:

        A: {saw the advertisement}
        S_1: {stage 1 decision to purchase}
        S_2: {stage 2 decision to purchase}
        S_3: {stage 3 decision to purchase}
        S_4: {stage 4 decision to purchase}
        S_5: {stage 5 decision to purchase}

$P(A \cap S_1 \cap S_2 \cap S_3 \cap S_3 \cap S_5)$

      $= P(A)P(S_1)P(S_2)P(S_3)P(S_4)P(S_5)$
      $= .9(.7)(.7)(.7)(.7)(.7)$
      $= .151263$

4.53   Starting in row 5, column 2, of Table I of Appendix B and reading across, take the first 20 single digit numbers.

The 20 digits selected for the random sample are:

      3, 9, 9, 7, 5, 8, 1, 8, 3, 7, 1, 6, 6, 5, 6, 0, 6, 1, 2, 1

4.55 a. In a random sample, all 12 people have an equal chance of being selected. Therefore the probability of selecting any one of the 12 people in the population is 1/12.

Since only one person in the population has a weekly income of $900 (Jerry), the probability of selecting a person with a weekly income of $900 is 1/12.

Two people in the population have weekly incomes of $1500 (Carl and Paul). Therefore the probability of selecting a person with a weekly income of $1500 is $\frac{1}{12} + \frac{1}{12} = \frac{2}{12} = \frac{1}{6}$

b. Since there are 12 people in the population, the number of samples of size 3 is a combination of 12 things taken 3 at a time or

$$\binom{12}{3} = \frac{12!}{3!(12 - 3)!} = \frac{12!}{3!9!}$$

$$= \frac{12 \cdot 11 \cdot 10 \cdot 9 \cdot 8 \cdot 7 \cdot 6 \cdot 5 \cdot 4 \cdot 3 \cdot 2 \cdot 1}{(3 \cdot 2 \cdot 1)(9 \cdot 8 \cdot 7 \cdot 6 \cdot 5 \cdot 4 \cdot 3 \cdot 2 \cdot 1)} = 220$$

c. Since there are 220 possible samples of size 3 that can be selected, the probability of any one of them being selected is 1/220.

The probability of selecting Norm, Art, and John is 1/220.

The probability of selecting Rema, Shawn, and David is 1/220.

d. First, assign each person in the population a number from 01 to 12.

Norm	01		Art	07
Carl	02		John	08
Maureen	03		David	09
Paul	04		George	10
Rema	05		Chris	11
Shawn	06		Jerry	12

Using Table I of Appendix B, start in row 15, column 1 and read across. Group the numbers in sets of two digits and take the first three numbers from 01 to 12.

The following two digit numbers were found in Table I using the above procedure.

07, 11, 99, 73, 36, 71, 04

The random sample of size 3 from this population is Art (07), Chris (11), and Paul (04).

4.57 a. Decide on a starting point on the random number table. Then take the first n numbers reading down, and this would be the sample. Group the digits on the random number table into groups of 7 (for part (b)) or groups of 4 (for part (c)). Eliminate any duplicates and numbers that begin with zero since they are not valid telephone numbers.

b. Starting in Row 6, column 5, take the first 10 seven-digit numbers reading down. The telephone numbers are:

```
277-5653
988-7231
188-7620
174-5318
530-6059
709-9779
496-2669
889-7433
482-3752
772-3313
```

c. Starting in Row 10, column 7, take the first 5 four-digit numbers reading down. The 5 telephone numbers are:

```
373-3886
373-5686
373-1866
373-3632
373-6768
```

4.59 b. On page 1 of your local telephone directory, give each nonbusiness telephone subscriber a number (from 1 to n). Using Table I of Appendix B, pick a starting point and read down until you have 5 different numbers. If n is less than 1000, you need to look at groups of 3 digits. If n is more than 999, then you need to look at groups of 4 digits.

c. It would be very time consuming to go through the entire telephone directory and number each nonbusiness telephone subscriber.

4.61 (1) The probabilities of all simple events must lie between 0 and 1, inclusive.

(2) The probabilities of all the simple events in the sample space must sum to 1.

4.63 $P(A \cap B) = .4$, $P(A|B) = .8$

Since the $P(A|B) = \dfrac{P(A \cap B)}{P(B)}$, substitute the given probabilities into the formula and solve for $P(B)$.

$$.8 = \frac{.4}{P(B)}$$

Therefore, $P(B) = .50$.

4.65 Define the following events:

A: {the watch is accurate}
N: {the watch is not accurate}

Assuming the manufacturer's claim is correct,

$P(N) = .05$ and $P(A) = 1 - P(N) = 1 - .05 = .95$

The sample space for the purchase of 4 of the manufacturer's watches is listed below.

(A, A, A, A)	(A, N, A, A)	(N, A, A, A)	(N, N, A, A)
(A, A, A, N)	(A, N, A, N)	(N, A, A, N)	(N, N, A, N)
(A, A, N, A)	(A, N, N, A)	(N, A, N, A)	(N, N, N, A)
(A, A, N, N)	(A, N, N, N)	(N, A, N, N)	(N, N, N, N)

a. All 4 watches being accurate as claimed is the simple event (A, A, A, A).

Assuming the watches purchased operate independently and the manufacturer's claim is correct,

$$P(A, A, A, A) = P(A)P(A)P(A)P(A) = (.95)^4 = .8145$$

b. The simple events in the sample space that consist of exactly two watches failing to meet the claim are listed below.

(A, A, N, N)	(N, A, A, N)
(A, N, A, N)	(N, A, N, A)
(A, N, N, A)	(N, N, A, A)

The probability that exactly two of the four watches fail to meet the claim is the sum of the probabilities of these six simple events.

Assuming the watches purchased operate independently and the manufacturer's claim is correct,

$$P(A, A, N, N) = P(A)P(A)P(N)P(N) = (.95)(.95)(.05)(.05)$$
$$= .00225625$$

All six of the simple events will have the same probability. Therefore, the probability that exactly two of the four watches fail to meet the claim when the manufacturer's claim is correct is

$$6(0.00225625) = .0135$$

c. The simple events in the sample space that consist of three of the four watches failing to meet the claim are listed below.

(A, N, N, N)   (N, N, A, N)
(N, A, N, N)   (N, N, N, A)

The probability that three of the four watches fail to meet the claim is the sum of the probabilities of the four simple events.

Assuming the watches purchased operate independently and the manufacturer's claim is correct,

$$P(A, N, N, N) = P(A)P(N)P(N)P(N) = (.95)(.05)(.05)(.05)$$
$$= .00011875$$

All four of the simple events will have the same probability. Therefore, the probability that three of the four watches fail to meet the claim when the manufacturer's claim is correct is

$$4(.00011875) = .000475$$

If this event occurred, we would tend to doubt the validity of the manufacturer's claim since its probability of occurring is so small.

d. All 4 watches tested failing to meet the claim is the simple event (N, N, N, N).

Assuming the watches purchased operate independently and the manufacturer's claim is correct,

$$P(N, N, N, N) = P(N)P(N)P(N)P(N) = (.05)^4 = .00000625$$

Since the probability of observing this event is so small if the claim is true, we have strong evidence against the validity of the claim. However, we do not have conclusive proof that the claim is false. There is still a chance the event can occur (with probability .00000625) although it is extremely small.

4.67 Define the following events:

        T: {Technical staff}
        N: {Nontechnical staff}
        U: {Under 20 years with company}
        O: {Over 20 years with company}
        R_1: {Retire at age 65}
        R_2: {Retire at age 68}

The probabilities for each simple event are given in table form.

	U		O	
	T	N	T	N
R_1	$\frac{31}{200}$	$\frac{5}{200}$	$\frac{45}{200}$	$\frac{12}{200}$
R_2	$\frac{59}{200}$	$\frac{25}{200}$	$\frac{15}{200}$	$\frac{8}{200}$

Each simple event consists of 3 characteristics: type of staff (T or N), years with the company, (U or O), and age plan to retire (R_1 or R_2).

a. $P(T) = P(T \cap U \cap R_1) + P(T \cap U \cap R_2) + P(T \cap O \cap R_1)$
           $+ P(T \cap O \cap R_2)$

$$= \frac{31}{200} + \frac{59}{200} + \frac{45}{200} + \frac{15}{200} = \frac{150}{200}$$

b. $P(O) = P(O \cap T \cap R_1) + P(O \cap T \cap R_2) + P(O \cap N \cap R_1)$
           $+ P(O \cap N \cap R_2)$

$$= \frac{45}{200} + \frac{15}{200} + \frac{12}{200} + \frac{8}{200} = \frac{80}{200}$$

$$P(R_2 \cap O) = P(R_2 \cap O \cap T) + P(R_2 \cap O \cap N) = \frac{15}{200} + \frac{8}{200} = \frac{23}{200}$$

Thus, $P(R_2 | O) = \dfrac{P(R_2 \cap O)}{P(O)} = \dfrac{\frac{23}{200}}{\frac{80}{200}} = \dfrac{23}{80}$

c. $P(T) = \dfrac{150}{200}$ from a.

$$P(U \cap T) = P(U \cap T \cap R_1) + P(U \cap T \cap R_2) = \frac{31}{200} + \frac{59}{200} = \frac{90}{200}$$

Thus, $P(U | T) = \dfrac{P(U \cap T)}{P(T)} = \dfrac{\frac{90}{200}}{\frac{150}{200}} = \dfrac{90}{150}$

d. $P(O \cap N \cap R_1) = \dfrac{12}{200}$

4.69 The number of different ways to select 5 stocks from 10 stocks is a combination of 10 things taken 5 at a time or

$$\binom{10}{5} = \frac{10!}{5!(10-5)!} = \frac{10 \cdot 9 \cdot 8 \cdot 7 \cdot 6 \cdot 5 \cdot 4 \cdot 3 \cdot 2 \cdot 1}{5 \cdot 4 \cdot 3 \cdot 2 \cdot 1 \cdot 5 \cdot 4 \cdot 3 \cdot 2 \cdot 1} = 252$$

4.71 Define the following events:

L: {under 30}
M: {30-50}
H: {over 50}
N: {Noticed the ad}
N^C: {Did not notice the ad}

a. The simple events are:

(L, N), (M, N), (H, N), (L, N^C), (M, N^C), (H, N^C)

b. The set of all possible simple events is called the sample space.

c. $P(L, N) = .25$ $P(L, N^C) = .05$
    $P(M, N) = .20$ $P(M, N^C) = .15$
    $P(H, N) = .10$ $P(H, N^C) = .25$

4.73 Define the following events:

G: {regularly use the golf course}
T: {regularly use the tennis courts}

Given: $P(G) = .7$ and $P(T) = .5$

The event 'uses neither facility' can be written as $G^C \cap T^C$ or $(G \cup T)^C$. We are given $P(G^C \cap T^C) = P[(G \cup T)^C] = .05$. The complement of the event 'uses neither facility' is the event 'uses at least one of the two facilities' which can be written as $G \cup T$.

$P(G \cup T) = 1 - P[(G \cup T)^C] = 1 - .05 = .95$

From the additive rule, $P(G \cup T) = P(G) + P(T) - P(G \cap T)$

=> $.95 = .7 + .5 - P(G \cap T)$
=> $P(G \cap T) = .25$

a. The Venn Diagram is:

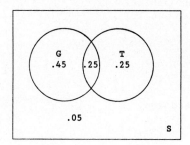

b. P(G ∪ T) = .95 from above.

c. P(G ∩ T) = .25 from above.

d. $P(G|T) = \dfrac{P(G \cap T)}{P(T)} = \dfrac{.25}{.5} = .5$

4.75 The statement would be valid if 1/50th of all U.S. citizens reside in New Hampshire. However, this is not true. Therefore, the statement is invalid.

4.77 Define the following events:

O_1: Component #1 operates properly
O_2: Component #2 operates properly
O_3: Component #3 operates properly

$P(O_1) = 1 - P(O_1^C) = 1 - .12 = .88$
$P(O_2) = 1 - P(O_2^C) = 1 - .09 = .91$
$P(O_3) = 1 - P(O_3^C) = 1 - .11 = .89$

a. P(system operates properly) = $P(O_1 \cap O_2 \cap O_3)$
    = $P(O_1)P(O_2)P(O_3)$ (since the three components operate
                                    independently)
    = (.88)(.91)(.89)
    = .7127

b. P(system fails) = 1 - P(system operates properly)
                    = 1 - .7127 (see part (a))
                    = .2873

4.79 Define the following events:

A: {product A is accepted by the public}
B: {product B is accepted by the public}

Given:

$P(A \cap B^C) = .3$
$P(A^C \cap B) = .4$
$P(A \cap B) = .2$

The simple events of the sample space are.

A, B
A, B^C
A^C, B
A^C, B^C

Since the sum of the probabilities of these 4 events is 1,

$P(A^C \cap B^C) = 1 - P(A \cap B) - P(A \cap B^C) - P(A^C \cap B)$
$= 1 - .2 - .3 - .4 = .1$

This probability is not equal to .01. Therefore, we would disagree with the manager.

4.81 a. $P(A|B) = \dfrac{P(A \cap B)}{P(B)} = \dfrac{.06}{.05 + .06 + .03 + 0} = \dfrac{.06}{.14} = .429$

b. $P(B|A) = \dfrac{P(A \cap B)}{P(A)} = \dfrac{.06}{.06 + .15 + .04} = \dfrac{.06}{.25} = .24$

c. $P(A|C) = \dfrac{P(A \cap C)}{P(C)} = \dfrac{.15 + .04}{.10 + .15 + .12 + .05 + .25 + .04 + .05 + .10}$

$= \dfrac{.19}{.86} = .221$

d. $P(C|D) = \dfrac{P(C \cap D)}{P(D)} = \dfrac{.10 + .25}{.05 + .10 + .25} = .875$

4.83 Define the following events:

A: {Trailer worth $12,000 - $17,999}
B: {Trailer worth more than $17,999}
C: {Owner does not own a generator}
D: {Owner plans to buy a generator}

$P(C) = \dfrac{5 + 65 + 78 + 36 + 18 + 10 + 14 + 160 + 175 + 62 + 21 + 6}{829}$

$= \dfrac{650}{829}$

a. $P(A|C) = \dfrac{P(A \cap C)}{P(C)} = \dfrac{\frac{78}{829} + \frac{175}{829}}{\frac{650}{829}} = \dfrac{\frac{253}{829}}{\frac{650}{829}} = \dfrac{253}{650}$

b. $P(B|C) = \dfrac{P(B \cap C)}{P(C)} = \dfrac{\dfrac{36 + 18 + 10 + 62 + 21 + 6}{829}}{\dfrac{650}{829}} = \dfrac{\dfrac{153}{829}}{\dfrac{650}{829}} = \dfrac{153}{650}$

c. $P(A \cap D)|C) = \dfrac{P(A \cap D \cap C)}{P(C)} = \dfrac{P(A \cap D)}{P(C)} = \dfrac{\dfrac{78}{829}}{\dfrac{650}{829}} = \dfrac{78}{650}$

d. $P((A \cup D)|C) = \dfrac{P((A \cup D) \cap C)}{P(C)} = \dfrac{\dfrac{5 + 65 + 78 + 36 + 18 + 10 + 175}{829}}{\dfrac{650}{829}}$

$$= \dfrac{\dfrac{387}{829}}{\dfrac{650}{829}} = \dfrac{387}{650}$$

4.85 No, this claim cannot be true. The probability that at least 2 local firms go bankrupt next year is the same as 2 or more go bankrupt. This event includes the event that exactly 2 firms go bankrupt. Therefore, the probability that at least 2 firms go bankrupt must be the same or larger than the probability that exactly 2 firms go bankrupt.

4.87 a. Consecutive tosses of a coin are independent events since what occurs one time would not affect the next outcome.

b. If the individuals are randomly selected, then what one individual says should not affect what the next person says. They are independent events.

c. The results in 2 consecutive at-bats are probably not independent. The player may have faced the same pitcher both times which may affect the outcome.

d. The amount of gain and loss for 2 different stocks bought and sold on the same day are probably not independent. The market might be way up or down on a certain day so that all stocks are affected.

e. The amount of gain or loss for 2 different stocks that are bought and sold in different time periods are independent. What happens to one stock should not affect what happens to the other.

f. The prices bid by two different development firms in response to the same building construction proposal would probably not be independent. The same variables would be present for both firms to consider in their bids (materials, labor, etc.).

CHAPTER 5

RANDOM VARIABLES AND PROBABILITY DISTRIBUTIONS

5.1   A random variable is a rule that assigns one and only one value to each simple event of an experiment.

5.3   a.   The number of houses sold by a real estate developer is countable (1, 2, 3, ...), so this is a *discrete* random variable.

       b.   This is a *continuous* random variable because we cannot count all the possible values.

       c.   Although a quart of milk is supposed to be 32 ounces, it can take on any value within an acceptable limit of 32 ounces, e.g., 32.09 ounces. Therefore, this is a *continuous* random variable.

       d.   The possible values for this random variable can be counted (e.g., 0, 7, 10, etc.). Hence, the variable is *discrete.*

5.5   The number of occupied units in an apartment complex at any time is a discrete random variable, as is the number of shares of stock traded on the New York Stock Exchange on a particular day. Two examples of continuous random variables are the length of time to complete a building project and the weight of a truckload of oranges.

5.7   An economist might be interested in the percentage of the work force that is unemployed, or the current inflation rate, both of which are continuous random variables.

5.9   The manager of a clothing store might be concerned with the number of employees on duty at a specific time of day, or the number of articles of a particular type of clothing that are on hand.

5.11   a.   The eight simple events and the corresponding values of x are
            shown in the following table.

SIMPLE EVENT	x
(H, H, H)	3
(H, H, T)	2
(H, T, H)	2
(T, H, H)	2
(T, T, H)	1
(T, H, T)	1
(H, T, T)	1
(T, T, T)	0

b.   Since the 8 simple events are equally likely,

$p(0) = P(x = 0) = P(T, T, T) = \frac{1}{8}$

$p(1) = P(x = 1) = P(T, T, H) + P(T, H, T) + P(H, T, T)$

$$= \frac{1}{8} + \frac{1}{8} + \frac{1}{8} = \frac{3}{8}$$

$p(2) = P(x = 2) = P(H, H, T) = P(H, T, H) + P(T, H, H)$

$$= \frac{1}{8} + \frac{1}{8} + \frac{1}{8} = \frac{3}{8}$$

$p(3) = P(x = 3) = P(H, H, H) = \frac{1}{8}$

The probability distribution of x may now be summarized in tabular
form:

x	p(x)
0	1/8
1	3/8
2	3/8
3	1/8

c. The probability distribution of x may also be presented in graphical form:

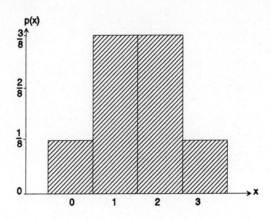

5.13 a. This is *not* a valid distribution because $\sum p(x) \neq 1$.

b. This is a *valid* distribution because $p(x) \geq 0$ for all values of x and $\sum p(x) = 1$.

c. This is *not* a valid distribution because one of the probabilities is negative.

d. The sum of the probabilities over all possible values of the random variable is greater than 1, so this is *not* a valid probability distribution.

5.15 a. $\mu = \sum_{\text{All } x} xp(x) = -2(.05) + (-1)(.20) + 0(.20) + 1(.30) + 2(.25)$
$= -.1 - .2 + .3 + .5$
$= .5$

b.
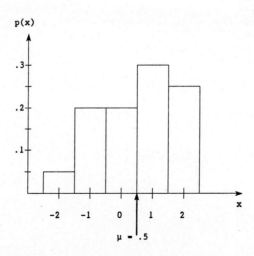

c. The average value of x is .5

d. No, the random variable x cannot assume the value of μ in this problem. According to the probability distribution, x is -2, -1, 0, 1, or 2. It cannot be .5.

e. Yes, in general a random variable can assume its expected value. The expected value is average value of x. Sometimes it is a value the random variable can assume, sometimes not.

5.17 a. The probability distribution for x in graphical form:

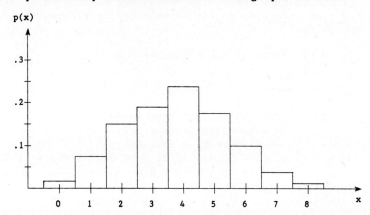

b. $P(x > 3) = p(4) + p(5) + p(6) + p(7) + p(8)$
    $= .24 + .17 + .10 + .04 + .01$
    $= .56$

$P(x > 4) = p(5) + p(6) + p(7) + p(8)$
    $= .17 + .10 + .04 + .01 = .32$

5.19 a. Let x equal the value of the prize. Since there are 300,000 brochures mailed, 3 people will win $5,000, 3 will win a microwave oven, 3 will win a television, 3 will win a computer, 3 will win a video recorder, 3 will win a moped, and 299,982 will win a raft. Since the winning numbers are randomly assigned to brochures, the probability distribution of x is given below in tabular form:

x	5000	795	769	699	500	49.95
p(x)	$\frac{3}{300,000}$	$\frac{3}{300,000}$	$\frac{3}{300,000}$	$\frac{6}{300,000}$	$\frac{3}{300,000}$	$\frac{299,982}{300,000}$

b. P(not win an inflatable raft)
    = 1 - P(will win an inflatable raft)
    = 1 - p(49.95)

    $= 1 - \dfrac{299,982}{300,000}$

    $= \dfrac{18}{300,000} = .00006$

c. No, the answer would not change if 1,000,000 instead of 300,000 brochures are mailed. When the number of brochures is increased, the number of winners also increases, but the ratio always stays the same. Therefore, the probability of winning the prizes will not change.

5.21 a. $E(x) = \sum_{\text{All } x} xp(x)$

Bank borrowers:

$$\begin{aligned}
E(x) &= 210(.109) + 200(.117) + 190(.109) + 180(.113) \\
&\quad + 170(.219) + 160(.102) + 150(.102) + 140(.074) \\
&\quad + 130(.035) + 120(.020) \\
&= 22.89 + 23.4 + 20.71 + 20.34 + 37.23 + 16.32 + 15.3 \\
&\quad + 10.36 + 4.55 + 2.4 \\
&= 173.5
\end{aligned}$$

The average credit score for the bank borrowers is 173.5.

Finance Company borrowers:

$$\begin{aligned}
E(x) &= 210(.000) + 200(.023) + 190(.034) + 180(.034) \\
&\quad + 170(.184) + 160(.069) + 150(.161) + 140(.172) \\
&\quad + 130(.105) + 120(.218) \\
&= 0 + 4.6 + 6.46 + 6.12 + 31.28 + 11.04 + 24.15 + 24.08 \\
&\quad + 13.65 + 26.16 \\
&= 147.54
\end{aligned}$$

The average credit score for the finance company borrowers is 147.54.

b. $\sigma = \sqrt{\sigma^2}$, $\sigma^2 = \sum\limits_{\text{All } x} (x - \mu)^2 p(x)$

Bank Borrowers:

$$\begin{aligned}
\sigma^2 &= (210 - 173.5)^2(.109) + (200 - 173.5)^2(.117) \\
&\quad + (190 - 173.5)^2(.109) + (180 - 173.5)^2(.113) \\
&\quad + (170 - 173.5)^2(.219) + (160 - 173.5)^2(.102) \\
&\quad + (150 - 173.5)^2(.102) + (140 - 173.5)^2(.074) \\
&\quad + (130 - 173.5)^2(.035) + (120 - 173.5)^2(.020) \\
&= 145.21525 + 82.16325 + 29.67525 + 4.77425 + 2.68275 \\
&\quad + 18.5895 + 56.3295 + 83.0465 + 66.22875 + 57.245 \\
&= 545.95 \\
\sigma &= 23.37
\end{aligned}$$

Finance Company Borrowers:

$$\begin{aligned}
\sigma^2 &= (210 - 147.54)^2(.000) + (200 - 147.54)^2(.023) \\
&\quad + (190 - 147.54)^2(.034) + (180 - 147.54)^2(.034) \\
&\quad + (170 - 147.54)^2(.184) + (160 - 147.54)^2(.069) \\
&\quad + (150 - 147.54)^2(.161) + (140 - 147.54)^2(.172) \\
&\quad + (130 - 147.54)^2(.105) + (120 - 147.54)^2(.218) \\
&= 0 + 63.2972 + 61.2970 + 35.8242 + 92.8191 + 10.7124 \\
&\quad + .9743 + 9.7785 + 32.3034 + 165.3424 \\
&= 472.3485 \\
\sigma &= 21.73
\end{aligned}$$

c. On the average, the bank borrowers have a larger credit score than the finance company borrowers. This would indicate that the bank borrowers have a smaller credit risk. The standard deviation is slightly higher for the bank borrowers, but they still seem to be more credit-worthy than the finance company borrowers.

5.23 a. Let x = profit from the concert. The probability distribution for the random variable x is

x	(Rain)	(No Rain)
x	-12,000	20,000
p(x)	.4	.6

The producer's expected profit from the concert is

$$\begin{aligned}
E(x) = \sum\limits_{\text{All } x} xp(x) &= -12000(.4) + 20000(.6) \\
&= -4800 + 12000 \\
&= \$7200
\end{aligned}$$

b. Let x = profit from the concert. The probability distribution for the random variable x if the producer buys insurance is

	(Rain)	(No Rain)
x	-1,000	19,000
p(x)	.4	.6

The producer's expected profit form the concert if she buys insurance is

$$E(x) = \sum_{\text{All } x} xp(x) = -1000(.4) + 19000(.6)$$
$$= -400 + 11400$$
$$= \$11,000$$

c. The insurance company has charged too little for the policy since the producer's expected profit has increased by 11000 - 7200 = $3800 by buying insurance.

5.25   a. $p(x) = \binom{n}{x} p^x (1 - p)^{n-x}$

$P(x = 0) = p(0) = \binom{5}{0}.2^0.8^5 = \frac{5!}{0!5!}.2^0.8^5 = 1(1)(.32768) = .32768$

$P(x = 1) = p(1) = \binom{5}{1}.2^1.8^4 = \frac{5!}{1!4!}.2^1.8^4 = 5(.2)(.4096) = .4096$

$P(x = 2) = p(2) = \binom{5}{2}.2^2.8^3 = \frac{5!}{2!3!}.2^2.8^3 = 10(.04)(.512) = .2048$

$P(x = 3) = p(3) = \binom{5}{3}.2^3.8^2 = \frac{5!}{3!2!}.2^3.8^2 = 10(.008)(.64) = .0512$

$P(x = 4) = p(4) = \binom{5}{4}.2^4.8^1 = \frac{5!}{4!1!}.2^4.8^1 = 5(.0016)(.8) = .0064$

$P(x = 5) = p(5) = \binom{5}{5}.2^5.8^0 = \frac{5!}{5!0!}.2^5.8^0 = 1(.00032)(1) = .00032$

In tabular form, the probability distribution for x is

x	0	1	2	3	4	5
p(x)	.32768	.4096	.2048	.0512	.0064	.00032

b.   p(x)

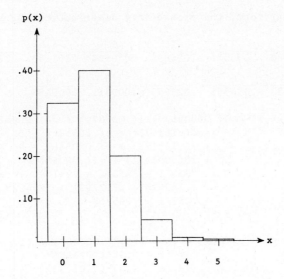

5.27   a. $p(x) = \binom{11}{x}.5^x.5^{11-x}$ $x = 0, 1, 2, \dots, 11$

$P(x = 0) = p(0) = \binom{11}{0}.5^0.5^{11} = \frac{11!}{0!11!}.5^{11} = (.5)^{11} = .000488$

$P(x = 1) = p(1) = \binom{11}{1}.5^1.5^{10} = \frac{11!}{1!10!}.5^{11} = 11(.5)^{11} = .005371$

$P(x = 2) = p(2) = \binom{11}{2}.5^2.5^9 = \frac{11!}{2!9!}.5^{11} = 55(.5)^{11} = .026855$

$P(x = 3) = p(3) = \binom{11}{3}.5^3.5^8 = \frac{11!}{3!8!}.5^{11} = 165(.5)^{11} = .080566$

$P(x = 4) = p(4) = \binom{11}{4}.5^4.5^7 = \frac{11!}{4!7!}.5^{11} = 330(.5)^{11} = .161133$

$P(x = 5) = p(5) = \binom{11}{5}.5^5.5^6 = \frac{11!}{5!6!}.5^{11} = 462(.5)^{11} = .225586$

$P(x = 6) = p(6) = \binom{11}{6}.5^6.5^5 = \frac{11!}{6!5!}.5^{11} = 462(.5)^{11} = .225586$

$P(x = 7) = p(7) = \binom{11}{7}.5^7.5^4 = \frac{11!}{7!4!}.5^{11} = 330(.5)^{11} = .161133$

$P(x = 8) = p(8) = \binom{11}{8}.5^8.5^3 = \frac{11!}{8!3!}.5^{11} = 165(.5)^{11} = .080566$

$P(x = 9) = p(9) = \binom{11}{9}.5^9.5^2 = \frac{11!}{9!2!}.5^{11} = 55(.5)^{11} = .026855$

$P(x = 10) = p(10) = \binom{11}{10}.5^{10}.5^1 = \frac{11!}{10!1!}.5^{11} = 11(.5)^{11} = .005371$

$P(x = 11) = p(11) = \binom{11}{11}.5^{11}.5^0 = \frac{11!}{11!0!}.5^{11} = (.5)^{11} = .000488$

In tabular form, the probability distribution for x is:

x	0	1	2	3	4	5	6
p(x)	.000488	.005371	.026855	.080566	.161133	.225586	.225586

7	8	9	10	11
.161133	.080566	.026855	.005371	.000488

b. $\mu = \sum\limits_{\text{All } x} x(px)$ = 0(.000488) + 1(.005371) + 2(.026855) + 3(.080566)
$\qquad$ + 4(.161133) + 5(.225586) + 6(.225586)
$\qquad$ + 7(.161133) + 8(.080566) + 9(.026855)
$\qquad$ + 10(.005371) + 11(.000488)
$\qquad$ = 0 + .005371 + .05371 + .241698 + .644532 + 1.12793
$\qquad$ + 1.353516 + 1.127931 + .644528 + .241695
$\qquad$ + .05371 + .005368
$\qquad$ = 5.5.

$\sigma^2 = \sum\limits_{\text{All } x} (x - \mu)^2 p(x)$ = $(0 - 5.5)^2(.000488) + (1 - 5.5)^2(.005371)$
$\qquad$ + $(2 - 5.5)^2(.026855) + (3 - 5.5)^2(.080566)$
$\qquad$ + $(4 - 5.5)^2(.161133) + (5 - 5.5)^2(.225586)$
$\qquad$ + $(6 - 5.5)^2(.225586) + (7 - 5.5)^2(.161133)$
$\qquad$ + $(8 - 5.5)^2(.080566) + (9 - 5.5)^2(.026855)$
$\qquad$ + $(10 - 5.5)^2(.005371)$
$\qquad$ + $(11 - 5.5)^2(.000488)$
$\qquad$ = .014762 + .10876275 + .32897375 + .5035375
$\qquad$ + .36254925 + .05363965 + .0563965
$\qquad$ + .36254925 + .5035375 + .32897375
$\qquad$ + .10876275 + .014762
$\qquad$ = 2.75

c.

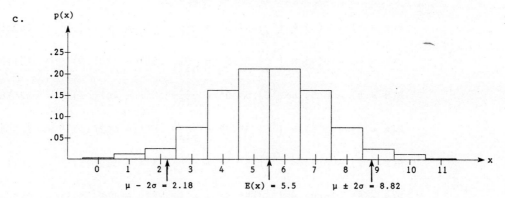

$\mu \pm 2\sigma \Rightarrow 5.5 \pm 2\sqrt{2.75} \Rightarrow 5.5 \pm 2(1.6583)$
$\qquad\qquad \Rightarrow 5.5 \pm 3.3166$
$\qquad\qquad \Rightarrow (2.1834, 8.8166)$

$\qquad\qquad\qquad\qquad\qquad\qquad\qquad\qquad\qquad$

d. $\mu \pm 2\sigma \Rightarrow (2.18, 8.82)$ (part (c))

$$P(2.18 < x < 8.82) = \sum_{x=3}^{8} p(x)$$
$$= .080566 + .161133 + .225586 + .225586$$
$$+ .161133 + .080566$$
$$= .93457$$

5.29 Using Table II in Appendix B with n = 15 and p = .40:

a. $P(x \leq 1) = \sum_{x=0}^{1} p(x) = .005$

b. $P(x \geq 3) = 1 - P(x \leq 2) = 1 - \sum_{x=0}^{2} p(x) = 1 - .027 = .973$

c. $P(x \leq 5) = \sum_{x=0}^{5} p(x) = .403$

d. $P(x < 10) = P(x \leq 9) = \sum_{x=0}^{9} p(x) = .966$

e. $P(x > 10) = 1 - P(x \leq 10) = 1 - \sum_{x=0}^{10} p(x) = 1 - .991 = .009$

f. $P(x = 6) = P(x \leq 6) - p(x \leq 5) = .610 - .403 = .207$

5.31 a. $P(\text{audited}|\text{income less than } \$50,000) = \frac{9}{1000} = .009$

$P(\text{audited}|\text{income of } \$50,000 \text{ or more}) = \frac{22}{1000} = .022$

b. Define x as the number of taxpayers with incomes under $50,000 that will be audited. The random variable x is a binomial random variable (the taxpayers are independently chosen and there are only two possible outcomes) with p = .02 and n = 5.

$$P(x = 1) = \binom{5}{1} .009^1 .991^4 = \frac{5!}{1!4!} .009^1 .991^4$$
$$= .0434$$
$$P(x > 1) = p(2) + p(3) + p(4) + p(5)$$
$$= 1 - (p(0) + p(1))$$
$$= 1 - (\binom{5}{0} .009^0 .991^5 + .0434)$$
$$= 1 - (\frac{5!}{0!5!} .009^0 .991^5 + .0434)$$
$$= 1 - .9992$$
$$= .0008$$

RANDOM VARIABLES AND PROBABILITY DISTRIBUTIONS

c. Define y as the number of taxpayers with incomes of \$50,000 or more that will be audited. The random variable y is a binomial random variable with p = .022 and n = 5.

$$P(y = 1) = \binom{5}{1} .022^1 .978^4 = \frac{5!}{1!4!} .022^1 .978^4$$

$$= .1006$$

$$P(y > 1) = 1 - (p(0) + p(1))$$

$$= 1 - (\binom{5}{0} .022^0 .978^5 + .1006)$$

$$= 1 - (\frac{5!}{0!5!} .022^0 .978^5 + .1006)$$

$$= 1 - .9953$$

$$= .0047$$

d. P(none of the taxpayers will be audited)
= P(x = 0 ∩ y = 0)
= P(x = 0)P(y = 0) (using independence)

$$= (\binom{2}{0} .009^0 .991^2) \binom{2}{0} (.022^0 .978^2)$$

$$= (\frac{2!}{0!2!} .009^0 .991^2)(\frac{2!}{0!2!} .022^0 .978^2)$$

$$= (.982081)(.956484)$$

$$= .9393$$

e. We must assume the taxpayers are chosen independently.

5.33 Define the following events:

J: Stock market is up in January
Y: Stock market is up for the whole year

If there is no truth to the "January" theory, there are four equally likely events that could occur in any a given year:

J, Y   J, Y^c J^c, Y J^c, Y^c

Thus, the probability of perfect agreement with the "January" theory if, in fact, there is no truth to the theory is

$$P(J, Y) + P(J^c, Y^c) = \frac{1}{4} + \frac{1}{4} = \frac{1}{2}$$

Let x equal the number of years that the January and annual movements are in perfect agreement during a period of 15 years.

The random variable x is a binomial random variable with p = .5, q = 5, and n = 15.

a. $p(x) = \binom{n}{x} p^x q^{n-x}$

$P(x = 15) = \binom{15}{15} .5^{15} .5^0 = \dfrac{15!}{15!0!} .5^{15} .5^0$

$= 1(.5^{15})(1) = .00003052 \approx 0$

b. $P(x \geq 10) = 1 - P(x \leq 9)$

$= 1 - \sum\limits_{x=0}^{9} p(x)$

$= 1 - .849 \quad$ (Table II, Appendix B)

$= .151$

5.35 a. We must assume that the probability that a specific type of ball meets the requirements is always the same from trial to trial and the trials are independent. To use the binomial probability distribution, we need to know the probability that a specific type of golf ball meets the requirements.

b. For a binomial distribution,

$\mu = np$
$\sigma = \sqrt{npq}$

In this example, n = two dozen = 2 · 12 = 24.

p = .10   (Success here means the golf ball *does not* meet
q = .90   standards.)

$\mu = np = 24(.10) = 2.4$

$\sigma = \sqrt{npq} = \sqrt{24(.10)(.90)} = 1.47$

c. In this situation,

p = Probability of success
  = Probability golf ball *does* meet standards
  = .90
q = 1 - .90 = .10
n = 24
$\mu = np = 24(.90) = 21.60$

$\sigma = \sqrt{npq} = \sqrt{24(.10)(.90)} = 1.47$ (Note that this is the same
                                         as in part (b).)

5.37 The random variable x = number of defective fuses is a binomial random variable with n = 25. We will accept a lot if x < 3.

Using Table II, Appendix B:

a. P(accepting a lot) = P(x < 3) = $\sum\limits_{x=0}^{2} p(x)$ = 0   when p = 1

b. P(accepting a lot) = P(x < 3) = $\sum\limits_{x=0}^{2} p(x)$ ≈ 0   when p = .8

c. P(accepting a lot) = P(x < 3) = $\sum\limits_{x=0}^{2} p(x)$ ≈ 0   when p = .5

d. P(accepting a lot) = P(x < 3) = $\sum\limits_{x=0}^{2} p(x)$ = .098   when p = .2

e. P(accepting a lot) = P(x < 3) = $\sum\limits_{x=0}^{2} p(x)$ = .873   when p = .05

f. P(accepting a lot) = P(x < 3) = $\sum\limits_{x=0}^{2} p(x)$ = 1   when p = 0

A graph of the operating characteristic curve for this sampling plan is shown below.

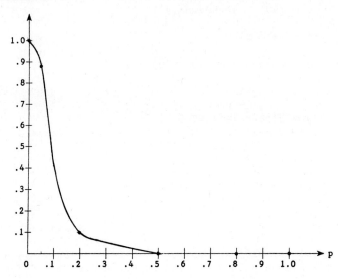

5.39   The random variable x (the number that prefer the beverage) is a
        binomial random variable with n = 400, p = .12, and q = .88 if the
        market analyst's claim is correct.

$$\mu = np = 400(.12) = 48$$

$$\sigma = \sqrt{npq} = \sqrt{400(.12)(.88)} = \sqrt{42.24} = 6.4992$$

If the market analyst's claim is true, it is not likely we would
observe a value of $x \leq 31$. The value 31 is almost 3 standard
deviations below the mean value of 48. Therefore, the survey does not
agree with the market analyst's claim.

5.41 $\mu = \lambda = 1.5$

Using Table III of Appendix B:

a. $P(x \leq 2) = .809$

b. $P(x \geq 2) = 1 - P(x \leq 1) = 1 - .558 = .442$

c. $P(x = 2) = P(x \leq 2) - P(x \leq 1) = .809 - .558 = .251$

d. $P(x = 0) = .223$

e. $P(x > 0) = 1 - P(x = 0) = 1 - .223 = .777$

f. $P(x > 5) = 1 - P(x \leq 5) = 1 - .996 = .004$

5.43   a. To graph the Poisson probability distribution with $\lambda = 4$, we need
            to calculate p(x) for x = 0 to 10. Using Table III, Appendix B,

            p(0) = .018
            p(1) = P(x ≤ 1) - P(x = 0) = .092 - .018 = .074
            p(2) = P(x ≤ 2) - P(x ≤ 1) = .238 - .092 = .146
            p(3) = P(x ≤ 3) - P(x ≤ 2) = .433 - .238 = .195
            p(4) = P(x ≤ 4) - P(x ≤ 3) = .629 - .433 = .196
            p(5) = P(x ≤ 5) - P(x ≤ 4) = .785 - .629 = .156
            p(6) = P(x ≤ 6) - P(x ≤ 5) = .889 - .785 = .104
            p(7) = P(x ≤ 7) - P(x ≤ 6) = .949 - .889 = .060
            p(8) = P(x ≤ 8) - P(x ≤ 7) = .979 - .949 = .030
            p(9) = P(x ≤ 9) - P(x ≤ 8) = .992 - .979 = .013
            p(10) = P(x ≤ 10) - P(x ≤ 9) = .997 - .992 = .005

The graph is shown below.

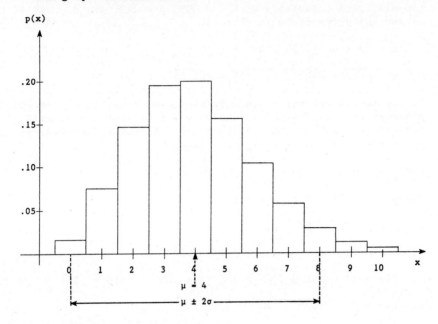

b. $\mu = \lambda = 4$

$\sigma = \sqrt{\lambda} = \sqrt{4} = 2$

$\mu \pm 2\sigma \Rightarrow 4 \pm 2(2) \Rightarrow (0, 8)$

c. $P(\mu - 2\sigma < x < \mu + 2\sigma)$
    $= P(0 < x < 8)$
    $= P(1 \leq x \leq 7)$
    $= P(x \leq 7) - p(x = 0)$
    $= .949 - .018$
    $= .931$

5.45 a. $E(x) = \mu = \lambda = 67.6$

$\sigma = \sqrt{\lambda} = \sqrt{67.6} = 8.222$

b. Using the formula with $\lambda = 67.6$,

$$P(x = 120) = \frac{\lambda^x e^{-\lambda}}{x!} = \frac{67.6^{120} e^{-67.6}}{120!}$$

c. $z = \dfrac{x - \mu}{\sigma} = \dfrac{120 - 67.6}{8.222} = 6.373$

d. Using the formula with with λ = 67.6,

$P(x \leq 48) = P(x = 0) + P(x = 1) + \ldots + P(x = 48)$

$$= \frac{67.6^0 e^{-67.6}}{0!} + \frac{67.6^1 e^{-67.6}}{1!} + \ldots + \frac{67.6^{48} e^{-67.6}}{48!}$$

e. The experiment consists of counting the number of bank failures per year. We assume the probability a bank fails in a year is the same for each year. We must also assume that the number of bank failures in one year is independent of the number in any other year.

5.47 a. $\mu = \lambda = 8.25$

$$p(x) = \frac{\lambda^x e^{-\lambda}}{x!} \qquad x = 0, 1, 2, \ldots$$

$$p(x = 0) = \frac{8.25^0 e^{-8.25}}{0!} = e^{-8.25} = .000261$$

b. $E(x) = \lambda = 8.25$

$\sigma = \sqrt{\lambda} = \sqrt{8.25} = 2.87$

c. Since we expect 8.25 fatalities with a standard deviation of 2.87, the probability of as many as 20 fatalities would be quite small. The z-score is

$$z = \frac{x - \mu}{\sigma} = \frac{20 - 8.25}{2.87} = 4.09$$

Twenty fatalities would be an extreme occurrence. The probability of as many as 20 fatalities or more occurring is approximately 0.

d. The experiment consists of counting the number of fatalities in one month. We assume the probability of a fatality in one month is the same for each month. We must also assume that the number of fatalities in one month is independent of the number in any other month.

5.49 Let x = number of minor flaws in one square foot of a door's surface. Then x has a Poisson distribution with λ = .5.

$\mu = \lambda = .5$, using Table III, Appendix B:

P(fail inspection)
= P(2 or more minor flaws in the square foot inspected)
= $P(x \geq 2)$
= $1 - P(x \leq 1)$
= $1 - .910$
= $.090$

P(pass inspection)
= P(x < 2)
= P(x ≤ 1)
= .910

5.51 $\mu = \lambda = 1$, using Table III, Appendix B:

$$P(x \geq 3) = 1 - P(x \leq 2)$$
$$= 1 - .920$$
$$= .08$$

$$P(x > 3) = 1 - P(x \leq 3)$$
$$= 1 - .981$$
$$= .019$$

Yes, the number of arrivals would rarely exceed 3 since the probability of this occurring is only .019.

5.53   Table IV in the text gives the area between $z = 0$ and $z = z_0$. In this exercise, the answers may thus be read directly from the table by looking up the appropriate z.

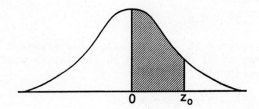

a. $P(0 < z < 2) = .4772$

b. $P(0 < z < 3.0) = .4987$

c. $P(0 < z < 1.5) = .4332$

d. $P(0 < z < .80) = .2881$

5.55   Using Table IV in Appendix B:

a. $P(z \geq 3) = .5 - P(0 \leq z \leq 3) = .5 - A_1$
$$= .5 - .4987$$
$$= .0013$$

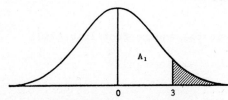

b. $P(z \leq -1.6) = .5 - P(-1.6 \leq z \leq 0) = .5 - P(0 \leq z \leq 1.6)$
$$= .5 - A_1$$
$$= .5 - .4452$$
$$= .0548$$

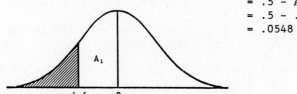

c. $P(z \geq 1.645) = .5 - P(0 \leq z \leq 1.645) = .5 - A_1$
$$= .5 - .45$$
$$= .05$$

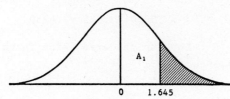

d. $P(z \geq 0) = .5$

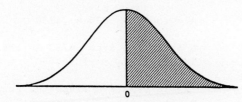

e. $P(z \leq -1.0) = .5 - P(-1.0 \leq z \leq 0) = .5 - P(0 \leq z \leq 1.0)$
$$= .5 - A_1$$
$$= .5 - .3413$$
$$= .1587$$

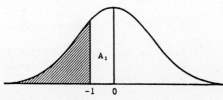

f. $P(z \leq -1.645) = P(z \geq 1.645) = .05$ (Refer to part (c).)

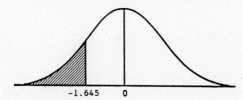

5.57   Using Table IV in Appendix B:

a. $P(z \geq z_0) = .05$

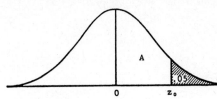

A = .5000 - .05 = .4500

Look up the area .45 in the body of Table IV; $z_0 = 1.645$.

.45 is half way between .4495 and .4505; therefore, we average the z-scores

$$\frac{1.64 + 1.65}{2} = 1.645$$

b. $P(z \geq z_0) = .025$

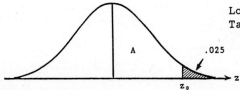

A = .5000 - .025 = .4750

Look up the area .4750 in the body of Table IV; $z_0 = 1.96$.

c. $P(z \leq z_0) = .025$

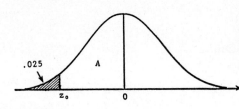

A = .5000 - .025 = .4750

Look up the area .4750 in the body of Table IV; $z_0 = -1.96$.

(z_0 is negative since the graph shows z_0 is on the left side of 0.)

d. $P(z \geq z_0) = .10$

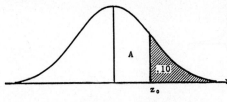

A = .5000 - .1000 = .4000

Look up the area .4000 in the body of Table IV; (take the closest value) $z_0 = 1.28$.

e. $P(z > z_0) = .10$ is equivalent to $P(z \geq z_0) = .10$; $z_0 = 1.28$ (Refer to part (d).)

5.59   From Exercise 5.58, x is described by a normal distribution with μ = 30 and σ = 4. The number of standard deviations away from the mean of x is the z-score for the given x value.

a. If x = 25, $z = \dfrac{x - \mu}{\sigma} = \dfrac{25 - 30}{4} = \dfrac{-5}{4} = -1.25$

Therefore, x is 1.25 standard deviations below the mean.

b. If x = 37.5, $z = \dfrac{x - \mu}{\sigma} = \dfrac{37.5 - 30}{4} = \dfrac{7.5}{4} = 1.875$

Therefore, x is 1.875 standard deviations above the mean.

c. If x = 30, $z = \dfrac{x - \mu}{\sigma} = \dfrac{30 - 30}{4} = 0$

Therefore, x is 0 standard deviations from the mean (x is the mean).

d. If x = 36, $z = \dfrac{x - \mu}{\sigma} = \dfrac{36 - 30}{4} = \dfrac{6}{4} = 1.5$

Therefore, x is 1.5 standard deviations above the mean.

5.61 Using Table IV of Appendix B:

a. To find the probability that x assumes a value more than 2 standard deviations from μ:

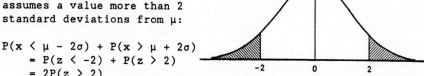

$P(x < \mu - 2\sigma) + P(x > \mu + 2\sigma)$
$= P(z < -2) + P(z > 2)$
$= 2P(z > 2)$
$= 2(.5000 - .4772)$
$= 2(.0228) = .0456$

To find the probability that x assumes a value more than 3 standard deviations from μ:

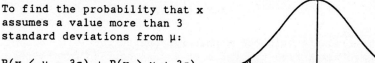

$P(x < \mu - 3\sigma) + P(x > \mu + 3\sigma)$
$= P(z < -3) + P(z > 3)$
$= 2P(z > 3)$
$= 2(.5000 - .4987)$
$= 2(.0013) = .0026$

b. To find the probability that x assumes a value within 1 standard deviation of its mean:

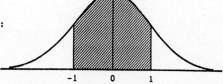

$P(\mu - \sigma < x < \mu + \sigma)$
$= P(-1 < z < 1)$
$= 2P(0 < z < 1)$
$= 2(.3413)$
$= .6826$

To find the probability that x
assumes a value within 2 standard
deviations of μ:

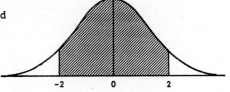

$$P(\mu - 2\sigma < x < \mu + 2\sigma)$$
$$= P(-2 < z < 2)$$
$$= 2P(0 < z < 2)$$
$$= 2(.4772)$$
$$= .9544$$

c. To find the value of x that represents the 80th percentile, we
    must first find the value of z that corresponds to the 80th
    percentile.

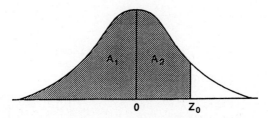

$P(z < z_0) = .80$. Thus, $A_1 + A_2 = .80$. Since $A_1 = .50$,
$A_2 = .80 - .50 = .30$. Using the body of Table IV, $z_0 = .84$. To
find x, we substitute the values into the z-score formula:

$$z = \frac{x - \mu}{\sigma}$$

$$.84 = \frac{x - 1000}{10} \Rightarrow x = .84(10) + 1000 = 1008.4$$

To find the value of x that represents the 10th percentile, we
must first find the value of z that corresponds to the 10th
percentile.

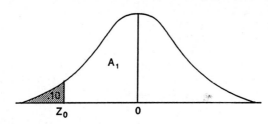

$P(z < z_0) = .10$. Thus, $A_1 = .50 - .10 = .40$. Using the body of Table IV, $z_0 = -1.28$. To find x, we substitute the values into the z-score formula:

$$z = \frac{x - \mu}{\sigma}$$

$$-1.28 = \frac{x - 1000}{10} \Rightarrow x = -1.28(10) + 1000 = 987.2$$

5.63 Let x = the score on the dexterity test. The random variable x is approximately normal with $\mu = 75$ and $\sigma = 7.5$.

a. The proportion of job candidates whose score exceeded 80 is:

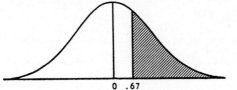

$$z = \frac{x - \mu}{\sigma} = \frac{80 - 75}{7.5} = .67$$

$$P(x > 80) = P(z > .67)$$
$$= .5000 - .2486$$
$$= .2514$$
(Table IV, Appendix B)

Therefore, $.2514 \times 100 = 25.14\%$ of the test scores exceeded 80.

b. Let x_0 be the score at the 98th percentile of the distribution of test scores.

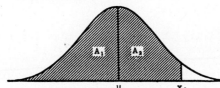

Find x_0 such that $P(x < x_0) = .98$. So, $A_1 + A_2 = .98$. Since $A_1 = .50$, $A_2 = .98 - .50 = .48$. Look up the area .48 in the body of Table IV, Appendix B; (take the closest value) $z_0 = 2.05$.

To find x_0, substitute into the z-score formula:

$$z = \frac{x - \mu}{\sigma}$$

$$2.05 = \frac{x_0 - 75}{7.5}$$

$$x_0 = 75 + 7.5(2.05) = 90.375$$

5.65 Let x = the amount of money tied up in outstanding insider loans. The random variable x is approximately normally distributed with $\mu = \$500,000$ and $\sigma = \$142,000$.

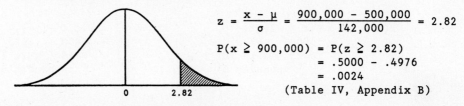

$$z = \frac{x - \mu}{\sigma} = \frac{900,000 - 500,000}{142,000} = 2.82$$

$$P(x \geq 900,000) = P(z \geq 2.82)$$
$$= .5000 - .4976$$
$$= .0024$$
(Table IV, Appendix B)

5.67 Let x = monthly rate of return to stock ABC and y = monthly rate of return to stock XYZ. The random variable x is normally distributed with μ = .05 and σ = .03 and y is normally distributed with μ = .07 and σ = .05. You have $100 invested in each stock.

a. The average monthly rate of return for ABC stock is .05.

The average monthly rate of return for XYZ stock is .07.

Therefore, stock XYZ has the higher average monthly rate of return.

b. E(x) = .05 for each $1.

Since we have $100 invested in stock ABC, the monthly rate of return would be 100(.05) = $5.

Therefore, the expected value of the investment in stock ABC at the end of 1 month is 100 + 5 = $105.

E(y) = .07 for each $1.

Since we have $100 invested in stock XYZ, the monthly rate of return would be 100(.07) = $7.

Therefore, the expected value of the investment in stock XYZ at the end of 1 month is 100 + 7 = $107.

c. We need to find the probability of incurring a loss for each stock and compare them.

P(incurring a loss on stock ABC)	P(incurring a loss on stock XYZ)
= P(monthly rate of return is negative on stock ABC)	= P(monthly rate of return is negative on stock XYZ)
= P(x < 0)	= P(y < 0)

$$z = \frac{x - \mu}{\sigma} = \frac{0 - .05}{.03} = -1.67 \qquad z = \frac{y - \mu}{\sigma} = \frac{0 - .07}{.05} = -1.4$$

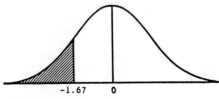

$$
\begin{aligned}
P(x < 0) &= P(z < -1.67) \\
&= .5000 - .4525 \\
&= .0475 \text{ (Table IV,} \\
&\qquad \text{Appendix B)}
\end{aligned}
\qquad
\begin{aligned}
P(y < 0) &= P(z < -1.4) \\
&= .5000 - .4192 \\
&= .0818 \text{ (Table IV,} \\
&\qquad \text{Appendix B)}
\end{aligned}
$$

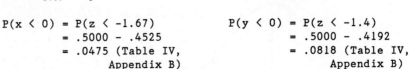

Since the probability of incurring a loss is smaller for stock ABC, stock ABC would have a greater protection against occurring a loss next month.

5.69 Let x = the additional time being charged to a long-distance phone call. The random variable x is normally distributed with μ = 25 and σ = 8 seconds.

a.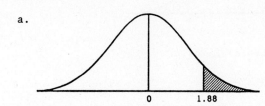

$$z = \frac{x - \mu}{\sigma} = \frac{40 - 25}{8} = 1.88$$

$$\begin{aligned} P(x \geq 40) &= P(z \geq 1.88) \\ &= .5000 - .4699 \\ &= .0301 \end{aligned}$$
(Table IV, Appendix B)

b.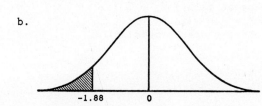

$$z = \frac{x - \mu}{\sigma} = \frac{10 - 25}{8} = -1.88$$

$$\begin{aligned} P(x \leq 10) &= P(z < -1.88) \\ &= P(z \geq 1.88) \\ &= .0301 \end{aligned}$$
(Refer to part (a).)

c. Eighty percent of long-distance calls are overcharged by 18.28 seconds or more.

We must find the time, x_0, such that $P(x > x_0) = P(z > z_0) = .80$. From the body of Table IV, $z_0 = -.84$.

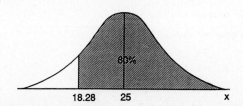

Using the z-score formula, $z = \frac{x - \mu}{\sigma}$

$$-.84 = \frac{x - 25}{8} \Rightarrow -.84(8) + 25 = 18.28$$

5.71   Let x = the amount of dye discharged. The random variable x is normally distributed with $\sigma^2 = .16$ ($\sigma = .4$).

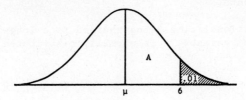

We want P(shade is unacceptable) $\leq$ .01

$$\Rightarrow P(x > 6) \leq .01$$

Then A = .50 − .01 = .49. Look up the area .49 in the body of Table IV, Appendix B; (take the closest value) $z_0 = 2.33$.

To find μ, substitute into the z-score formula:

$$z = \frac{x - \mu}{\sigma}$$

$$2.33 = \frac{6 - \mu}{.4}$$

$$\mu = 6 - .4(2.33) = 5.068$$

5.73   In order to approximate the binomial distribution with the normal distribution, the interval $\mu \pm 3\sigma \Rightarrow np \pm 3\sqrt{npq}$ should lie in the range 0 to n.

a.   When n = 50 and p = .01,

$$np \pm 3\sqrt{npq} \Rightarrow 50(.01) \pm 3\sqrt{50(.01)(1 - .01)}$$

$$\Rightarrow .5 \pm 3\sqrt{.495}$$
$$\Rightarrow 8.5 \pm 2.1107$$
$$\Rightarrow (-1.6107, 2.6107)$$

Since the interval calculated does not lie in the range 0 to 50, we should not use the normal approximation.

b.   When n = 20, p = .45

$$np \pm 3\sqrt{npq} \Rightarrow 20(.45) \pm 3\sqrt{20(.45)(1 - .45)}$$

$$\Rightarrow 9 \pm 3\sqrt{4.95}$$
$$\Rightarrow 9 \pm 6.6746$$
$$\Rightarrow (2.3254, 15.6746)$$

Since the interval calculated does lie in the range 0 to 20, we can use the normal approximation.

c. When n = 10, p = .40

$$np \pm 3\sqrt{npq} \Rightarrow 10(.40) \pm 3\sqrt{10(.40)(1 - .40)}$$
$$\Rightarrow 4 \pm 3\sqrt{2.4}$$
$$\Rightarrow 4 \pm 4.6479$$
$$\Rightarrow (-.6479, \ 8.6479)$$

Since the interval calculated does not lie in the range 0 to 10, we should not use the normal approximation.

d. If n = 1000 and p = .1,

$$np \pm 3\sqrt{npq} \Rightarrow 1000(.1) \pm 3\sqrt{1000(.1)(1 - .1)}$$
$$\Rightarrow 100 \pm 3\sqrt{90}$$
$$\Rightarrow 100 \pm 28.4605$$
$$\Rightarrow (71.5395, \ 128.4605)$$

Since the interval calculated does lie in the range 0 to 1000, we can use the normal approximation.

e. If n = 200 and p = .8,

$$np \pm 3\sqrt{npq} \Rightarrow 200(.8) \pm 3\sqrt{200(.8)(1 - .8)}$$
$$\Rightarrow 160 \pm 3\sqrt{32}$$
$$\Rightarrow 160 \pm 16.9706$$
$$\Rightarrow (143.0294, \ 166.9706)$$

Since the interval calculated does lie in the range 0 to 200, we can use the normal approximation.

f. If n = 35 and p = .7,

$$np \pm 3\sqrt{npq} \Rightarrow 35(.7) \pm 3\sqrt{35(.7)(1 - .7)}$$
$$\Rightarrow 24.5 \pm 3\sqrt{7.35}$$
$$\Rightarrow 24.5 \pm 8.1333$$
$$\Rightarrow (16.3667, \ 32.6333)$$

Since the interval calculated does lie in the range 0 to 35, we can use the normal approximation.

5.75 x is a binomial random variable with n = 25 and p = .5. Therefore, $\mu = np = 25(.5) = 12.5$ and

$$\sigma = \sqrt{npq} = \sqrt{25(.5)(.5)} = 2.5$$

a. $P(x \leq 12) = .500$ (using Table II in Appendix B)

To find the approximate probability with the normal approximation,

$$z = \frac{(a + .5) - \mu}{\sigma} = \frac{12.5 - 12.5}{2.5} = 0$$

$$P(x \leq 12) \approx P(z \leq 0) = .5$$

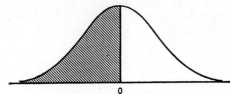

b. $P(x \geq 15) = 1 - P(x \leq 14) = 1 - .788 = .212$

(using Table II in Appendix B)

To find the approximate probability with the normal approximation,

$$z = \frac{(a - .5) - \mu}{\sigma} = \frac{14.5 - 12.5}{2.5} = .8$$

$$P(x \geq 15) \approx P(z \geq .8)$$
$$= .5000 - .2881 = .2119$$
(using Table IV in Appendix B)

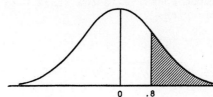

c. $P(9 \leq x \leq 15) = P(x \leq 15) - P(x \leq 8) = .885 - .054 = .831$

(using Table II in Appendix B)

To find the approximate probability with the normal approximation,

$$z = \frac{(a - .5) - \mu}{\sigma} = \frac{8.5 - 12.5}{2.5} = -1.6$$

$$z = \frac{(a + .5) - \mu}{\sigma} = \frac{15.5 - 12.5}{2.5} = 1.2$$

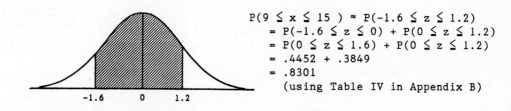

$$P(9 \leq x \leq 15) \approx P(-1.6 \leq z \leq 1.2)$$
$$= P(-1.6 \leq z \leq 0) + P(0 \leq z \leq 1.2)$$
$$= P(0 \leq z \leq 1.6) + P(0 \leq z \leq 1.2)$$
$$= .4452 + .3849$$
$$= .8301$$

(using Table IV in Appendix B)

5.77   x is a binomial random variable with n = 1000 and p = .50.

$$\mu \pm 3\sigma = np \pm 3\sqrt{npq} = 1000(.50) \pm 3\sqrt{1000(.5)(.5)}$$
$$= 500 \pm 3(15.8114)$$
$$= (452.5658, 547.4342)$$

Since the interval lies in the range 0 to 1000, we can use the normal approximation to approximate the probabilities.

a. $z = \dfrac{(a + .5) - \mu}{\sigma} = \dfrac{500.5 - 500}{15.8114} = .03$

(Using Table IV in Appendix B)
$$P(x > 500) \approx P(z > .03)$$
$$= .5000 - .012 = .488$$

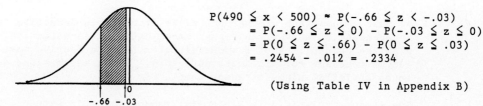

b. $z = \dfrac{(a - .5) - \mu}{\sigma} = \dfrac{489.5 - 500}{15.8114} = -.66$

$z = \dfrac{(a - .5) - \mu}{\sigma} = \dfrac{499.5 - 500}{15.8114} = -.03$

$$P(490 \leq x < 500) \approx P(-.66 \leq z < -.03)$$
$$= P(-.66 \leq z \leq 0) - P(-.03 \leq z \leq 0)$$
$$= P(0 \leq z \leq .66) - P(0 \leq z \leq .03)$$
$$= .2454 - .012 = .2334$$

(Using Table IV in Appendix B)

c. $P(x > 1000) = 0$

Since n = 1000, the random variable x can only take on the values 0, 1, 2, ... , 1000.

5.79   a.   Let x = the number of workers on the job on a particular day out of 50 workers. The random variable x is a binomial random variable with n = 50 and p = .80 (if 20% are absent, 80% are on the job).

90% of 50 workers = .9(50) = 45

μ = np = 50(.8) = 40
σ^2 = npq = 50(.8)(.2) = 8
σ = $\sqrt{\sigma^2}$ = $\sqrt{8}$ = 2.8284

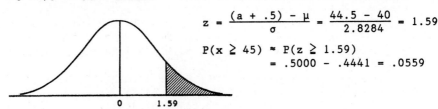

$z = \dfrac{(a + .5) - \mu}{\sigma} = \dfrac{44.5 - 40}{2.8284} = 1.59$

$P(x \geq 45) \approx P(z \geq 1.59)$
$= .5000 - .4441 = .0559$

b. $\mu \pm 3\sigma$ => np $\pm 3\sqrt{npq}$ => 40 $\pm$ 3(2.8284) (part (a))
       => (31.5148, 48.4852)

Since the interval lies in the range 0 to 50, we can use the normal approximation to approximate the probability in part (a).

c. If the absentee rate is 2%, then 98% of the workers are on the job. Hence, x is a binomial random variable with n = 50 and p = .98.

$\mu \pm 3\sigma$ => np $\pm 3\sqrt{npq}$ => 50(.98) $\pm 3\sqrt{50(.98)(1 - .98)}$
       => 49 $\pm$ 2.9698
       => (46.0302, 51.9698)

Since the interval does not lie in the range 0 to 50, we should not use the normal approximation to approximate the probability in part (a).

5.81 a. We must assume that whether one smoke detector is defective is independent of whether any other smoke detector is defective. Also the probability of a smoke detector being defective must remain constant for all smoke detectors. These assumptions seem to be satisfied since a random sample was taken.

b. The random variable x is a binomial random variable with n = 2000 and p = .40.

$\mu \pm 3\sigma$ => np $\pm 3\sqrt{npq}$ => 2000(.40) $\pm 3\sqrt{2000(.40)(1 - .40)}$
       => 800 $\pm$ 65.7267
       => (734.2733, 865.7267)

Since the interval does lie in the range 0 to 2000, we can use the normal approximation to approximate the probability.

$$z = \frac{(a + .5) - \mu}{\sigma} = \frac{4.5 - 800}{\sqrt{2000(.4)(1 - .4)}} = \frac{4.5 - 800}{21.9089} = -36.31$$

$$P(x \leq 4) \approx P(z \leq -36.31)$$
$$\approx .5 - .5 = 0$$

    c. No, it is not likely that 40% of their detectors are defective. If 40% really were defective, then the probability of four or fewer defectives is approximately zero. But there were only four defectives. Therefore, it is very unlikely that 40% are defective.

    d. Yes, it is possible that 40% of the detectors are defective. The probability of four or fewer defectives is approximately zero. It is possible but very unlikely.

5.83 a. $f(x) = \dfrac{1}{d - c}$ $(c \leq x \leq d)$

$$\frac{1}{d - c} = \frac{1}{45 - 20} = \frac{1}{25} = .04$$

So, $f(x) = .04$ $(20 \leq x \leq 45)$.

    b. $\mu = \dfrac{c + d}{2} = \dfrac{20 + 45}{2} = \dfrac{65}{2} = 32.5$

$$\sigma = \frac{d - c}{\sqrt{12}} = \frac{45 - 20}{\sqrt{12}} = 7.2169$$

$$\sigma^2 = (7.2169)^2 = 52.0833$$

    c.

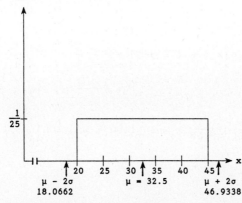

$$\mu \pm 2\sigma \Rightarrow 32.5 \pm 2(7.2169) \Rightarrow (18.0662, 46.9338)$$

$$P(18.0662 < x < 49.9338) = P(20 < x < 45)$$

$$= (45 - 20)\frac{1}{25} = 1$$

5.85　a.　$f(x) = \dfrac{1}{d - c}$　$(c \leqq x \leqq d)$

$$\dfrac{1}{d - c} = \dfrac{1}{5 - 2} = \dfrac{1}{3}$$

$$f(x) = \dfrac{1}{3}\quad(2 \leqq x \leqq 5)$$

　　b.　$\mu = \dfrac{c + d}{2} = \dfrac{2 + 5}{2} = \dfrac{7}{2} = 3.5$

$$\sigma = \dfrac{d - c}{\sqrt{12}} = \dfrac{5 - 2}{\sqrt{12}} = \dfrac{3}{\sqrt{12}} = .866$$

$$\sigma^2 = (.866)^2 = .75$$

　　c.

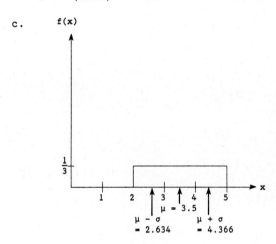

$$\mu \pm \sigma \Rightarrow 3.5 \pm .866 \Rightarrow (2.634,\ 4.366)$$

$$P(a < x < b) = P(2.634 < x < 4.366) = \dfrac{b - a}{d - c} = \dfrac{4.366 - 2.634}{5 - 2}$$

$$= \dfrac{1.732}{3} = .577$$

5.87　$f(x) = \dfrac{1}{d - c} = \dfrac{1}{200 - 100} = \dfrac{1}{100} = .01$　$(100 \leqq x \leqq 200)$

$$\mu = \frac{c + d}{2} = \frac{100 + 200}{2} = \frac{300}{2} = 150$$

$$\sigma = \frac{d - c}{\sqrt{12}} = \frac{200 - 100}{\sqrt{12}} = \frac{100}{\sqrt{12}} = 28.8675$$

a. $\mu \pm 2\sigma \Rightarrow 150 \pm 2\left(\dfrac{100}{\sqrt{12}}\right) \Rightarrow 150 \pm 57.735$

$\Rightarrow (92.265, 207.735)$

$P(x < 92.265) + P(x > 207.735) = P(x < 100) + P(x > 200)$
$$= \quad 0 \quad + \quad 0$$
$$= 0$$

b. $\mu \pm 3\sigma \Rightarrow 150 \pm 3\left(\dfrac{100}{\sqrt{12}}\right) \Rightarrow 150 \pm 86.6025$

$\Rightarrow (63.3975, 236.6025)$

$P(63.3975 < x < 236.6025) = P(100 < x < 200)$
$$= (200 - 100)(.01) = 1$$

c. From (a), $\mu \pm 2\sigma = (92.265, 207.735)$

$P(92.265 < x < 207.735) = P(100 < x < 200)$
$$= (200 - 100)(.01) = 1$$

5.89 To construct a relative frequency histogram for the data, we can use 7 measurement classes.

$$\text{Interval width} = \frac{\text{Largest number} - \text{smallest number}}{\text{Number of classes}}$$

$$= \frac{98.0716 - .7434}{7} = 13.9$$

We will use an interval width of 14 and a starting value of .74335.

The measurement classes, frequencies, and relative frequencies are given in the table below.

CLASS	MEASUREMENT CLASS	CLASS FREQUENCY	CLASS RELATIVE FREQUENCY
1	.74335 – 14.74335	6	6/40 = .15
2	14.74335 – 28.74335	4	.10
3	28.74335 – 42.74335	6	.15
4	42.74335 – 56.74335	6	.15
5	56.74335 – 70.74335	5	.125
6	70.74335 – 84.74335	4	.10
7	84.74335 – 98.74335	9	.225
		40	1.000

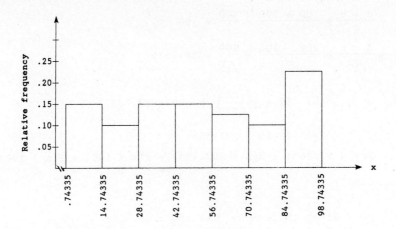

The histogram looks like the data could be from a uniform distribution. The last class (84.74335 - 98.74335) has a few more observations in it. However, we cannot expect a perfect graph from a sample of only 40 observations.

5.91   a.

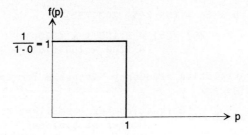

b. $\mu = \dfrac{c + d}{2} = \dfrac{0 + 1}{2} = .5$

$\sigma = \dfrac{d - c}{\sqrt{12}} = \dfrac{1 - 0}{\sqrt{12}} = .289 \qquad \sigma^2 = .289^2 = .083$

c. $P(p > .95) = (1 - .95)(1) = .05$
$P(p < .95) = (.95 - 0)(1) = .95$

d.   The analyst should use a uniform probability distribution with c = .90 and d = .95.

$$f(p) = \frac{1}{d - c} = \frac{1}{.95 - .90} = \frac{1}{.05} = 20 \ (.90 \le p \le .95)$$

5.93   Let x = the number of minutes you wait for the bus. The random variable x is best described by a uniform probability distribution with c = 0 and d = 30.

$$f(x) = \frac{1}{d - c} = \frac{1}{30 - 0} = \frac{1}{30} = .0333 \ (0 \le x \le 30)$$

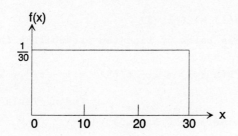

$$P(x > 20) = (30 - 20)\left(\frac{1}{30}\right) = \frac{10}{30} = .333$$

$$\mu = \frac{c + d}{2} = \frac{0 + 30}{2} = 15$$

You would expect to wait 15 minutes for the bus.

5.95 a. If $\lambda = 1$, $a = 1$, then $e^{-\lambda a} = e^{-1} = .367879$

b. If $\lambda = 1$, $a = 2.5$, then $e^{-\lambda a} = e^{-2.5} = .082085$

c. If $\lambda = 2.5$, $a = 3$, then $e^{-\lambda a} = e^{-7.5} = .000553$

d. If $\lambda = 5$, $a = .3$, then $e^{-\lambda a} = e^{-1.5} = .223130$

5.97 Using Table V in Appendix B:

a. $P(x \leq 3) = 1 - P(x > 3) = 1 - e^{-2.5(3)} = 1 - e^{-7.5} = 1 - .000553$
$$= .999447$$

b. $P(x \leq 4) = 1 - P(x > 4) = 1 - e^{-2.5(4)} = 1 - e^{-10} = 1 - .000045$
$$= .999955$$

c. $P(x \leq 1.6) = 1 - P(x > 1.6) = 1 - e^{-2.5(1.6)} = 1 - e^{-4}$
$$= 1 - .018316$$
$$= .981684$$

d. $P(x \leq .4) = 1 - P(x > .4) = 1 - e^{-2.5(.4)} = 1 - e^{-1} = 1 - .367879$
$$= .632121$$

5.99 $f(x) = \lambda e^{-\lambda x} = e^{-x}$ $(x > 0)$

$$\mu = \frac{1}{\lambda} = \frac{1}{1} = 1, \quad \sigma = \frac{1}{\lambda} = \frac{1}{1} = 1$$

a. $\mu \pm 3\sigma \Rightarrow 1 \pm 3(1) \Rightarrow (-2, 4)$

Since $\mu - 3\sigma$ lies below 0, find the probability that x is more than $\mu + 3\sigma = 4$.

$P(x > 4) = e^{-1(4)} = e^{-4} = .018316$ (using Table V in Appendix B)

b. $\mu \pm 2\sigma \Rightarrow 1 \pm 2(1) \Rightarrow (-1, 3)$

Since $\mu - 2\sigma$ lies below 0, find the probability that x is between 0 and 3.

$P(x < 3) = 1 - P(x \geq 3) = 1 - e^{-1(3)} = 1 - e^{-3} = 1 - .049787$
$$= .950213$$

(using Table V in Appendix B)

c. $\mu \pm .5\sigma \Rightarrow 1 \pm .5(1) \Rightarrow (.5, 1.5)$

$P(.5 < x < 1.5) = P(x > .5) - P(x > 1.5)$

$$= e^{-.5} - e^{-1.5}$$
$$= .606531 - .223130$$
$$= .383401 \quad \text{(using Table V in Appendix B)}$$

5.101 Let x = the shelf-life of bread. The mean of an exponential distribution is $\mu = 1/\lambda$. We know that $\mu = 2$; therefore, $\lambda = .5$. We want to find:

$P(x > 3) = e^{-.5(3)} = e^{-1.5} = .223130 \quad \text{(using Table V in Appendix B)}$

5.103 Let x = the time (in days) required to find the next error. The random variable x has an exponential distribution with $\lambda = .042$.

$f(x) = \lambda e^{-\lambda x} \qquad (x > 0)$

$f(x) = .042e^{-.042x}$

a. To graph the exponential distribution of x with $\lambda = .042$, we need to calculate f(x) for certain values of x. Using Table V, Appendix B:

$f(2.38) = .042e^{-.042(2.38)} = .042e^{-.1} = .042(.904837) = .038$

$f(11.9) = .042e^{-.042(11.9)} = .042e^{-.5} = .042(.606531) = .025$

$f(23.81) = .042e^{-.042(23.81)} = .042e^{-1} = .042(.367879) = .015$

$f(35.71) = .042e^{-.042(35.71)} = .042e^{-1.5} = .042(.22313) = .009$

$f(47.62) = .042e^{-.042(47.62)} = .042e^{-2} = .042(.135335) = .006$

The graph is given below.

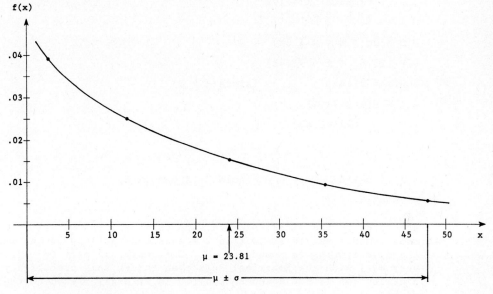

$$\mu = \frac{1}{\lambda} = \frac{1}{.042} = 23.81$$

$$\sigma = \mu = \frac{1}{\lambda} = 23.81$$

$$\mu \pm \sigma \Rightarrow 23.81 \pm 23.81$$
$$\Rightarrow (0, \ 47.62)$$

b. Since we have already found 26 errors, the average time to find the next error (the twenty-seventh error) is $\mu = 23.81$.

c. $P(x < 30) = 1 - P(x \geq 30) = 1 - e^{-.042(30)}$

$$= 1 - e^{-1.26} = 1 - .283654$$

$$= .716346$$

d. $P(\mu - \sigma < x < \mu + \sigma)$

$= P(0 < x < 47.62)$

$= P(x < 47.62)$ (since $x > 0$)

$= 1 - P(x \geq 47.62)$

$= 1 - e^{-.042(47.62)}$

$= 1 - e^{-2}$

$= 1 - .135335$ (Table V, Appendix B)

$= .864665$

e. $\mu \pm 2\sigma \Rightarrow 23.81 \pm 2(23.81)$ (Refer to part (a).)

$\qquad\quad \Rightarrow 23.81 \pm 47.62$

$\qquad\quad \Rightarrow (-23.81, 71.43)$

$P(\mu - 2\sigma < x < \mu + 2\sigma)$

$= P(-23.81 < x < 71.43)$

$= P(x < 71.43)$ $\qquad$ (since $x > 0$)

$= 1 - P(x \geq 71.43)$

$= 1 - e^{-.042(71.43)}$

$= 1 - e^{-3}$

$= 1 - .049787$ $\qquad$ (Table V, Appendix B)

$= .950213$

According to the Empirical Rule, approximately 95% of all measurements should lie within 2 standard deviations of the mean if the distribution is mound-shaped. Our answer in part (e) agrees very well with the Empirical Rule even though this probability distribution is not mound-shaped (it is strongly skewed to the right).

5.105 a. $R(x) = e^{-\lambda x} = R(x) = e^{-.5x}$

b. $P(x \geq 4) = e^{-.5(4)} = e^{-2} = .135335$ (Table V, Appendix B)

c. $\mu = \dfrac{1}{\lambda} = \dfrac{1}{.5} = 2$

$P(x > \mu) = P(x > 2) = e^{-.5(2)} = e^{-1} = .367879$ (Table V, Appendix B)

d. For all exponential distributions, $\mu = \dfrac{1}{\lambda}$

$P(x > \mu) = P(x > \dfrac{1}{\lambda}) = e^{-\lambda(1/\lambda)} = e^{-1} = .367879$.   Thus,

regardless of the value of λ, the probability that x is larger than the mean is always .367879.

e. $P(x > 5) = e^{-.5(5)} = e^{-2.5} = .082085$ (Table V, Appendix B)

If 10,000 units are sold, approximately $10,000(.082085) = 820.85$ will perform satisfactorily for more than 5 years.

$P(x \leq 1) = 1 - P(x > 1) = 1 - e^{-.5(1)} = 1 - e^{-.5} = 1 - .606531$

$\qquad\qquad\qquad\qquad\qquad\qquad\qquad\qquad\qquad\quad = .39469$

If 10,000 units are sold, approximately $10,000(.393469) = 3934.69$ will fail within 1 year.

f. $P(x < a) \leq .05$

$\Rightarrow 1 - P(x \geq a) \leq .05$
$\Rightarrow P(x \geq a) \geq .95$
$\Rightarrow e^{-.5a} \geq .95$

Using Table V, Appendix B, $e^{-.05}$ is closest to .95 (yet larger).

Thus, $.05 = .5a \Rightarrow a = .1$

The warranty should be for approximately .1 year or .1(365) = 36.5 or 37 days.

5.107 $p(x) = \binom{n}{x} p^x q^{n-x}$ $x = 0, 1, 2, \dots, n$

a. $P(x = 2) = p(2) = \binom{4}{2} .2^2 .8^2 = \frac{4!}{2!2!} .2^2 .8^2$

$= 6(.04)(.64) = .1536$

b. $P(x = 4) = p(4) = \binom{5}{4} .4^4 .6^1 = \frac{5!}{4!1!} .4^4 .6^1$

$= 5(.0256)(.6) = .0768$

c. $P(x = 0) = p(0) = \binom{3}{0} .5^0 .5^3 = \frac{3!}{0!3!} .5^0 .5^3$

$= 1(1)(.125) = .125$

5.109 Using Table III, Appendix B:

a. When $\lambda = 3$, $p(2) = P(x = 2) = P(x \leq 2) - P(x \leq 1)$
$= .423 - .199$
$= .224$

b. When $\lambda = 2$, $p(3) = P(x = 3) = P(x \leq 3) - P(x \leq 2)$
$= .857 - .677$
$= .180$

c. When $\lambda = .5$, $p(3) = P(x = 3) = P(x \leq 3) - P(x \leq 2)$
$= .998 - .986$
$= .012$

5.111 a. $f(x) = \frac{1}{d - c} = \frac{1}{90 - 10} = \frac{1}{80}$, $10 \leq x \leq 90$

b. $\mu = \dfrac{c + d}{2} = \dfrac{10 + 90}{2}$

$= 50$

$\sigma = \dfrac{d - c}{\sqrt{12}} = \dfrac{90 - 10}{\sqrt{12}}$

$= 23.094011$

c. The interval $\mu \pm 2\sigma \Rightarrow (50 \pm 2(23.1))$
$\Rightarrow (3.8, 96.2)$
is indicated on the graph.

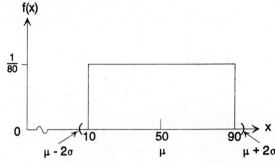

d. $P(x \leq 60) = \text{Base(height)} = (60 - 10)\dfrac{1}{80} = \dfrac{5}{8} = .625$

e. $P(x \geq 90) = 0$

f. $P(x \leq 80) = \text{Base(height)} = (80 - 10)\dfrac{1}{80} = \dfrac{7}{8} = .875$

g. $P(\mu - \sigma \leq x \leq \mu + \sigma) = P(50 - 23.1 \leq x \leq 50 + 23.1)$
$= P(26.9 \leq x \leq 73.1)$
$= \text{Base(height)}$

$= (73.1 - 26.9)(\dfrac{1}{80}) = \dfrac{46.2}{80} = .5775$

h. $P(x > 75) = \text{Base(height)} = (90 - 75)\dfrac{1}{80} = \dfrac{15}{80} = .1875$

5.113 x is a binomial random variable with n = 50 and p = .6.

$\mu \pm 3\sigma \Rightarrow np \pm 3\sqrt{npq} \Rightarrow 50(.6) \pm 3\sqrt{50(.6)(1 - .6)}$
$\Rightarrow 30 \pm 3(3.4641)$
$\Rightarrow (19.6077, 40.3923)$

Since the interval lies in the range 0 to 50, we can use the normal approximation to approximate the probabilities.

a. $z = \dfrac{(a + .5) - \mu}{\sigma} = \dfrac{35.5 - 30}{3.4641} = 1.59$

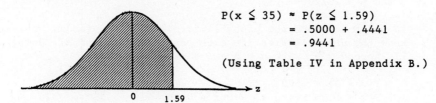

$P(x \leq 35) \approx P(z \leq 1.59)$
$\qquad\quad = .5000 + .4441$
$\qquad\quad = .9441$

(Using Table IV in Appendix B.)

b. $z = \dfrac{(a - .5) - \mu}{\sigma} = \dfrac{24.5 - 30}{3.4641} = -1.59$

$z = \dfrac{(a + .5) - \mu}{\sigma} = \dfrac{40.5 - 30}{3.4641} = 3.03$

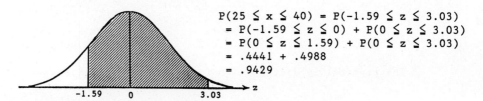

$P(25 \leq x \leq 40) = P(-1.59 \leq z \leq 3.03)$
$\qquad = P(-1.59 \leq z \leq 0) + P(0 \leq z \leq 3.03)$
$\qquad = P(0 \leq z \leq 1.59) + P(0 \leq z \leq 3.03)$
$\qquad = .4441 + .4988$
$\qquad = .9429$

c. $z = \dfrac{(a - .5) - \mu}{\sigma} = \dfrac{19.5 - 30}{3.4641} = -3.03$

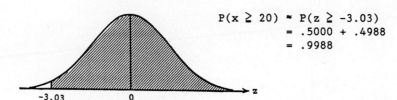

$P(x \geq 20) \approx P(z \geq -3.03)$
$\qquad\quad = .5000 + .4988$
$\qquad\quad = .9988$

d. $z = \dfrac{(a - .5) - \mu}{\sigma} = \dfrac{39.5 - 30}{3.4641} = 2.74$

$z = \dfrac{(a + .5) - \mu}{\sigma} = \dfrac{50.5 - 30}{3.4641} = 5.92$

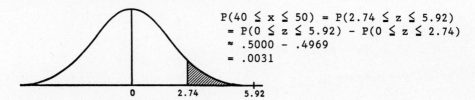

$P(40 \leq x \leq 50) = P(2.74 \leq z \leq 5.92)$
$\qquad = P(0 \leq z \leq 5.92) - P(0 \leq z \leq 2.74)$
$\qquad \approx .5000 - .4969$
$\qquad = .0031$

5.115 a. The random variable x is a binomial random variable (the boards are chosen independently and there are two possible outcomes) with n = 5 and p = 20/200 = .1.

In order to graph the probability distribution for x, we need to know the probabilities for each possible value of x. Using Table II, Appendix B, with n = 5 and p = .1:

$P(x = 0) = .590$
$P(x = 1) = P(x \leq 1) - P(x = 0) = .919 - .590 = .329$
$P(x = 2) = P(x \leq 2) - P(x \leq 1) = .991 - .919 = .072$
$P(x = 3) = P(x \leq 3) - P(x \leq 2) \approx 1 - .991 = .009$
$P(x = 4) = P(x \leq 4) - P(x \leq 3) \approx 1 - 1 = .000$
$P(x = 5) = P(x \leq 5) - P(x \leq 4) \approx 1 - 1 = .000$

The probability distribution for x in tabular form is:

x	0	1	2	3	4	5
p(x)	.590	.329	.072	.009	.000	.000

The probability distribution for x in graphical form is:

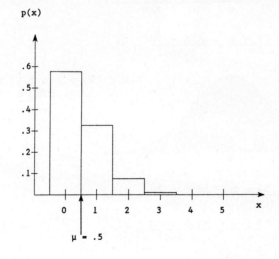

b. $\mu = np = 5(.1) = .5$

$\sigma^2 = npq = 5(.1)(.9) = .45$

5.117 a. For company A,

$E(x) = \sum_{\text{All } x} xp(x) = 2(.05) + 3(.15) + 4(.20) + 5(.35) + 6(.25)$
$= .10 + .45 + .80 + 1.75 + 1.50$
$= 4.60$

For company B,

$$E(x) = \sum_{\text{All } x} xp(x) = 2(.15) + 3(.30) + 4(.30) + 5(.20) + 6(.05)$$
$$= .30 + .90 + 1.20 + 1.00 + .30$$
$$= 3.70$$

b. The expected profit equals the expected value of x times the profit for each job.

For company A,

$$4.6(\$10,000) = \$46,000$$

For company B,

$$3.7(\$15,000) = \$55,500$$

c. For company A,

$$\sigma^2 = \sum_{\text{All } x} (x - \mu)^2 p(x) = (2 - 4.6)^2.05 + (3 - 4.6)^2.15$$
$$+ (4 - 4.6)^2.20 + (5 - 4.6)^2.35$$
$$+ (6 - 4.6)^2.25$$
$$= .338 + .384 + .072 + .056 + .49$$
$$= 1.34$$

$$\sigma = \sqrt{\sigma^2} = \sqrt{1.34} = 1.16$$

For company B,

$$\sigma^2 = \sum_{\text{All } x} (x - \mu)^2 p(x) = (2 - 3.7)^2.15 + (3 - 3.7)^2.30$$
$$+ (4 - 3.7)^2.30 + (5 - 3.7)^2.20$$
$$+ (6 - 3.7)^2.05$$
$$= .4335 + .147 + .027 + .338 + .2645$$
$$= 1.21$$

$$\sigma = \sqrt{\sigma^2} = \sqrt{1.21} = 1.10$$

d. For company A, the graph of p(x) is given below.

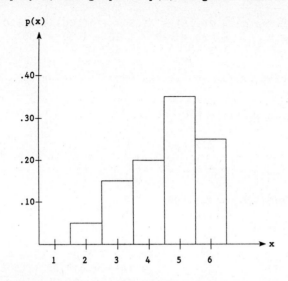

For company A,

    $\mu \pm 2\sigma \Rightarrow 4.6 \pm 2(1.16) \Rightarrow 4.6 \pm 2.32 \Rightarrow (2.28, 6.92)$

$P(2.28 < x < 6.92) = p(3) + p(4) + p(5) + p(6)$
$= .15 + .20 + .35 + .25$
$= .95$

For company B, the graph of p(x) is given below.

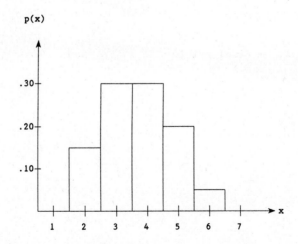

For company B,

$$\mu \pm 2\sigma \Rightarrow 3.70 \pm 2(1.10) \Rightarrow 3.67 \pm 2.2 \Rightarrow (1.5, 5.9)$$

$$P(1.5 < x < 5.9) = p(2) + p(3) + p(4) + p(5)$$
$$= .15 + .30 + .30 + .20$$
$$= .95$$

5.119 Let y be the profit on a metal part that is produced. Then y is $10, $-2, or $-1, depending where it falls with respect to the tolerance limits.

Let x be the tensile strength of a particular metal part. The random variable x is normally distributed with $\mu = 25$ and $\sigma = 2$.

$$z = \frac{x - \mu}{\sigma} = \frac{21 - 25}{2} = -2$$

$$z = \frac{x - \mu}{\sigma} = \frac{30 - 25}{2} = 2.5$$

$$P(y = 10) = P(x \text{ falls within the tolerance limits})$$

$$= P(21 < x < 30) = P(-2 < z < 2.5)$$
$$= P(-2 < z < 0) + P(0 < z < 2.5)$$
$$= P(0 < z < 2) + P(0 < z < 2.5)$$
$$= .4772 + .4938$$
$$= .9710$$

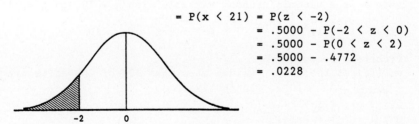

$$P(y = -2) = P(x \text{ falls below the lower tolerance limit})$$

$$= P(x < 21) = P(z < -2)$$
$$= .5000 - P(-2 < z < 0)$$
$$= .5000 - P(0 < z < 2)$$
$$= .5000 - .4772$$
$$= .0228$$

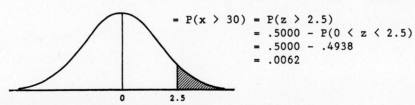

$$P(y = -1) = P(x \text{ falls above the upper tolerance limit})$$

$$= P(x > 30) = P(z > 2.5)$$
$$= .5000 - P(0 < z < 2.5)$$
$$= .5000 - .4938$$
$$= .0062$$

The probability distribution of y is given below:

y	10	-2	-1
p(y)	.9710	.0228	.0062

$$E(y) = \sum yp(y) = 10(.9710) + -2(.0228) + -1(.0062)$$
$$= 9.71 - .0456 - .0062$$
$$= 9.6582$$

5.121 a. There are 36 quality control inspectors who each have one observation for 8 weeks. Thus, the number of observations is 8 x 36 = 288.

b. Let x be the weekly average earnings.

$$z = \frac{x - \mu}{\sigma} = \frac{8.5 - 7.65}{1.25} = .68$$

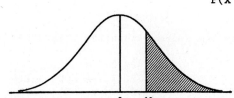

$$P(x > 8.5) = P(z > .68)$$
$$= .5000 - P(0 < z < .68)$$
$$= .5000 - .2517$$
$$= .2483$$

c. No, it is not possible to determine how many of the inspectors average over $8.50 per hour. In order to determine the number of inspectors who average over $8.50 per hour, we have to know the total number of inspectors.

5.123 Let x = the number of defective units in the sample. The random variable x is a binomial random variable with n = 10 and p = .11.

$$p(x) = \binom{10}{x}.11^x.89^{10-x} \qquad x = 0, 1, 2, \ldots, 10$$

P(correct decision)
= P(reject the lot)   (since more than 10% of the units are defective)
$$= P(x \geq 2)$$
$$= 1 - P(x \leq 1)$$
$$= 1 - [p(0) + p(1)]$$
$$= 1 - [\binom{10}{0}.11^0.89^{10} + \binom{10}{1}.11^1.89^9]$$
$$= 1 - [.312 + .385]$$
$$= 1 - .697$$
$$= .303$$

5.125 Let x = the number of typewriters the outlet sells tomorrow. The
random variable x is a Poisson random variable with $\mu = \lambda = 2.4$. Using
Table III, Appendix B:

P(outlet runs out of typewriters tomorrow)
= P(x > 5)
= 1 - P(x ≤ 5)
= 1 - .964
= .036

5.127 Let x be the time a worker is unemployed in weeks. The random variable
x is an exponential random variable with $\lambda = .075$.

a. $\mu = 1/\lambda = 1/.075 = 13.33$ weeks

b. $P(x \geq 2) = e^{-2\lambda} = e^{-2(.075)} = e^{-.15} = .860708$

$P(x > 6) = e^{-6\lambda} = e^{-6(.075)} = e^{-.45} = .637628$

c. $P(x < 12) = 1 - P(x \geq 12) = 1 - e^{-12(.075)}$

$= 1 - e^{-.9} = 1 - .40657$
$= .59343$

5.129 Let x = the number of delivery truck breakdowns today and y = the
number of delivery truck breakdowns tomorrow. The random variables x
and y are Poisson with $\mu = \lambda = 1.5$. Using Table III, Appendix B:

P(x = 2 ∩ y = 3)
= P(x = 2)P(y = 3) (by independence)

= [P(x ≤ 2) - P(x ≤ 1)][P(y ≤ 3) - P(y ≤ 2)]
= (.809 - .558)(.934 - .809)
= .251(.125)
= .0314

P(x < 2 ∩ y > 2)
= P(x < 2)P(y > 2) (by independence)
= P(x ≤ 1)[1 - P(y ≤ 2)]
= .558(1 - .809)
= .558(.191)
= .1066

5.131 The random variable x is a binomial random variable with n = 1600 and
p = .20.

$\mu = np = 1600(.20) = 320$

$\sigma = \sqrt{npq} = \sqrt{1600(.20)(1 - .20)} = \sqrt{256} = 16$

We observe that x = 400 out of the 1600 customers. This value is much larger than the mean value. It is 5 standard deviations above the mean.

The probability of observing a value this high or higher when p = .2 is (using the normal approximation)

$$P(x \geq 400) \approx P(z \geq 4.97) \approx 0$$

where $z = \dfrac{(a - .5) - \mu}{\sigma} = \dfrac{399.5 - 320}{16} = 4.97$

This would lead me to believe that p is really larger than .2 since x is 400.

5.133 The random variable x is a binomial random variable with n = 25, p = .20, and q = 1 - p = .80. (Assuming that whether a person refuses to take part in the poll is independent of any other person refusing.)

a. $\mu = np = 25(.20) = 5$
    $\sigma^2 = npq = 25(.20)(.80) = 4$

b. $P(x \leq 5) = .617$ Table II, Appendix B

c. $P(x > 10) = 1 - P(x \leq 10)$
                $= 1 - .994$
                $= .006$

CHAPTER 6

SAMPLING DISTRIBUTIONS

6.1   a.   "The sampling distribution of the sample statistic A" is the probability distribution of the variable A.

b.   "A" is an unbiased estimator of α because the mean of the sampling distribution of A is α.

c.   If both A and B are unbiased estimators of α, then the statistic whose standard deviation is smaller is a better estimator of α.

d.   No.   The Central Limit Theorem applies only to the sample mean.   If A is the sample mean, $\bar{x}$, and n is sufficiently large, then the Central Limit Theorem will apply.   However, both A and B cannot be sample means.   Thus, we cannot apply the Central Limit Theorem to both A and B.

6.3   a. $\mu_{\bar{x}} = \mu = 20$ $\qquad$ $\sigma_{\bar{x}} = \dfrac{\sigma}{\sqrt{n}} = \dfrac{3}{\sqrt{10}} = .949$

b. $\mu_{\bar{x}} = \mu = 100$ $\qquad$ $\sigma_{\bar{x}} = \dfrac{\sigma}{\sqrt{n}} = \dfrac{10}{\sqrt{40}} = 1.581$

c. $\mu_{\bar{x}} = \mu = 25$ $\qquad$ $\sigma_{\bar{x}} = \dfrac{\sigma}{\sqrt{n}} = \dfrac{2}{\sqrt{12}} = .577$

d. $\mu_{\bar{x}} = \mu = 400$ $\qquad$ $\sigma_{\bar{x}} = \dfrac{\sigma}{\sqrt{n}} = \dfrac{9}{\sqrt{100}} = .900$

6.5   We know that the sampling distribution of $\bar{x}$ will be normal since the sampled population is normal.   We also know that the sampling distribution will have mean and standard deviation

$$\mu_{\bar{x}} = \mu = 15 \qquad \sigma_{\bar{x}} = \dfrac{\sigma}{\sqrt{n}} = \dfrac{3}{\sqrt{25}} = .6$$

a. $P(\bar{x} > 16) = P\left(z > \dfrac{16 - \mu}{\sigma_{\bar{x}}}\right) = P\left(z > \dfrac{16 - 15}{.6}\right) = P(z > 1.67)$

$\qquad\qquad = .5 - P(0 < z < 1.67) = .5 - .4525 = .0475$

b. $P(\bar{x} < 16) = P\left(z < \dfrac{16 - \mu}{\sigma_{\bar{x}}}\right) = P\left(z < \dfrac{16 - 15}{.6}\right) = P(z < 1.67)$

$$= .5 + P(0 < z < 1.67) = .5 + .4525 = .9525$$

Note: $\bar{x} < 16$ is the complement of $\bar{x} > 16$; therefore,
$P(\bar{x} < 16) = 1 - P(\bar{x} > 16) = 1 - .0475 = .9525$.

c. $P(\bar{x} > 14.2) = P\left(z > \dfrac{14.2 - \mu}{\sigma_{\bar{x}}}\right) = P\left(z > \dfrac{14.2 - 15}{.6}\right) = P(z > -1.33)$

$$= .5 + P(-1.33 < z < 0) = .5 + P(0 < z < 1.33)$$
$$= .5 + .4082 = .9082$$

d. $P(14 < \bar{x} < 16) = P\left(\dfrac{14 - \mu}{\sigma_{\bar{x}}} < z < \dfrac{16 - \mu}{\sigma_{\bar{x}}}\right) = P\left(\dfrac{14 - 15}{.6} < z < \dfrac{16 - 15}{.6}\right)$

$$= P(-1.67 < z < 1.67) = 2P(0 < z < 1.67)$$
$$= 2(.4525) = .9050$$

e. $P(\bar{x} < 14) = P\left(z < \dfrac{14 - \mu}{\sigma_{\bar{x}}}\right) = P\left(z < \dfrac{14 - 15}{.6}\right) = p(z < -1.67)$

$$= .5 - P(-1.67 < z < 0) = .5 - P(0 < z < 1.67)$$
$$= .5 - .4525 = .0475$$

Note: Because the normal distribution is symmetric,
$p(\bar{x} < 14) = P(\bar{x} > 16)$ (see part (a)).

6.7 Though we do not know the relative frequency distribution of the sampled population, we know by the Central Limit Theorem that the sampling distribution of $\bar{x}$ will be approximately normal since $n \geq 30$. Also the sampling distribution will have mean and standard deviation

$$\mu_{\bar{x}} = \mu = 200 \qquad \sigma_{\bar{x}} = \dfrac{\sigma}{\sqrt{n}} = \dfrac{20}{\sqrt{49}} = 2.86$$

a. $P(\bar{x} \leq 200) = P\left(z \leq \dfrac{200 - \mu}{\sigma_{\bar{x}}}\right) = P\left(z \leq \dfrac{200 - 200}{2.86}\right) = P(z \leq 0) = .5$

b. $P(\bar{x} < 200) = P\left(z \leq \dfrac{200 - \mu}{\sigma_{\bar{x}}}\right) = P\left(z \leq \dfrac{200 - 200}{2.86}\right) = P(z < 0) = .5$

Recall that $p(x = a) = 0$ for a continuous distribution; hence (a) and (b) are identical problems. Also, notice that the probability of observing a sample mean greater than or less than μ is .5 as the symmetric normal distribution is split into two equal parts by its mean.

c. $P(\bar{x} < 205) = P\left(z < \dfrac{205 - \mu}{\sigma_{\bar{x}}}\right) = P\left(z \leq \dfrac{205 - 200}{2.86}\right) = P(z < 1.75)$

$$= .5 + P(0 < z < 1.75) = .5 + .4599 = .9599$$

d. $P(\bar{x} > 190) = P\left(z < \dfrac{190 - \mu}{\sigma_{\bar{x}}}\right) = P\left(z > \dfrac{190 - 200}{2.86}\right) = P(z > -3.50)$

$= .5 + P(-3.50 < z < 0) = .5 + P(0 < z < 3.50)$
$= .5 + \text{approx. } .5 = \text{approx. } 1$

e. $P(\bar{x} > 209) = P\left(z > \dfrac{209 - \mu}{\sigma_{\bar{x}}}\right) = P\left(z > \dfrac{209 - 200}{2.86}\right) = P(z > 3.15)$

$= .5 - P(0 < z < 3.15) = .5 - \text{approx. } .5 = \text{approx. } 0$

f. $P(193 \leq \bar{x} \leq 200) = P\left(\dfrac{193 - \mu}{\sigma_{\bar{x}}} \leq z \leq \dfrac{200 - \mu}{\sigma_{\bar{x}}}\right)$

$= P\left(\dfrac{193 - 200}{2.86} \leq z \leq \dfrac{200 - 200}{2.86}\right)$

$= P(-2.45 \leq z \leq 0) = P(0 \leq z \leq 2.45) = .4929$

g. $P(197.1 \leq \bar{x} \leq 202.9) = P\left(\dfrac{197.1 - \mu}{\sigma_{\bar{x}}} \leq z \leq \dfrac{202.9 - \mu}{\sigma_{\bar{x}}}\right)$

$= P\left(\dfrac{197.1 - 200}{2.86} \leq z \leq \dfrac{202.9 - 200}{2.86}\right)$

$= P(-1.01 \leq z \leq 1.01) = 2P(0 \leq z \leq 1.01)$
$= 2(.3438) = .6876$

h. $P(205 \leq \bar{x} \leq 210) = P\left(\dfrac{205 - \mu}{\sigma_{\bar{x}}} \leq z \leq \dfrac{210 - \mu}{\sigma_{\bar{x}}}\right)$

$= P\left(\dfrac{205 - 200}{2.86} \leq z \leq \dfrac{210 - 200}{2.86}\right)$

$= P(1.75 \leq z \leq 3.50) = P(0 \leq z \leq 3.50) - P(0 \leq z \leq 1.75)$
$= \text{approx } .5 - .4599 = \text{approx. } .0401$

6.9 Recall that $\bar{x} = \frac{\Sigma x}{n}$. The following sample means are computed. The results are arranged in the same manner as the data sets in the exercise.

4.83	4.50	4.50	5.67
4.67	5.00	4.17	5.00
5.17	4.67	5.33	4.17
4.50	5.33	3.83	2.50
5.67	3.83	4.33	2.67
5.00	4.17	4.83	5.50
7.33	4.00	3.50	2.17
5.83	3.33	3.50	7.00
4.00	4.33	6.83	5.83
6.17	4.00	6.83	2.67
3.17	3.83	5.83	5.67
4.83	5.17	3.83	5.50
5.50	3.50		

a. The following relative frequency histogram can be obtained.

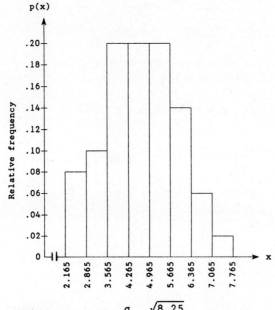

b. $\mu_{\bar{x}} = \mu = 4.5$ $\sigma_{\bar{x}} = \frac{\sigma}{\sqrt{n}} = \frac{\sqrt{8.25}}{\sqrt{6}} = 1.172$

The center of the histogram appears to be around 4.5, and the standard deviation of 1.172 appears reasonable.

c. The mean and standard deviation of the 50 medians are 4.78 and 1.642, respectively.

The actual mean and standard deviation of the 50 means are 4.68 and 1.172, respectively.

From this information, it appears the sample means are closer to the true mean than the sample medians.

6.11 The sample means are:

4.75	4.83	4.33	5.33
4.83	4.58	4.58	3.33
5.33	4.08	4.58	4.08
6.58	3.83	3.50	4.58
5.08	3.92	6.83	4.25
4.00	4.33	4.83	5.58
5.00			

a. We will graph the relative frequency histogram using the same measurement classes used in Exercise 6.9 to provide a good comparison.

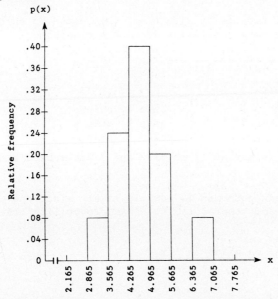

The means based on n = 12 are much less variable than those based on n = 6.

b. Let $\bar{\bar{x}}$ = mean of the 25 sample means, $\bar{\bar{x}} = \dfrac{\sum \bar{x}_i}{n} = \dfrac{116.94}{25} = 4.68$

Let $s_{\bar{x}}^2$ = variance of the 25 sample means.

$$s_{\bar{x}}^2 = \frac{\sum \bar{x}_i^2 - \dfrac{\left(\sum \bar{x}_i\right)^2}{n}}{n-1} = \frac{563.388 - \dfrac{116.94^2}{25}}{25-1} = \frac{16.389456}{24} = .682894$$

$$s_{\bar{x}} = \sqrt{s_{\bar{x}}^2} = \sqrt{.682894} = .8264$$

Notice that the standard deviation of the means is close to

$$\sigma_{\bar{x}} = \frac{\sigma}{\sqrt{n}} = \frac{2.872}{\sqrt{12}} = .829$$

The standard deviation of the mean, $\sigma_{\bar{x}} = \dfrac{\sigma}{\sqrt{n}}$ will decrease as the sample size increases. In this case, as n doubled, we expect $\sigma_{\bar{x}}$ to decrease by $\dfrac{1}{\sqrt{2}}$. Notice that $\dfrac{1.172}{\sqrt{2}} = .829$

6.17 a. The number of samples of size n = 2 that could be selected without replacement from a population of size N = 4 is:

$$\binom{N}{n} = \binom{4}{2} = \frac{4!}{2!(4-2)!} = 6$$

The samples are:

chip 1, chip 2	chip 2, chip 3
chip 1, chip 3	chip 2, chip 4
chip 1, chip 4	chip 3, chip 4

where chip 1 is marked 1, chips 2 and 3 are marked 2, and chip 4 is marked 3.

b. Each of the six outcomes is equally likely since the chips are chosen at random; therefore, each has probability 1/6.

c.

Sample (Number marked on chip)	$\bar{x}$
1, 2	1.5
1, 2	1.5
1, 3	2
2, 2	2
2, 3	2.5
2, 3	2.5

d.

$\bar{x}$	$p(\bar{x})$
1.5	$\frac{2}{6} = \frac{1}{3}$
2	$\frac{2}{6} = \frac{1}{3}$
2.5	$\frac{2}{6} = \frac{1}{3}$

e.   Population Probability Distribution

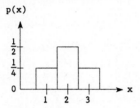

Sampling Distribution

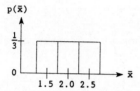

6.19   a.   Tossing a coin three times can result in:

3 heads (3 ones)
3 tails (3 zeros)
2 heads, 1 tail (2 ones, 1 zero)
2 tails, 1 head (2 zeros, 1 one)

b. $\bar{x}_{3 \text{ heads}} = 1$; $\bar{x}_{3 \text{ tails}} = 0$; $\bar{x}_{2H, 1T} = \frac{2}{3}$; $\bar{x}_{1H, 2T} = \frac{1}{3}$

c.   There are eight possible combinations for one coin tossed three times, as shown below:

Coin Tosses	$\bar{x}$	$\bar{x}$	$p(\bar{x})$
H, H, H	1	1	1/8
H, H, T	2/3	2/3	3/8
H, T, H	2/3	1/3	3/8
T, H, H	2/3	0	1/8
T, T, H	1/3		
T, H, T	1/3		
H, T, T	1/3		
T, T, T	0		

d. The sampling distribution of $\bar{x}$ is given in the histogram below:

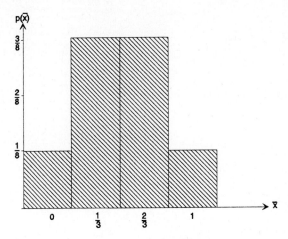

6.21 No, for n = 5, $\sigma_{\bar{x}} = \dfrac{10}{\sqrt{5}} = 4.472$ and for n = 25, $\sigma_{\bar{x}} = \dfrac{10}{\sqrt{25}} = 2$.

The standard deviation of $\bar{x}$ decreases by 2.47 when n increases from 5 to 25.

For n = 30, $\sigma_{\bar{x}} = \dfrac{10}{\sqrt{30}} = 1.826$ and for n = 50, $\sigma_{\bar{x}} = \dfrac{10}{\sqrt{50}} = 1.414$.

The standard deviation of $\bar{x}$ decreases by .412 when n increases from 30 to 50.

6.23 The mean, μ, of the internal strength of bottles is 157 psi with a standard deviation of 3 psi. By the Central Limit Theorem, the sampling distribution of $\bar{x}$ is approximately normal since n $\geq$ 30 and

$$\mu_{\bar{x}} = \mu = 157 \qquad \sigma_{\bar{x}} = \frac{\sigma}{\sqrt{n}} = \frac{3}{\sqrt{40}} = .474$$

a. A sample mean that is 1.3 psi below the process mean indicates that $\bar{x} - \mu = -1.3$.

We want to find $P(\bar{x} - \mu \leq -1.3)$.

$$P(\bar{x} - \mu \leq -1.3) = P\left(z \leq \frac{-1.3}{\sigma_{\bar{x}}}\right) = P\left(z \leq \frac{-1.3}{.474}\right) = P(z \leq -2.74)$$

$$= .5 - P(-2.74 \leq z \leq 0) = .5 - .4969 = .0031$$

Since the probability of observing this sample mean is very small if μ is indeed 157 psi, we might doubt the manufacturer's claim.

b. The sample mean observed was $\bar{x} = 157 - 1.3 = 155.7$ psi. If $\mu = 156$, the observed sample mean is closer to μ; hence, the sample mean would be more likely.

If $\mu = 158$, the observed sample mean is farther from μ making the sample mean less likely.

c. As the standard deviation decreases, the calculated value of z would increase indicating a less likely value. As the standard deviation increases, the calculated value of z would decrease indicating a more likely value.

6.25 a. The risk would increase. If $n = 5$, a measure of the risk was $\sigma^2/n = 3.2$, with $\sigma^2 = 5(3.2) = 16.0$. If $n = 3$, this number would increase to $\sigma^2/n = 16/3 = 5.33$. Risk will increase as sample size decreases.

b. The risk would be $\sigma^2/n = 16/10 = 1.6$. By doubling the sample size, we have reduced the risk by half.

6.27 The mean, μ, of the savings account balances is \$1000 with a standard deviation, σ, of \$240. By the Central Limit Theorem, the sampling distribution of $\bar{x}$ is approximately normal since $n \geq 30$, and

$$\mu_{\bar{x}} = \mu = 1000 \qquad \sigma_{\bar{x}} = \frac{\sigma}{\sqrt{n}} = \frac{240}{\sqrt{64}} = 30$$

The auditors will certify the bank if the sample mean balance is within \$60 of the reported mean of \$1000, i.e., the sample mean is between \$940 and \$1060.

Also, notice that the event {auditors don't certify the bank} is the complement of the event {auditors do certify the bank}; hence,

P(auditors don't certify) = 1 - P(auditors do certify)

$$= 1 - P(940 \leq \bar{x} \leq 1060) = 1 - P\left(\frac{940 - \mu}{\sigma_{\bar{x}}} \leq z \leq \frac{1060 - \mu}{\sigma_{\bar{x}}}\right)$$

$$= 1 - P\left(\frac{940 - 1000}{30} \leq z \leq \frac{1060 - 1000}{30}\right) = 1 - P(-2.00 \leq z \leq 2.00)$$

$$= 1 - 2P(0 \leq z \leq 2.00) = 1 - 2(.4772) = 1 - .9544 = .0456$$

6.29 The mean, μ, of the starting salaries of men who received college degrees last years is \$22,000 with a standard deviation, σ, of \$1,200. The sampling distribution of $\bar{x}$ is approximately normal by the Central Limit Theorem since $n \geq 30$ and

$$\mu_{\bar{x}} = \mu = \$22,000 \qquad \sigma_{\bar{x}} = \frac{\sigma}{\sqrt{n}} = \frac{1,200}{\sqrt{36}} = 200$$

a. $P(\bar{x} \geq 22{,}600) = P\!\left(z \geq \dfrac{22600 - \mu}{\sigma_{\bar{x}}}\right) = P\!\left(z \geq \dfrac{22600 - 22000}{200}\right)$

   $= P(z \geq 3.00) = .5 - P(0 \leq z \leq 3.00) = .5 - .4987 = .0013$

b. The probability of observing a sample mean of \$22,600 or larger is so small given the population information that we might believe the starting salaries of women should be characterized by a different probability distribution.

6.31 The mean, μ, of the diameter of the bearings is actually .501 with a standard deviation, σ, of .001. By the Central Limit Theorem, the sampling distribution of $\bar{x}$ is approximately normal since $n \geq 30$ and

   $\mu_{\bar{x}} = \mu = .501 \qquad \sigma_{\bar{x}} = \dfrac{\sigma}{\sqrt{n}} = \dfrac{.001}{\sqrt{36}} = .000167$

Notice that the machine is actually out-of-control if the mean diameter of bearings is .501. The test will fail to imply this if the sample mean is between .4994 and .5006. Then the probability of interest is:

   $P(.4994 \leq \bar{x} \leq .5006) = P\!\left(\dfrac{.4994 - \mu}{\sigma_{\bar{x}}} \leq z \leq \dfrac{.5006 - \mu}{\sigma_{\bar{x}}}\right)$

   $= P\!\left(\dfrac{.4994 - .501}{.000167} \leq z \leq \dfrac{.5006 - .501}{.000167}\right) = P(-9.58 \leq z \leq -2.40)$

   $= P(0 \leq z \leq 9.58) - P(0 \leq z \leq 2.40) = \text{approx. } .5 - .4918$

   $= \text{approx. } .0082$

6.33 a. The population of interest is the market value of all single-family homes in a particular county in 1991.

   b. By the Central Limit Theorem, the sampling distribution of $\bar{x}$ is approximately normal. The probability of observing a value higher than μ is .5.

   c. Having the sample mean fall within \$4000 of μ implies $|\bar{x} - \mu| \leq 4000$ or $-4000 \leq \bar{x} - \mu \leq 4000$.

   $P(-4000 \leq \bar{x} - \mu \leq 4000) = P\!\left(\dfrac{-4000}{\sigma_{\bar{x}}} \leq z \leq \dfrac{4000}{\sigma_{\bar{x}}}\right)$

   $= P\!\left(\dfrac{-4000}{\frac{50{,}000}{\sqrt{400}}} \leq z \leq \dfrac{4000}{\frac{50{,}000}{\sqrt{400}}}\right) = P(-1.60 \leq z \leq 1.60)$

   $= 2P(0 \leq z \leq 1.60) = 2(.4452) = .8904$

6.35 a. If the company is willing to risk a .10 probability that $\bar{x}$ will fall outside the control limits, then we must find z_0 such that $P(-z_0 < z < z_0) = .90$. Using Table IV, $z_0 = 1.645$. The control limits are located $1.645\sigma_{\bar{x}}$ above and below μ.

$$\mu_{\bar{x}} = \mu = 2 \qquad \sigma_{\bar{x}} = \frac{\sigma}{\sqrt{n}} = \frac{1}{\sqrt{5}} = .4472$$

$$1.645\sigma_{\bar{x}} = 1.645(.4472) = .7356$$

Therefore, the control limits are located .7356% above and below the mean of 2%, or the limits are 1.2644 and 2.7356.

b. If $\mu = 3\%$ and $n = 5$, then the probability that $\bar{x}$ will fall outside the control limits is

$$P(\bar{x} < 1.2644) + P(\bar{x} > 2.7356)$$

$$= P\left(z < \frac{1.2644 - 3}{.4472}\right) + P\left(z > \frac{2.7356 - 3}{.4472}\right)$$

$$= P(z < -3.88) + P(z > -.59) = .5 \quad - .5 + .2224 + .5$$

$$= .7224$$

If $n = 10$, then $\sigma_{\bar{x}} = \frac{\sigma}{\sqrt{n}} = \frac{1}{\sqrt{10}} = .3162$

$$1.645\sigma_{\bar{x}} = 1.645(.3162) = .5201$$

Therefore, the control limits are located .5201% above and below the mean of 2%, or the limits are 1.4799% and 2.5201%.

If $\mu = 3\%$ and $n = 10$, then the probability that $\bar{x}$ will fall outside the control limits is

$$P(\bar{x} < 1.4799) + P(\bar{x} > 2.5201)$$

$$= P\left(z < \frac{1.4799 - 3}{.3162}\right) + P\left(z > \frac{2.5201 - 3}{.3162}\right)$$

$$= P(z < -4.81) + P(z > -1.52) = .5 - .5 + .4357 + .5$$

$$= .9357$$

6.37 a. Because $n = 36$ is sufficiently large, the sampling distribution of the sample mean, $\bar{x}$, is approximately normal with

$$\mu_{\bar{x}} = \mu = 75.05 \qquad \sigma_{\bar{x}} = \frac{\sigma}{\sqrt{n}} = \frac{.12}{\sqrt{36}} = .02$$

b. $P(\bar{x} < 75) = P\left(z < \frac{75 - 75.05}{.02}\right) = P(z < -2.50) = .5 - .4938 = .0062$

c. Yes. In part (b), we found that the probability of observing a sample mean less than 75 is .0062. A sample mean of 74.97 is less than 75. Therefore, it would be very unlikely (probability of .0062) to observe a sample mean of 74.97 if the true mean were 75.05 feet. There is evidence to indicate the manufacturer's claim is incorrect.

6.39 Using figure (a), $\mu_A = \dfrac{20,000 + 25,000}{2} = \dfrac{45,000}{2} = 22,500$

Drawing a figure similar to (a) for supplier B, we obtain

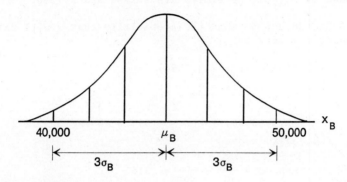

$6\sigma_B = 50,000 - 40,000 = 10,000 \Rightarrow \sigma_B = 10,000/6 = 1666.7$

$\mu_B = \dfrac{40,000 + 50,000}{2} = \dfrac{90,000}{2} = 45,000$

Adding to figure (b), we get

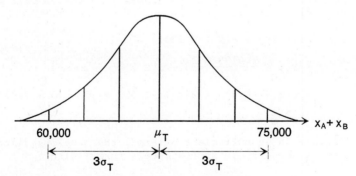

Lower limit = 20,000 + 40,000 = 60,000
Upper limit = 25,000 + 50,000 = 75,000

$$\mu_T = \mu_A + \mu_B = 22,500 + 45,000 = 67,500$$

$$\sigma_T = \sigma_A + \sigma_B = 833.3 + 1666.7 = 2500$$

or $6\sigma_T = 75,000 - 60,000 \Rightarrow \sigma_T = 15,000/6 = 2500$

6.41 a. Since n = 30 is sufficiently large, the Central Limit Theorem says that the sampling distribution of the total $\sum x_i$, is approximately normal with a mean of $n\mu = 30(250) = 7500$ and a variance of $n\sigma^2 = 30(45^2) = 60,750$. The standard deviation of the total is $\sqrt{60,750} = 246.475$.

b. $P(7000 < \sum x_i < 8000) = P\left(\dfrac{7000 - 7500}{246.475} < z < \dfrac{8000 - 7500}{246.475}\right)$

$$= P(-2.03 < z < 2.03) = .4788 + .4788$$

$$= .9576$$

c. $P(\sum x_i > 8100) = P\left(z > \dfrac{8100 - 7500}{246.475}\right) = P(z > 2.43)$

$$= .5 - .4925 = .0075$$

CHAPTER 7

INFERENCES BASED ON
A SINGLE SAMPLE:
ESTIMATION

7.1   a. $\alpha = .10$, $\alpha/2 = .05$, then $z_{.05}$ is the z value that locates .05 in one tail of the standard normal distribution. Since the total area to the right of the mean is .5, $z_{.05}$ will be the z value corresponding to the tabulated area to the right of the mean equal to $.5 - .05 = .4500$. Using Table IV of Appendix B, this z value is 1.645.

      b. $\alpha = .01$, $\alpha/2 = .005$. Then $z_{.005}$ is the z value that locates .005 in one tail of the standard normal distribution. Looking up an area of $.5 - .005 = .4950$ in Table IV, Appendix B, $z_{.005}$ is 2.575.

      c. $\alpha = .05$, $\alpha/2 = .025$. Looking up an area of $.5 - .025 = .4750$ in Table IV, Appendix B, $z_{.025}$ is 1.96.

      d. $\alpha = .20$, $\alpha/2 = .10$. Looking up an area of $.5 - .10 = .4000$ in Table IV, Appendix B, $z_{.10}$ is 1.28.

7.3   a.   For confidence coefficient .95, $\alpha = 1 - .95 = .05$ and $\alpha/2 = .05/2 = .025$. From Table IV, Appendix B, $z_{.025} = 1.96$. The 95% confidence interval for μ is:

$$\bar{x} \pm z_{.025}\sigma_{\bar{x}}$$

$$\Rightarrow \bar{x} \pm 1.96 \frac{\sigma}{\sqrt{n}}$$

$$\Rightarrow 14.1 \pm 1.96 \frac{2.6}{\sqrt{80}}$$

$$\Rightarrow 14.1 \pm .57 \Rightarrow (13.53, 14.67)$$

b. For confidence coefficient, .99, $\alpha = 1 - .99 = .01$ and $\alpha/2 = .01/2 = .005$. From Table IV, Appendix B, $z_{.005} = 2.575$. The 99% confidence interval for μ is:

$$\bar{x} \pm z_{.005}\sigma_{\bar{x}}$$

$$\Rightarrow \bar{x} \pm 2.575 \frac{\sigma}{\sqrt{n}}$$

$$\Rightarrow 14.1 \pm 2.575 \frac{2.6}{\sqrt{80}}$$

$$\Rightarrow 14.1 \pm .749 \Rightarrow (13.351, 14.849)$$

c. As the confidence coefficient is increased, the width of a confidence interval also increases. The more confident we want to be that μ is contained in the interval, the more values we need in the interval.

d. The confidence intervals in parts (a) and (b) are valid regardless of the distribution of the original population. By the Central Limit Theorem, the sampling distribution of $\bar{x}$ is approximately normal when $n \geq 30$.

7.5   If we were to repeatedly draw samples from the population and form the interval $\bar{x} \pm 1.96 \sigma_{\bar{x}}$ each time, approximately 95% of the intervals would contain μ. We have no way of knowing whether our interval estimate is one of the 95% that contain μ or one of the 5% that do not.

7.7   As the confidence coefficient increases, the width of the interval increases. As the confidence coefficient decreases, the width of the interval decreases.

7.9   a. The population consists of the changes in rent for two-bedroom apartments in metropolitan Minneapolis between May 1989 and May 1990.

b. First, compute the mean and standard deviation of the sample.

$$\bar{x} = \frac{\sum x}{n} = \frac{48.01}{32} = 1.5$$

$$s^2 = \frac{\sum x^2 - \frac{(\sum x)^2}{n}}{n - 1} = \frac{160.9639 - \frac{(48.01)^2}{32}}{32 - 1} = 2.8688$$

$$s = \sqrt{2.8688} = 1.6938$$

For confidence coefficient .95, $\alpha = 1 - .95 = .05$ and $\alpha/2 = .05/2$
= .025. From Table IV, Appendix B, $z_{.025} = 1.96$. The 95%
confidence interval is:

$$\bar{x} \pm z_{.025}\sigma_{\bar{x}}$$

$$=> \bar{x} \pm 1.96 \, \frac{\sigma}{\sqrt{n}}$$

$$=> 1.5 \pm 1.96 \, \frac{1.6938}{\sqrt{32}}$$

$$=> 1.5 \pm .587 => (.913, 2.087)$$

c. The confidence interval in part (b) is valid regardless of the
distribution of the population. By the Central Limit Theorem, the
sampling distribution of $\bar{x}$ is approximately normal when $n \geq 30$.

7.11 a. First, compute the mean and standard deviation of the sample.

$$\bar{x} = \frac{\sum x}{n} = \frac{1045.875}{36} = 29.0521$$

$$s^2 = \frac{\sum x^2 - \frac{(\sum x)^2}{n}}{n - 1} = \frac{42419.48445 - \frac{1045.875^2}{36}}{36 - 1} = 343.84676$$

$$s = \sqrt{343.84676} = 18.5431$$

For confidence coefficient .80, $\alpha = 1 - .80 = .20$ and $\alpha/2 = .20/2$
= .10. From Table IV, Appendix B, $z_{.10} = 1.28$. The 80%
confidence interval for μ is:

$$\bar{x} \pm z_{.10}\sigma_{\bar{x}}$$

$$=> \bar{x} \pm 1.28 \, \frac{\sigma}{\sqrt{n}}$$

$$=> 29.0521 \pm 1.28 \, \frac{18.5431}{\sqrt{36}}$$

$$=> 29.0521 \pm 3.9559 => (25.0962, 33.0080)$$

7.13 a. For confidence coefficient .90, $\alpha = 1 - .90 = .10$ and $\alpha/2 = .10/2 = .05$. From Table IV, Appendix B, $z_{.05} = 1.645$. The 90% confidence interval for μ is:

$$\bar{x} \pm z_{.05}\sigma_{\bar{x}}$$

$$\Rightarrow \bar{x} \pm 1.645\,\frac{\sigma}{\sqrt{n}}$$

$$\Rightarrow 23.43 \pm 1.645\,\frac{10.82}{\sqrt{96}}$$

$$\Rightarrow 23.43 \pm 1.817 \Rightarrow (21.613,\ 25.247)$$

b. We are 90% confident the true mean number of years of service lies in the interval 21.613 to 25.247.

c. That you have chosen a random sample where n is sufficiently large to use the normal distribution.

d. Yes, $\bar{x}$ is an unbiased estimate of μ; therefore, $E(\bar{x}) = \mu = E(x)$.

7.15 To compute the necessary sample size, use

$$n = \frac{4(z_{\alpha/2})^2\sigma^2}{W^2} \quad \text{where } \alpha = 1 - .95 = .05 \text{ and } \alpha/2 = .05/2 = .025.$$

From Table IV, Appendix B, $z_{.025} = 1.96$. Thus,

$$n = \frac{4(1.96)^2(6.1)}{.2^2}$$

$$= 2343.376 \approx 2344$$

In Exercise 7.14, the bound is .2 which means the width is .4. The confidence interval resulting from the sample will be wider in Exercise 7.14 than in this exercise. Therefore, the sample size in Exercise 7.14 is smaller. As the sample size decreases, the width of the confidence interval increases.

7.17 a. An estimate of σ is obtained from:

$$\text{range} \approx 4s$$

$$s \approx \frac{\text{range}}{4}$$

$$= \frac{27 - 24}{4}$$

$$= .75$$

To compute the necessary sample size, use

$$n = \frac{(z_{\alpha/2})^2\sigma^2}{B^2} \quad \text{where } \alpha = 1 - .90 = .10 \text{ and } \alpha/2 = .05.$$

From Table IV, Appendix B, $z_{.05} = 1.645$. Thus,

$$n = \frac{(1.645)^2(.75)^2}{.15^2}$$

$$= 67.65 \approx 68$$

b. A less conservative estimate of σ is obtained from:

range $\approx 6s$

$$s \approx \frac{range}{6}$$

$$= \frac{27 - 24}{6}$$

$$= .5$$

Thus,

$$n = \frac{(z_{\alpha/2})^2\sigma^2}{B^2}$$

$$= \frac{(1.645)^2(.5)^2}{.15^2}$$

$$= 30.07 \approx 31$$

7.19   a. To compute the needed sample size, use

$$n = \frac{(z_{\alpha/2})^2\sigma^2}{B^2} \quad \text{where } \alpha = 1 - .80 = .20 \text{ and } \alpha/2 = .10.$$

From Table IV, Appendix B, $z_{.10} = 1.28$. Thus,

$$n = \frac{(1.28)^2(2)^2}{.1^2}$$

$$= 655.36 \approx 656$$

b. As the sample size decreases, the width of the confidence interval increases. Therefore, if we sample 100 parts instead of 656, the confidence interval would be wider.

c. To compute the maximum confidence level that could be attained meeting the management's specifications,

$$n = \frac{(z_{\alpha/2})^2 \sigma^2}{B^2}$$

$$\Rightarrow 100 = \frac{(z_{\alpha/2})^2 (2)^2}{.1^2}$$

$$\Rightarrow (z_{\alpha/2})^2 = \frac{100(.01)}{4} = .25$$

$$\Rightarrow z_{\alpha/2} = .5$$

Using Table IV, Appendix B, $P(0 \le z \le .5) = .1915$. Thus, $\alpha/2 = .5000 - .1915 = .3085$, $\alpha = 2(.3085) = .617$, and $1 - \alpha = 1 - .617 = .383$.

The maximum confidence level would be 38.3%.

7.21 An estimate of σ is obtained from:

range $\approx 4s$

$$s \approx \frac{range}{4}$$

$$= \frac{180 - 60}{4}$$

$$= 30$$

To compute the necessary sample size, use

$$n = \frac{(z_{\alpha/2})^2 \sigma^2}{B^2} \quad \text{where } \alpha = 1 - .95 = .05 \text{ and } \alpha/2 = .025.$$

From Table IV, Appendix B, $z_{.025} = 1.96$. Thus,

$$n = \frac{(1.96)^2 (30)^2}{5^2}$$

$$= 138.298$$

You would need to take 139 cups of coffee.

7.23 a. If x is normally distributed, the sampling distribution of $\bar{x}$ is normal, regardless of the sample size.

b. If nothing is known about the distribution of x, the sampling distribution of $\bar{x}$ is approximately normal if n is sufficiently large. If n is not large, the distribution of $\bar{x}$ is unknown if the distribution of x is not known.

7.25   a. $P(t \geq t_0) = .025$ where df $= 8$

$$t_0 = 2.306$$

b. $P(t \geq t_0) = .01$ where df $= 10$

$$t_0 = 2.764$$

c. $P(t \leq t_0) = .005$ where df $= 17$

Because of symmetry, the statement can be rewritten

$$P(t \geq -t_0) = .005 \text{ where df} = 17$$

$$t_0 = -2.898$$

d. $P(t \leq t_0) = .05$ where df $= 14$

$$t_0 = -1.761$$

7.27   For this sample,

$$\bar{x} = \frac{\sum x}{n} = \frac{2400}{24} = 100$$

$$s^2 = \frac{\sum x^2 - \frac{(\sum x)^2}{n}}{n - 1} = \frac{244,382 - \frac{2400^2}{24}}{24 - 1} = 190.5217$$

$$s = \sqrt{s^2} = 13.8030$$

a.   For confidence coefficient, .80, $\alpha = 1 - .80 = .20$ and $\alpha/2 = .20/2$ $= .10$. From Table VI, Appendix B, with df $= n - 1 = 24 - 1 = 23$, $t_{.10} = 1.319$. The 80% confidence interval for μ is:

$$\bar{x} \pm t_{.10} \frac{s}{\sqrt{n}}$$

$$\Rightarrow 100 \pm 1.319 \frac{13.803}{\sqrt{24}}$$

$$\Rightarrow 100 \pm 3.72 \Rightarrow (96.28, \ 103.72)$$

b.   For confidence coefficient, .95, $\alpha = 1 - .95 = .05$ and $\alpha/2 = .05/2$ $= .025$. From Table VI, Appendix B, with df $= n - 1 = 24 - 1 = 23$, $t_{.025} = 2.069$. The 95% confidence interval for μ is:

$$\bar{x} \pm t_{.025} \frac{s}{\sqrt{n}}$$

$$\Rightarrow 100 \pm 2.069 \frac{13.808}{\sqrt{24}}$$

$$\Rightarrow 100 \pm 5.83 \Rightarrow (94.17, \ 105.83)$$

The 95% confidence interval for μ is wider than the 80% confidence interval for μ found in part (a).

c. For part (a),

> We are 80% confident that the true population mean lies in the interval 96.28 to 103.72.

For part (b),

> We are 95% confident that the true population mean lies in the interval 94.17 to 105.83.

The 95% confidence interval is wider than the 80% confidence interval because the more confident you want to be that μ lies in the interval, the more numbers must be in the interval. The more confident you are, the larger the t-value, which makes the interval wider.

7.29 a. For confidence coefficient .99, $\alpha = 1 - .99 = .01$ and $\alpha/2 = .01/2 = .005$. From Table VI, Appendix B, with df $= n - 1 = 15 - 1 = 14$, $t_{.005} = 2.977$. The 99% confidence interval is:

$$\bar{x} \pm t_{.005} \frac{s}{\sqrt{n}}$$

$$\Rightarrow 23.8 \pm 2.977 \frac{9.4}{\sqrt{15}}$$

$$\Rightarrow 23.8 \pm 7.225 \Rightarrow (16.575, 31.025)$$

b. We are 99% confident that the mean percentage of 1990 revenues from foreign sales for all large U.S. firms is between 16.575% and 31.025%.

c. We must assume the distribution of percentages of 1990 revenues from foreign sales is normal and the sample is a random sample.

7.31 a. The population of interest is all the costs of hiring secretaries in the corporation for the last 2 years.

b. First, compute the sample mean and standard deviation:

$$\bar{x} = \frac{\sum x}{n} = \frac{15215}{8} = 1901.88$$

$$s^2 = \frac{\sum x^2 - \frac{(\sum x)^2}{n}}{n - 1} = \frac{29649475 - \frac{(15215)^2}{8}}{7} = 101778.12$$

$$s = \sqrt{s^2} = 319.027$$

For confidence coefficient .90, α = .10 and $\alpha/2$ = .05. From Table VI, Appendix B, with df = n − 1 = 8 − 1 = 7, $t_{.05}$ = 1.895. The 90% confidence interval is:

$$\bar{x} \pm t_{.05} \frac{s}{\sqrt{n}}$$

$$\Rightarrow 1901.88 \pm 1.895 \frac{319.027}{\sqrt{8}}$$

$$\Rightarrow 1901.88 \pm 213.74 \Rightarrow (1688.14, \ 2115.62)$$

c. The width of the confidence interval is

$$2115.62 - 1688.14 = 427.48 = 2(213.74)$$

A 95% confidence interval would be wider because increasing the confidence level causes the use of a larger $t_{\alpha/2}$ value in every case; thus, increasing the width of the confidence interval.

7.33 a. For confidence coefficient .95, α = 1 − .95 = .05 and $\alpha/2$ = .05/2 = .025. From Table VI, Appendix B, with df = n − 1 = 23 − 1 = 22, $t_{.025}$ = 2.074. The 95% confidence interval is:

$$\bar{x} \pm t_{.025} \frac{s}{\sqrt{n}}$$

$$\Rightarrow 135 \pm 2.074 \frac{32}{\sqrt{23}}$$

$$\Rightarrow 135 \pm 13.839 \Rightarrow (121.161, \ 148.839)$$

b. We must assume a random sample was selected and that the population of all health insurance costs per worker per month is normally distributed.

c. "95% confidence interval" means that if repeated samples of size 23 were selected from the population and 95% confidence intervals formed, 95% of all confidence intervals will contain the true value of μ.

7.35 An unbiased estimator is one in which the mean of the sampling distribution is the parameter of interest, i.e., $E(\hat{p})$ = p.

7.37 The sample size is large enough if $\hat{p} \pm 3\sigma_{\hat{p}}$ lies within the interval (0, 1).

$$\hat{p} \pm 3\sigma_{\hat{p}} \Rightarrow \hat{p} \pm 3\sqrt{\frac{pq}{n}} \Rightarrow \hat{p} \pm 3\sqrt{\frac{\hat{p}\hat{q}}{n}}$$

a. When n = 500, $\hat{p}$ = .05:

$$.05 \pm 3\sqrt{\frac{.05(1 - .05)}{500}}$$

$$=> .05 \pm .0292 => (.0208, .0792)$$

Since the interval lies completely in the interval (0, 1), the normal approximation will be adequate.

b. When n = 100, $\hat{p}$ = .05:

$$.05 \pm 3\sqrt{\frac{.05(1 - .05)}{100}}$$

$$=> .05 \pm .0654 => (-.0154, .1154)$$

Since the interval does not lie completely in the interval (0, 1), the normal approximation will not be adequate.

c. When n = 10, $\hat{p}$ = .5:

$$.5 \pm 3\sqrt{\frac{.5(1 - .5)}{10}}$$

$$=> .5 \pm .4743 => (.0257, .9743)$$

Since the interval lies completely in the interval (0, 1), the normal approximation will be adequate.

d. When n = 10, $\hat{p}$ = .3:

$$.3 \pm 3\sqrt{\frac{.3(1 - .3)}{10}}$$

$$=> .3 \pm .4347 => (-.1347, .7347)$$

Since the interval does not lie completely in the interval (0, 1), the normal approximation will not be adequate.

7.39 $\hat{p}$ = x/n = 76/122 = .623

a. We first check to see if the sample size is sufficiently large.

$$\hat{p} \pm 3\sigma_{\hat{p}} \approx \hat{p} \pm 3\sqrt{\frac{\hat{p}\hat{q}}{n}}$$

$$=> .623 \pm 3\sqrt{\frac{(.623)(.377)}{122}}$$

$$=> .623 \pm .132 => (.491, .755)$$

Since the interval is wholly contained in the interval (0, 1), we may conclude that the normal approximation is reasonable.

For confidence coefficient .95, $\alpha = 1 - .95 = .05$ and $\alpha/2 = .05/2 = .025$. From Table IV, Appendix B, $z_{.025} = 1.96$. The 95% confidence interval is:

$$\hat{p} \pm z_{.025} \sqrt{\frac{\hat{p}\hat{q}}{n}}$$

$$\Rightarrow .623 \pm 1.96 \sqrt{\frac{(.623)(.377)}{122}}$$

$$\Rightarrow .623 \pm .086 \Rightarrow (.537, .709)$$

b. We are 95% confident the proportion of all Illinois law firms which used microcomputers at the time of the survey is between .537 and .709.

c. "95% confidence interval" means that if repeated samples of size 122 were selected from the population and 95% confidence intervals formed, 95% of all confidence intervals will contain the true value of p.

d. Probably not. The sample was selected only from Illinois law firms. The only way the interval could be used to estimate the proportion of all U.S. law firms which were using microcomputers at the time of the survey would be if the Illinois law firms are very similar to all U.S. law firms.

7.41 a. Check to see if the normal approximation will be adequate.

$$\hat{p} \pm 3\sigma_{\hat{p}} \Rightarrow \hat{p} \pm 3\sqrt{\frac{pq}{n}} \Rightarrow p \pm 3\sqrt{\frac{\hat{p}\hat{q}}{n}} \text{ where } \hat{p} = \frac{120}{300} = 0.4$$

$$\Rightarrow .4 \pm 3\sqrt{\frac{.4(.6)}{300}}$$

$$\Rightarrow .4 \pm .085 \Rightarrow (.315, .485)$$

Since the interval lies within the interval (0, 1), the normal approximation will be adequate.

For confidence coefficient .90, $\alpha = .10$ and $\alpha/2 = .05$. From Table IV, Appendix B, $z_{.05} = 1.645$. The 90% confidence interval is:

$$\hat{p} \pm z_{.05} \sqrt{\frac{pq}{n}}$$

$$\Rightarrow \hat{p} \pm 1.645 \sqrt{\frac{\hat{p}\hat{q}}{n}}$$

$$\Rightarrow .4 \pm 1.645 \sqrt{\frac{.4(.6)}{300}}$$

$$\Rightarrow .4 \pm .047 \Rightarrow (.353, .447)$$

b. The width of the confidence interval is:

$$.447 - .353 = .094 = 2(.047)$$

An 80% confidence interval would be narrower. As the confidence level decreases, the $z_{\alpha/2}$ value decreases causing the confidence interval to be narrower.

7.43 First, check to see if the normal approximation is adequate:

$$\hat{p} \pm 3\sigma_{\hat{p}} \Rightarrow \hat{p} \pm 3\sqrt{\frac{pq}{n}} \Rightarrow \hat{p} \pm 3\sqrt{\frac{\hat{p}\hat{q}}{n}} \text{ where } \hat{p} = \frac{2}{25} = .08 \text{ and } n = 500.$$

$$\Rightarrow .08 \pm 3\sqrt{\frac{.08(.92)}{500}}$$

$$\Rightarrow .08 \pm .036 \Rightarrow (.044, .116)$$

Since the interval does not include 0 or 1, the normal approximation can be used to form the confidence interval:

$$\hat{p} \pm 1.96\sqrt{\frac{\hat{p}\hat{q}}{n}} \Rightarrow .08 \pm 1.96\sqrt{\frac{(.08)(.92)}{500}} \Rightarrow .08 \pm .024 \Rightarrow (.056, .104)$$

7.45 The sample size will be larger than necessary for any p other than .5.

7.47 a. To compute the needed sample size, use:

$$n = \frac{4(z_{\alpha/2})^2 pq}{W^2} \text{ where } z_{.025} = 1.96 \text{ from Table IV, Appendix B.}$$

Thus,
$$n = \frac{4(1.96)^2(.3)(.7)}{.12^2}$$

$$= 224.1$$

You would need to take n = 225 samples.

b. To compute the needed sample size, use:

$$n = \frac{4(z_{\alpha/2})^2 pq}{W^2} = \frac{4(1.96)^2(.5)(.5)}{.12^2}$$

$$= 266.8$$

You would need to take 267 samples.

7.49 a. To compute the needed sample size, use:

$$n = \frac{4(z_{\alpha/2})^2 pq}{W^2} \text{ where } z_{.05} = 1.645 \text{ from Table IV, Appendix B.}$$

Thus,

$$n = \frac{4(1.645)^2(.17)(.83)}{.06^2}$$

$$= 424.2$$

You would need to sample 425 IRS offices.

7.51   a.   To compute the necessary sample size, use:

$$n = \frac{4(z_{\alpha/2})^2(pq)}{W^2}$$ where $z_{.025} = 1.96$ from Table IV, Appendix B.

Thus,

$$n = \frac{4(1.96)^2(.3)(.7)}{.01^2}$$

$$= 32,269.4$$

You would need to sample 32,270 viewers.

7.53   First, compute the necessary sample size. Use:

$$n = \frac{(z_{\alpha/2})^2(pq)}{B^2}$$ where $z_{.025} = 1.96$ from Table IV, Appendix B.

Thus,

$$n = \frac{(1.96)^2(.05)(.95)}{.02^2}$$

$$= 456.19 \approx 457$$

NHSA needs to sample n = 457 tires to meet the desired specifications.

At $25 a tire, 25(457) = $11,425 is needed. Since NHSA only has $10,000, it cannot attain its goal while staying within the budget.

7.55   a.   The average number of checks the bank processed per week for the 50 randomly sampled weeks.

b.   The proportion of weeks the bank processed more than 100,000 checks in the 50 randomly sampled weeks.

c.   The standard deviation of the number of checks the bank processes each week.

d.   The average number of checks the bank processes per week.

e.   The number of weeks that are randomly sampled (n = 50).

f.   The standard deviation of the average number of checks the bank processed each week for the 50 randomly selected weeks.

g. The proportion of weeks the bank processes more than 100,000 checks.

h. The standard deviation of the number of checks the bank processed each week in the 50 randomly sampled weeks.

7.57   a. For confidence coefficient .90, α = .10 and $\alpha/2$ = .05. From Table IV, Appendix B, $z_{.05}$ = 1.645. The 90% confidence interval is:

$$\bar{x} \pm z_{.05} \frac{\sigma}{\sqrt{n}}$$

$$\Rightarrow \bar{x} \pm 1.645 \frac{s}{\sqrt{n}}$$

$$\Rightarrow 12.2 \pm 1.645 \frac{10}{\sqrt{100}}$$

$$\Rightarrow 12.2 \pm 1.645 \Rightarrow (10.555, 13.845)$$

b. To compute the necessary sample size, use:

$$n = \frac{(z_{\alpha/2})^2 \sigma^2}{B^2} \quad \text{where } z_{.005} = 2.575 \text{ from Table IV, Appendix B.}$$

Thus,

$$n = \frac{(2.575)^2 (10)^2}{2^2}$$

$$= 165.8$$

You would need to sample 166 personnel files.

7.59   a. To compute the needed sample size, use:

$$n = \frac{(z_{\alpha/2})^2 (pq)}{B^2} \quad \text{where } z_{.05} = 1.645 \text{ from Table IV, Appendix B.}$$

Thus,

$$n = \frac{(1.645)^2 (.6)(.4)}{.03^2}$$

$$= 721.61 \approx 722$$

b. To compute the needed sample size, use:

$$n = \frac{(z_{\alpha/2})^2 \sigma^2}{B^2}$$

Thus,

$$n = \frac{(1.645)^2 (2)}{.25^2}$$

$$= 173.19 \approx 174$$

Therefore, the sample size determined in part (a) is large enough to also estimate μ with the desired specifications.

7.61   To satisfy all specifications to estimate both μ and p, all we need do is choose the larger of the two computed sample sizes.

To estimate μ, we compute:

$$n = \frac{4(z_{\alpha/2})^2\sigma^2}{W^2} \text{ where } z_{.025} = 1.96 \text{ from Table IV, Appendix B.}$$

Thus,

$$n = \frac{4(1.96)^2(10)^2}{6^2}$$

$$= 42.7$$

We would need 43 samples.

To estimate p, we compute:

$$n = \frac{4(z_{\alpha/2})^2(pq)}{W^2} \text{ where } z_{.05} = 1.645 \text{ from Table IV, Appendix B.}$$

Thus,

$$n = \frac{4(1.645)^2(.4)(.6)}{.1^2}$$

$$= 259.8$$

We would need 260 samples.

Then to estimate both μ and p to specifications, we would need to take 260 samples.

7.63   a.   The point estimate for the mean wear is $\bar{x} = 42,250$ miles.

b.   For confidence coefficient .90, $\alpha = 1 - .90 = .10$ and $\alpha/2 = .10/2 = .05$. From Table VI, Appendix B, with df $= n - 1 = 20 - 1 = 19$, $t_{.05} = 1.729$. The 90% confidence interval is:

$$\bar{x} \pm t_{.05}\frac{s}{\sqrt{n}}$$

$$\Rightarrow 42,250 \pm 1.729\frac{4355}{\sqrt{20}}$$

$$\Rightarrow 42,250 \pm 1683.713 \Rightarrow (40,566.287, \ 43,933.713)$$

c.   Interval estimation is better. The probability of estimating the true mean exactly with a single number is 0. With a confidence interval, we can estimate the true mean using a range of values. We are then fairly confident the true mean will fall in this range.

7.65   To compute the needed sample size, use:

$$n = \frac{4(z_{\alpha/2})^2 pq}{W^2}$$ where $z_{.025} = 1.96$ from Table IV, Appendix B.

Thus, $n = \frac{4(1.96)^2(.094)(.906)}{.04^2} \approx 817.9 \approx 818$

7.67   a. To compute the necessary sample size, use:

$$n = \frac{(z_{\alpha/2})^2 \sigma^2}{B^2}$$ where $\alpha = 1 - .99 = .01$ and $\alpha/2 = .01/2 = .005$

From Table IV, Appendix B, $z_{.005} = 2.575$. Thus,

$$n = \frac{(2.575)^2 11.34^2}{1^2} = 852.7 \approx 853.$$

        b. We would have to assume the sample was a random sample.

C H A P T E R 8

INFERENCES BASED ON A SINGLE SAMPLE: TESTS OF HYPOTHESES

8.1 The null hypothesis is the "status quo" hypothesis, while the alternative hypothesis is the research hypothesis.

8.3 The "level of significance" of a test is α. This is the probability that the test statistic will fail in the rejection region when the null hypothesis is true.

8.5 The four possible results are:

1. Rejecting the null hypothesis when it is true. This would be a Type I error.

2. Accepting the null hypothesis when it is true. This would be a correct decision.

3. Rejecting the null hypothesis when it is false. This would be a correct decision.

4. Accepting the null hypothesis when it is false. This would be a Type II error.

8.7 When you reject the null hypothesis in favor of the alternative hypothesis, this does not prove the alternative hypothesis is correct. We are $100(1 - α)$% confident that there is sufficient evidence to conclude that the alternative hypothesis is correct.

If we were to repeatedly draw samples from the population and perform the test each time, approximately $100(1 - α)$% of the tests performed would yield the correct decision.

8.9 a. Since the company must give proof the drug is safe, the null hypothesis would be the drug is unsafe. The alternative hypothesis would be the drug is safe.

b. A Type I error would be concluding the drug is safe when it is not safe. A Type II error would be concluding the drug is not safe when it is. α is the probability of concluding the drug is safe when it is not. β is the probability of concluding the drug is not safe when it is.

c. In this problem, it would be more important for α to be small. We would want the probability of concluding the drug is safe when it is not to be as small as possible.

8.11 a. H_0: $\mu = 100$
H_a: $\mu > 100$

The test statistic is $z = \dfrac{\bar{x} - \mu_0}{\sigma_{\bar{x}}} = \dfrac{\bar{x} - \mu_0}{\sigma/\sqrt{n}} = \dfrac{110 - 100}{60/\sqrt{100}} = 1.67$

The rejection region requires $\alpha = .05$ in the upper tail of the z distribution. From Table IV, Appendix B, $z_{.05} = 1.645$. The rejection region is $z > 1.645$.

Since the observed value of the test statistic falls in the rejection region, ($z = 1.67 > 1.645$), H_0 is rejected. There is sufficient evidence to indicate the true population mean is greater than 100 at $\alpha = .05$.

b. H_0: $\mu = 100$
H_a: $\mu \neq 100$

The test statistic is $z = \dfrac{\bar{x} - \mu_0}{\sigma_{\bar{x}}} = \dfrac{110 - 100}{60/\sqrt{100}} = 1.67$

The rejection region requires $\alpha/2 = .05/2 = .025$ in each tail of the z distribution. From Table IV, Appendix B, $z_{.025} = 1.96$. The rejection region is $z < -1.96$ or $z > 1.96$.

Since the observed value of the test statistic does not fall in the rejection region, ($z = 1.67 \not> 1.96$), H_0 is not rejected. There is insufficient evidence to indicate μ does not equal 0 at $\alpha = .05$.

c. In part (a), we rejected H_0 and concluded the mean was greater than 100. In Part (b), we did not reject H_0. There was insufficient evidence to conclude the mean was different from 100. Because the alternative hypothesis in part (a) is more specific than the one in (b), it is easier to reject H_0.

8.13 First, we must find the sample mean and standard deviation.

$$\bar{x} = \frac{\sum x}{n} = \frac{27.4}{60} = .4567$$

$$s^2 = \frac{\sum x^2 - \dfrac{(\sum x)^2}{n}}{n - 1} = \frac{14.3 - \dfrac{27.4^2}{60}}{60 - 1} = .0303$$

$$s = \sqrt{s^2} = .1741$$

a. We want to test:

H_0: $\mu = .40$
H_a: $\mu > .40$

The test statistic is $z = \dfrac{\bar{x} - \mu_0}{\sigma_{\bar{x}}} = \dfrac{\bar{x} - \mu_0}{\sigma/\sqrt{n}} \approx \dfrac{\bar{x} - \mu_0}{s/\sqrt{n}} = \dfrac{.4567 - .40}{.1741/\sqrt{60}}$

$$= 2.52$$

The rejection region requires $\alpha = .05$ in the upper tail of the z distribution. From Table IV, Appendix B, $z_{.05} = 1.645$. The rejection region is $z > 1.645$.

Since the observed value of the test statistic falls in the rejection region ($z = 2.52 > 1.645$), H_0 is rejected. There is sufficient evidence to indicate the true population mean is greater than .40 at $\alpha = .05$.

b. We want to test:

H_0: $\mu = .40$
H_a: $\mu \neq .40$

The test statistic is 2.52. (Refer to part (a)).

The rejection region requires $\alpha/2 = .05/2 = .025$ in each tail of the z distribution. From Table IV, Appendix B, $z_{.025} = 1.96$. The rejection region is $z < -1.96$ or $z > 1.96$.

Since the observed value of the test statistic falls in the rejection region ($z = 2.52 > 1.96$), H_0 is rejected. There is sufficient evidence to indicate the true population mean is not equal to .40 at $\alpha = .05$.

8.15 a. The null hypothesis is H_0: $\mu = 35$ mpg. The alternative hypothesis is H_a: $\mu > 35$ mpg.

b. We want to test:

H_0: $\mu = 35$
H_a: $\mu > 35$

The test statistic is $z = \dfrac{\bar{x} - \mu_0}{\sigma_{\bar{x}}} = \dfrac{\bar{x} - \mu_0}{\sigma/\sqrt{n}} \approx \dfrac{\bar{x} - \mu_0}{s/\sqrt{n}} = \dfrac{36.8 - 35}{6/\sqrt{36}}$

$$= 1.8$$

The rejection region requires $\alpha = .05$ in the upper tail of the z distribution. From Table IV, Appendix B, $z_{.05} = 1.645$. The rejection region is $z > 1.645$.

Since the observed value of the test statistic falls in the rejection region ($z = 1.8 > 1.645$), H_0 is rejected. There is sufficient evidence to support the auto manufacturer's claim that the mean miles per gallon for the car exceeds the EPA estimate of 35 at $\alpha = .05$.

8.17 a. To determine if the sample data refutes the manufacturer's claim, we want to test:

$$H_0: \mu = 10$$
$$H_a: \mu < 10$$

b. A Type I error results if we decide that the equipment can inspect less than 10 joints per second on the average when it can inspect at least 10 joints per second.

A Type II error results if we decide that the equipment can inspect at least 10 joints per second on the average but it really cannot.

c. First, compute the sample mean and standard deviation.

$$\bar{x} = \frac{\sum x}{n} = \frac{446}{48} = 9.2917$$

$$s^2 = \frac{\sum x^2 - \frac{(\sum x)^2}{n}}{n - 1} = \frac{4352 - \frac{446^2}{48}}{48 - 1} = 4.4238$$

$$s = \sqrt{s^2} = 2.1033$$

The test statistic is $z = \dfrac{\bar{x} - \mu_0}{\sigma_{\bar{x}}} = \dfrac{\bar{x} - \mu_0}{\sigma/\sqrt{n}} \approx \dfrac{\bar{x} - \mu_0}{s/\sqrt{n}} = \dfrac{9.2917 - 10}{2.1033/\sqrt{48}}$

$$= -2.33$$

The rejection region requires $\alpha = .05$ in the lower tail of the z distribution. From Table IV, Appendix B, $z_{.05} = 1.645$. The rejection region is $z < -1.645$.

Since the observed value of the test statistic falls in the rejection region ($z = -2.33 < -1.645$), H_0 is rejected. There is sufficient evidence to indicate the equipment can inspect less than 10 joints per second on the average at $\alpha = .05$.

8.19 We will reject H_0 if the p-value $< \alpha$.

a. $.06 \not< .05$, do not reject H_0

b. $.10 \not< .05$, do not reject H_0

c. $.01 < .05$, reject H_0

d. $.001 < .05$, reject H_0

e. $.251 \not< .05$, do not reject H_0

f. $.042 < .05$, reject H_0

8.23 p-value = $P(z \geq 2.26)$ = .5 - $P(0 < z < 2.26)$

$\qquad\qquad\qquad\qquad\qquad$ = .5 - .4881

$\qquad\qquad\qquad\qquad\qquad$ = .0119

8.25 p-value = $P(z \leq -1.11)$ = .5 - $P(0 < z < 1.11)$

$\qquad\qquad\qquad\qquad\qquad$ = .5 - .3665

$\qquad\qquad\qquad\qquad\qquad$ = .1335

8.27 First, find the value of the test statistic:

$$z = \frac{\bar{x} - \mu_0}{\sigma_{\bar{x}}} = \frac{\bar{x} - \mu_0}{\sigma/\sqrt{n}} \approx \frac{\bar{x} - \mu_0}{s/\sqrt{n}}$$

$$= \frac{9.5 - 10}{2.1/\sqrt{50}}$$

$$= -1.68$$

p-value = $P(z \leq -1.68$ or $z \geq 1.68)$

$\qquad$ = $2P(z \geq 1.68)$

$\qquad$ = $2[.5 - P(0 < z < 1.68)]$

$\qquad$ = $2(.5 - .4535)$

$\qquad$ = $2(.0465)$ = .093

8.29 From Exercise 8.14, z = 7.02 for a two-tailed test.

$\qquad$ p-value = $P(z \leq -7.02$ or $z \geq 7.02)$

$\qquad\qquad$ = $2P(z \geq 7.02)$

$\qquad\qquad$ = $2[.5 - P(0 < z < 7.02)]$

$\qquad\qquad$ = $2[.5 - $ approx. $.5]$

$\qquad\qquad$ = $2[$approx. $0]$

$\qquad\qquad$ $\approx$ 0

8.31 a. H_0: μ = \$90,380
$\qquad\quad$ H_a: μ > \$90,380

$\qquad$ b. First, find the value of the test statistic:

$$z = \frac{\bar{x} - \mu_0}{\sigma_{\bar{x}}} = \frac{\bar{x} - \mu_0}{\sigma/\sqrt{n}} \approx \frac{\bar{x} - \mu_0}{s/\sqrt{n}}$$

$$= \frac{93,290 - 90,380}{6,500/\sqrt{30}}$$

$$= 2.45$$

$$\text{p-value} = P(z \geq 2.45) = .5 - P(0 < z < 2.45)$$
$$= .5 - .4929$$
$$= .0071$$

There is a strong indication that the mean cost of a new home in Florida is greater than \$90,380, since we would observe a test statistic this extreme or more extreme only 71 in 10,000 times if the mean is \$90,380.

8.33 From Exercise 8.18, we want to test H_0: μ = \$30,000 against H_a: μ > \$30,000, z = 2.44.

$$\text{p-value} = P(z \geq 2.44)$$
$$= .5 - P(0 \leq z \leq 2.44)$$
$$= .5 - .4927 = .0073$$

8.37 a. For this sample,

$$\bar{x} = \frac{\sum x}{n} = \frac{24}{5} = 4.8$$

$$s^2 = \frac{\sum x^2 - \frac{(\sum x)^2}{n}}{n - 1} = \frac{126 - \frac{(24)^2}{5}}{4} = 2.7$$

$$s = \sqrt{s^2} = 1.643$$

H_0: $\mu = 6$
H_a: $\mu < 6$

The test statistic is $t = \dfrac{\bar{x} - \mu_0}{s/\sqrt{n}} = \dfrac{4.8 - 6}{1.643/\sqrt{5}} = -1.63$

The rejection region requires α =.05 in the lower tail of the t distribution with df = n - 1 = 5 - 1 = 4. From Table VI, Appendix B, $t_{.05}$ = 2.132. The rejection region is t < -2.132.

Since the observed value of the test statistic does not fall in the rejection region, (t = -1.63 ≮ -2.132), H_0 is not rejected. There is insufficient evidence to indicate μ is less than 6.

b. H_0: $\mu = 6$
H_a: $\mu \neq 6$

Test statistic: t = -1.63

The rejection region requires $\alpha/2$ =.05/2 = .025 in each tail of the t distribution with df = n - 1 = 5 - 1 = 4. From Table VI, Appendix B, $t_{.025}$ = 2.776. The rejection region is t < -2.776 or t > 2.776.

Since the observed value of the test statistic does not fall in the rejection region, ($t = -1.63 \not< -2.776$), H_0 is not rejected. There is insufficient evidence to indicate μ differs from 6.

8.39 For this sample,

$$\bar{x} = \frac{\sum x}{n} = \frac{11}{6} = 1.8333$$

$$s^2 = \frac{\sum x^2 - \frac{(\sum x)^2}{n}}{n - 1} = \frac{41 - \frac{11^2}{6}}{6 - 1} = 4.1667$$

$$s = \sqrt{s^2} = 2.0412$$

a. H_0: $\mu = 3$
    H_a: $\mu < 3$

The test statistic is $t = \dfrac{\bar{x} - \mu_0}{s/\sqrt{n}} = \dfrac{1.8333 - 3}{2.0412/\sqrt{6}} = -1.40$

The rejection region requires $\alpha = .05$ in the lower tail of the t distribution with df = $n - 1 = 6 - 1 = 5$. From Table VI, Appendix B, $t_{.05} = 2.015$. The rejection region is $t < -2.015$.

Since the observed value of the test statistic does not fall in the rejection region ($t = -1.40 \not< -2.015$), H_0 is not rejected. There is insufficient evidence to indicate μ is less than 3.

b. H_0: $\mu = 3$
    H_a: $\mu \neq 3$

Test statistic: $t = -1.40$ (Refer to part (a).)

The rejection region requires $\alpha/2 = .05/2 = .025$ in each tail of the t distribution with df = $n - 1 = 6 - 1 = 5$. From Table VI, Appendix B, $t_{.025} = 2.571$. The rejection region is $t < -2.571$ or $t > 2.571$.

Since the observed value of the test statistic does not fall in the rejection region ($t = -1.40 \not< -2.571$), H_0 is not rejected. There is insufficient evidence to indicate μ differs from 3.

8.41 To determine if the sample information disagrees with the manufacturer's claim, we test:

H_0: $\mu = 4$
H_a: $\mu > 4$

The test statistic is $t = \dfrac{\bar{x} - \mu_0}{s/\sqrt{n}} = \dfrac{4.16 - 4}{.3/\sqrt{25}} = 2.67$

The rejection region requires α =.05 in the upper tail of the t distribution with df = n - 1 = 25 - 1 = 24. From Table VI, Appendix B, $t_{.05}$ = 1.711. The rejection region is t > 1.711.

Since the observed value of the test statistic falls in the rejection region (t = 2.67 > 1.711), H_0 is rejected. There is sufficient evidence to indicate the average milligrams of tar in the cigarette is more than 4. That is, the sample information disagrees with the manufacturer's claim at α = .05.

Assumption: The sample is a random sample selected from a normally distributed population.

8.43 a. First, compute the sample mean and standard deviation:

$$\bar{x} = \frac{\sum x}{n} = \frac{37663}{12} = 3138.5833$$

$$s^2 = \frac{\sum x^2 - \frac{(\sum x)^2}{n}}{n - 1} = \frac{119161829 - \frac{37663^2}{12}}{12 - 1} = 86669.53818$$

$$s = \sqrt{s^2} = 294.3969$$

To determine if the sample data provides evidence that the average interest deduction in 1986 is greater than in 1980 for taxpayers in the $25,000-$30,000 bracket, we test:

H_0: μ = $3,011
H_a: μ > $3,011

The test statistic is $t = \dfrac{\bar{x} - \mu_0}{s/\sqrt{n}} = \dfrac{3138.5833 - 3011}{294.3969/\sqrt{12}} = 1.50$

The rejection region requires α =.05 in the upper tail of the t distribution with df = n - 1 = 12 - 1 = 11. From Table VI, Appendix B, $t_{.05}$ = 1.796. The rejection region is t > 1.796.

Since the observed value of the test statistic does not fall in the rejection region (t = 1.50 ≯ 1.796), H_0 is not rejected. There is insufficient evidence to indicate the average interest deduction in 1986 is greater than in 1980 for taxpayers in the $25,000-$30,000 bracket at α = .05.

Assumption: The sample is a random sample selected from a population with a relative frequency distribution that is approximately normal.

b. p-value = $P(t \geq 1.50)$ where df = 11

           .05 < p-value < .10   (Table VI, Appendix B)

The results are not highly significant, but at α = .10, we would reject H_0.

8.45 a. First, compute the sample mean and standard deviation for plant 1's arsenic level:

$$\bar{x} = \frac{\sum x}{n} = \frac{.015}{2} = .0075$$

$$s^2 = \frac{\sum x^2 - \frac{(\sum x)^2}{n}}{n - 1} = \frac{.000125 - \frac{.015^2}{2}}{2 - 1} = .0000125$$

$$s = \sqrt{s^2} = .003536$$

To determine if plant 1 fails to meet OSHA standards, we test:

     H_0: μ = .004
     H_a: μ > .004

The test statistic is $t = \dfrac{\bar{x} - \mu_0}{s/\sqrt{n}} = \dfrac{.0075 - .004}{.003536/\sqrt{2}} = 1.40$

The rejection region requires α = .05 in the upper tail of the t distribution with df = n - 1 = 2 - 1 = 1. From Table VI, Appendix B, $t_{.05}$ = 6.314. The rejection region is t > 6.314.

Since the observed value of the test statistic does not fall in the rejection region (t = 1.40 $\not>$ 6.314), H_0 is not rejected. There is insufficient evidence to indicate the mean level of exposure to arsenic per cubic meter of air is more than .004 milligrams. Thus, there is insufficient evidence that plant 1 fails to meet the OSHA standard at α = .05.

Assumption: The sample is a random sample selected from a population with a relative frequency distribution that is approximately normal.

b. First, compute the sample mean and standard deviation for plant 2's arsenic level:

$$\bar{x} = \frac{\sum x}{n} = \frac{.14}{2} = .07$$

$$s^2 = \frac{\sum x^2 - \frac{(\sum x)^2}{n}}{n - 1} = \frac{.0106 - \frac{.14^2}{2}}{2 - 1} = .0008$$

$$s = \sqrt{s^2} = .0283$$

To determine if plant 2 fails to meet OSHA standards, we test:

$H_0: \mu = .004$
$H_a: \mu > .004$

The test statistic is $t = \dfrac{\bar{x} - \mu_0}{s/\sqrt{n}} = \dfrac{.07 - .004}{.0283/\sqrt{2}} = 3.3$

The rejection region is $t > 6.314$. (Refer to part (a).)

Since the observed value of the test statistic does not fall in the rejection region ($t = 3.3 \not> 6.314$), H_0 is not rejected. There is insufficient evidence to indicate the mean level of exposure to arsenic per cubic meter of air is more than .004 milligrams. Thus, there is insufficient evidence that plant 2 fails to meet the OSHA standard at $\alpha = .05$.

Assumption: The sample is a random sample selected from a population with a relative frequency distribution that is approximately normal.

c. Part (a) (plant 1)

p-value = $P(t \geq 1.40)$ where df = 1

p-value > .10   (Table VI, Appendix B)

The results are not statistically significant.

Part (b) (plant 2)

p-value = $P(t \geq 3.30)$ where df = 1

.05 < p-value < .10   (Table VI, Appendix B)

The results are not highly significant, but at $\alpha = .10$ we would reject H_0.

8.47 a. Since the normal distribution is symmetric, the probability that a randomly selected observation exceeds the mean of a normal distribution is .5.

b. By the definition of "median," the probability that a randomly selected observation exceeds the median of a normal distribution is .5.

c. If the distribution is not normal, the probability that a randomly selected observation exceeds the mean depends on the distribution. With the information given, the probability cannot be determined.

d. By definition of "median," the probability that a randomly selected observation exceeds the median of a non-normal distribution is .5.

8.49 a. H_0: $M = 10$
H_a: $M > 10$

The test statistic is S = {Number of observations greater than 10} = 6.

The p-value = $P(x \geq 6)$ where x is a binomial random variable with n = 10 and p = .5. From Table II,

$$\text{p-value} = P(x \geq 6) = 1 - P(x \leq 5) = 1 - .623 = .377$$

Since the p-value = .377 > α = .05, H_0 is not rejected. There is insufficient evidence to indicate the median is greater than 10 at α = .05.

b. H_0: $M = 10$
H_a: $M \neq 10$

S_1 = {Number of observations less than 10} = 4 and
S_2 = {Number of observations greater than 10} = 6

The test statistic is S = larger of S_1 and S_2 = 6.

The p-value = $2P(x \geq 6)$ where x is a binomial random variable with n = 10 and p = .5. From Table II,

$$\text{p-value} = 2P(x \geq 6) = 2(1 - P(x \leq 5)) = 2(1 - .623) = .754$$

Since the p-value = .754 > α = .05, H_0 is not rejected. There is insufficient evidence to indicate the median is different than 10 at α = .05.

c. H_0: $M = 18$
H_a: $M < 18$

The test statistic is S = {Number of observations less than 18} = 9

The p-value = $P(x \geq 9)$ where x is a binomial random variable with n = 10 and p = .5. From Table II,

$$\text{p-value} = P(x \geq 9) = 1 - P(x \leq 8) = 1 - .989 = .011$$

Since the p-value = .011 < α = .05, H_0 is rejected. There is sufficient evidence to indicate the median is less than 18 at α = .05.

d. H_0: $M = 18$
    H_a: $M \neq 18$

S_1 = {Number of observations less than 18} = 9 and
S_2 = {Number of observations greater than 18} = 1

The test statistic is S = larger of S_1 and S_2 = 9.

The p-value = $2P(x \geq 9)$ where x is a binomial random variable with n = 10 and p = .5. From Table II,

$$\text{p-value} = 2P(x \geq 9) = 2(1 - P(x \leq 8)) = 2(1 - .989) = .022$$

Since the p-value = .022 < α = .05, H_0 is rejected. There is sufficient evidence to indicate the median is different than 18 at α = .05.

e. For all parts, $\mu = np = 10(.5) = 5$ and $\sigma = \sqrt{npq} = \sqrt{10(.5)(.5)}$ = 1.581.

For part (a), $P(x \geq 6) \approx P\left(z > \dfrac{(6 - .5) - 5}{1.581}\right)$

$$= P(z \geq .32) = .5 - .1255 = .3745$$

This is close to the probability .377 in part (a). The conclusion is the same.

For part (b), $2P(x \geq 6) \approx 2P\left(z > \dfrac{(6 - .5) - 5}{1.581}\right)$

$$= 2P(z \geq .32) = 2(.5 - .1255) = .7890$$

This is close to the probability .754 in part (b). The conclusion is the same.

For part (c), $P(x \geq 9) \approx P\left(z > \dfrac{(9 - .5) - 5}{1.581}\right)$

$$= P(z \geq 2.21) = .5 - .4864 = .0136$$

This is close to the probability .011 in part (c). The conclusion is the same.

For part (d), $2P(x \geq 9) \approx 2P\left(z > \dfrac{(9 - .5) - 5}{1.581}\right)$

$$= 2P(z \geq 2.21) = 2(.5 - .4864) = .0272$$

This is close to the probability .022 in part (d). The conclusion is the same.

f. We must assume only that the sample is selected randomly from a continuous probability distribution.

8.51   a.   To determine if the test is too hard, we test:

H_0:   M = 60
H_a: M < 60

b.   The test statistic is S = number of measurements less than 60.

Reject H_0 if the p-value < α = .05.

c.   We must assume the sample was randomly selected from a continuous probability distribution.

d.   The test statistic is S = 14.

The p-value = $P(x \geq 14)$ where x is a binomial random variable with n = 20 and p = .5. From Table II,

p-value = $P(x \geq 14) = 1 - P(x \leq 13) = 1 - .942 = .058$

Since the p-value = .058 is not less than α = .05, H_0 is not rejected. There is insufficient evidence to indicate the test is too hard.

e.   The observed significance level is the p-value = .058. If the test is in fact not too hard (M = 60), the probability of observing our test statistic or anything more unusual is .058.

f.   Since the p-value is very close to α = .05, we would probably want to sample more teachers before making a recommendation.

8.53   a.   To determine if the median height exceeds 40 feet, we test:

H_0:   M = 40
H_a: M > 40

The test statistic is S = {Number of measurements greater than 40} = 17.

The p-value = $P(x \geq 17)$ where x is a binomial random variable with n = 24 and p = .5. Since we do not have a table for n = 24 (and n is sufficiently large), we will use the large-sample approximation.

μ = np = 24(.5) = 12 and $\sigma = \sqrt{npq} = \sqrt{24(.5)(.5)} = 2.4495$

p-value = $P(x \geq 17) \approx P\left(z \geq \dfrac{(17 - .5) - 12}{2.4495}\right)$

$= P(z \geq 1.84) = .5 - .4671 = .0329$

Since the p-value = .0329 is less than α = .05, H_0 is rejected. There is sufficient evidence to indicate the median height of the trees is more than 40 feet at α = .05.

b. The p-value = .0329. If the true median of the trees is 40 feet, the probability of seeing 17 or more out of 24 trees taller than 40 feet is .0329.

c. We must assume the sample of 24 tree heights was randomly selected from a continuous probability distribution.

8.55 b. First, check to see if n is large enough.

$$p_0 \pm 3\sigma_{\hat{p}} \Rightarrow p_0 \pm 3\sqrt{\frac{pq}{n}} \Rightarrow p_0 \pm 3\sqrt{\frac{p_0 q_0}{100}}$$

$$\Rightarrow .70 \pm 3\sqrt{\frac{.70(.30)}{100}}$$

$$\Rightarrow .70 \pm .137 \Rightarrow (.563, .837)$$

Since the interval lies within the interval (0, 1), the normal approximation will be adequate.

H_0: $p = .70$
H_a: $p < .70$

The test statistic is $z = \dfrac{\hat{p} - p_0}{\sigma_{\hat{p}}} = \dfrac{\hat{p} - p_0}{\sqrt{\dfrac{pq}{n}}} \approx \dfrac{\hat{p} - p_0}{\sqrt{\dfrac{p_0 q_0}{n}}}$

$$= \frac{.63 - .70}{\sqrt{\dfrac{.70(.30)}{100}}}$$

$$= -1.53$$

The rejection region requires $\alpha = .05$ in the lower tail of the z distribution. From Table IV, Appendix B, $z_{.05} = 1.645$. The rejection region is $z < -1.645$.

Since the observed value of the test statistic does not fall in the rejection region, ($z = -1.53 \nless -1.645$), H_0 is not rejected. There is insufficient evidence to indicate p is less than .70.

c. p-value = $P(z \leq -1.53)$ = $.5 - P(0 < z < 1.53)$
$$= .5 - .4370$$
$$= .0630$$

8.57 a. To determine if the percentage of shoppers using cents-off coupons exceeds 65%, we test:

$$H_0: \quad p = .65$$
$$H_a: \quad p > .65$$

The test statistic is $z = \dfrac{\hat{p} - p_0}{\sigma_{\hat{p}}} = \dfrac{\hat{p} - p_0}{\sqrt{\dfrac{pq}{n}}} \approx \dfrac{\hat{p} - p_0}{\sqrt{\dfrac{p_0 q_0}{n}}}$

$$= \dfrac{.76 - .65}{\sqrt{\dfrac{.65(.35)}{100}}} = 2.31$$

The rejection requires $\alpha = .05$ in the upper tail of the z distribution. From Table IV, Appendix B, $z_{.05} = 1.645$. The rejection region is $z > 1.645$.

Since the observed value of the test statistic falls in the rejection region ($z = 2.31 > 1.645$), H_0 is rejected. There is sufficient evidence to indicate the proportion of shoppers using cents-off coupons exceeds .65 at $\alpha = .05$.

b. The sample size is large enough if the interval does not include 0 or 1.

$$p_0 \pm 3\sigma_{\hat{p}} \Rightarrow p \pm 3\sqrt{\dfrac{pq}{n}} \Rightarrow \hat{p} \pm 3\sqrt{\dfrac{\hat{p}\hat{q}}{n}} \quad \text{where } \hat{p} = \dfrac{76}{100} = .76$$

$$\Rightarrow .76 \pm 3\sqrt{\dfrac{.76(.24)}{100}}$$

$$\Rightarrow .76 \pm .128 \Rightarrow (.632, .888)$$

Since the interval lies completely in the interval (0, 1), the normal approximation will be adequate.

c. p-value $= P(z \geq 2.31) = .5 - P(0 < z < 2.31)$
$$= .5 - .4896$$
$$= .0104$$

The smallest value α could assume where the conclusion is to reject H_0 is .0104. The results are highly significant.

8.59 From 8.58, $z = 1.72$ for the one-tailed, upper tail test.

p-value $= P(z \geq 1.72) = .5 - P(0 < z < 1.72)$
$$= .5 - .4573$$
$$= .0427$$

8.61   a.   First, check to see if the normal approximation is adequate:

$$p_0 \pm 3\sigma_{\hat{p}} \Rightarrow p_0 \pm 3\sqrt{\frac{pq}{n}} \Rightarrow p_0 \pm 3\sqrt{\frac{p_0 q_0}{n}}$$

$$\Rightarrow .2 \pm 3\sqrt{\frac{.2(.8)}{200}}$$

$$\Rightarrow .2 \pm .085 \Rightarrow (.115, .285)$$

Since the interval lies completely in the interval (0, 1), the normal approximation will be adequate.

To determine if the proportion of orange juice drinkers who prefer the producer's brand is less than .2, we test:

H_0: $p = .20$
H_a: $p < .20$

The test statistic is $z = \dfrac{\hat{p} - p_0}{\sigma_{\hat{p}}} = \dfrac{\hat{p} - p_0}{\sqrt{\dfrac{pq}{n}}} \approx \dfrac{\hat{p} - p_0}{\sqrt{\dfrac{p_0 q_0}{n}}}$

where $\hat{p} = \dfrac{33}{200} = .165$

$$= \frac{.165 - .2}{\sqrt{\dfrac{.2(.8)}{200}}}$$

$$= -1.24$$

The rejection requires $\alpha = .10$ in the lower tail of the z distribution. From Table IV, Appendix B, $z_{.10} = 1.28$. The rejection region is $z < -1.28$.

Since the observed value of the test statistic does not fall in the rejection region, ($z = -1.24 \not< -1.28$), H_0 is not rejected. There is insufficient evidence to indicate the proportion of orange juice drinkers who prefer the producer's brand is less than .20 at $\alpha = .10$.

b.   p-value = $P(z \leq -1.24) = .5 - P(0 < z < 1.24)$
$$= .5 - .3925$$
$$= .1075$$

This is the smallest value α could assume where we would still reject H_0. The results are not highly significant.

8.63   As β increases, the power = $1 - \beta$ decreases. As β decreases, the power of the test increases.

8.65 a.

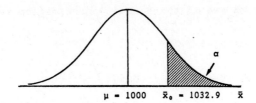

$$\mu = 1000 \qquad \bar{x}_0 = 1032.9 \qquad \bar{x}$$

b. $\bar{x}_0 = \mu_0 + z_\alpha \sigma_{\bar{x}} = \mu_0 + z_\alpha \dfrac{\sigma}{\sqrt{n}}$ where $z_\alpha = z_{.05} = 1.645$ from Table IV, Appendix B.

Thus, $\bar{x}_0 = 1000 + 1.645 \dfrac{120}{\sqrt{36}}$

$$= 1032.9$$

c.

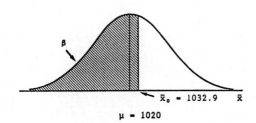

$$\bar{x}_0 = 1032.9 \qquad \bar{x}$$
$$\mu = 1020$$

d. $\beta = P(\bar{x}_0 < 1032.9 \text{ when } \mu = 1020)$

$$z = \frac{\bar{x}_0 - \mu_a}{\sigma_{\bar{x}}} = \frac{\bar{x}_0 - \mu_a}{\sigma/\sqrt{n}}$$

$$= \frac{1032.9 - 1020}{120/\sqrt{36}}$$

$$= .645$$

$\beta = P(z < .645) = .5 + P(0 < z < .645)$

$$= .5 + \frac{.2389 + .2422}{2}$$

$$= .5 + .24055$$

$$= .74055$$

e. power $= 1 - \beta$
$$= 1 - .74055$$
$$= .25945$$

8.67 a. The sampling distribution of $\bar{x}$ will be approximately normal (by the Central Limit Theorem) with $\mu_{\bar{x}} = \mu = 50$ and $\sigma_{\bar{x}} = \dfrac{\sigma}{\sqrt{n}} = \dfrac{20}{\sqrt{64}} = 2.5$.

    b. The sampling distribution of $\bar{x}$ will be approximately normal (by the Central Limit Theorem) with $\mu_{\bar{x}} = \mu = 45$ and $\sigma_{\bar{x}} = \dfrac{\sigma}{\sqrt{n}} = \dfrac{20}{\sqrt{64}} = 2.5$.

    c. First, find

$$\bar{x}_0 = \mu_0 - z_\alpha \sigma_{\bar{x}} = \mu_0 - z_\alpha \frac{\sigma}{\sqrt{n}} \text{ where } z_{.10} = 1.28 \text{ from Table IV,}$$

Appendix B.

Thus, $\bar{x}_0 = 50 - 1.28 \dfrac{20}{\sqrt{64}}$

$$= 46.8$$

Now, find

$\beta = P(\bar{x}_0 > 46.8 \text{ when } \mu = 45)$

$$z = \frac{\bar{x}_0 - \mu_a}{\sigma_{\bar{x}}} = \frac{\bar{x}_0 - \mu_a}{\sigma/\sqrt{n}}$$

$$= \frac{46.8 - 45}{20/\sqrt{64}}$$

$$= .72$$

$$\beta = P(z > .72) = .5 - P(0 < z < .72)$$
$$= .5 - .2642$$
$$= .2358$$

    d. power $= 1 - \beta - .2358 = .7642$

8.69 a. The sampling distribution of $\bar{x}$ will be approximately normal (by the Central Limit Theorem) with $\mu_{\bar{x}} = \mu = 10$ and $\sigma_{\bar{x}} = \dfrac{\sigma}{\sqrt{n}} = \dfrac{1.00}{\sqrt{100}} = 0.1$.

    b. The sampling distribution of $\bar{x}$ will be approximately normal (CLT) with $\mu_{\bar{x}} = \mu = 9.9$ and $\sigma_{\bar{x}} = \dfrac{\sigma}{\sqrt{n}} = \dfrac{1.0}{\sqrt{100}} = 0.1$.

    c. First, find

$$\bar{x}_{0,L} = \mu_0 - z_{\alpha/2}\sigma_{\bar{x}} = \mu_0 - z_{\alpha/2} \frac{\sigma}{\sqrt{n}} \text{ where } = z_{.05/2} = z_{.025} = 1.96$$

from Table IV, Appendix B.

Thus, $\bar{x}_{0,L} = 10 - 1.96 \dfrac{1.0}{\sqrt{100}}$

$\qquad\qquad = 9.804$

$\bar{x}_{0,U} = \mu_0 + z_{\alpha/2}\sigma_{\bar{x}} = \mu_0 + z_{\alpha/2}\dfrac{\sigma}{\sqrt{n}}$

$\qquad\qquad\qquad = 10 + 1.96 \dfrac{1.0}{\sqrt{100}}$

$\qquad\qquad\qquad = 10.196$

Now, find

$\qquad \beta = P(9.804 < \bar{x} < 10.196 \text{ when } \mu = 9.9)$

$z = \dfrac{\bar{x}_{0,L} - \mu_a}{\sigma_{\bar{x}}} = \dfrac{\bar{x}_0 - \mu_a}{\sigma/\sqrt{n}}$

$\qquad\qquad = \dfrac{9.804 - 9.9}{1.0/\sqrt{100}}$

$\qquad\qquad = -0.96$

$z = \dfrac{\bar{x}_{0,U} - \mu_a}{\sigma_{\bar{x}}} = \dfrac{\bar{x}_0 - \mu_a}{\sigma/\sqrt{n}}$

$\qquad\qquad = \dfrac{10.196 - 9.9}{1.0/\sqrt{100}}$

$\qquad\qquad = 2.96$

$\qquad \beta = P(-0.96 < z < 2.96) = P(0 < z < 2.96) + P(0 < z < 0.96)$

$\qquad\qquad\qquad\qquad\qquad\qquad\quad = .4985 + .3315$

$\qquad\qquad\qquad\qquad\qquad\qquad\quad = .8300$

d. $\quad \beta = P(9.804 < \bar{x} < 10.196 \text{ when } \mu = 10.1)$

$\qquad z = \dfrac{\bar{x}_{0,L} - \mu_a}{\sigma_{\bar{x}}} = \dfrac{\bar{x}_{0,L} - \mu_a}{\sigma/\sqrt{n}}$

$\qquad\qquad\quad = \dfrac{9.804 - 10.1}{1.0/\sqrt{100}}$

$\qquad\qquad\quad = -2.96$

$\qquad z = \dfrac{\bar{x}_{0,U} - \mu_a}{\sigma_{\bar{x}}} = \dfrac{\bar{x}_{0,U} - \mu_a}{\sigma/\sqrt{n}}$

$\qquad\qquad\quad = \dfrac{10.196 - 10.1}{1.0/\sqrt{100}}$

$\qquad\qquad\quad = 0.96$

$$\beta = P(-2.96 < z < 0.96) = P(0 < z < 0.96) + P(0 < z < 2.96)$$
$$= .3315 + .4985$$
$$= .8300$$

8.71 a. We have failed to reject H_0 when it is not true. This is a Type II error.

To compute β, first find:

$$\bar{x}_0 = \mu_0 - z_\alpha \sigma_{\bar{x}} = \mu_0 - z_\alpha \frac{\sigma}{\sqrt{n}} \text{ where } z_{.05} = 1.645 \text{ from Table IV,}$$

Appendix B.

Thus, $\bar{x}_0 = 5.0 - 1.645 \dfrac{.01}{\sqrt{100}}$

$$= 4.998355$$

Then find:

$$\beta = P(\bar{x}_0 > 4.9984 \text{ when } \mu = 4.9975)$$

$$z = \frac{\bar{x}_0 - \mu_a}{\sigma_{\bar{x}}} = \frac{\bar{x}_0 - \mu_a}{\sigma/\sqrt{n}}$$

$$= \frac{4.998355 - 4.9975}{.01/\sqrt{100}}$$

$$= .855$$

$$\beta = P(z > 0.855) = .5 - P(0 < z < 0.855)$$

$$= .5 - \frac{.3023 + .3051}{2}$$

$$= .5 - .3037$$

$$= .1963$$

b. We have rejected H_0 when it is true. This is a Type I error. The probability of a Type I error is $\alpha = .05$.

c. A departure of .0025 below 5.0 is $\mu = 4.9975$. Using (a), β when $\mu = 4.9975$ is .1963. The power of the test is $1 - \beta = 1 - .1963 = .8037$.

8.73 a. First, find:

$$\bar{x}_0 = \mu_0 + z_\alpha \sigma_{\bar{x}} \approx \mu_0 + z_\alpha \frac{\sigma}{\sqrt{n}} \text{ where } z_{.05} = 1.645 \text{ from Table IV,}$$
Appendix B.

Thus, $\bar{x}_0 = 35 + 1.645 \dfrac{6}{\sqrt{36}}$

$$= 36.645$$

Now, find β for each value of μ_a.

$\underline{\mu = 35.5}$

$\beta = P(\bar{x}_0 < 36.645 \text{ when } \mu = 35.5)$

$$z = \frac{\bar{x}_0 - \mu_a}{\sigma_{\bar{x}}} = \frac{\bar{x}_0 - \mu_a}{\sigma/\sqrt{n}} \approx \frac{\bar{x}_0 - \mu_a}{s/\sqrt{n}}$$

$$= \frac{36.645 - 35.5}{6/\sqrt{36}}$$

$$= 1.145$$

$\beta = P(z < 1.145) = .5 + P(0 < z < 1.145)$

$$= .5 + \frac{.3729 + .3749}{2}$$

$$= .8739$$

power $= 1 - \beta = 1 - .8739 = .1261$

$\underline{\mu = 36.0}$

$\beta = P(\bar{x}_0 < 36.645 \text{ when } \mu = 36.0)$

$$z = \frac{\bar{x}_0 - \mu_a}{\sigma_{\bar{x}}} = \frac{\bar{x}_0 - \mu_a}{\sigma/\sqrt{n}} \approx \frac{\bar{x}_0 - \mu_a}{s/\sqrt{n}}$$

$$= \frac{36.645 - 36.0}{6/\sqrt{36}}$$

$$= 0.645$$

$\beta = P(z < 0.645) = .5 + P(0 < z < 0.645)$

$$= .5 + \frac{.2389 + .2422}{2}$$

$$= .74055$$

power $= 1 - \beta = 1 - .74055 = .25945 \approx .2595$

$\underline{\mu = 36.5}$

$\beta = P(\bar{x}_0 < 36.645 \text{ when } \mu = 36.5)$

$$z = \frac{\bar{x}_0 - \mu_a}{\sigma_{\bar{x}}} = \frac{\bar{x}_0 - \mu_a}{\sigma/\sqrt{n}} \approx \frac{\bar{x}_0 - \mu_a}{s/\sqrt{n}}$$

$$= \frac{36.645 - 36.5}{6/\sqrt{36}}$$

$$= 0.145$$

$$\beta = P(z < 0.145) = .5 + P(0 < z < 0.145)$$

$$= .5 + \frac{.0557 + .0596}{2}$$

$$= .55765$$

power $= 1 - \beta = 1 - .55765 = .44235 \approx .4424$

$\underline{\mu = 37.0}$

$$\beta = P(\bar{x}_0 < 36.645 \text{ when } \mu = 37.0)$$

$$z = \frac{\bar{x}_0 - \mu_a}{\sigma_{\bar{x}}} = \frac{\bar{x}_0 - \mu_a}{\sigma/\sqrt{n}} \approx \frac{\bar{x}_0 - \mu_a}{s/\sqrt{n}}$$

$$= \frac{36.645 - 37.0}{6/\sqrt{36}}$$

$$= -.355$$

$$\beta = P(z < -.355) = .5 - P(0 < z < .355)$$

$$= .5 - \frac{.1368 + .1406}{2}$$

$$= .3613$$

power $= 1 - \beta = 1 - .3613 = .6387$

$\underline{\mu = 37.5}$

$$\beta = P(\bar{x}_0 < 36.645 \text{ when } \mu = 37.5)$$

$$z = \frac{\bar{x}_0 - \mu_a}{\sigma_{\bar{x}}} = \frac{\bar{x}_0 - \mu_a}{\sigma/\sqrt{n}} \approx \frac{\bar{x}_0 - \mu_a}{s/\sqrt{n}}$$

$$= \frac{36.645 - 37.5}{6/\sqrt{36}}$$

$$= -.855$$

$$\beta = P(z < -.855) = .5 - P(0 < z < .855)$$

$$= .5 - \frac{.3023 + .3051}{2}$$

$$= .1963$$

power $= 1 - \beta = 1 - .1963 = .8037$

b.

c. $\beta = P(\bar{x}_0 < 36.645 \text{ when } \mu = 36.75)$

$$z = \frac{\bar{x}_0 - \mu_a}{\sigma_{\bar{x}}} = \frac{\bar{x}_0 - \mu_a}{\sigma/\sqrt{n}} \approx \frac{\bar{x}_0 - \mu_a}{s/\sqrt{n}}$$

$$= \frac{36.645 - 36.75}{6/\sqrt{36}}$$

$$= -.105$$

$$\beta = P(z < -.105) = .5 - P(0 < z < .105)$$

$$= .5 - \frac{.0398 + .0438}{2}$$

$$= .4582$$

$$\text{power} = 1 - \beta = 1 - .4582 = .5418$$

d. $\beta = P(\bar{x}_0 < 36.645 \text{ when } \mu = 40)$

$$z = \frac{\bar{x}_0 - \mu_a}{\sigma_{\bar{x}}} = \frac{\bar{x}_0 - \mu_a}{\sigma/\sqrt{n}} \approx \frac{\bar{x}_0 - \mu_a}{s/\sqrt{n}}$$

$$= \frac{36.645 - 40}{6/\sqrt{36}}$$

$$= -3.355$$

$$\beta = P(z < -3.355) = .5 - P(0 < z < 3.355)$$

$$= .5 - \text{approx. } .5$$

$$= \text{approx. } 0$$

8.75 The elements of the test of hypothesis that should be specified prior
to analyzing the data are: null hypothesis, alternative hypothesis,
and rejection region.

8.77 For a large sample test of hypothesis about a population mean, no
      assumptions are necessary because the Central Limit Theorem assures
      that the test statistic will be approximately normally distributed.
      For a small sample test of hypothesis about a population mean, we must
      assume that the population being sampled from is normal. The test
      statistic for the large sample test is the z statistic, and the test
      statistic for the small sample test is the t statistic.

8.79 α = P(Type I error) = P(rejecting H_0 when it is true). Thus, if
      rejection of H_0 would cause your firm to go out of business, you would
      want this probability to be small.

8.81 a. H_0: $\mu = 3$
          H_a: $\mu > 3$

          The test statistic is $z = \dfrac{\bar{x} - \mu_0}{\sigma_{\bar{x}}} = \dfrac{\bar{x} - \mu_0}{\sigma/\sqrt{n}} \approx \dfrac{\bar{x} - \mu_0}{s/\sqrt{n}}$

          $$= \frac{3.1 - 3}{.5/\sqrt{50}}$$

          $$= 1.41$$

          The rejection region requires α =.01 in the upper tail of the z
          distribution. From Table IV, Appendix B, $z_{.01}$ = 2.33. The
          rejection region is z > 2.33.

          Since the observed value of the test statistic does not fall in the
          rejection region, (z = 1.41 $\not>$ 2.33), H_0 is not rejected. There is
          insufficient evidence to indicate the mean amount of PCB in the
          effluent is more than 3 parts per million. Do not halt the
          manufacturing process.

      b. As plant manager, I do not want to shut down the plant
          unnecessarily. Therefore, I want α = P(shut down plant when $\mu = 3$)
          to be small.

      c. p-value = P(z $\geq$ 1.41) = .5 - P(0 < z < 1.41)
                                    = .5 - .4207
                                    = .0793

          The smallest value α could assume where the conclusion is to reject
          H_0 is .0793. The results are not highly significant, but at α =
          .10 we would reject H_0.

8.83 a. No, it increases the risk of falsely rejecting H_0, i.e., closing
          the plant unnecessarily.

b. First, find

$$\bar{x}_0 = \mu_0 + z_\alpha \sigma_{\bar{x}} \approx \mu_0 + z_{.05} \frac{s}{\sqrt{n}} \quad \text{where } z_{.05} = 1.645 \text{ from Table}$$

IV, Appendix B.

$$\bar{x} = 3 + 1.645 \frac{.5}{\sqrt{50}}$$

$$= 3.116$$

Then, compute

$$\beta = P(\bar{x}_0 < 3.116 \text{ when } \mu = 3.1)$$

$$z = \frac{\bar{x}_0 - \mu_a}{\sigma_{\bar{x}}} \approx \frac{\bar{x}_0 - \mu_a}{s/\sqrt{n}}$$

$$= \frac{3.116 - 3.1}{.5/\sqrt{50}}$$

$$= .23$$

$$\beta = P(z < .23) = .5 + P(0 < z < .23)$$
$$= .5 + .0910$$
$$= .5910$$

$$\text{power} = 1 - \beta = 1 - .5910 = .4090$$

c. The power of the test increases as α increases.

8.85 From Exercise 8.84, $z = 1.07$ for a one-tailed, upper tail test.

$$\text{p-value} = P(z \geq 1.07) = .5 - P(0 < z < 1.07)$$
$$= .5 - .3577$$
$$= .1423$$

The smallest value of α for which we could reject H_0 is .1423. The results are not statistically significant.

8.87 To determine if the mean waiting time was less than two minutes, we test:

$$H_0: \quad \mu = 120$$
$$H_a: \quad \mu < 120$$

The test statistic is $t = \dfrac{x - \mu_0}{s/\sqrt{n}} = \dfrac{112 - 120}{28/\sqrt{20}} = -1.28$

The rejection region requires $\alpha = .05$ in the lower tail of the t distribution with df $= n - 1 = 20 - 1 = 19$. From Table VI, Appendix B, $t_{.05} = 1.729$. The rejection region is $t < -1.729$.

Since the observed value of the test statistic does not fall in the rejection region (t = -1.28 ≮ -1.729), H_0 is not rejected. There is insufficient evidence to indicate the mean waiting time is less than two minutes at α = .05.

8.89   a. To determine if the mean daily yield for the new process is less than for the old one, we test:

H_0: μ = 880
H_a: μ < 880

The test statistic is $z = \dfrac{\bar{x} - \mu_0}{\sigma_{\bar{x}}} = \dfrac{\bar{x} - \mu_0}{\sigma/\sqrt{n}} \approx \dfrac{\bar{x} - \mu_0}{s/\sqrt{n}} = \dfrac{871 - 880}{21/\sqrt{50}}$

$= -3.03$

p-value = P(z < -3.03) = .5 - P(0 < z < 3.03)
                       = .5 - .4988
                       = .0012

Reject H_0 of p-value < α

   .0012 < .01

Reject H_0. There is sufficient evidence to indicate the mean daily yield is less than 880 pounds. Thus, there is sufficient evidence to indicate the new process has a smaller mean daily yield than the old process at α = .01.

   b. We must assume that a random sample is chosen where n is sufficiently large to use the normal distribution.

8.91   From Exercise 8.89, we are testing H_0: μ = 880 against H_a: μ < 880, α = .01, s = 21, and n = 50.

First, find

$\bar{x}_0 = \mu_0 - z_\alpha \sigma_{\bar{x}} \approx \mu_0 - z_\alpha \dfrac{s}{\sqrt{n}}$ where $z_\alpha = z_{.01}$ = 2.33 from Table IV, Appendix B.

$\bar{x}_0 = 880 - 2.332\dfrac{21}{\sqrt{50}}$

   = 873.08

Then, compute

$$\beta = P(\bar{x}_0 > 873.08 \text{ when } \mu = 875)$$

$$z = \frac{\bar{x}_0 - \mu_a}{\sigma_{\bar{x}}} = \frac{\bar{x}_0 - \mu_a}{\sigma/\sqrt{n}} \approx \frac{\bar{x}_0 - \mu_a}{s/\sqrt{n}}$$

$$= \frac{873.08 - 875}{21/\sqrt{50}}$$

$$= -.65$$

$$\beta = P(z > -.65) = .5 + P(0 < z < .65)$$
$$= .5 + .2422$$
$$= .7422$$

$$\text{power} = 1 - \beta = 1 - .7422 = .2578$$

8.93 a. To determine if the median level differs from the target, we test:

$$H_0: \quad M = .75$$
$$H_a: \quad M \neq .75$$

b. S_1 = number of observations less than .75 and S_2 = number of observations greater than .75.

The test statistic is S = larger of S_1 and S_2.

The p-value = $2P(x \geq S)$ where x is a binomial random variable with n = 25 and p = .5. If the p-value is less than α = .10, reject H_0.

c. A Type I error would be concluding the median level is not .75 when it is. If a Type I error were committed, the supervisor would correct the fluoridation process when it was not necessary. A Type II error would be concluding the median level is .75 when it is not. If a Type II error were committed, the supervisor would not correct the fluoridation process when it was necessary.

d. S_1 = number of observations less than .75 = 7 and S_2 = number of observations greater than .75 = 18.

The test statistic is S = larger of S_1 and S_2 = 18.

The p-value = $2P(x \geq 18)$ where x is a binomial random variable with n = 25 and p = .5. From Table II,

$$\text{p-value} = 2P(x \geq 18) = 2(1 - P(x \leq 17)) = 2(1 - .978)$$

$$= 2(.022) = .044$$

Since the p-value = .044 < α = .10, H_0 is rejected. There is sufficient evidence to indicate the median level of fluoridation differs from the target of .75 at α = .10.

e. A distribution heavily skewed to the right might look something like the following:

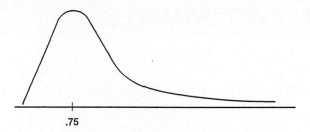

.75

One assumption necessary for the t-test is that the distribution from which the sample is drawn is normal. A distribution which is heavily skewed in one direction is not normal. Thus, the sign test would be preferred.

8.95 a. The value of the test statistic is t = 2.408. The p-value is .0304, which corresponds to a two-tailed test. $P(t \geq 2.408) + P(t \leq -2.408) = .0304$. Since the p-value is less than α = .10, H_0 is rejected. There is sufficient evidence to indicate the mean beta coefficient of high technology stock is different than 1.

b. The p-value would be .0304/2 = .0152.

8.97 Using Table IV, Appendix B, the p-value is $P(z > 1.41) = .5 - .4207 = .0793$. The probability of observing a test statistic of 1.41 or anything more unusual is .0793. This is not particularly small. There is no evidence to reject H_0.

CHAPTER 9

INFERENCES FOR MEANS
BASED ON TWO SAMPLES

9.1　a.　From Chapter 6, $\sigma_{\bar{x}_1} = \dfrac{\sigma_1}{\sqrt{n_1}} = \dfrac{\sqrt{900}}{\sqrt{100}} = \dfrac{30}{10} = 3$

$\mu_1 \pm 2\sigma_{\bar{x}_1}$ => 150 ± 2(3) => 150 ± 6 => (144, 156)

b.　$\sigma_{\bar{x}_2} = \dfrac{\sigma_2}{\sqrt{n_2}} = \dfrac{\sqrt{1600}}{\sqrt{100}} = \dfrac{40}{10} = 4$

$\mu_2 \pm 2\sigma_{\bar{x}_2}$ => 150 ± 2(4) => 150 ± 8 => (142, 158)

c.　$\mu_{\bar{x}_1-\bar{x}_2} = \mu_1 - \mu_2 = 150 - 150 = 0$

$\sigma_{\bar{x}_1-\bar{x}_2} = \sqrt{\dfrac{\sigma_1^2}{n_1} + \dfrac{\sigma_2^2}{n_2}} = \sqrt{\dfrac{900}{100} + \dfrac{1600}{100}} = \sqrt{25} = 5$

d.　$\mu_{\bar{x}_1-\bar{x}_2} \pm 2\sigma_{\bar{x}_1-\bar{x}_2}$ => 0 ± 2(5) => 0 ± 10 => (-10, 10)

e.　In general, the variability of the difference between independent sample means is larger than the variability of individual sample means.

9.3　From Exercise 9.2, $\sigma_{\bar{x}_1-\bar{x}_2} = \sqrt{\dfrac{\sigma_1^2}{n_1} + \dfrac{\sigma_2^2}{n_2}} = \sqrt{\dfrac{4^2}{64} + \dfrac{3^2}{64}} = \sqrt{\dfrac{25}{64}} = \dfrac{5}{8}$

$\mu_{\bar{x}_1-\bar{x}_2} = \mu_1 - \mu_2 = 12 - 10 = 2$

a.　$z = \dfrac{(\bar{x}_1 - \bar{x}_2) - (\mu_1 - \mu_2)}{\sigma_{\bar{x}_1-\bar{x}_2}} = \dfrac{1.5 - 2}{\frac{5}{8}} = -.8$

b.　$P[(\bar{x}_1 - \bar{x}_2) > 1.5] = P(z > -.8) = .5 + .2881 = .7881$ (from Table IV, Appendix B).

c.　$P[(\bar{x}_1 - \bar{x}_2) < 1.5] = P(z < -.8) = .5 - .2881 = .2119$ (from Table IV, Appendix B).

d. $z = \dfrac{1 - 2}{\frac{5}{8}} = -1.6$ $\qquad$ $z = \dfrac{-1 - 2}{\frac{5}{8}} = -4.8$

$P[(\bar{x}_1 - \bar{x}_2) < -1] + P[(\bar{x}_1 - \bar{x}_2) > 1] = P(z < -4.8) + P(z > -1.6)$

$\qquad = (.5 - .5) + (.5 + .4452) = .9452$ (from Table IV, Appendix B).

9.5 a. To determine if the merged firms generally have smaller price earnings ratios, we test:

$H_0: \quad \mu_1 = \mu_2$
$H_a: \quad \mu_1 < \mu_2$

where μ_1 = mean price earnings ratio for merged firms, and
μ_2 = mean price earnings ratio for nonmerged firms.

The test statistic is $z = \dfrac{(\bar{x}_1 - \bar{x}_2) - 0}{\sqrt{\dfrac{\sigma_1^2}{n_1} + \dfrac{\sigma_2^2}{n_2}}} = \dfrac{(7.295 - 14.666) - 0}{\sqrt{\dfrac{7.374^2}{44} + \dfrac{16.089^2}{44}}}$

$\qquad = \dfrac{-7.371}{2.6681} = -2.76$

The rejection region requires $\alpha = .05$ in the lower tail of the z distribution. From Table IV, Appendix B, $z_{.05} = -1.645$. The rejection region is $z < -1.645$.

Since the observed value of the test statistic falls in the rejection region ($z = -2.76 < -1.645$), H_0 is rejected. There is sufficient evidence to indicate the mean price earnings ratio for merged firms is smaller than that for nonmerged firms at $\alpha = 05$.

b. The p-value is $P(z \leq -2.76) = .5 - .4971 = .0029$.

c. We must assume the samples are randomly selected.

d. No. If the price-earnings ratios cannot be negative, the populations cannot be normal because the standard deviations for both groups are larger than the means. Thus, there can be no observations more than one standard deviation below the mean.

9.7 For confidence coefficient .90, $\alpha = 1 - .90 = .1$ and $\alpha/2 = .1/2 = .05$. From Table IV, Appendix B, $z_{.05} = 1.645$. The confidence interval is:

$(\bar{x}_1 - \bar{x}_2) \pm z_{\alpha/2} \sqrt{\dfrac{\sigma_1^2}{n_1} + \dfrac{\sigma_2^2}{n_2}} \Rightarrow (25.4 - 27.3) \pm 1.645\sqrt{\dfrac{3.1^2}{50} + \dfrac{3.7^2}{50}}$

$\qquad \Rightarrow -1.9 \pm 1.123 \Rightarrow (-3.023, -.777)$

9.9   To determine if there is a difference in job satisfaction for the 2
       groups, we test:

$$H_0: \quad \mu_1 - \mu_2 = 0$$
$$H_a: \quad \mu_1 - \mu_2 \neq 0$$

where μ_1 = mean rating for workers that believe in an existence of a
              class system, and
      μ_2 = mean rating for workers that do not believe in an existence
              of a class system.

The test statistic is $z = \dfrac{(\bar{x}_1 - \bar{x}_2) - 0}{\sqrt{\dfrac{\sigma_1^2}{n_1} + \dfrac{\sigma_2^2}{n_2}}} \approx \dfrac{(5.42 - 5.19) - 0}{\sqrt{\dfrac{1.24^2}{175} + \dfrac{1.17^2}{277}}} = 1.96$

The rejection region requires $\alpha/2$ = .10/2 = .05 in each tail of the z
distribution. From Table IV, Appendix B, $z_{.05}$ = 1.645. The rejection
region is z < -1.645 or z > 1.645.

Since the observed value of the test statistic falls in the rejection
region (z = 1.96 > 1.645), H_0 is rejected. There is sufficient
evidence to indicate a difference in job satisfaction for the two
different sociocultural types of workers at α = .10.

Since the test statistic is positive, workers with belief in class
systems are more satisfied with their jobs.

9.11   From Exercise 9.10, $\bar{x}_1$ = 365, s_1 = 23, and n_1 = 100.

To determine if the mean strength of firm A's corrugated fiberboard is
more than 360 pounds, we test:

$$H_0: \quad \mu_1 = 360$$
$$H_a: \quad \mu_1 > 360$$

The test statistic is $z = \dfrac{\bar{x}_1 - \mu_0}{\sigma_{\bar{x}_1}} = \dfrac{\bar{x}_1 - \mu_0}{\sigma_1/\sqrt{n_1}} = \dfrac{\bar{x}_1 - \mu_0}{s_1/\sqrt{n_1}}$

$$= \dfrac{365 - 360}{23/\sqrt{100}} = 2.17$$

The rejection region requires α = .10 in the upper tail of the z
distribution. From Table IV, Appendix B, $z_{.10}$ = 1.28. The rejection
region is z > 1.28.

Since the observed value of the test statistic falls in the rejection
region (z = 2.17 > 1.28), H_0 is rejected. There is sufficient
evidence to indicate the mean strength of firm A's corrugated
fiberboard is more than 360 pounds at α = .10.

9.13   The two populations must have relative frequency distributions that
       are approximately normal and the population variances must be equal.

The samples must be randomly and independently selected from the populations.

9.15 The pooled variance (s_p^2) is simply a weighted average of the two sample variances, s_1^2 and s_2^2. The pooled variance, s_p^2, should be closer to σ^2 than s_1^2 or s_2^2 since it is based on a larger sample size.

9.17 a. First, compute the mean and variance for each sample.

$$\bar{x}_1 = \frac{\sum x_1}{n_1} = \frac{16.2}{6} = 2.7 \qquad \bar{x}_2 = \frac{\sum x_2}{n_2} = \frac{17.9}{5} = 3.58$$

$$s_1^2 = \frac{\sum x_1^2 - \frac{(\sum x_1)^2}{n}}{n_1 - 1} = \frac{46.98 - \frac{16.2^2}{6}}{6 - 1} = .648$$

$$s_2^2 = \frac{\sum x_2^2 - \frac{(\sum x_2)^2}{n_2}}{n_2 - 1} = \frac{64.83 - \frac{17.9^2}{5}}{5 - 1} = .187$$

$$s_p^2 = \frac{(n_1 - 1)s_1^2 + (n_2 - 1)s_2^2}{n_1 + n_2 - 2} = \frac{(6 - 1).648 + (5 - 1)(.187)}{6 + 5 - 2} = \frac{3.988}{9}$$
$$= .443$$

b. H_0: $\mu_1 = \mu_2$
H_a: $\mu_1 < \mu_2$

The test statistic is $t = \dfrac{(\bar{x}_1 - \bar{x}_2) - D_0}{\sqrt{s_p^2\left(\frac{1}{n_1} + \frac{1}{n_2}\right)}} = \dfrac{(2.7 - 3.58) - 0}{\sqrt{.443\left(\frac{1}{6} + \frac{1}{5}\right)}}$

$$= \frac{-.88}{.403} = -2.18$$

The rejection region requires $\alpha = .10$ in the lower tail of the t distribution with df = $n_1 + n_2 - 2 = 6 + 5 - 2 = 9$. From Table VI, Appendix B, $t_{.10} = 1.383$. The rejection region is $t < -1.383$.

Since the observed value of the test statistic falls in the rejection region ($t = -2.18 < -1.383$), H_0 is rejected. There is sufficient evidence to indicate that $\mu_1 < \mu_2$ ($\mu_2 > \mu_1$) at $\alpha = .10$.

Assumption: the population variances are equal.

c. The approximate observed significance level is $P(t \leq -2.18) = P(t \geq 2.18)$. From Table VI, Appendix B, with df = 9, $.025 < \text{p-value} < .05$.

The results are statistically significant. We would reject H_0 if α is larger than .05.

9.19 a. $s_p^2 = \dfrac{(n_1 - 1)s_1^2 + (n_2 - 1)s_2^2}{n_1 + n_2 - 2} = \dfrac{(12 - 1)4.2^2 + (16 - 1)3.7^2}{12 + 16 - 2}$

$$= \dfrac{399.39}{26} = 15.36$$

b. $H_0: \mu_1 = \mu_2$
$H_a: \mu_1 \neq \mu_2$

The test statistic is $t = \dfrac{(\bar{x}_1 - \bar{x}_2) - D_0}{\sqrt{s_p^2\left(\dfrac{1}{n_1} + \dfrac{1}{n_2}\right)}} = \dfrac{(35 - 43) - 0}{\sqrt{15.36\left(\dfrac{1}{12} + \dfrac{1}{16}\right)}}$

$$= \dfrac{-8}{1.4967} = -5.35$$

The rejection region requires $\alpha/2 = .05/2$ in each tail of the t distribution with df = $n_1 + n_2 - 2 = 12 + 16 - 2 = 26$. From Table VI, Appendix B, $t_{.025} = 2.056$. The rejection region is $t < -2.056$ or $t > 2.056$.

Since the observed value of the test statistic falls in the rejection region ($t = -5.35 < -2.056$), H_0 is rejected. There is sufficient evidence to indicate that $\mu_1 \neq \mu_2$ at $\alpha = .05$.

Assumption: the population variances are equal.

c. The approximate p-value is $P(t \leq -5.35$ or $t \geq 5.35)$
$\Rightarrow 2P(t \geq 5.35)$.
From Table VI, Appendix B, with df = 26,
p-value $= 2P(t \geq 5.35) < 2(.005)$ (Approximately 0)
$\Rightarrow$ p-value $< .01$.

The results are highly significant.

9.21 a. Let μ_1 = mean investment per quad for electric plants and μ_2 = mean investment per quad for gas plants.

$s_p^2 = \dfrac{(n_1 - 1)s_1^2 + (n_2 - 1)s_2^2}{n_1 + n_2 - 2} = \dfrac{(11 - 1)17.5 + (16 - 1)15}{11 + 16 - 2} = \dfrac{400}{25}$

$$= 16$$

To determine if a difference exists in average investment per quad between plans using gas and those using electric, we test:

$H_0: \mu_1 - \mu_2 = 0$
$H_a: \mu_1 - \mu_2 \neq 0$

The test statistic is $t = \dfrac{(\bar{x}_1 - \bar{x}_2) - D_0}{\sqrt{s_p^2\left(\dfrac{1}{n_1} + \dfrac{1}{n_2}\right)}} = \dfrac{(225 - 17.5) - 0}{\sqrt{16\left(\dfrac{1}{11} + \dfrac{1}{16}\right)}}$

$$= \dfrac{5}{1.5667} = 3.19$$

The rejection region requires $\alpha/2 = .05/2$ in each tail of the t distribution with df $= n_1 + n_2 - 2 = 11 + 16 - 2 = 25$. From Table VI, Appendix B, $t_{.025} = 2.060$. The rejection region is $t < -2.060$ or $t > 2.060$.

Since the observed value of the test statistic falls in the rejection region ($t = 3.19 > 2.060$), H_0 is rejected. There is sufficient evidence to indicate the mean investment per quad differs between plants using gas and those using electric at $\alpha = .05$.

b. For confidence coefficient .90, $\alpha = 1 - .90 = .10$ and $\alpha/2 = .10/2 = .05$. From Table VI, Appendix B, with df $= 25$, $t_{.05} = 1.708$. The confidence interval is:

$$(\bar{x}_1 - \bar{x}_2) \pm t_{.05}\sqrt{s_p^2\left(\frac{1}{n_1} + \frac{1}{n_2}\right)}$$

$$\Rightarrow (22.5 - 17.5) \pm 1.708\sqrt{16\left(\frac{1}{11} + \frac{1}{16}\right)}$$

$$\Rightarrow 5 \pm 2.676 \Rightarrow (2.304, 7.676)$$

We are 90% confident the mean investment per quad for electric plants exceeds that for gas plants by anywhere from 2.304 to 7.676.

9.23 a. Let μ_1 = mean change in bond prices handled by underwriter 1 and μ_2 = mean change in bond prices handled by underwriter 2.

$$s_p^2 = \frac{(n_1 - 1)s_1^2 + (n_2 - 1)s_2^2}{n_1 + n_2 - 2} = \frac{(27 - 1).0098 + (23 - 1).002465}{27 + 23 - 2}$$

$$= \frac{.30903}{48} = .006438$$

To determine if there is a difference in the mean change in bond prices handled by the 2 underwriters, we test:

H_0: $\mu_1 - \mu_2 = 0$
H_a: $\mu_1 - \mu_2 \neq 0$

The test statistic is $t = \dfrac{(\bar{x}_1 - \bar{x}_2) - D_0}{\sqrt{s_p^2\left(\frac{1}{n_1} + \frac{1}{n_2}\right)}} = \dfrac{-.0491 - (-.0307) - 0}{\sqrt{.006438\left(\frac{1}{27} + \frac{1}{23}\right)}}$

$$= -.81$$

The rejection region requires $\alpha/2 = .05/2 = .025$ in each tail of the t distribution with df $= n_1 + n_2 - 2 = 27 + 23 - 2 = 48$. From Table VI, Appendix B, $t_{.025} \approx 1.96$. The rejection region is $t < -1.96$ or $t > 1.96$.

Since the observed value of the test statistic does not fall in the rejection region (t = -.81 $\not< $ -1.96), H_0 is not rejected. There is insufficient evidence to indicate there is a difference in the mean change in bond prices handled by the 2 underwriters at α = .05.

b. For confidence coefficient .95, α = 1 - .95 = .05 and $\alpha/2$ = .05/2 = .025. From Table VI, Appendix B, with df = 48, $t_{.025} \approx 1.96$. The confidence interval is:

$$(\bar{x}_1 - \bar{x}_2) \pm t_{.025}\sqrt{s_p^2\left(\frac{1}{n_1} + \frac{1}{n_2}\right)}$$

$$\Rightarrow (-.0491 - (-.0307)) \pm 1.96\sqrt{.006438\left(\frac{1}{27} + \frac{1}{23}\right)}$$

$$\Rightarrow -.0184 \pm .0446 \Rightarrow (-.063, .0262)$$

I am 95% confident the mean difference in bond prices handled by underwriter 1 and underwriter 2 is somewhere between -.063 and .0262.

9.25 a. $s_1^2 = \dfrac{\sum x_1^2 - \dfrac{(\sum x_1)^2}{n_1}}{n_1 - 1} = \dfrac{2436 - \dfrac{128^2}{10}}{10 - 1} = 88.6222$

$s_2^2 = \dfrac{\sum x_2^2 - \dfrac{(\sum x_2)^2}{n_2}}{n_2 - 1} = \dfrac{1698 - \dfrac{104^2}{10}}{10 - 1} = 68.4889$

b. $s_p^2 = \dfrac{(n_1 - 1)s_1^2 + (n_2 - 1)s_2^2}{n_1 + n_2 - 2} = \dfrac{(10 - 1)88.6222 + (10 - 1)68.4889}{10 + 10 - 2}$

$$= 78.5556$$

$s_p = \sqrt{s_p^2} = 8.86$

The estimate of $\sigma(s_p = 8.86)$ appears to be a reasonable value for σ.

c. H_0: $\mu_1 = \mu_2$
H_a: $\mu_1 > \mu_2$

The test statistic is $t = \dfrac{(\bar{x}_1 - \bar{x}_2) - D_0}{\sqrt{s_p^2\left(\frac{1}{n_1} + \frac{1}{n_2}\right)}} = \dfrac{(12.8 - 10.4) - 0}{\sqrt{78.5556\left(\frac{1}{10} + \frac{1}{10}\right)}}$

$$= .61$$

The rejection region requires α = .05 in the upper tail of the t distribution with df = $n_1 + n_2 - 2$ = 10 + 10 - 2 = 18. From Table VI, Appendix B, $t_{.05}$ = 1.734. The rejection region is t > 1.734.

Since the observed value of the test statistic does not fall in the rejection region (t = .61 $\not> $ 1.734), H_0 is not rejected. There is insufficient evidence to indicate that $\mu_1 > \mu_2$. That is, there is insufficient evidence to indicate the mean number of sick days is larger for the night shift at $\alpha = .05$.

d. The necessary assumptions are:

1. Both sampled populations are approximately normal.
2. The population variances are equal.
3. The samples are randomly and independently sampled.

e. If the assumptions are not satisfied, use the Wilcoxon rank sum test for independent samples to test for a shift in population distributions (see Section 9.5).

9.27   a. The rejection region requires $\alpha = .05$ in the upper tail of the t distribution with df $= n_D - 1 = 10 - 1 = 9$. From Table VI, Appendix B, $t_{.05} = 1.833$. The rejection region is $t > 1.833$.

b. From Table VI, with df $= n_D - 1 = 20 - 1 = 19$, $t_{.10} = 1.328$. The rejection region is $t > 1.328$.

c. From Table VI, with df $= n_D - 1 = 5 - 1 = 4$, $t_{.025} = 2.776$. The rejection region is $t > 2.776$.

d. From Table VI, with df $= n_D - 1 = 9 - 1 = 8$, $t_{.01} = 2.896$. The rejection region is $t > 2.896$.

9.29   From Exercise 9.28, $\bar{x}_D = -7.6$ and $s_D = 4.56$.

For confidence coefficient .95, $\alpha = 1 - .95 = .05$ and $\alpha/2 = .05/2 = .025$. From Table VI, Appendix B, with df $= n_D - 1 = 5 - 1 = 4$, $t_{.025} = 2.776$. The confidence interval is:

$$\bar{x}_D \pm t_{.025} \frac{s_D}{\sqrt{n_D}} \Rightarrow -7.6 \pm 2.776\left(\frac{4.56}{\sqrt{5}}\right)$$

$$\Rightarrow -7.6 \pm 5.66 \Rightarrow (-13.26, -1.94)$$

9.31   A paired difference experiment provides more information if there is much variation among the experimental units. By pairing, the variation from experimental unit to experimental unit is eliminated. If there is little variation among the experimental units, pairing may not provide as much information. When pairing is used, degrees of freedom are reduced.

9.33   a. The samples are not independent, because each pair came from the same house.

b. The samples are paired on houses.

c. Some preliminary calculations are:

SINGLE-FAMILY HOME	DIFFERENCE (ASKING - SALE)
1	3700
2	2700
3	4900
4	-2000
5	0
6	10000
7	3700
8	-1300
9	0
10	4900

$$\bar{x}_D = \frac{\sum x_D}{n_D} = \frac{26600}{10} = 2660$$

$$s_D^2 = \frac{\sum x_D^2 - \frac{(\sum x_D)^2}{n_D}}{n_D - 1} = \frac{188,380,000 - \frac{26600^2}{10}}{10 - 1} = \frac{117,624,000}{9}$$

$$= 13,069,333.333$$

$$s_D = \sqrt{13,069,333.333} = 3615.1533$$

To determine if people generally receive the asking price, we test:

$$H_0: \quad \mu_D = 0$$
$$H_a: \quad \mu_D > 0$$

The test statistic is $t = \dfrac{\bar{x}_D - 0}{\dfrac{s_D}{\sqrt{n_D}}} = \dfrac{2660 - 0}{\dfrac{3615.1533}{\sqrt{10}}} = 2.327$

The rejection region requires $\alpha = .05$ in the upper tail of the t distribution with df $= n_D - 1 = 10 - 1 = 9$. From Table VI, Appendix B, $t_{.05} = 1.833$. The rejection region is $t > 1.833$.

Since the observed value of the test statistic falls in the rejection region ($t = 2.327 > 1.833$), H_0 is rejected. There is sufficient evidence to indicate in general people do not receive their asking price at $\alpha = .05$.

9.35   Some preliminary calculations are:

TRAINEE	DIFFERENCE (BEFORE - AFTER)
1	-12
2	-2
3	2
4	-1
5	4
6	-9
7	5
8	-3
9	7
10	7

$$\bar{x}_D = \frac{\sum x_D}{n_D} = \frac{-2}{10} = -.2$$

$$s_D^2 = \frac{\sum x_D^2 - \frac{(\sum x_D)^2}{n_D}}{n_D - 1} = \frac{382 - \frac{(-2)^2}{10}}{10 - 1} = 42.4$$

$$s_D = \sqrt{42.4} = 6.5115$$

a.   To determine if the trainees are more assertive after taking the course, we test:

$$H_0: \quad \mu_D = 0$$
$$H_a: \quad \mu_D < 0$$

The test statistic is $t = \dfrac{\bar{x}_D - 0}{\dfrac{s_D}{\sqrt{n_D}}} = \dfrac{-.2 - 0}{\dfrac{6.5115}{\sqrt{10}}} = -.10$

The rejection region requires $\alpha = .05$ in the lower tail of the t distribution with df = $n_D - 1 = 10 - 1 = 9$. From Table VI, Appendix B, $t_{.05} = 1.833$. The rejection region is $t < -1.833$.

Since the observed value of the test statistic does not fall in the rejection region ($t = -.10 \nless -1.833$), H_0 is not rejected. There is insufficient evidence to indicate the trainees are more assertive after taking the course at $\alpha = .05$.

b.   The p-value is $P(t \leq -.10)$. From Table VI, with df = 9, $P(t \leq -.10) > .10$. Thus, the p-value is greater than .10.

c.   No. There is no evidence the training program is effective.

d. The necessary assumptions are:

1. The population of differences is normal.
2. The differences are randomly selected.

9.37 Some preliminary calculations are:

CAR	DIFFERENCE (MANUFACTURER - COMPETITOR)
1	.4
2	.4
3	.5
4	.4
5	.6
6	.2

$$\bar{x}_D = \frac{\sum x_D}{n_D} = \frac{2.5}{6} = .4167$$

$$s_D^2 = \frac{\sum x_D^2 - \frac{(\sum x_D)^2}{n_D}}{n_D - 1} = \frac{1.13 - \frac{2.5^2}{6}}{6 - 1} = .0177$$

$$s_D = \sqrt{.0177} = .1329$$

a. To determine if there is a difference in the mean strength of the two types of shocks, we test:

$H_0: \mu_D = 0$
$H_a: \mu_D \neq 0$

The test statistic is $t = \dfrac{\bar{x}_D - 0}{\frac{s_D}{\sqrt{n}}} = \dfrac{.4167 - 0}{\frac{.1329}{\sqrt{6}}} = 7.68$

The rejection region requires $\alpha/2 = .05/2 = .025$ in each tail of the t distribution with df = $n_D - 1 = 6 - 1 = 5$. From Table VI, Appendix B, $t_{.025} = 2.571$. The rejection region is $t < -2.571$ or $t > 2.571$.

Since the observed value of the test statistic falls in the rejection region ($t = 7.68 > 2.571$), H_0 is rejected. There is sufficient evidence to indicate a difference in mean strength of the two shocks at $\alpha = .05$.

b. The observed significance level is $2P(t \geq 7.68)$. From Table VI, with df = 5, $2P(t \geq 7.68) < 2(.005) = .01$.

c. The necessary assumptions are:

   1. The population of differences is normal.
   2. The differences are randomly selected.

d. For confidence coefficient .95, $\alpha = 1 - .95 = .05$ and $\alpha/2 = .05/2 = .025$. From Table VI, with df = 5, $t_{.025} = 2.571$. The confidence interval is:

$$\bar{x}_D \pm t_{.025}\frac{s_D}{\sqrt{n_D}} \Rightarrow .4167 \pm 2.571\left(\frac{.1329}{\sqrt{6}}\right)$$

$$\Rightarrow .4167 \pm .1395 \Rightarrow (.2772, .5562)$$

We are 95% confident the difference in mean strength between the manufacturer's shock and that of the competitor's shock is between .2772 and .5562.

9.39 Some preliminary calculations are:

PAIR	DIFFERENCE PRIVATE - GOVERNMENT
1	750
2	1400
3	-300
4	2400
5	-700
6	800
7	1300
8	-400
9	1900
10	-1100
11	1600
12	300

$$\bar{x}_D = \frac{\sum x_D}{n_D} = \frac{7950}{12} = 662.5$$

$$s_D^2 = \frac{\sum x_D^2 - \frac{(\sum x_D)^2}{n_D}}{n_D - 1} = \frac{18,822,500 - \frac{7950^2}{12}}{12 - 1} = 1,232,329.545$$

$$s_D = \sqrt{1232329.545} = 1110.1034$$

a. For confidence coefficient .99, $\alpha = 1 - .99 = .01$ and $\alpha/2$ = .01/2 = .005. From Table VI, Appendix B, with df = $n_D - 1$ = 12 - 1 = 11, $t_{.005}$ = 3.106. The confidence interval is:

$$\bar{x}_D \pm t_{.005} \frac{s_D}{\sqrt{n_D}} \Rightarrow 662.5 \pm 3.106\left(\frac{1110.1034}{\sqrt{12}}\right)$$

$$\Rightarrow 662.5 \pm 995.35 \Rightarrow (-332.85, 1656.85)$$

b. The necessary assumptions are:

1. The population of differences is normal.
2. The differences are randomly selected.

9.41 $\quad n_1 = n_2 = \dfrac{(z_{\alpha/2})^2(\sigma_1^2 + \sigma_2^2)}{B^2}$

For confidence coefficient .95, $\alpha = 1 - .95 = .05$ and $\alpha/2 = .05/2 =$ .025. From Table IV, Appendix B, $z_{.025} = 1.96$.

$$n_1 = n_2 = \frac{1.96^2(12 + 12)}{1.5^2} = 40.98 \approx 41$$

9.43 $\quad R \approx 60 \Rightarrow s_D \approx \dfrac{R}{4} = \dfrac{60}{4} = 15$

$$n_D = \frac{(z_{\alpha/2})^2\sigma_D^2}{B^2}$$

For confidence coefficient .95, $\alpha = 1 - .95 = .05$ and $\alpha/2 = .05/2 =$ .025. From Table IV, Appendix B, $z_{.025} = 1.96$.

$$n_D = \frac{1.96^2(15^2)}{4.7^2} = 39.13 \approx 40$$

9.45 For confidence coefficient .95, $\alpha = 1 - .95 = .05$ and $\alpha/2 = .05/2 =$ .025. From Table IV, Appendix B, $z_{.025} = 1.96$.

$$n_1 = n_2 = \frac{4(z_{\alpha/2})^2(\sigma_1^2 + \sigma_2^2)}{W^2} = \frac{4(1.96^2)(6.25^2 + 6.25^2)}{6^2} = 33.3 \approx 34$$

9.47 From 9.34, $s_D = 1.5736$

$$n_D = \frac{(z_{\alpha/2})^2\sigma_D^2}{B^2}$$

For confidence coefficient .95, $\alpha = 1 - .95 = .05$ and $\alpha/2 = .05/2 =$ .025. From Table IV, Appendix B, $z_{.025} = 1.96$.

$$n_D = \frac{1.96^2(1.5736^2)}{.5^2} = 38.05 \approx 38$$

9.49   a.   The test statistic is T_B, the rank sum of population B (because $n_B < n_A$).

The rejection region is $T_B \leq 32$ or $T_B \geq 58$, from Table XI, Appendix B, with $n_A = 8$, $n_B = 6$, and $\alpha = .10$.

b.   The test statistic is T_A, the rank sum of population A (because $n_A < n_B$).

The rejection region is $T_A \geq 40$, from Table XI, Appendix B, with $n_A = 5$, $n_B = 6$, and $\alpha = .05$.

c.   The test statistic is T_B, the rank sum of population B (because $n_B < n_A$).

The rejection region is $T_B \geq 98$.

d.   Since $n_A = n_B = 20$, the test statistic is

$$z = \frac{T_A - \dfrac{n_1(n_1 + n_2 + 1)}{2}}{\sqrt{\dfrac{n_1 n_2 (n_1 + n_2 + 1)}{12}}}$$

The rejection region is $z < -z_{\alpha/2}$ or $z > z_{\alpha/2}$. For $\alpha = .05$ and $\alpha/2 = .05/2 = .025$, $z_{.025} = 1.96$ from Table IV, Appendix B. The rejection region is $z < -1.96$ or $z > 1.96$.

9.51   The alternative hypotheses differ for one- and two-tailed versions of the Wilcoxon rank sum test. For a two-tailed test, the alternative hypothesis is H_a: The probability distribution for one population is shifted to the right or left of the other distribution. For a one-tailed test, the alternative hypothesis is H_a: The probability distribution for one population is shifted to the right (left) of the other distribution.

The rejection regions are also different. For a two-tailed test, the rejection region is $T \leq T_L$ or $T \geq T_U$ where T is the rank sum of the sample with the smallest sample size. For a one-tailed test, the rejection region is $T \geq T_U$ (or $T \leq T_L$).

9.53   a.   We first rank all observations:

| NEIGHBORHOOD A | | NEIGHBORHOOD B | |
OBSERVATION	RANK	OBSERVATION	RANK
.850	11	.911	16
1.060	18	.770	3
.910	15	.815	8
.813	7	.748	2
.787	1	.835	9
.880	13	.800	6
.895	14	.793	4
.844	10	.769	5
.965	17		
.875	12		
	$T_A = 118$		$T_B = 53$

To determine the fairness of the assessments between the two neighborhoods, we test:

H_0: Two sampled populations have identical probability distributions

H_a: The probability distribution for Neighborhood A is shifted to the right or left of that for Neighborhood B

The test statistic is $T_B = 53$ because $n_B < n_A$.

The rejection region is $T_B \leq 54$ or $T_B \geq 98$ from Table XI, Appendix B, with $n_A = 10$, $n_B = 5$, and $\alpha = .05$.

Since the observed value of the test statistic falls in the rejection region ($T = 53 \leq 54$), H_0 is rejected. There is sufficient evidence to indicate the fairness of the assessments are not the same for the two neighborhoods at $\alpha = .05$.

b.   In order to use the two-sample t-test, we have to have normal distributions for both neighborhoods A and B, the samples must be independent, and the population variances must be equal.

c.   We must assume the two samples are random and independent, and the two probability distributions are continuous.

9.55   We first rank all data:

BEFORE RIGHT-TURN LAW	RANK	AFTER RIGHT-TURN LAW	RANK
150	3	145	2
500	11	390	8
250	5	680	13
301	7	560	12
242	4	899	14
435	10	1250	16
100	1	290	6
402	9	963	15
	50		86

To determine whether the damages tended to increase after the enactment of the law, we test:

H_0:   The distributions before and after the right-turn law are identical

H_a: The distribution after the right-turn law is shifted to the right of that before the right-turn law

The test statistic is T_{After} = 86.

The rejection region is $T \geq 84$ from Table XI, Appendix B, with $n_A = n_B = 8$ and $\alpha = .05$.

Since the observed value of the test statistic falls in the rejection region ($T = 86 \geq 84$), H_0 is rejected. There is sufficient evidence to indicate the damages tended to increase after the enactment of the law at $\alpha = .05$.

9.57   a.   Some preliminary calculations are:

$T_A = 1594.5$ $T_B = 1033.5$

After ranking all observations, the sum of the ranks for the data associated with the NYSE is $T_A = 1594.5$ and the sum of the ranks for the data associated with the ASE is $T_B = 1033.5$.

To determine if there is a shift in the locations of the distributions of closing prices for the two stock exchanges, we test:

H_0:   The two sampled populations have identical probability distributions

H_a: The probability distribution for the NYSE is shifted to the right or left of that for the ASE

INFERENCES FOR MEANS BASED ON TWO SAMPLES

The test statistic is

$$z = \frac{T_A - \dfrac{n_1(n_1 + n_2 + 1)}{2}}{\sqrt{\dfrac{n_1 n_2 (n_1 + n_2 + 1)}{12}}} = \frac{1594.5 - \dfrac{36(36 + 36 + 1)}{2}}{\sqrt{\dfrac{36(36)(36 + 36 + 1)}{12}}} = 3.159$$

The rejection region requires $\alpha/2 = .05/2 = .025$ in each tail of the z distribution. From Table IV, Appendix B, $z_{.025} = 1.96$. The rejection region is $z < -1.96$ or $z > 1.96$.

Since the observed value of the test statistic falls in the rejection region ($z = 3.159 > 1.96$), H_0 is rejected. There is sufficient evidence to indicate a shift in the locations of the distributions of closing prices for the stock exchanges at $\alpha = .05$.

b. A Type I error would be concluding there was a shift in the locations of the distributions of closing prices for the two stock exchanges when there is not a shift.

A Type II error would be concluding there was not shift in the locations of the distributions of closing prices for the two stock exchanges when there is a shift.

c. The probability of committing a Type I error is $\alpha = .05$.

9.59 a. The test statistic is T_- or T_+, the smaller of the two.

The rejection region is $T \leq 101$, from Table XII, Appendix B, with $n = 25$, $\alpha = .10$, and two-tailed.

b. The test statistic is T_-.

The rejection region is $T_- \leq 303$, from Table XII, Appendix B, with $n = 41$, $\alpha = .05$, and one-tailed.

c. The test statistic is T_+.

The rejection region is $T_+ \leq 0$, from Table XII, Appendix B, with $n = 8$, $\alpha = .005$, and one-tailed.

9.61 The difference between a one- and two-tailed Wilcoxon signed rank test is the following:

A one-tailed test is used to test if one population distribution is shifted in a specified direction. A two-tailed test is used to test if one population distribution is sifted in either direction.

9.63 a. H_0: The two sampled populations have identical probability
           distributions
      H_a: The probability distribution for population A is located to
           the right of that for population B

      b. The test statistic is

$$z = \frac{T_+ - \dfrac{n(n + 1)}{4}}{\sqrt{\dfrac{n(n + 1)(2n + 1)}{24}}} = \frac{354 - \dfrac{30(30 + 1)}{4}}{\sqrt{\dfrac{30(30 + 1)(60 + 1)}{24}}}$$

$$= \frac{121.5}{48.6184} = 2.499$$

The rejection region requires $\alpha = .05$ in the upper tail of the
z distribution. From Table IV, Appendix B, $z_{.05} = 1.645$. The
rejection region is $z > 1.645$.

Since the observed value of the test statistic falls in the
rejection region ($z = 2.499 > 1.645$), H_0 is rejected. There is
sufficient evidence to indicate Population A is located to the
right of that for population B at $\alpha = .05$.

      c. The p-value = $P(z \geq 2.499) = .5 - .4938 = .0062$.

      d. The necessary assumptions are:

          1. The sample of differences is randomly selected from the
              population of differences.
          2. The probability distribution from which the sample of paired
              differences is drawn is continuous.

9.65 a. Some preliminary calculations are:

CITY	CORPORATE LAWYERS	LAWYERS WITH LAW FIRMS	DIFFERENCE CL - L	RANK OF ABSOLUTE DIFFERENCES
Atlanta	$45,500	$45,500	0	(Eliminated)
Chicago	43,000	48,000	-5,000	5
Cincinnati	43,500	45,000	-1,500	1
Dallas/Ft. Worth	49,500	46,500	3,000	3
Los Angeles	47,000	60,000	-13,000	9
Milwaukee	37,500	50,000	-12,500	8
Minneapolis/St. Paul	47,500	43,500	4,000	4
New York	43,500	54,000	-10,500	6
Pittsburgh	42,000	44,000	-2,000	2
San Francisco	47,500	59,500	-12,000	7
				$T_+ = 7$

To determine whether the salaries of corporate lawyers differ from those of lawyers working for law firms, we test:

H_0: The two sampled populations have identical probability distributions

H_a: The probability distribution for the salaries of corporate lawyers is shifted to the right or left of the salaries of lawyers working for law firms.

The test statistic is $T_+ = 7$.

The rejection region is $T_+ \leq 6$ from Table XII, Appendix B, with $n = 9$ and $\alpha = .05$.

Since the observed value of the test statistic does not fall in the rejection region ($T_+ = 7 \nleq 6$), H_0 is not rejected. There is insufficient evidence to indicate the salaries of corporate lawyers differ from those of lawyers working for law firms at $\alpha = .05$.

b. If the distribution of the differences is normal, the paired t test could be used.

9.67   a.   Some preliminary calculations are:

WEEK	1986	1987	DIFFERENCE 1986 - 1987	RANK OF ABSOLUTE DIFFERENCES
2	6	8	-2	2.5
8	3	5	-2	2.5
22	2	2	0	(Eliminated)
35	1	0	1	1
48	4	7	-3	4.5
51	7	10	-3	4.5
				$T_+ = 1$

To determine whether the probability distribution of the number of accidents per week after the law is located above that of the number of accidents before the law, we test:

H_0: The two sampled populations have identical probability distributions

H_a: The probability distribution for the number of accidents per week after the law is shifted to the right of that for the number of accidents per week before the law

The test statistic is $T_+ = 1$.

The rejection region is $T_+ \leq 1$ from Table XII, Appendix B, with $n = 5$ and $\alpha = .05$.

Since the observed value of the test statistic falls in the rejection region ($T_+ = 1 \leq 1$), H_0 is rejected. There is sufficient evidence to indicate the probability distribution for the number of accidents per week after the law is shifted to the right of that for the number of accidents per week before the law at $\alpha = .05$.

b. The paired difference design was used to eliminate variation in number of accidents due to weeks. There are some weeks (such as weeks including holidays) that have more accidents than others. The pairing eliminates this difference.

9.69 Some preliminary calculations are:

LOCATION	A	B	DIFFERENCE A - B	RANK OF ABSOLUTE DIFFERENCES
1	879	1085	-206	6
2	445	325	120	2
3	692	848	-156	5
4	1565	1421	144	4
5	2326	2778	-452	8
6	857	992	-135	3
7	1250	1303	-53	1
8	773	1215	-442	7
				$T_+ = 6$

To determine whether one of the chains tends to have more customers than the other, we test:

H_0: The two sampled populations have identical probability distributions

H_a: The probability distribution for chain A is shifted to the right or left of that for chain B

The test statistic is $T_+ = 6$.

The rejection region is $T_+ \leq 4$ from Table XII, Appendix B, with $n = 8$ and $\alpha = .05$.

Since the observed value of the test statistic does not fall in the rejection region ($T_+ = 6 \not\leq 4$), H_0 is not rejected. There is insufficient evidence to indicate one of the chains tends to have more customers than the other at $\alpha = .05$.

9.71 a. The necessary assumptions are that the two samples are randomly selected in an independent manner from the two populations.

b. The necessary assumptions are:

1. Both sampled populations have relative frequency distributions that are approximately normal.
2. The population variances are equal.
3. The samples are randomly and independently selected from the populations.

c. The necessary assumptions are:

1. The relative frequency distribution of the population of differences is normal.
2. The differences are randomly selected from the population of differences.

9.73 From Exercise 9.72, $\bar{x}_D = 2.55$, $s_D^2 = 11.3383$ and $s_D = 3.3672$.

For confidence coefficient .95, $\alpha = 1 - .95 = .05$ and $\alpha/2 = .05/2 = .025$. From Table IV, Appendix B, with df $= n_D - 1 = 10 - 1 = 9$, $t_{.025} = 2.262$. The confidence interval is:

$$\bar{x}_D \pm t_{.025} \frac{s_D}{\sqrt{n_D}} \Rightarrow 2.55 \pm 2.262\left(\frac{3.3672}{\sqrt{10}}\right)$$

$$\Rightarrow 2.55 \pm 2.409 \Rightarrow (.141, 4.959)$$

We are 95% confident the difference between 1985 and 1984 R & D expenditures is between .141 and 4.959.

9.75 For confidence coefficient .90, $\alpha = 1 - .90 = .10$ and $\alpha/2 = .10/2 = .05$. From Table IV, Appendix B, $z_{.05} = 1.645$.

An estimate of σ_1 and σ_2 is obtained from:

range $\approx 4s$

$$s \approx \frac{range}{4}$$

$$= \frac{6}{4} = 1.5$$

$$n_1 = n_2 = \frac{4(z_{\alpha/2})^2(\sigma_1^2 + \sigma_2^2)}{W^2} = \frac{4(1.645^2)(1.5^2 + 1.5^2)}{1^2} = 48.71 \approx 49$$

9.77 a. In order to use the t test, the data must be normally distributed. It is doubtful that the number of accidents is normally distributed.

b. Some preliminary calculations:

BEFORE		AFTER	
OBSERVATION	RANK	OBSERVATION	RANK
12	10	4	3
5	4	2	1
10	9	7	6
9	8	3	2
14	11	8	7
6	5		
$T_A = \overline{47}$		$T_B = \overline{19}$	

To determine if the traffic light aided in reducing the number of accidents, we test:

H_0: The two sampled populations have identical probability distributions

H_a: The probability distribution after the traffic light was installed is shifted to the left of that before

The test statistic is $T_B = 19$.

The rejection region is $T_B \leq 19$ from Table XI, Appendix B, with $n_A = 6$, $n_B = 5$, and $\alpha = .025$.

Since the observed value of the test statistic falls in the rejection region ($T_B = 19 \leq 19$), H_0 is rejected. There is sufficient evidence to indicate the traffic light aided in reducing the number of accidents at $\alpha = .025$.

9.79 To determine if the average number of services used by bank 1's customers is greater than that for bank 2's customers, we test:

H_0: $\mu_1 - \mu_2 = 0$
H_a: $\mu_1 - \mu_2 > 0$

The test statistic is $z = \dfrac{(\bar{x}_1 - \bar{x}_2) - 0}{\sqrt{\dfrac{\sigma_1^2}{n_1} + \dfrac{\sigma_2^2}{n_2}}} \approx \dfrac{(2.2 - 1.8) - 0}{\sqrt{\dfrac{1.15^2}{40} + \dfrac{1.10^2}{50}}} = 1.67$

The rejection region requires $\alpha = .10$ in the upper tail of the z distribution. From Table IV, Appendix B, $z_{.10} = 1.28$. The rejection region is $z > 1.28$.

Since the observed value of the test statistic falls in the rejection region ($z = 1.67 > 1.28$), H_0 is rejected. There is sufficient evidence to indicate the mean number of services used by bank 1's customers is greater than that for bank 2's customers at $\alpha = .10$.

INFERENCES FOR MEANS BASED ON TWO SAMPLES

9.81 To determine if the mean housing price per square foot differs in the
two locales, we test:

$H_0: \mu_1 - \mu_2 = 0$
$H_a: \mu_1 - \mu_2 \neq 0$

The test statistic is $z = \dfrac{(\bar{x}_1 - \bar{x}_2) - 0}{\sqrt{\dfrac{\sigma_1^2}{n_1} + \dfrac{\sigma_2^2}{n_2}}} \approx \dfrac{(50.4 - 53.7) - 0}{\sqrt{\dfrac{4.5^2}{63} + \dfrac{5.3^2}{78}}} = -4.00$

The rejection region requires $\alpha/2 = .01/2 = .005$ in each tail of the z
distribution. From Table IV, Appendix B, $z_{.005} = 2.575$. The
rejection region is $z < -2.575$ or $z > 2.575$.

Since the observed value of the test statistic falls in the rejection
region ($z = -4.00 < -2.575$), H_0 is rejected. There is sufficient
evidence to indicate the mean housing price per square foot differs
for the two locales at $\alpha = .01$.

9.83 a. Some preliminary calculations are:

DAY	DIFFERENCE HIGHWAY 1 - HIGHWAY 2
1	-25
2	4
3	-23
4	-16
5	-16

$\bar{d} = \dfrac{\sum d_i}{n} = \dfrac{-76}{5} = -15.2$

$s_d^2 = \dfrac{\sum d_i^2 - \dfrac{(\sum d_i)^2}{n}}{n - 1} = \dfrac{1682 - \dfrac{(-76)^2}{5}}{5 - 1}$

$= 131.7$

$s_d = \sqrt{131.7} = 11.4761$

To determine if the mean number of speeders per 100 cars differ
for the two highways, we test:

$H_0: \mu_1 = \mu_2$
$H_a: \mu_1 \neq \mu_2$

The test statistic is $t = \dfrac{\bar{d} - 0}{s_d/\sqrt{n}} = \dfrac{-15.2}{\dfrac{11.4761}{\sqrt{5}}} = -2.96$

The rejection region requires $\alpha/2 = .05/2 = .025$ in each tail of
the t distribution with df $= n - 1 = 5 - 1 = 4$. From Table VI,
Appendix B, $t_{.025} = 2.776$. The rejection region is $t > 2.776$ and
$t < -2.776$. Since the observed value of the test statistic falls
in the rejection region ($t = -2.96 < -2.776$), H_0 is rejected.

There is sufficient evidence to indicate the mean number of speeders per 100 cars differ for the 2 highways at $\alpha = .05$.

We must assume the population of differences is normally distributed. It is fairly doubtful that the differences are normally distributed.

b. Some preliminary calculations are:

DIFFERENCE HIGHWAY 1 - HIGHWAY 2	RANK OF ABSOLUTE DIFFERENCES
-25	5
4	1
-23	4
-16	2.5
-16	2.5
	$T_+ = 1$

The hypotheses are:

H_0: The two sampled populations have identical probability distributions

H_a: The probability distribution for highway 1 is shifted to the right or left of that for highway 2

The test statistic is $T_+ = 1$.

The rejection region is $T_+ \leq 1$ from Table XII, Appendix B, with n = 5 and $\alpha = .10$.

Since the observed value of the test statistic falls in the rejection region ($T_+ = 1 \leq 1$), H_0 is rejected. There is sufficient evidence to indicate the probability distribution for highway 1 is shifted to the right or left of that for highway 2 at $\alpha = .10$.

9.85 $s_p^2 = \dfrac{(n_1 - 1)s_1^2 + (n_2 - 1)s_2^2}{n_1 + n_2 - 2} = \dfrac{(15 - 1)10.3^2 + (15 - 1)13.4^2}{15 + 15 - 2}$

$$= 142.825$$

a. To determine if a difference in mean time until spoilage begins exists for the 2 preservatives, we test:

H_0: $\mu_1 - \mu_2 = 0$

H_a: $\mu_1 - \mu_2 \neq 0$

The test statistic is $t = \dfrac{(\bar{x}_1 - \bar{x}_2) - 0}{\sqrt{s_p^2\left(\dfrac{1}{n_1} + \dfrac{1}{n_2}\right)}} = \dfrac{(106.4 - 96.5) - 0}{\sqrt{142.825\left(\dfrac{1}{15} + \dfrac{1}{15}\right)}}$

$= \dfrac{9.9}{4.3639} = 2.27$

The rejection region requires $\alpha/2 = .05/2 = .025$ in each tail of the t distribution with df $= n_1 + n_2 - 2 = 15 + 15 - 2 = 28$. From Table VI, Appendix B, $t_{.025} = 2.048$. The rejection region is t < -2.048 or t > 2.048.

Since the observed value of the test statistic falls in the rejection region (t = 2.27 > 2.048), H_0 is rejected. There is sufficient evidence to indicate a difference in mean time until spoilage begins for the two preservatives at $\alpha = .05$.

b. The processor could have used a paired difference design to reduce variability. Each cut of meat could be cut in 2 pieces, with one piece receiving preservative A and the other preservative B.

9.87   Some preliminary calculations are:

MONTH	DIFFERENCE MEN'S - SPORT	MONTH	DIFFERENCE MEN'S - SPORT
1	-1,807	7	-1,249
2	348	8	-424
3	2,876	9	314
4	1,994	10	-841
5	-6,249	11	1,403
6	-7,934	12	-2,131

$\bar{x}_D = \dfrac{\sum x_D}{n_D} = \dfrac{-13700}{12} = -1,141.67$

$s_D^2 = \dfrac{\sum x_D^2 - \dfrac{(\sum x_D)^2}{n_D}}{n_D - 1} = \dfrac{126687346 - \dfrac{(-13700)^2}{12}}{12 - 1} = 10,095,137.51$

$s_D = \sqrt{s_D^2} = 3,177.2846$

a. For confidence coefficient .95, $\alpha = 1 - .95 = .05$ and $\alpha/2 = .05/2 = .025$. From Table VI, Appendix B, with df $= n_D - 1 = 12 - 1 = 11$, $t_{.025} = 2.201$. The confidence interval is:

$$\bar{x}_D \pm t_{.025}\frac{s_D}{\sqrt{n_D}} \Rightarrow -1,141.67 \pm 2.201\left(\frac{3,177.2846}{\sqrt{12}}\right)$$

$$\Rightarrow -1,141.67 \pm 2,018.76 \Rightarrow (-3,160.43, 877.09)$$

b. We cannot make a decision based on the confidence interval in part (a) since we cannot determine which department has the greater mean sales.

c. The necessary assumptions are:

1. The population of differences is normal.
2. The differences are randomly selected.

9.89 a. $$s_p^2 = \frac{(n_1 - 1)s_1^2 + (n_2 - 1)s_2^2}{n_1 + n_2 - 2} = \frac{(15 - 1)2300^2 + (22 - 1)3100^2}{15 + 22 - 2}$$

$$= 7,882,000$$

To determine if the mean salary of male first-level managers exceeds that of females, we test:

$$H_0: \quad \mu_1 - \mu_2 = 0$$
$$H_a: \quad \mu_1 - \mu_2 < 0$$

The test statistic is $t = \dfrac{(\bar{x}_1 - \bar{x}_2) - 0}{\sqrt{s_p^2\left(\frac{1}{n_1} + \frac{1}{n_2}\right)}} = \dfrac{(23,400 - 24,700) - 0}{\sqrt{7,882,000\left(\frac{1}{15} + \frac{1}{22}\right)}}$

$$= -1.38$$

The rejection region requires $\alpha = .05$ in the lower tail of the t distribution with df $= n_1 + n_2 - 2 = 15 + 22 - 2 = 35$. From Table VI, Appendix B, $t_{.05} \approx 1.645$. The rejection region is $t < -1.645$.

Since the observed value of the test statistic does not fall in the rejection region ($t = -1.38 \not< -1.645$), H_0 is not rejected. There is insufficient evidence to indicate the mean salary of male first-level managers exceeds the mean salary of females at $\alpha = .05$.

b. The necessary assumptions are:

1. Both sampled populations are approximately normal.
2. The population variances are equal.
3. The samples are randomly and independently sampled.

COMPARING POPULATION PROPORTIONS

10.1   The characteristics of a binomial experiment are:

   1.   The experiment consists of n identical trials.
   2.   There are only two possible outcomes on each trial; one denoted
        S(Success) and one denoted F(Failure).
   3.   The probability of S remains the same from trial to trial. This
        probability is denoted by p.
   4.   The trials are independent.
   5.   The binomial random variable x is the number of S's in n trials.

10.3   From Chapter 7, it was given that the distribution of $\hat{p}$ is
       approximately normal if the interval $\hat{p} \pm 3\sigma_{\hat{p}}$ does not contain 0 or 1.

   a. $\sigma_{\hat{p}_1} \approx \sqrt{\dfrac{\hat{p}_1 \hat{q}_1}{n_1}} = \sqrt{\dfrac{.5(.5)}{10}} = .158$ $\hat{p}_1 \pm 3\sigma_{\hat{p}_1} \Rightarrow .5 \pm 3(.158)$

   $\Rightarrow .5 \pm .474 \Rightarrow (.026, .974)$

   $\sigma_{\hat{p}_2} \approx \sqrt{\dfrac{\hat{p}_2 \hat{q}_2}{n_2}} = \sqrt{\dfrac{.42(.58)}{12}} = .142$ $\hat{p}_2 \pm 3\sigma_{\hat{p}_2} \Rightarrow .42 \pm 3(.142)$

   $\Rightarrow .42 \pm .426 \Rightarrow (-.006, .846)$

   No. The interval $\hat{p}_2 \pm 3\sigma_{\hat{p}_2}$ contains 0.

   b. $\sigma_{\hat{p}_1} \approx \sqrt{\dfrac{.1(.9)}{10}} = .095$ $\hat{p}_1 \pm 3\sigma_{\hat{p}_1} \Rightarrow .1 \pm 3(.095)$

   $\Rightarrow .1 \pm .285 \Rightarrow (-.185, .385)$

   $\sigma_{\hat{p}_2} \approx \sqrt{\dfrac{.08(.92)}{12}} = .078$ $\hat{p}_2 \pm 3\sigma_{\hat{p}_2} \Rightarrow .08 \pm 3(.078)$

   $\Rightarrow .08 \pm .156 \Rightarrow (-.076, .236)$

   No. Both intervals contain 0.

c. $\sigma_{\hat{p}_1} \approx \sqrt{\dfrac{.2(.8)}{30}} = .073$ $\hat{p}_1 \pm 3\sigma_{\hat{p}_1} \Rightarrow .2 \pm 3(.073)$

$\Rightarrow .2 \pm .219 \Rightarrow (-.019, .419)$

$\sigma_{\hat{p}_2} \approx \sqrt{\dfrac{.3(.7)}{30}} = .084$ $\hat{p}_2 \pm 3\sigma_{\hat{p}_2} \Rightarrow .3 \pm 3(.084)$

$\Rightarrow .3 \pm .252 \Rightarrow (.048, .552)$

No. The interval $\hat{p}_1 \pm 3\sigma_{\hat{p}_1}$ contains 0.

d. $\sigma_{\hat{p}_1} \approx \sqrt{\dfrac{.05(.95)}{100}} = .022$ $\hat{p}_1 \pm 3\sigma_{\hat{p}_1} \Rightarrow .05 \pm 3(.022)$

$\Rightarrow .05 \pm .066 \Rightarrow (-.016, .116)$

$\sigma_{\hat{p}_2} \approx \sqrt{\dfrac{.09(.91)}{200}} = .020$ $\hat{p}_2 \pm 3\sigma_{\hat{p}_2} \Rightarrow .09 \pm 3(.020)$

$\Rightarrow .09 \pm .06 \Rightarrow (.03, .15)$

No. The interval $\hat{p}_1 \pm 3\sigma_{\hat{p}_1}$ contains 0.

e. $\sigma_{\hat{p}_1} \approx \sqrt{\dfrac{.95(.05)}{100}} = .022$ $\hat{p}_1 \pm 3\sigma_{\hat{p}_1} \Rightarrow .95 \pm 3(.022)$

$\Rightarrow .95 \pm .066 \Rightarrow (.884, 1.016)$

$\sigma_{\hat{p}_2} \approx \sqrt{\dfrac{.91(.09)}{200}} = .020$ $\hat{p}_2 \pm 3\sigma_{\hat{p}_2} \Rightarrow .91 \pm 3(.020)$

$\Rightarrow .91 \pm .06 \Rightarrow (.85, .97)$

No. The interval $\hat{p}_1 \pm 2\sigma_{\hat{p}_1}$ contains 1.

10.5 a. $\hat{p}_1 = \dfrac{x_1}{n_1} = \dfrac{38}{200} = .19,$ $\hat{p}_2 = \dfrac{x_1}{n_2} = \dfrac{71}{220} = .323$

b. The rejection region requires $\alpha/2 = .10/2 = .05$ in each tail of the z distribution. From Table IV, Appendix B, $z_{.05} = 1.645$. The rejection region is $z < -1.645$ or $z > 1.645$.

c. The test statistic is $z = \dfrac{(\hat{p}_1 - \hat{p}_2) - 0}{\sqrt{\hat{p}\hat{q}\left(\dfrac{1}{n_1} + \dfrac{1}{n_2}\right)}}$

where $\hat{p} = \dfrac{x_1 + x_2}{n_1 + n_2} = \dfrac{38 + 71}{200 + 220} = .2595$ and

$\hat{q} = 1 - \hat{p} = 1 - .2595 = .7405$.

Thus, $z = \dfrac{.19 - .323}{\sqrt{.2595(.7405)\left(\dfrac{1}{200} + \dfrac{1}{220}\right)}} = \dfrac{-.133}{.0428} = -3.11$

Since the observed value of the test statistic falls in the rejection region ($z = -3.11 < -1.645$), H_0 is rejected. There is sufficient evidence to indicate the 2 population proportions differ at $\alpha = .10$.

d. The p-value is $2P(z \leq -3.11)$. From Table IV, Appendix B,

$$2P(z \leq -3.11) < 2(.5000 - .4990) = .002.$$

The probability of observing this test statistic or anything more unusual is less than .002.

e. We must assume the two samples are independent random samples from binomial distributions. Also, the intervals $\hat{p}_1 \pm 3\sigma_{\hat{p}_1}$ and $\hat{p}_2 \pm 3\sigma_{\hat{p}_2}$ must not contain 0 or 1.

10.7 a. The rejection region requires $\alpha = .025$ in the lower tail of the z distribution. From Table IV, $z_{.025} = 1.96$. The rejection region is $z < -1.96$.

c. The test statistic is $z = \dfrac{(\hat{p}_1 - \hat{p}_2) - 0}{\sqrt{\hat{p}\hat{q}\left(\dfrac{1}{n_1} + \dfrac{1}{n_2}\right)}}$

where $\hat{p}_1 = \dfrac{x_1}{n_1} = \dfrac{140}{500} = .28$, $\hat{p}_2 = \dfrac{x_2}{n_2} = \dfrac{192}{500} = .384$,

$\hat{p} = \dfrac{x_1 + x_2}{n_1 + n_2} = \dfrac{140 + 192}{500 + 500} = .332$, and

$\hat{q} = 1 - \hat{p} = 1 - .332 = .668$

Thus, $z = \dfrac{(.28 - .384) - 0}{\sqrt{.332(.668)\left(\dfrac{1}{500} + \dfrac{1}{500}\right)}} = \dfrac{-.104}{.0298} = -3.49$

Since the observed value of the test statistic falls in the rejection region ($z = -3.49 < -1.96$), H_0 is rejected. There is sufficient evidence to indicate the proportion of population 1 is less than that of population 2.

c. The observed significance level is $P(z < -3.49) \approx .5000 - .5000 = 0$.

d. The intervals $\hat{p}_i \pm 3\sigma_{\hat{p}_i}$ must not contain 0 or 1.

$\hat{p}_1 \pm 3\sigma_{\hat{p}_1} \Rightarrow .28 \pm 3\sqrt{\dfrac{.28(.72)}{500}} \Rightarrow .28 \pm .060 \Rightarrow (.22, .34)$

$\hat{p}_2 \pm 3\sigma_{\hat{p}_2} \Rightarrow .384 \pm 3\sqrt{\dfrac{.384(.616)}{500}} \Rightarrow .384 \pm .022 \Rightarrow (.362, .406)$

Since neither interval contains 0 or 1, the above test is valid.

10.9 $\hat{p} = \dfrac{n_1\hat{p}_1 + n_2\hat{p}_2}{n_1 + n_2} = \dfrac{50(.4) + 60(.3)}{50 + 60} = \dfrac{38}{110} = .345$

$\hat{q} = 1 - \hat{p} = 1 - .345 = .655$

The test statistic is $z = \dfrac{(\hat{p}_1 - \hat{p}_2) - 0}{\sqrt{\hat{p}\hat{q}\left(\frac{1}{n_1} + \frac{1}{n_2}\right)}} = \dfrac{(.4 - .3) - 0}{\sqrt{.345(.655)\left(\frac{1}{50} + \frac{1}{60}\right)}}$

$= \dfrac{.1}{.091} = 1.10$

The rejection region requires $\alpha = .05$ in the upper tail of the z distribution. From Table IV, Appendix B, $z_{.05} = 1.645$. The rejection region is $z > 1.645$.

Since the observed value of the test statistic does not fall in the rejection region ($z = 1.10 \ngtr 1.645$), H_0 is not rejected. There is insufficient evidence to indicate the proportion from population 1 is greater than that for population 2 at $\alpha = .05$.

10.11 From Exercise 10.10,

$\hat{p}_1 = \dfrac{x_1}{n_1} = \dfrac{19}{207} = .092 \qquad \hat{p}_2 = \dfrac{x_2}{n_2} = \dfrac{96}{153} = .627$

For confidence coefficient .95, $\alpha = 1 - .95 = .05$ and $\alpha/2 = .05/2 = .025$. From Table IV, Appendix B, $z_{.025} = 1.96$. The confidence interval is:

$(\hat{p}_1 - \hat{p}_2) \pm z_{.025} \sqrt{\dfrac{\hat{p}_1\hat{q}_1}{n_1} + \dfrac{\hat{p}_2\hat{q}_2}{n_2}}$

$\Rightarrow (.092 - .627) \pm 1.96\sqrt{\dfrac{.092(.908)}{207} + \dfrac{.627(.373)}{153}}$

$\Rightarrow -.535 \pm .086 \Rightarrow (-.621, -.449)$

10.13 Some preliminary calculations are:

$\hat{p}_1 = \dfrac{x_1}{n_1} = \dfrac{81}{100} = .81, \qquad \hat{p}_2 = \dfrac{x_2}{n_2} = \dfrac{51}{100} = .51$

$\hat{p} = \dfrac{x_1 + x_2}{n_1 + n_2} = \dfrac{81 + 51}{100 + 100} = .66, \qquad \hat{q} = 1 - \hat{p} = 1 - .66 = .34$

a. To determine if the ability to identify food decreases with age, we test:

H_0: $p_1 - p_2 = 0$
H_a: $p_1 - p_2 > 0$

The test statistic is $z = \dfrac{(\hat{p}_1 - \hat{p}_2) - 0}{\sqrt{\hat{p}\hat{q}\left(\dfrac{1}{n_1} + \dfrac{1}{n_2}\right)}}$

$$= \dfrac{(.81 - .51) - 0}{\sqrt{.66(.34)\left(\dfrac{1}{100} + \dfrac{1}{100}\right)}} = \dfrac{.30}{.067} = 4.48$$

The rejection requires $\alpha = .05$ in the upper tail of the z distribution. From Table IV, Appendix B, $z_{.05} = 1.645$. The rejection region is $z > 1.645$.

Since the observed value of the test statistic falls in the rejection region ($z = 4.48 > 1.645$), H_0 is rejected. There is sufficient evidence to indicate the ability to identify food decreases with age at $\alpha = .05$.

b. The p-value is $P(z \geq 4.48) \approx 0$ (from Table IV, Appendix B). The probability of observing a test statistic of 4.48 or higher is ≈ 0 if the proportions are equal.

c. The intervals $\hat{p}_i \pm 3\sigma_{\hat{p}_i}$ cannot contain 0 or 1.

$\hat{p}_1 \pm 3\sigma_{\hat{p}_1} \Rightarrow .81 \pm 3\sqrt{\dfrac{.81(.19)}{100}} \Rightarrow .81 \pm .118 \Rightarrow (.692, .928)$

$\hat{p}_2 \pm 3\sigma_{\hat{p}_2} \Rightarrow .51 \pm 3\sqrt{\dfrac{.51(.49)}{100}} \Rightarrow .51 \pm .050 \Rightarrow (.46, .56)$

Since neither interval contains 0 or 1, the above test is valid.

10.15   From Exercise 10.14,

$\hat{p}_1 = \dfrac{x_1}{n_1} = \dfrac{475}{1000} = .475, \qquad \hat{p}_2 = \dfrac{x_2}{n_2} = \dfrac{305}{1000} = .305$

$\hat{p} = \dfrac{x_1 + x_2}{n_1 + n_2} = \dfrac{475 + 305}{1000 + 1000} = .39, \qquad \hat{q} = 1 - \hat{p} = 1 - .39 = .61$

To determine if the switch has hurt the firm's market share, we test:

H_0: $p_1 - p_2 = 0$
H_a: $p_1 - p_2 > 0$

The test statistic is $z = \dfrac{(\hat{p}_1 - \hat{p}_2) - 0}{\sqrt{\hat{p}\hat{q}\left(\dfrac{1}{n_1} + \dfrac{1}{n_2}\right)}}$

$$= \dfrac{(.475 - .305) - 0}{\sqrt{.39(.61)\left(\dfrac{1}{1000} + \dfrac{1}{1000}\right)}} = \dfrac{.17}{.0218} = 7.79$$

The rejection requires $\alpha = .05$ in the upper tail of the
z distribution. From Table IV, Appendix B, $z_{.05} = 1.645$. The
rejection region is $z > 1.645$.

Since the observed value of the test statistic falls in the rejection
region ($z = 7.79 > 1.645$), H_0 is rejected. There is sufficient
evidence to indicate the switch to the box has hurt the firm's market
share at $\alpha = .05$.

10.17 From Exercise 10.16,

$$\hat{p}_1 = \frac{1653}{9542} = .173, \qquad \hat{p}_2 = \frac{501}{6631} = .076$$

$$\hat{p} = \frac{x_1 + x_2}{n_1 + n_2} = \frac{1653 + 501}{9542 + 6631} = .133, \qquad \hat{q} = 1 - \hat{p} = 1 - .133 = .867$$

To determine if a difference exists between the true percentage of
shipments resulting in claims made against Company A and Company
B, we test:

$H_0: \quad p_1 - p_2 = 0$
$H_a: \quad p_1 - p_2 \neq 0$

The test statistic is $z = \dfrac{(\hat{p}_1 - \hat{p}_2) - 0}{\sqrt{\hat{p}\hat{q}\left(\frac{1}{n_1} + \frac{1}{n_2}\right)}}$

$$= \frac{(.173 - .076) - 0}{\sqrt{.133(.867)\left(\frac{1}{9542} + \frac{1}{6631}\right)}} = \frac{.097}{.0054} = 17.96$$

The rejection requires $\alpha/2 = .05/2 = .025$ in each tail of the z
distribution. From Table IV, Appendix B, $z_{.025} = 1.96$. The rejection
region is $z < -1.96$ or $z > 1.96$.

Since the observed value of the test statistic falls in the rejection
region ($z = 17.96 > 1.96$), H_0 is rejected. There is sufficient
evidence to indicate the true percentage of shipments resulting in
claims made against company A and company B differ at $\alpha = .05$.

Since there is a difference, and $\hat{p}_1 = .173$ is greater than $\hat{p}_2 = .076$,
company A has more claims made against it. Company B is superior.

10.19 Let p_1 = proportion of miners with respiratory symptoms and
p_2 = proportion of Duluth area men with respiratory symptoms. To
determine if the proportion of miners with respiratory symptoms
differs from the proportion of Duluth area men with respiratory
symptoms, we test:

$H_0: \quad p_1 - p_2 = 0$
$H_a: \quad p_1 - p_2 \neq 0$

The test statistic is $z = \dfrac{(\hat{p}_1 - \hat{p}_2) - 0}{\sqrt{\hat{p}\hat{q}\left(\dfrac{1}{n_1} + \dfrac{1}{n_2}\right)}}$ where $n_1 = 307$ and $n_2 = 35$

The rejection region requires $\alpha/2$ in each tail of the z distribution. The rejection region is $z < -z_{\alpha/2}$ or $z > z_{\alpha/2}$.

10.21 a. For confidence coefficient .99, $\alpha = .01$ and $\alpha/2 = .005$. From Table IV, Appendix B, $z_{.005} = 2.58$.

$$n_1 = n_2 = \frac{4(z_{.005})^2(p_1 q_1 + p_2 q_2)}{W^2} = \frac{4(2.58)^2(.3(.7) + .6(.4))}{.2^2}$$

$$= 299.538 \approx 300$$

      b. For confidence coefficient .90, $\alpha = .10$ and $\alpha/2 = .05$. From Table IV, Appendix B, $z_{.05} = 1.645$. Since no prior information is available for p_1 and p_2, we will approximate them with .5.

$$n_1 = n_2 = \frac{z_{.05}^2(p_1 q_1 + p_2 q_2)}{B^2} = \frac{1.645^2(.5(.5) + .5(.5))}{.05^2}$$

$$= 541.2 \approx 542$$

      c. For confidence coefficient .90, $\alpha = .10$ and $\alpha/2 = .05$. From Table IV, Appendix B, $z_{.05} = 1.645$.

$$n_1 = n_2 = \frac{z_{.05}^2(p_1 q_1 + p_2 q_2)}{B^2} = \frac{1.645^2(.1(.9) + .2(.8))}{.05^2}$$

$$= 270.6 \approx 271$$

10.23 For confidence coefficient .90, $\alpha = 1 - .90 = .10$ and $\alpha/2 = .10/2 = .05$. From Table IV, Appendix B, $z_{.05} = 1.645$.

$$n_1 = n_2 = \frac{(z_{\alpha/2})^2(p_1 q_1 + p_2 q_2)}{B^2} = \frac{1.645^2(.4(.6) + .4(.6))}{.04^2}$$

$$= 811.8 \approx 812$$

10.25 a. For confidence coefficient .80, $\alpha = 1 - .80 = .20$ and $\alpha/2 = .20/2 = .10$. From Table IV, Appendix B, $z_{.10} = 1.28$.

$$n_1 = n_2 = \frac{4(z_{\alpha/2})^2(p_1 q_1 + p_2 q_2)}{W^2}$$

Since we have no information on p_1 and p_2, we will use $p_1 = p_2 = .5$ to be conservative.

$$n_1 = n_2 = \frac{4(1.28^2)(.5(.5) + .5(.5))}{.06^2} = 910.2 \approx 911$$

The total number included should be $2(911) = 1822$.

b. For confidence coefficient .9, $\alpha = 1 - .9 = .1$ and $\alpha/2 = .1/2$ = .05. From Table IV, Appendix B, $z_{.05} = 1.645$.

$$n_1 = \frac{(z_{\alpha/2})^2(p_1 q_1)}{B^2} = \frac{1.645^2(.5(.5))}{.02^2} = 1691.3 \approx 1692$$

Thus, the necessary sample size is 1692 for both men and women.
This is much greater than the sample size of 911 each in part (a).

10.27 For confidence coefficient .95, $\alpha = 1 - .95 = .05$ and $\alpha/2 = .05/2 =$
.025. From Table IV, Appendix B, $z_{.025} = 1.96$. We estimate $p_1 = p_2 =$
.5 to be conservative.

$$n_1 = n_2 = \frac{(z_{\alpha/2})^2(p_1 q_1 + p_2 q_2)}{B^2} = \frac{1.96^2(.5(.5) + .5(.5))}{.02^2} = 4802$$

10.29 a. For df = 15, $\chi^2_{.05} = 24.9958$

b. For df = 100, $\chi^2_{.990} = 70.0648$

c. For df = 12, $\chi^2_{.10} = 18.5494$

d. For df = 2, $\chi^2_{.005} = 10.5966$

10.31 The characteristics of the multinomial experiment are:

1. The experiment consists of n identical trials.

2. There are k possible outcomes to each trial.

3. The probabilities of the k outcomes, denoted $p_1, p_2, \ldots, p_k$, remain the same from trial to trial, where $p_1 + p_2 + \ldots + p_k = 1$.

4. The trials are independent.

5. The random variables of interest are the counts $n_1, n_2, \ldots, n_k$ in each of the k cells.

The characteristics of the binomial are the same as those for the multinomial with k = 2.

10.33 a. Some preliminary calculations are:

$$E(n_1) = np_{1,0} = 300(.15) = 45$$
$$E(n_2) = np_{2,0} = 300(.25) = 75$$
$$E(n_3) = np_{3,0} = 300(.30) = 90$$
$$E(n_4) = np_{4,0} = 300(.20) = 60$$
$$E(n_5) = np_{5,0} = 300(.10) = 30$$

H_0: $p_1 = .15$, $p_2 = .25$, $p_3 = .30$, $p_4 = .20$, $p_5 = .10$

H_a: At least one of the multinomial probabilities does not equal its hypothesized value

The test statistic is $\chi^2 = \dfrac{\sum[n_i - E(n_i)]^2}{E(n_i)}$

$$= \frac{(48 - 45)^2}{45} + \frac{(69 - 75)^2}{75} + \frac{(83 - 90)^2}{90} + \frac{(61 - 60)^2}{60} + \frac{(39 - 30)^2}{30}$$

$= 3.941$

The rejection region requires $\alpha = .05$ in the upper tail of the χ^2 distribution with df $= k - 1 = 5 - 1 = 4$. From Table XIII, Appendix B, $\chi^2_{.05} = 9.48773$. The rejection region is $\chi^2 > 9.48773$.

Since the observed value of the test statistic does not fall in the rejection region ($\chi^2 = 3.941 \not> 9.48773$), H_0 is not rejected. There is insufficient evidence to indicate the multinomial probabilities differ from their hypothesized values at $\alpha = .05$.

b. The observed significance level is $P(\chi^2 \geq 3.941)$. From Table XIII, with df $= 4$, $P(\chi^2 \geq 3.941) > .10$.

10.35 For confidence coefficient .95, $\alpha = .05$ and $\alpha/2 = .05/2 = .025$. From Table IV, Appendix B, $z_{.025} = 1.96$.

$\hat{p}_3 = 60/206 = .291$

The confidence interval is

$$\hat{p} \pm z_{.025}\sqrt{\frac{\hat{p}\hat{q}}{n}} \Rightarrow .2913 \pm 1.96\sqrt{\frac{.291(.709)}{206}}$$

$\Rightarrow .2913 \pm .0620 \Rightarrow (.2293, .3533)$

10.37 a. To determine if the number of overweight trucks per week is distributed over the 7 days of the week in direct proportion to the volume of truck traffic, we test:

H_0: $p_1 = .191$, $p_2 = .198$, $p_3 = .187$, $p_4 = .180$, $p_5 = .155$, $p_6 = .043$, and $p_7 = .046$

H_a: At least one of the probabilities differs from the hypothesized value

$E(n_1) = np_{1,0} = 414(.191) = 79.074$
$E(n_2) = np_{2,0} = 414(.198) = 81.972$
$E(n_3) = np_{3,0} = 414(.187) = 77.418$
$E(n_4) = np_{4,0} = 414(.180) = 74.520$
$E(n_5) = np_{5,0} = 414(.155) = 64.170$
$E(n_6) = np_{6,0} = 414(.043) = 17.802$
$E(n_7) = np_{7,0} = 414(.046) = 19.044$

The test statistic is $\chi^2 = \sum \dfrac{(n_i - E(n_i))^2}{E(n_i)}$

$= \dfrac{(90 - 79.074)^2}{79.074} + \dfrac{(82 - 81.972)^2}{81.972} + \dfrac{(72 - 77.418)^2}{77.418}$

$+ \dfrac{(70 - 74.520)^2}{74.520} + \dfrac{(51 - 64.170)^2}{64.170} + \dfrac{(18 - 17.802)^2}{17.802}$

$+ \dfrac{(31 - 19.044)^2}{19.044} = 12.374$

The rejection region requires $\alpha = .05$ in the upper tail of the χ^2 distribution with df = $k - 1 = 7 - 1 = 6$. From Table XIII, Appendix B, $\chi^2_{.05} = 12.5916$. The rejection region is $\chi^2 > 12.5916$.

Since the observed value of the test statistic does not fall in the rejection region ($\chi^2 = 12.374 \not> 12.5916$), H_0 is not rejected. There is insufficient evidence to indicate the number of overweight trucks per week is distributed over the 7 days of the week is not in direct proportion to the volume of truck traffic at $\alpha = .05$.

b. The p-value is $P(\chi^2 \geq 12.374)$. From Table XIII, Appendix B, with df = $k - 1 = 7 - 1 = 6$, $.05 < P(\chi^2 \geq 12.374) = .10$.

10.39 a. Some preliminary calculations are:

$E(n_1) = np_{1,0} = 300(.90) = 270$
$E(n_2) = np_{2,1} = 300(.04) = 36$
$E(n_3) = np_{3,0} = 300(.03) = 9$
$E(n_4) = np_{4,0} = 300(.02) = 6$
$E(n_5) = np_{5,0} = 300(.005) = 1.5$
$E(n_6) = np_{6,0} = 300(.005) = 1.5$

To determine if the proportions of printed invoices in the six error categories differ from the proportions using the previous format, we test:

H_0: $p_1 = .9$, $p_2 = .04$, $p_3 = .03$, $p_4 = .02$, $p_5 = .005$, and $p_6 = .005$
H_a: At least one of the proportions differs from the hypothesized value

The test statistic is $\chi^2 = \sum \dfrac{(n_i - E(n_i))^2}{E(n_i)} = \dfrac{(150 - 270)^2}{270}$

$+ \dfrac{(120 - 36)^2}{36} + \dfrac{(15 - 9)^2}{9} + \dfrac{(7 - 6)^2}{6} + \dfrac{(4 - 1.5)^2}{1.5}$

$+ \dfrac{(4 - 1.5)^2}{1.5} = 1038$

The rejection region requires α = .05 in the upper tail of the χ^2 distribution with df = k - 1 = 6 - 1 = 5. From Table XIII, Appendix B, $\chi^2_{.05}$ = 11.0705. The rejection region is $\chi^2 > 11.0705$.

Since the observed value of the test statistic falls in the rejection region (χ^2 = 1038 > 11.0705), H_0 is rejected. There is sufficient evidence to indicate the proportions of printed invoices in the six error categories differ from the proportions using the previous format at α = .05.

b. The observed significance level is $P(\chi^2 > 1038)$. From Table XIII, Appendix B, with df = 5, $P(\chi^2 > 1038) < .005$. Since $P(\chi^2 > 16.7496)$ = .005, we know $P(\chi^2 > 1038)$ is much smaller than .005 or approximately 0.

10.41 Some preliminary calculations are:

$E(n_1) = np_{1,0} = 6478(.25) = 1619.5$
$E(n_2) = np_{2,0} = 6478(.60) = 3886.8$
$E(n_3) = np_{3,0} = 6478(.15) = 971.7$

To determine if the proportions of the readership in the three categories have changed since the previous survey, we test

H_0: p_1 = .25, p_2 = .60, p_3 = .15
H_a: At least one of the multinomial probabilities differs from the hypothesized value

The test statistic is $\chi^2 = \sum \dfrac{[n_i - E(n_i)]^2}{E(n_i)}$

$= \dfrac{(1653 - 1619.5)^2}{1619.5} + \dfrac{(3946 - 3886.8)^2}{3886.8} + \dfrac{(879 - 971.7)^2}{971.7} = 10.44$

The rejection region requires α = .05 in the upper tail of the χ^2 distribution with df = k - 1 = 3 - 1 = 2. From Table XIII, Appendix B, $\chi^2_{.05}$ = 5.99147. The rejection region is $\chi^2 > 5.99147$.

Since the observed value of the test statistic falls in the rejection region (χ^2 = 10.44 > 5.99147), H_0 is rejected. There is sufficient evidence to indicate the proportions of the readership in the three categories have changed since the previous survey at α = .05.

10.43 a. H_0: The row and column variables are independent
H_a: The row and column variables are dependent

b. The test statistic is $\chi^2 = \sum\sum \dfrac{[n_{ij} - \hat{E}(n_{ij})]^2}{\hat{E}(n_{ij})}$

The rejection region requires α = .01 in the upper tail of the χ^2 distribution with df = (r - 1)(c - 1) = (2 - 1)(3 - 1) = 2. From

Table XIII, Appendix B, $\chi^2_{.01} = 9.21034$. The rejection region is $\chi^2 > 9.21034$.

c. The estimated expected cell counts are:

$$\hat{E}(n_{11}) = \frac{r_1 c_1}{n} = \frac{95(25)}{165} = 14.39$$

$$\hat{E}(n_{12}) = \frac{r_1 c_2}{n} = \frac{95(62)}{165} = 35.70$$

$$\hat{E}(n_{13}) = \frac{r_1 c_3}{n} = \frac{95(78)}{165} = 44.91$$

$$\hat{E}(n_{21}) = \frac{r_2 c_1}{n} = \frac{70(25)}{165} = 10.61$$

$$\hat{E}(n_{22}) = \frac{r_2 c_2}{n} = \frac{70(62)}{165} = 26.30$$

$$\hat{E}(n_{23}) = \frac{r_2 c_3}{n} = \frac{70(78)}{165} = 33.09$$

d. The test statistic is $\chi^2 = \frac{(10 - 14.39)^2}{14.39} + \frac{(32 - 35.70)^2}{35.70}$

$$+ \frac{(53 - 44.91)^2}{44.91} + \frac{(15 - 10.61)^2}{10.61} + \frac{(30 - 26.30)^2}{26.30}$$

$$+ \frac{(25 - 33.09)^2}{33.09} = 7.49$$

Since the observed value of the test statistic does not fall in the rejection region ($\chi^2 = 7.49 \not> 9.21034$), H_0 is not rejected. There is insufficient evidence to indicate the row and column classifications are dependent at $\alpha = .01$.

10.45 Some preliminary calculations are:

$$\hat{E}(n_{11}) = \frac{r_1 c_1}{n} = \frac{156(132)}{437} = 47.121 \qquad \hat{E}(n_{23}) = \frac{r_2 c_3}{n} = \frac{184(141)}{437} = 59.368$$

$$\hat{E}(n_{12}) = \frac{r_1 c_2}{n} = \frac{156(164)}{437} = 58.545 \qquad \hat{E}(n_{31}) = \frac{r_3 c_1}{n} = \frac{97(132)}{437} = 29.300$$

$$\hat{E}(n_{13}) = \frac{r_1 c_3}{n} = \frac{156(141)}{437} = 50.334 \qquad \hat{E}(n_{32}) = \frac{r_3 c_2}{n} = \frac{97(164)}{437} = 36.403$$

$$\hat{E}(n_{21}) = \frac{r_2 c_1}{n} = \frac{184(132)}{437} = 55.579 \qquad \hat{E}(n_{33}) = \frac{r_3 c_3}{n} = \frac{97(141)}{437} = 31.297$$

$$\hat{E}(n_{22}) = \frac{r_2 c_2}{n} = \frac{184(164)}{437} = 69.053$$

H_0: The classifications A and B are independent
H_a: The classifications A and B are dependent

The test statistic is $\chi^2 = \sum\sum \dfrac{[n_{ij} - \hat{E}(n_{ij})]^2}{\hat{E}(n_{ij})}$

$$= \frac{(39 - 47.121)^2}{47.121} + \frac{(75 - 58.545)^2}{58.545} + \cdots + \frac{(29 - 31.297)^2}{31.297} = 15.27$$

The rejection region requires $\alpha = .05$ in the upper tail of the χ^2 distribution with df $= (r - 1)(c - 1) = (3 - 1)(3 - 1) = 4$. From Table XIII, Appendix B, $\chi^2_{.05} = 9.48773$. The rejection region is $\chi^2 > 9.48773$.

Since the observed value of the test statistic falls in the rejection region ($\chi^2 = 15.27 > 9.48773$), H_0 is rejected. There is sufficient evidence to indicate the classifications A and B are dependent at $\alpha = .05$.

10.47 Some preliminary calculations are:

$\hat{E}(n_{11}) = \dfrac{r_1 c_1}{n} = \dfrac{140(90)}{611} = 20.622$ $\hat{E}(n_{23}) = \dfrac{r_2 c_3}{n} = \dfrac{190(199)}{611} = 61.882$

$\hat{E}(n_{12}) = \dfrac{r_1 c_2}{n} = \dfrac{140(150)}{611} = 34.370$ $\hat{E}(n_{24}) = \dfrac{r_2 c_4}{n} = \dfrac{190(172)}{611} = 53.486$

$\hat{E}(n_{13}) = \dfrac{r_1 c_3}{n} = \dfrac{140(199)}{611} = 45.597$ $\hat{E}(n_{31}) = \dfrac{r_3 c_1}{n} = \dfrac{281(90)}{611} = 41.391$

$\hat{E}(n_{14}) = \dfrac{r_1 c_4}{n} = \dfrac{140(172)}{611} = 39.411$ $\hat{E}(n_{32}) = \dfrac{r_3 c_2}{n} = \dfrac{281(150)}{611} = 68.985$

$\hat{E}(n_{21}) = \dfrac{r_2 c_1}{n} = \dfrac{190(90)}{611} = 27.987$ $\hat{E}(n_{33}) = \dfrac{r_3 c_3}{n} = \dfrac{281(199)}{611} = 91.520$

$\hat{E}(n_{22}) = \dfrac{r_2 c_2}{n} = \dfrac{190(150)}{611} = 46.645$ $\hat{E}(n_{34}) = \dfrac{r_3 c_4}{n} = \dfrac{281(172)}{611} = 79.103$

To determine if the two classifications are dependent, we test:

H_0: The classifications A and B are independent
H_a: The classifications A and B are dependent

The test statistic is $\chi^2 = \sum\sum \dfrac{[n_{ij} - \hat{E}(n_{ij})]^2}{\hat{E}(n_{ij})}$

$$= \frac{(22 - 20.622)^2}{20.622} + \frac{(38 - 34.370)^2}{34.370} + \cdots + \frac{(68 - 79.103)^2}{79.103} = 38.02$$

The rejection region requires $\alpha = .05$ in the upper tail of the χ^2 distribution with df $= (r - 1)(c - 1) = (3 - 1)(4 - 1) = 6$. From Table XIII, Appendix B, $\chi^2_{.05} = 12.5916$. The rejection region is $\chi^2 > 12.5916$.

Since the observed value of the test statistic falls in the rejection region ($\chi^2 = 38.02 > 12.5916$), H_0 is rejected. There is sufficient evidence to indicate the two classifications A and B are dependent at $\alpha = .05$.

10.49 The estimated expected cell counts are computed assuming the two classifications are independent. Thus, the test statistic is also calculated assuming the two classifications are independent. The distribution of the test statistic has a chi-square distribution only if the two classifications are independent.

10.51 a. Some preliminary calculations are:

For union members:

$\hat{E}(n_{11}) = \dfrac{r_1 c_1}{n} = \dfrac{44(155)}{314} = 21.72$ $\hat{E}(n_{23}) = \dfrac{r_2 c_3}{n} = \dfrac{189(28)}{314} = 16.85$

$\hat{E}(n_{12}) = \dfrac{r_1 c_2}{n} = \dfrac{44(116)}{314} = 16.25$ $\hat{E}(n_{24}) = \dfrac{r_2 c_4}{n} = \dfrac{189(15)}{314} = 9.03$

$\hat{E}(n_{13}) = \dfrac{r_1 c_3}{n} = \dfrac{44(28)}{314} = 3.92$ $\hat{E}(n_{31}) = \dfrac{r_3 c_1}{n} = \dfrac{81(155)}{314} = 39.98$

$\hat{E}(n_{14}) = \dfrac{r_1 c_4}{n} = \dfrac{44(15)}{314} = 2.10$ $\hat{E}(n_{32}) = \dfrac{r_3 c_2}{n} = \dfrac{81(116)}{314} = 29.92$

$\hat{E}(n_{21}) = \dfrac{r_2 c_1}{n} = \dfrac{189(155)}{314} = 93.30$ $\hat{E}(n_{33}) = \dfrac{r_3 c_3}{n} = \dfrac{81(28)}{314} = 7.22$

$\hat{E}(n_{22}) = \dfrac{r_2 c_2}{n} = \dfrac{189(116)}{314} = 69.82$ $\hat{E}(n_{34}) = \dfrac{r_3 c_4}{n} = \dfrac{81(15)}{314} = 3.87$

H_0: Level of confidence and job satisfaction are independent
H_a: Level of confidence and job satisfaction are dependent

The test statistic is $\chi^2 = \sum\sum \dfrac{[n_{ij} - \hat{E}(n_{ij})]^2}{\hat{E}(n_{ij})}$

$= \dfrac{(26 - 21.72)^2}{21.72} + \dfrac{(15 - 16.25^2}{16.25} + \dfrac{(2 - 3.92)^2}{3.92}$

$+ \ldots + \dfrac{(9 - 3.87)^2}{3.87} = 13.36$

The rejection region requires $\alpha = .05$ in the upper tail of the χ^2 distribution with df $= (r - 1)(c - 1) = (3 - 1)(4 - 1) = 6$. From Table XIII, Appendix B, $\chi^2_{.05} = 12.5916$. The rejection region is $\chi^2 > 12.5916$.

Since the observed value of the test statistic falls in the rejection region ($\chi^2 = 13.36 > 12.5916$), H_0 is rejected. There is sufficient evidence to indicate the level of confidence and job satisfaction are related at $\alpha = .05$ for union members.

For nonunion members:

$$\hat{E}(n_{11}) = \frac{r_1 c_1}{n} = \frac{180(430)}{775} = 99.87 \quad \hat{E}(n_{23}) = \frac{r_2 c_3}{n} = \frac{443(69)}{775} = 39.44$$

$$\hat{E}(n_{12}) = \frac{r_1 c_2}{n} = \frac{180(245)}{775} = 56.90 \quad \hat{E}(n_{24}) = \frac{r_2 c_4}{n} = \frac{443(31)}{775} = 17.72$$

$$\hat{E}(n_{13}) = \frac{r_1 c_3}{n} = \frac{180(69)}{775} = 16.03 \quad \hat{E}(n_{31}) = \frac{r_3 c_1}{n} = \frac{152(430)}{775} = 84.34$$

$$\hat{E}(n_{14}) = \frac{r_1 c_4}{n} = \frac{180(31)}{775} = 7.20 \quad \hat{E}(n_{32}) = \frac{r_3 c_2}{n} = \frac{152(245)}{775} = 48.05$$

$$\hat{E}(n_{21}) = \frac{r_2 c_1}{n} = \frac{443(430)}{775} = 245.79 \quad \hat{E}(n_{33}) = \frac{r_3 c_3}{n} = \frac{152(69)}{775} = 13.53$$

$$\hat{E}(n_{22}) = \frac{r_2 c_2}{n} = \frac{443(245)}{775} = 140.05 \quad \hat{E}(n_{34}) = \frac{r_3 c_4}{n} = \frac{152(31)}{775} = 6.08$$

H_0: Level of confidence and job satisfaction are independent
H_a: Level of confidence and job satisfaction are dependent

The test statistic is $\chi^2 = \sum\sum \dfrac{[n_{ij} - \hat{E}(n_{ij})]^2}{\hat{E}(n_{ij})}$

$$= \frac{(111 - 99.87)^2}{99.87} + \frac{(52 - 56.90)^2}{56.90} + \frac{(13 - 16.03)^2}{16.03}$$

$$+ \ldots + \frac{(9 - 6.08)^2}{6.08} = 9.16$$

The rejection region is $\chi^2 > 12.5916$. Since the observed value of the test statistic does not fall in the rejection region ($\chi^2 = 9.16 \not> 12.5916$), H_0 is not rejected. There is insufficient evidence to indicate the level of confidence and job satisfaction are related for nonunion workers at $\alpha = .05$.

b. For the union workers, the p-value = $P(\chi^2 \geq 13.36)$. Using Table XIII, Appendix B, with df = 6, $.025 < P(\chi^2 \geq 13.36) < .05$.

For the nonunion workers, the p-value = $P(\chi^2 \geq 9.16)$.
$.1 < P(\chi^2 \geq 9.16) < .9$

10.53 Some preliminary calculations are:

$$\hat{E}(n_{11}) = \frac{r_1 c_1}{n} = \frac{67(83)}{311} = 17.88 \quad \hat{E}(n_{12}) = \frac{67(117)}{311} = 25.21$$

$$\hat{E}(n_{21}) = \frac{69(83)}{311} = 18.41 \quad \hat{E}(n_{22}) = \frac{69(117)}{311} = 25.96$$

$$\hat{E}(n_{31}) = \frac{104(83)}{311} = 27.76 \quad \hat{E}(n_{32}) = \frac{104(117)}{311} = 39.13$$

$$\hat{E}(n_{41}) = \frac{71(83)}{311} = 18.95 \quad \hat{E}(_{42}) = \frac{71(117)}{311} = 26.71$$

$$\hat{E}(n_{13}) = \frac{67(79)}{311} = 17.02 \qquad \hat{E}(n_{14}) = \frac{67(32)}{311} = 6.89$$

$$\hat{E}(n_{23}) = \frac{69(79)}{311} = 17.53 \qquad \hat{E}(n_{24}) = \frac{69(32)}{311} = 7.10$$

$$\hat{E}(n_{33}) = \frac{104(79)}{311} = 26.42 \qquad \hat{E}(n_{34}) = \frac{104(32)}{311} = 10.70$$

$$\hat{E}(n_{43}) = \frac{71(79)}{311} = 18.04 \qquad \hat{E}(n_{44}) = \frac{71(32)}{311} = 7.31$$

To determine if there is a relationship between length of stay and hospitalization coverage, we test:

H_0: Length of stay and hospitalization coverage are independent
H_a: Length of stay and hospitalization coverage are dependent

The test statistic is $\chi^2 = \sum\sum \dfrac{(n_{ij} - \hat{E}(n_{ij}))^2}{\hat{E}(n_{ij})}$

$$= \frac{(26 - 17.88)^2}{17.88} + \frac{(21 - 18.41)^2}{18.41} + \frac{(25 - 27.76)^2}{27.76} + \cdots$$

$$+ \frac{(11 - 7.31)^2}{7.31} = 40.70$$

The rejection region requires $\alpha = .01$ in the upper tail of the χ^2 distribution with df $= (r - 1)(c - 1) = (4 - 1)(4 - 1) = 9$. From Table XIII, Appendix B, $\chi^2_{.01} = 21.666$. The rejection region is $\chi^2 > 21.666$.

Since the observed value of the test statistic falls in the rejection region ($\chi^2 = 40.70 > 21.666$), H_0 is rejected. There is sufficient evidence to indicate length of stay and hospitalization coverage are dependent at $\alpha = .01$.

10.55 Some preliminary calculations are:

$$\hat{p}_1 = \frac{x_1}{n_1} = \frac{12}{500} = .024 \qquad \hat{p}_2 = \frac{x_2}{n_2} = \frac{15}{450} = .0333$$

$$\hat{p} = \frac{x_1 + x_2}{n_1 + n_2} = \frac{12 + 15}{500 + 450} = .0284$$

To determine if there is a difference in the proportions preferring the new brand between the 2 regions, we test:

H_0: $p_1 - p_2 = 0$
H_a: $p_1 - p_2 \neq 0$

The test statistic is $z = \dfrac{(\hat{p}_1 - \hat{p}_2) - 0}{\sqrt{\hat{p}\hat{q}\left(\dfrac{1}{n_1} + \dfrac{1}{n_2}\right)}}$

$$= \frac{(.024 - .0333) - 0}{\sqrt{.0284(.9716)\left(\frac{1}{500} + \frac{1}{450}\right)}} = -.86$$

The rejection region requires $\alpha/2 = .05/2 = .025$ in each tail of the z distribution. From Table IV, Appendix B, $z_{.025} = 1.96$. The rejection region is $z < -1.96$ or $z > 1.96$.

Since the observed value of the test statistic does not fall in the rejection region ($z = -.86 \not< -1.96$), H_0 is not rejected. There is insufficient evidence to indicate there is a difference in the proportions preferring the new brand between the two regions at $\alpha = .05$.

Since there is no evidence to indicate a difference in the proportions preferring the new brand, the two advertising agencies are equally effective.

10.57 a. No. If January change is down, half the next 11-month changes are up and half are down.

   b. The percentages of years for which the 11-month movement is up based on January change are found by dividing the numbers in the first column by the corresponding row total and multiplying by 100. We also divide the first column total by the overall total and multiply by 100.

   January Change:

   Up $\dfrac{25}{35} \cdot 100 = 71.4\%$

   Down $\dfrac{9}{18} \cdot 100 = 50\%$

   Total $\dfrac{34}{53} \cdot 100 = 64.2\%$

   c. H_0: The January change and the next 11-month change are independent
      H_a: The January change and the next 11-month change are dependent

   d. Some preliminary calculations are:

   $\hat{E}(n_{11}) = \dfrac{r_1 c_1}{n} = \dfrac{35(34)}{53} = 22.453$ $\hat{E}(n_{12}) = \dfrac{35(19)}{53} = 12.547$

   $\hat{E}(n_{21}) = \dfrac{18(34)}{53} = 11.547$ $\hat{E}(n_{22}) = \dfrac{18(19)}{53} = 6.453$

The test statistic is $\chi^2 = \sum\sum \dfrac{(n_{ij} - \hat{E}(n_{ij}))^2}{\hat{E}(n_{ij})}$

$$= \frac{(25 - 22.453)^2}{22.453} + \frac{(9 - 11.547)^2}{11.547} + \frac{(10 - 12.547)^2}{12.547}$$

$$+ \frac{(9 - 6.453)^2}{6.453} = 2.373$$

The rejection region requires $\alpha = .05$ in the upper tail of the χ^2 distribution with df = $(r - 1)(c - 1) = (2 - 1)(2 - 1) = 1$. From Table XIII, Appendix B, $\chi^2_{.05} = 3.84146$. The rejection region is $\chi^2 > 3.84146$.

Since the observed value of the test statistic does not fall in the rejection region ($\chi^2 = 2.373 \ngtr 3.84146$), H_0 is not rejected. There is insufficient evidence to indicate the January change and the next 11-month change are dependent at $\alpha = .05$.

e.   Yes. For $\alpha = .10$, the rejection region is $\chi^2 > \chi^2_{.10} = 2.70554$, from Table XIII, Appendix B, with df = 1. Since the observed value of the test statistic does not fall in the rejection region ($\chi^2 = 2.373 \ngtr 2.70554$), H_0 is not rejected. The conclusion is the same.

10.59   a.   The contingency table is:

		Committee		
		Acceptable	Rejected	Totals
Inspector	Acceptable	101	23	124
	Rejected	10	19	29
	Totals	111	42	153

b.   Yes. To plot the percentages, first convert frequencies to percentages by dividing the numbers in each column by the column total and multiplying by 100. Also, divide the row totals by the overall total and multiply by 100.

		Acceptable	Rejected	
Inspector	Acceptable	$\frac{101}{111} \cdot 100 = 90.99\%$	$\frac{23}{42} \cdot 100 = 54.76\%$	$\frac{124}{153} \cdot 100 = 81.05\%$
	Rejected	$\frac{10}{100} \cdot 100 = 9.01\%$	$\frac{19}{42} \cdot 100 = 45.23\%$	$\frac{29}{153} \cdot 100 = 18.95\%$

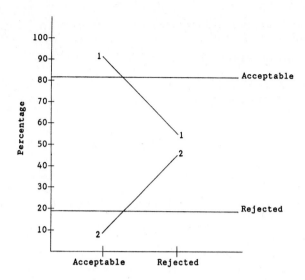

From the plot, it appears there is a relationship.

c. Some preliminary calculations are:

$$\hat{E}(n_{11}) = \frac{r_1 c_1}{n} = \frac{124(111)}{153} = 89.961 \quad \hat{E}(n_{12}) = \frac{r_1 c_2}{n} = \frac{124(42)}{153} = 34.039$$

$$\hat{E}(n_{21}) = \frac{r_2 c_1}{n} = \frac{29(111)}{153} = 21.039 \quad \hat{E}(n_{22}) = \frac{r_2 c_2}{n} = \frac{29(42)}{153} = 7.961$$

To determine if the inspector's classifications and the committee's classifications are related, we test:

H_0: The inspector's and committee's classification are independent

H_a: The inspector's and committee's classifications are dependent

The test statistic is $\chi^2 = \sum\sum \dfrac{[n_{ij} - \hat{E}(n_{ij})]^2}{\hat{E}(n_{ij})}$

$$= \frac{(101 - 89.961)^2}{89.961} + \frac{(23 - 34.039)^2}{34.039} + \frac{(10 - 21.039)^2}{21.039}$$

$$+ \frac{(19 - 7.961)^2}{7.961} = 26.034$$

The rejection region requires $\alpha = .05$ in the upper tail of the χ^2 distribution with df $= (r - 1)(c - 1) = (2 - 1)(2 - 1) = 1$. From Table XIII, Appendix B, $\chi^2_{.05} = 3.84146$. The rejection region is $\chi^2 > 3.84146$.

Since the observed value of the test statistic falls in the rejection region ($\chi^2 = 26.034 > 3.84146$), H_0 is rejected. There is sufficient evidence to indicate the inspector's and committee's classifications are related at $\alpha = .05$. This indicates that the inspector and committee tend to make the same decisions.

10.61 a. $\hat{p}_1 = .45 + .24 = .69$

For confidence coefficient .90, $\alpha = 1 - .90 = .10$ and $\alpha/2 = .10/2 = .05$. From Table IV, Appendix B, $z_{.05} = 1.645$. The confidence interval is:

$$\hat{p}_1 \pm z_{.05}\sqrt{\frac{\hat{p}_1\hat{q}_1}{n_1}} \Rightarrow .69 \pm 1.645\sqrt{\frac{.69(.31)}{387}}$$

$$\Rightarrow .69 \pm .039 \Rightarrow (.651, .729)$$

b. $\hat{p}_2 = .23 + .47 = .70$. The confidence interval is:

$$(\hat{p}_1 - \hat{p}_2) \pm z_{.05}\sqrt{\frac{\hat{p}_1\hat{q}_1}{n_1} + \frac{\hat{p}_2\hat{q}_2}{n_2}}$$

$$\Rightarrow (.69 - .70) \pm 1.645\sqrt{\frac{.69(.31)}{387} + \frac{.7(.3)}{311}}$$

$$\Rightarrow -.01 \pm .058 \Rightarrow (-.068, .048)$$

c. The intervals $\hat{p}_i \pm 3\sigma_{\hat{p}_i}$ cannot contain 0 or 1.

$$\hat{p}_1 \pm 3\sigma_{\hat{p}_1} \Rightarrow .69 \pm 3\sqrt{\frac{.69(.31)}{387}} \Rightarrow .69 \pm .071 \Rightarrow (.619, .761)$$

$$\hat{p}_2 \pm 3\sigma_{\hat{p}_2} \Rightarrow .70 \pm 3\sqrt{\frac{.70(.30)}{311}} \Rightarrow .70 \pm .078 \Rightarrow (.622, .778)$$

Since neither interval contains 0 or 1, the results are valid.

10.63 a. First, we arrange the data in a table.

| | | FIRM'S LEGAL STRUCTURE | | | |
		Sole Proprietorship	Partnership	Corporation	
Loan Status	Defaulted	14	10	12	36
	Paid off or current	13	1	14	28
		27	11	26	64

$$\hat{E}(n_{11}) = \frac{r_1 c_1}{n} = \frac{36(27)}{64} = 15.1875$$

$$\hat{E}(n_{12}) = \frac{36(11)}{64} = 6.1875$$

$$\hat{E}(n_{13}) = \frac{36(26)}{64} = 14.625$$

$$\hat{E}(n_{21}) = \frac{28(27)}{64} = 11.8125$$

$$\hat{E}(n_{22}) = \frac{28(11)}{64} = 4.8125$$

$$\hat{E}(n_{23}) = \frac{28(26)}{64} = 11.375$$

To determine if a relationship exists between the legal structure and the success or failure of the loan, we test:

H_0: Legal structure and loan success or failure are independent

H_a: Legal structure and loan success or failure are dependent

The test statistic is $\chi^2 = \sum\sum \dfrac{(n_{ij} - \hat{E}(n_{ij}))^2}{\hat{E}(n_{ij})}$

$$= \frac{(14 - 15.1875)^2}{15.1875} + \frac{(10 - 6.1875)^2}{6.1875} + \frac{(12 - 14.625)^2}{14.625}$$

$$+ \frac{(13 - 11.8125)^2}{11.8125} + \frac{(1 - 4.8125)^2}{4.8125} + \frac{(14 - 11.375)^2}{11.375} = 6.66$$

The rejection region requires $\alpha = .05$ in the upper tail of the χ^2 distribution with df $= (r - 1)(c - 1) = (2 - 1)(3 - 1) = 2$. From Table XIII, Appendix B, $\chi^2_{.05} = 5.99147$. The rejection region is $\chi^2 > 5.99147$.

Since the observed value of the test statistic falls in the rejection region ($\chi^2 = 6.66 > 5.99147$), H_0 is rejected. There is sufficient evidence to indicate a relationship exists between the legal structure and the success or failure of the loan at $\alpha = .05$.

b.   The observed significance level is $P(\chi^2 > 6.66)$. From Table XIII, Appendix B, with df $= 2$, $.025 < P(\chi^2 > 6.66) < .05$.

c.   The necessary assumption is:

1.   The sample size will be large enough so that, for every cell, the expected cell count, $E(n_{ij})$, will be equal to 5 or more.

10.65   Some preliminary calculations are:

$$\hat{E}(n_{11}) = \frac{r_1 c_1}{n} = \frac{75(152)}{300} = 38 = \hat{E}(n_{21}) = \hat{E}(n_{31}) = \hat{E}(n_{41})$$

$$\hat{E}(n_{12}) = \frac{r_1 c_2}{n} = \frac{75(122)}{300} = 30.5 = \hat{E}(n_{22}) = \hat{E}(n_{32}) = \hat{E}(n_{42})$$

$$\hat{E}(n_{13}) = \frac{r_1 c_3}{n} = \frac{75(26)}{300} = 6.5 = \hat{E}(n_{23}) = \hat{E}(n_{33}) = \hat{E}(n_{43})$$

To determine if customer preferences are different for the four restaurants, we test:

H_0: Customer preferences and restaurants are independent
H_a: Customer preferences and restaurants are dependent

The test statistic is $\chi^2 = \sum\sum \dfrac{[n_{ij} - \hat{E}(n_{ij})]^2}{\hat{E}(n_{ij})}$

$$= \frac{(38 - 38)^2}{38} + \frac{(32 - 30.5)^2}{30.5} + \frac{(5 - 6.5)^2}{6.5} + \ldots + \frac{(8 - 6.5)^2}{6.5}$$

$$= 2.60$$

The rejection region requires $\alpha = .10$ in the upper tail of the χ^2 distribution with df $= (r - 1)(c - 1) = (4 - 1)(3 - 1) = 6$. From Table XIII, Appendix B, $\chi^2_{.10} = 10.6446$. The rejection region is $\chi^2 > 10.6466$.

Since the observed value of the test statistic does not fall in the rejection region ($\chi^2 = 2.60 \not> 10.6446$), H_0 is not rejected. There is insufficient evidence to indicate the customer preferences are different for the four restaurants at $\alpha = .10$.

10.67   Some preliminary calculations are:

$$\hat{p}_1 = \frac{x_1}{n_1} = \frac{47}{525} = .0895 \qquad \hat{p}_2 = \frac{x_2}{n_2} = \frac{22}{375} = .0587$$

For confidence coefficient .95, $\alpha = 1 - .95 = .05$ and $\alpha/2 = .05/2 = .025$. From Table IV, Appendix B, $z_{.025} = 1.96$. The confidence interval is:

$$(\hat{p}_1 - \hat{p}_2) \pm z_{.025}\sqrt{\frac{\hat{p}_1\hat{q}_1}{n_1} + \frac{\hat{p}_2\hat{q}_2}{n_2}}$$

$$\Rightarrow (.0895 - .0587) \pm 1.96\sqrt{\frac{.0895(.9105)}{525} + \frac{.0587(.9413)}{375}}$$

$$\Rightarrow .0308 \pm .0341 \Rightarrow (-.0033, .0649)$$

10.69   Some preliminary calculations are:

$$\hat{E}(n_{11}) = \frac{r_1 c_1}{n} = \frac{200(300)}{600} = 100 = \hat{E}(n_{21}) = \hat{E}(n_{31})$$

$$\hat{E}(n_{12}) = \frac{r_1 c_2}{n} = \frac{200(175)}{600} = 58.333 = \hat{E}(n_{22}) = \hat{E}(n_{32})$$

$$\hat{E}(n_{13}) = \frac{r_1 c_3}{n} = \frac{200(125)}{600} = 41.667 = \hat{E}(n_{23}) = \hat{E}(n_{33})$$

To determine if a relationship exists between income and view on government regulation of private enterprise, we test:

H₀: Income and view on government regulation of private enterprise are independent
H_a: Income and view on government regulation of private enterprise are dependent

The test statistic is $\chi^2 = \sum\sum \dfrac{[n_{ij} - \hat{E}(n_{ij})]^2}{\hat{E}(n_{ij})}$

$$= \frac{(125 - 100)^2}{100} + \frac{(48 - 58.333)^2}{58.333} + \frac{(27 - 41.667)^2}{41.667}$$

$$+ \ldots + \frac{(59 - 41.667)^2}{41.667} = 30.507$$

The rejection region requires $\alpha = .05$ in the upper tail of the χ^2 distribution with df $= (r - 1)(c - 1) = (3 - 1)(3 - 1) = 4$. From Table XIII, Appendix B, $\chi^2_{.05} = 9.48773$. The rejection region is $\chi^2 > 9.48773$.

Since the observed value of the test statistic falls in the rejection region ($\chi^2 = 30.507 > 9.48773$), H₀ is rejected. There is sufficient evidence to indicate income and view on government regulation of private enterprise are dependent at $\alpha = .05$.

10.71 Some preliminary calculations are:

$\hat{E}(n_{11}) = \dfrac{r_1 c_1}{n} = \dfrac{117(155)}{300} = 60.45$ $\qquad$ $\hat{E}(n_{13}) = \dfrac{117(31)}{300} = 12.09$

$\hat{E}(n_{21}) = \dfrac{120(155)}{300} = 62$ $\qquad$ $\hat{E}(n_{23}) = \dfrac{120(31)}{300} = 12.4$

$\hat{E}(n_{31}) = \dfrac{63(155)}{300} = 32.55$ $\qquad$ $\hat{E}(n_{33}) = \dfrac{63(31)}{300} = 6.51$

$\hat{E}(n_{12}) = \dfrac{117(114)}{300} = 44.46$

$\hat{E}(n_{22}) = \dfrac{120(114)}{300} = 45.6$

$\hat{E}(n_{32}) = \dfrac{63(114)}{300} = 23.94$

To determine if time and size of purchase are related, we test:

H₀: Time and size of purchase are independent
H_a: Time and size of purchase are dependent

The test statistic is $\chi^2 = \sum\sum \dfrac{(n_{ij} - \hat{E}(n_{ij}))^2}{\hat{E}(n_{ij})}$

$$= \frac{(65 - 60.45)^2}{60.45} + \frac{(61 - 62)^2}{62} + \frac{(29 - 32.55)^2}{32.55} + \cdots$$

$$+ \frac{(7 - 6.51)^2}{6.51} = 3.13$$

The rejection region requires $\alpha = .05$ in the upper tail of the χ^2 distribution with df $= (r - 1)(c - 1) = (3 - 1)(3 - 1) = 4$. From Table XIII, Appendix B, $\chi^2_{.05} = 9.48773$. The rejection region is $\chi^2 > 9.48773$.

Since the observed value of the test statistic does not fall in the rejection region ($\chi^2 = 3.13 \ngtr 9.48773$), H_0 is not rejected. There is insufficient evidence to indicate time and size of purchase are related at $\alpha = .05$.

10.73   a.   Some preliminary calculations are:

$\hat{E}(n_{11}) = \dfrac{r_1 c_1}{n} = \dfrac{819(331)}{1600} = 169.4306$ $\hat{E}(n_{22}) = \dfrac{781(60)}{1600} = 29.2875$

$\hat{E}(n_{12}) = \dfrac{781(331)}{1600} = 161.5694$ $\hat{E}(n_{31}) = \dfrac{819(1209)}{1600} = 618.8569$

$\hat{E}(n_{21}) = \dfrac{819(60)}{1600} = 30.7125$ $\hat{E}(n_{32}) = \dfrac{78(1209)}{1600} = 590.1431$

To determine if life insurance preference of students depends on their sex, we test:

H_0:   Life insurance preference of students and students' sex are independent

H_a: Life insurance preference of students and students' sex are dependent

The test statistic is $\sum\sum \dfrac{(n_{ij} - \hat{E}(n_{ij}))^2}{\hat{E}(n_{ij})}$

$$= \frac{(116 - 169.4306)^2}{169.4306} + \frac{(215 - 161.5694)^2}{161.5694} + \cdots$$

$$+ \frac{(533 - 590.1431)^2}{590.1431} = 46.25$$

The rejection region requires $\alpha = .05$ in the upper tail of the χ^2 distribution with df $= (r - 1)(c - 1) = (2 - 1)(3 - 1) = 2$. From Table XIII, Appendix B, $t^2_{.05} = 5.99147$. The rejection region is $\chi^2 > 5.99147$.

Since the observed value of the test statistic falls in the rejection region ($\chi^2 = 46.25 > 5.99147$), H_0 is rejected. There is sufficient evidence to indicate life insurance preference of students depends on their sex at $\alpha = .05$.

b. The observed significance level is $P(\chi^2 > 46.25)$. From Table XIII, Appendix B, with df = 2, $P(\chi^2 > 46.25) < .005$.

c. To calculate the appropriate percentages, divide the numbers in each column by the total for that column and multiply by 100. Divide each row total by the total sample size and multiply by 100.

	Preferred a Term Policy	Preferred Whole Life	No Preference	
Females	$\frac{116}{331} \cdot 100 = 35.0\%$	$\frac{27}{60} \cdot 100 = 45\%$	$\frac{676}{1209} \cdot 100 = 55.9\%$	$\frac{819}{1600} \cdot 100 = 51.2\%$
Males	$\frac{215}{331} \cdot 100 = 65\%$	$\frac{33}{60} \cdot 100 = 55\%$	$\frac{533}{1209} \cdot 100 = 44.1\%$	$\frac{781}{1600} \cdot 100 = 48.8\%$

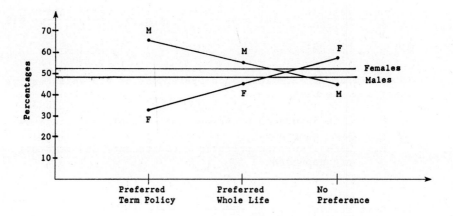

REGRESSION ANALYSIS

11.1   a.

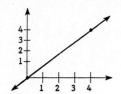

b.

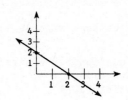

c.

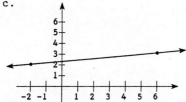

d.

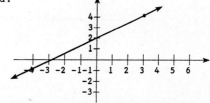

11.3   a.   The equation for a straight line (deterministic) is

$$y = \beta_0 + \beta_1 x$$

If the line passes through (0, 0), then

$$0 = \beta_0 + \beta_1(0) \Rightarrow 0 = \beta_0$$

Likewise, through (4, 4),

$$4 = \beta_0 + \beta_1(4)$$

$$4 = \beta_1(4) \Rightarrow \beta_1 = 1$$

Thus, $y = 0 + 1x$ or $y = x$

   b.   The equation for a straight line is $y = \beta_0 + \beta_1 x$. If the line passes through (0, 2), then $2 = \beta_0 + \beta_1(0)$, which implies $\beta_0 = 2$. Likewise, through the point (2, 0), then $0 = \beta_0 + 2\beta_1$ or $-\beta_0 = 2\beta_1$. Substituting $\beta_0 = 2$, we get $-2 = 2\beta_1$ or $\beta_1 = -1$. Therefore, the line passing through (0, 2) and (2, 0) is $y = 2 - x$.

c. The equation for a straight line is $y = \beta_0 + \beta_1 x$. If the line passes through $(-2, 2)$, then $2 = \beta_0 + \beta_1(-2)$. Likewise through the point $(6, 3)$, $3 = \beta_0 + \beta_1(6)$. Solving for these 2 equations

$$3 = \beta_0 + \beta_1 6$$
$$\underline{-(2 = \beta_0 - \beta_1 2)}$$
$$1 = \qquad 8\beta_1 \quad \text{or} \quad \beta_1 = \frac{1}{8}$$

Solving for β_0, $2 = \beta_0 + \frac{1}{8}(-2)$ or $2 = \beta_0 - \frac{1}{4}$ or $\beta_0 = 2 + \frac{1}{4} = \frac{9}{4}$

The equation, with $\beta_0 = \frac{9}{4}$ and $\beta_1 = \frac{1}{8}$, is $y = \frac{9}{4} + \frac{1}{8}x$

d. The equation for a straight line is $y = \beta_0 + \beta_1 x$. If the line passes through $(-4, -1)$, then $-1 = \beta_0 - \beta_1 4$. Likewise, through the point $(3, 4)$, $4 = \beta_0 + \beta_1 3$. Solving these equations simultaneously,

$$4 = \beta_0 + \beta_1 3$$
$$\underline{-[(-1) = \beta_0 - \beta_1 4]}$$
$$5 = \qquad 7\beta_1 \quad \text{or} \quad \beta_1 = \frac{5}{7}$$

Solving for β_0, $4 = \beta_0 + 3\left(\frac{5}{7}\right) \Rightarrow 4 - \frac{15}{7} = \beta_0$ or $\beta_0 = \frac{13}{7}$.

Therefore, $y = \frac{13}{7} + \frac{5}{7}x$.

11.5 a. $y = 3 + 2x$. The slope is the value for β_1 or $\beta_1 = 2$. The intercept is that value for β_0 or $\beta_0 = 3$.

b. $y = 3 - 2x$. The slope is the value for β_1, which is -2; the intercept is the value for β_0 or 3.

c. $y = -3 + 2x$. The slope is the value for β_1, which is 2; the intercept is the value β_0 or -3.

d. $y = -x$. We note $\beta_0 = 0$, so the intercept is 0. The slope, $\beta_1 = -1$.

e. $y = 2x$. We note $\beta_0 = 0$, so the intercept is 0. The slope, $\beta_1 = 2$.

f. $y = .5 + 1.25x$. The slope, $\beta_1 = 1.25$, and the intercept $\beta_0 = .5$.

11.7 The "line of means" is the deterministic component of the probabilistic model, because the mean of y, $E(y)$, is equal to the straight-line component of the model. That is, $E(y) = \beta_0 + \beta_1 x$.

11.9 a.

x_i	y_i	x_i^2	x_iy_i
7	2	$7^2 = 49$	$7(2) = 14$
4	4	$4^2 = 16$	$4(4) = 16$
6	2	$6^2 = 36$	$6(2) = 12$
2	5	$2^2 = 4$	$2(5) = 10$
1	7	$1^2 = 1$	$1(7) = 7$
1	6	$1^2 = 1$	$1(6) = 6$
3	5	$3^2 = 9$	$3(5) = 15$

Totals: $\sum x_i = 7 + 4 + 6 + 2 + 1 + 1 + 3 = 24$

$\sum y_i = 2 + 4 + 2 + 5 + 7 + 6 + 5 = 31$

$\sum x_i^2 = 49 + 16 + 36 + 4 + 1 + 1 + 9 = 116$

$\sum x_iy_i = 14 + 16 + 12 + 10 + 7 + 6 + 15 = 80$

b. $SS_{xy} = \sum_{i=1}^{n} x_iy_i - \frac{\left(\sum_{i=1}^{n} x_i\right)\left(\sum_{i=1}^{n} y_i\right)}{n} = 80 - \frac{(24)(31)}{7} = 80 - 106.2857$

$= -26.2857$

c. $SS_{xx} = \sum x_i^2 - \frac{(\sum x_i)^2}{7} = 116 - \frac{(24)^2}{7} = 116 - 82.2857 = 33.7143$

d. $\hat{\beta}_1 = \frac{SS_{xy}}{SS_{xx}} = \frac{-26.2857}{33.7143} = -.7796$

e. $\bar{x} = \frac{\sum x_i}{n} = \frac{24}{7} = 3.4286$ $\bar{y} = \frac{\sum y_i}{n} = \frac{31}{7} = 4.4286$

f. $\hat{\beta}_0 = \bar{y} - \hat{\beta}_1\bar{x} = 4.4286 - (-.7796)(3.4286) = 4.4286 - (-2.6729)$
$= 7.102$

g. The least squares line is $\hat{y} = \hat{\beta}_0 + \hat{\beta}_1x = 7.102 - .7796x$

11.11 a.

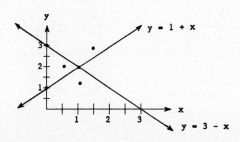

b. Choose y = 1 + x since it best describes the relation of x and y.

c.

y	x	$\hat{y} = 1 + x$	$y - \hat{y}$
2	.5	1.5	2 - 1.5 = .5
1	1	2	1 - 2 = -1
3	1.5	2.5	3 - 2.5 = .5

Sum of errors = 0

y	x	$\hat{y} = 3 - x$	$y - \hat{y}$
2	.5	3 - .5 = 2.5	2 - 2.5 = .5
1	1	3 - 1 = 2	1 - 2 = -1
3	1.5	3 - 1.5 = 1.5	3 - 1.5 = 1.5

Sum of errors = 0

d. SSE = $\sum (y - \hat{y})^2$

SSE for 1st model: y = 1 + x, SSE = $(.5)^2 + (-1)^2 + (.5)^2 = 1.5$

SSE for 2nd model: y = 3 - x, SSE = $(.5)^2 + (-1)^2 + (1.5)^2 = 3.5$

e. The best fitting straight line is the one that has the least squares. The model y = 1 + x has a smaller SSE, and therefore it verifies the visual check in part (a). The least squares line,

$$\hat{\beta}_1 = \frac{SS_{xy}}{SS_{xx}} \qquad \sum x_i = 3 \quad \sum y_i = 6 \quad \sum x_i y_i = 6.5 \quad \sum x_i^2 = 3.5 \quad \sum y_i^2 = 14$$

$$SS_{xy} = \sum x_i y_i - \frac{(\sum x_i)(\sum y_i)}{n} = 6.5 - \frac{(3)(6)}{3} = .5$$

$$SS_{xx} = \sum x_i^2 - \frac{(\sum x_i)^2}{n} = 3.5 - \frac{(3)^2}{3} = .5$$

$$\hat{\beta}_1 = \frac{.5}{.5} = 1 \qquad \bar{x} = \frac{\sum x_i}{3} = \frac{3}{3} = 1 \qquad \bar{y} = \frac{\sum y_i}{3} = \frac{6}{3} = 2$$

$$\hat{\beta}_0 = \bar{y} - \hat{\beta}_1 \bar{x} = 2 - 1(1) = 1 \Rightarrow \hat{y} = \hat{\beta}_0 + \hat{\beta}_1 x = 1 + x$$

11.13 a.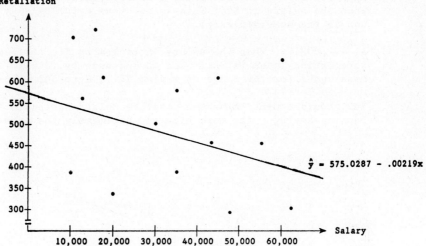

It appears as salary increases, the retaliation index decreases.

b. $\sum x = 516,100 \qquad \sum y = 7497 \qquad \sum xy = 248,409,000$

$\sum x^2 = 22,119,490,000$

$\bar{x} = \dfrac{\sum x}{n} = \dfrac{516,100}{15} = 34,406.667 \qquad \bar{y} = \dfrac{\sum y}{n} = \dfrac{7,497}{15} = 499.8$

$SS_{xy} = \sum xy - \dfrac{(\sum x)(\sum y)}{n} = 248,409,000 - \dfrac{(516,100)(7,497)}{15}$

$\qquad = 248,409,000 - 257,946,780 = -9,537,780$

$SS_{xx} = \sum x^2 - \dfrac{(\sum x)^2}{n} = 22,119,490,000 - \dfrac{(516,000)^2}{15}$

$\qquad\qquad = 22,119,490,000 - 17,757,281,000$

$\qquad\qquad = 4,362,209,300$

$\hat{\beta}_1 = \dfrac{SS_{xy}}{SS_{xx}} = \dfrac{-9,537,780}{4,362,200,300} = -.00219$

$\hat{\beta}_0 = \bar{y} - \hat{\beta}_1\bar{x} = 499.8 - (-.002186456)(34,406.667)$

$\qquad\qquad = 499.8 + 75.22867 = 575.0287$

$\hat{y} = 575.0287 - .00219x$

c. The least squares line supports the answer because the line has a negative slope.

d. $\hat{\beta}_0 = 575.0287$. The estimated mean retaliation index is 575.0287 when the salary is \$0. This is not meaningful because x = 0 is not in the observed range.

e. $\hat{\beta}_1 = -.00219$. When the salary increases by \$1, the mean retaliation index is estimated to decrease by .00219. This is meaningful for the range of x from \$11,900 to \$62,000.

11.15 a. You should expect to have a positive relationship since the higher batting average, the more hits and ultimately the more games won.

b.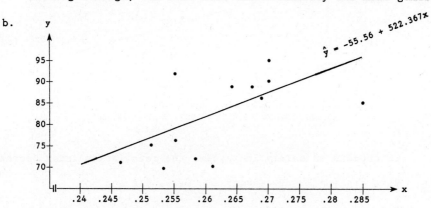

Yes, it seems there is a relationship as batting averages increase, the number of games won also increases.

c. $SS_{xy} = \sum xy - \dfrac{(\sum x)(\sum y)}{n} = 296.734 - \dfrac{(3.658)(1,133)}{14}$

$$= 296.734 - 296.0367143 = .6972857$$

$SS_{xx} = \sum x^2 - \dfrac{(\sum x)^2}{n} = .957118 - \dfrac{(3.658)^2}{14}$

$$= .957118 - .955783142 = .001334857$$

$\hat{\beta}_1 = \dfrac{SS_{xy}}{SS_{xx}} = \dfrac{.6972857}{.001334857} = 522.367$

$\hat{\beta}_0 = \bar{y} - \hat{\beta}_1 \bar{x} = \dfrac{1133}{14} - 522.3673006\left(\dfrac{3.658}{14}\right) = 80.9286 - 136.487$

$$= -55.56$$

Therefore, $\hat{y} = -55.56 + 522.367x$.

d. The line presents an adequate fit.

e. There are more factors to a game than batting, such as pitcher's performance.

11.17 $s^2 = \dfrac{SSE}{n - 2} = \dfrac{.507}{12 - 2} = \dfrac{.507}{10} = .0507$

11.19 $SSE = SS_{yy} - \hat{\beta}_1 SS_{xy}$

where $SS_{yy} = \sum y_i^2 - \dfrac{(\sum y_i)^2}{n}$

For Exercise 11.9,

$\sum y_i^2 = 159 \qquad \sum y_i = 31 \qquad SS_{yy} = 159 - \dfrac{31^2}{7} = 159 - 137.285714$
$$= 21.714286$$

$SS_{xy} = 26.285714 \qquad \hat{\beta}_1 = -.77966$

Therefore, $SSE = 21.714286 - (-.77966)(-26.285714)$
$$= 21.714286 - 20.49392 = 1.2203662 \approx 1.2204$$
$$s^2 = \dfrac{SSE}{n - 2} = \dfrac{1.2203662}{5} = .2441, \quad s = \sqrt{.2441} = .4940$$

For Exercise 11.12,

$\sum x_i = 26 \quad \sum y_i = 24 \quad \sum x_i y_i = 129 \quad \sum x_i^2 = 140 \quad \sum y_i^2 = 124$

$SS_{xy} = \sum x_i y_i - \dfrac{(\sum x_i \sum y_i)}{n} = 129 - \dfrac{(26)(24)}{7} = 129 - 89.142857$
$$= 39.857143$$

$SS_{xx} = \sum x_i^2 - \dfrac{(\sum x_i)^2}{n} = 140 - \dfrac{(26)^2}{7} = 140 - 96.571429$
$$= 43.428571$$

$S_{yy} = \sum y_i^2 - \dfrac{(\sum y_i)^2}{n} = 124 - \dfrac{(24)^2}{7} = 124 - 82.285714$
$$= 41.714286$$

$\hat{\beta}_1 = \dfrac{SS_{xy}}{S_{xx}} = \dfrac{39.857143}{43.428571} = .9177632$

$SSE = SS_{yy} - \hat{\beta}_1 SS_{xy} = 41.714286 - (.9177632)(39.857143)$
$$= 41.714286 - 36.579418$$
$$= 5.1348681 \approx 5.1349$$
$$s^2 = \dfrac{SSE}{n - 2} = \dfrac{5.1348681}{5} = 1.0270 \quad s = \sqrt{1.0270} = 1.0134$$

11.21 a.

BRAND A

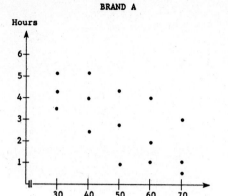

BRAND B

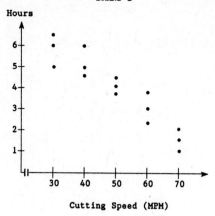

b. For Brand A,

$$\sum x_i = 750 \quad \sum y_i = 44.8 \quad \sum x_i y_i = 2022 \quad \sum x_i^2 = 40,500$$

$$\sum y_i^2 = 168.7$$

$$SS_{xx} = \sum x_i^2 - \frac{(\sum x_i)^2}{n} = 40,500 - \frac{750^2}{15} = 40,500 - 37,500 = 3000$$

$$SS_{xy} = \sum x_i y_i - \frac{(\sum x_i)(\sum y_i)}{n} = 2022 - \frac{(750)(44.8)}{15} = 2022 - 2240$$
$$= -218$$

$$\hat{\beta}_1 = \frac{SS_{xy}}{SS_{xx}} = \frac{-218}{3000} = -.0726667$$

$$\hat{\beta}_0 = \bar{y} - \hat{\beta}_1 \bar{x} = \frac{44.8}{15} - (-.0726667)\left(\frac{750}{15}\right) = 2.9866667 + 3.633333$$
$$= 6.62$$

$$\hat{y} = 6.62 - .0727x$$

For Brand B,

$$\sum x_i = 750 \quad \sum y_i = 58.9 \quad \sum x_i y_i = 2622 \quad \sum x_i^2 = 40,500$$

$$\sum y_i^2 = 270.89$$

$$SS_{xx} = \sum x_i^2 - \frac{(\sum x_i)^2}{n} = 40,500 - \frac{(750)^2}{15} = 40,500 - 37,500 = 3000$$

$$SS_{xy} = \sum xy - \frac{(\sum x)(\sum y)}{n} = 2622 - \frac{(750)(58.9)}{15} = 2622 - 2945$$
$$= -323$$

$$\hat{\beta}_1 = \frac{SS_{xy}}{SS_{xx}} = \frac{-323}{3000} = -.1076667$$

$$\hat{\beta}_0 = \bar{y} - \hat{\beta}_1\bar{x} = \left(\frac{59.9}{15}\right) - (-.1076667)\left(\frac{750}{15}\right) = 3.92667 + 5.38333$$
$$= 9.31$$
$$\hat{y} = 9.31 - .1077x$$

c. For Brand A,

$$SS_{yy} = \sum y_i^2 - \frac{(\sum y_i)^2}{n} = 168.7 - \frac{(44.8)^2}{15} = 168.7 - 133.80267$$
$$= 34.897333$$

$$SSE = SS_{yy} - \hat{\beta}_1 SS_{xy} = 34.897333 - (-.0726667)(-218)$$
$$= 34.897333 - 15.841341$$
$$= 19.055992 \approx 19.056$$

$$s^2 = \frac{SSE}{n-2} = \frac{19.055992}{13} = 1.4658 \qquad s = \sqrt{1.4658} = 1.211$$

For Brand B,

$$SS_{yy} = \sum y_i^2 - \frac{(\sum y_i)^2}{n} = 270.89 - \frac{(58.9)^2}{15} = 270.89 - 231.280667$$
$$= 39.609333$$

$$SSE = SS_{yy} - \hat{\beta}_1 SS_{xy} = 39.609333 - (-.1076667)(-323)$$
$$= 39.609333 - 34.776344 = 4.8329889$$

$$s^2 = \frac{SSE}{n-2} = \frac{4.8329889}{13} = .3717 \qquad s = \sqrt{.3717} = .610$$

d. For Brand A,

$\hat{y} = 6.62 - .0727x$. For $x = 70$, $\hat{y} = 6.62 - .0727(70) = 1.531$

$2s = 2(1.211) = 2.422$

Therefore, $\hat{y} \pm 2s \Rightarrow 1.531 \pm 2.422 \Rightarrow (-.891, 3.953)$

For Brand B,

$\hat{y} = 9.31 - .1077x$. For $x = 70$, $\hat{y} = 9.31 - .1077(70) = 1.771$

$2s = 2(.61) = 1.22$

Therefore, $\hat{y} \pm 2s \Rightarrow 1.771 \pm 1.22 \Rightarrow (.551, 2.991)$

e. More confident with Brand B since there is less variation.

11.23 a. First, we compute percentage of channels watched by dividing the number of channels watched by the number of channels available and multiplying by 100. The percentages are:

Household	% Channels Watched	Household	% Channels Watched
1	50	11	40
2	34.5	12	75
3	75	13	80
4	40	14	40
5	30	15	56.25
6	60	16	100
7	83.3	17	20
8	100	18	28.9
9	57.1	19	14.3
10	30	20	20

$\sum x_i = 357$ $\sum x_i^2 = 10535$ $\sum x_i y_i = 13100.7$

$\sum y_i = 1034.35$ $\sum y_i^2 = 66743.3125$

$$SS_{xy} = \sum x_i y_i - \frac{\sum x_i \sum y_i}{n} = 13100.7 - \frac{357(1034.35)}{20} = -5362.4475$$

$$SS_{xx} = \sum x_i^2 - \frac{(\sum x_i)^2}{n} = 10535 - \frac{357^2}{20} = 4162.55$$

$$SS_{yy} = \sum y_i^2 - \frac{(\sum y_i)^2}{n} = 66743.3125 - \frac{1034.35^2}{20} = 13249.3164$$

$$\hat{\beta}_1 = \frac{SS_{xy}}{SS_{xx}} = \frac{-5362.4475}{4162.55} = -1.2882602$$

$$\hat{\beta}_0 = \bar{y} - \hat{\beta}_1 \bar{x} = \frac{1034.35}{20} - (-1.2882602)\left(\frac{357}{20}\right) = 74.712945$$

The least squares line is $\hat{y} = 74.7129 - 1.2883x$. Because our estimate for β_1 is negative, -1.2883, this supports the Nielsen findings.

b.

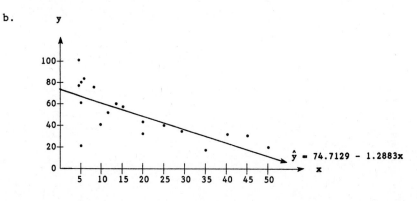

c. $SSE = SS_{yy} - \hat{\beta}_1 SS_{xy} = 13249.3164 - (-1.2882602)(-5362.4475)$

$$= 6341.0883$$

$$s^2 = \frac{SSE}{n-2} = \frac{6341.0883}{20-2} = 352.2827$$

$$s = \sqrt{352.2827} = 18.769$$

We would expect the least squares line to be able to predict the percentage of channels watched to within 2 standard deviations or ±2(18.769) = ±37.538.

11.25   a.   For confidence coefficient .95, $\alpha = 1 - .95 = .05$ and $\alpha/2 = .05/2 = .025$. From Table VI, Appendix B, with $df = n - 2 = 10 - 2 = 8$, $t_{.025} = 2.306$.

The 95% confidence interval for β_1 is:

$$\hat{\beta}_1 \pm t_{.025} s_{\hat{\beta}_1} \quad \text{where} \quad s_{\hat{\beta}_1} = \frac{s}{\sqrt{SS_{xx}}} = \frac{3}{\sqrt{35}} = .5071$$

$$\Rightarrow 31 \pm 2.306(.5071) \Rightarrow 31 \pm 1.17 \Rightarrow (29.83, 32.17)$$

For confidence coefficient .90, $\alpha = 1 - .90 = .10$ and $\alpha/2 = .10/2 = .05$. From Table VI, Appendix B, with $df = 8$, $t_{.05} = 1.860$.

The 90% confidence interval for β_1 is:

$$\hat{\beta}_1 \pm t_{.05} s_{\hat{\beta}_1}$$

$$\Rightarrow 31 \pm 1.860(.5071) \Rightarrow 31 \pm .94 \Rightarrow (30.06, 31.94)$$

b. $s^2 = \dfrac{SSE}{n-2} = \dfrac{1,960}{14-2} = 163.3333$, $s = \sqrt{s^2} = 12.7802$

For confidence coefficient .95, $\alpha = 1 - .95 = .05$ and $\alpha/2 = .05/2 = .025$. From Table VI, Appendix B, with $df = n - 2 = 14 - 2 = 12$, $t_{.025} = 2.179$. The 95% confidence interval for β_1 is:

$$\hat{\beta}_1 \pm t_{.025} s_{\hat{\beta}_1} \quad \text{where} \quad s_{\hat{\beta}_1} = \frac{s}{\sqrt{SS_{xx}}} = \frac{12.7802}{\sqrt{30}} = 2.3333$$

$$\Rightarrow 64 \pm 2.179(2.3333) \Rightarrow 64 \pm 5.08 \Rightarrow (58.92, 69.08)$$

For confidence coefficient .90, $\alpha = 1 - .90 = .10$ and $\alpha/2 = .10/2 = .05$. From Table VI, Appendix B, with $df = 12$, $t_{.05} = 1.782$.

The 90% confidence interval for β_1 is:

$$\hat{\beta}_1 \pm t_{.05}s_{\hat{\beta}_1}$$

$$\Rightarrow 64 \pm 1.782(2.3333) \Rightarrow 64 \pm 4.16 \Rightarrow (59.84, 68.16)$$

c. $s^2 = \dfrac{SSE}{n-2} = \dfrac{146}{20-2} = 8.1111$, $s = \sqrt{s^2} = 2.848$

For confidence coefficient .95, $\alpha = 1 - .95 = .05$ and $\alpha/2 = .05/2 = .025$. From Table VI, Appendix B, with df = n - 2 = 20 - 2 = 18, $t_{.025} = 2.776$. The 95% confidence interval for β_1 is:

$$\hat{\beta}_1 \pm t_{.025}s_{\hat{\beta}_1} \quad \text{where } s_{\hat{\beta}_1} = \frac{s}{\sqrt{SS_{xx}}} = \frac{2.848}{\sqrt{64}} = .356$$

$$\Rightarrow -8.4 \pm 2.101(.356) \Rightarrow -8.4 \pm .75 \Rightarrow (-9.15, -7.65)$$

For confidence coefficient .90, $\alpha = 1 - .90 = .10$ and $\alpha/2 = .10/2 = .05$. From Table VI, Appendix B, with df = 18, $t_{.05} = 1.734$.

The 90% confidence interval for β_1 is:

$$\hat{\beta}_1 \pm t_{.05}s_{\hat{\beta}_1}$$

$$\Rightarrow -8.4 \pm 1.734(.356) \Rightarrow -8.4 \pm .62 \Rightarrow (-9.02, -7.78)$$

11.27   From Exercise 11.26, $\hat{\beta}_1 = .8214$, $s = 1.1922$, $SS_{xx} = 28$, and n = 7.

For confidence coefficient .80, $\alpha = 1 - .80 = .20$ and $\alpha/2 = .20/2 = .10$. From Table VI, Appendix B, with df = n - 2 = 7 - 2 = 5, $t_{.10} = 1.476$. The 80% confidence interval for β_1 is:

$$\hat{\beta}_1 \pm t_{.10}s_{\hat{\beta}_1} \quad \text{where } s_{\hat{\beta}_1} = \frac{s}{\sqrt{SS_{xx}}} = \frac{1.1922}{\sqrt{28}} = .2253$$

$$\Rightarrow .8214 \pm 1.476(.2253) \Rightarrow .8214 \pm .3325 \Rightarrow (.4889, 1.1539)$$

For confidence coefficient .98, $\alpha = 1 - .98 = .02$ and $\alpha/2 = .02/2 = .01$. From Table VI, Appendix B, with df = 5, $t_{.01} = 3.365$.

The 98% confidence interval for β_1 is:

$$\hat{\beta}_1 \pm t_{.01}s_{\hat{\beta}_1}$$

$$\Rightarrow .8214 \pm 3.365(.2253) \Rightarrow .8214 \pm .7581 \Rightarrow (.0633, 1.5795)$$

11.29 a.

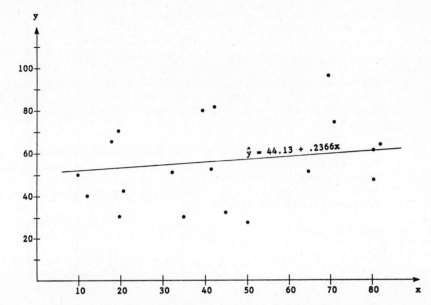

b. $\hat{\beta}_1 = \dfrac{SS_{xy}}{SS_{xx}} = \dfrac{2,561.2632}{10,824.5263} = .236617$

$\hat{\beta}_0 = \bar{y} - \hat{\beta}_1 \bar{x} = 54.5789 - .236617(44.1579) = 44.13$

The least squares line is $\hat{y} = 44.13 + .2366x$.

c. $SSE = SS_{yy} - \hat{\beta}_1 SS_{xy} = 7,006.6316 - .236617(2,561.2632)$

$\qquad\qquad = 6,400.6367$

$s^2 = \dfrac{SSE}{n-2} = \dfrac{6400.6367}{19-2} = 376.508$

$s = 19.4038$

The standard deviation s represents the spread of the manager success index about the least squares line. Approximately 95% of the manager success indexes should lie within $2s = 2(19.40) = 38.8$ of the least squares line.

d. Refer to the scattergram in part (a). The number of interactions with outsiders might contribute some information in the prediction of managerial success, but it does not look like a very strong relationship.

e. To determine if the number of interactions contributes information for the prediction of managerial success, we test:

H_0: $\beta_1 = 0$
H_a: $\beta_1 \neq 0$

The test statistic is $t = \dfrac{\hat{\beta}_1 - 0}{s_{\hat{\beta}_1}} = \dfrac{.2366 - 0}{\dfrac{19.40}{\sqrt{10,824.5263}}} = 1.27$

The rejection region requires $\alpha/2 = .05/2 = .025$ in each tail of the t distribution with df $= n - 2 = 19 - 2 = 17$. From Table VI, Appendix B, $t_{.025} = 2.110$. The rejection region is $t > 2.110$ or $t < -2.110$.

Since the observed value of the test statistic does not fall in the rejection region ($t = 1.27 \not> 2.110$), H_0 is not rejected. There is insufficient evidence to indicate the number of interactions contributes information for the prediction of managerial success at $\alpha = .05$.

f. The confidence interval for β_1 is

$\hat{\beta}_1 \pm t_{\alpha/2} s_{\hat{\beta}_1}$ where $s_{\hat{\beta}_1} = \dfrac{s}{\sqrt{SS_{xx}}} = \dfrac{19.40}{\sqrt{10,824.5263}} = .1865$

For confidence coefficient .95, $\alpha = 1 - .95 = .05$ and $\alpha/2 = .05/2 = .025$. From Table VI, Appendix B, with df $= 17$, $t_{.025} = 2.110$. The 95% confidence interval is:

$\Rightarrow .2366 \pm 2.110(.1865) \Rightarrow .2366 \pm .3935 \Rightarrow (-.1569, .6301)$

We are 95% confident the change in the mean manager success index for each additional interaction with outsiders is between $-.1569$ and $.6301$.

11.31 a. <u>For Conoco:</u>

H_0: $\beta_1 = 0$
H_a: $\beta_1 \neq 0$

The test statistic is $t = 21.93$.

The rejection region requires $\alpha/2 = .01/2 = .005$ in each tail of the t distribution. From Table VI, Appendix B, with df $= 2 = 504 - 2 = 502$, $t_{.005} \approx 2.576$. The rejection region is $t > 2.576$ or $t < -2.576$.

Since the observed value of the test statistic falls in the rejection region ($t = 21.93 > 2.576$), H_0 is rejected. There is sufficient evidence to indicate that $\beta_1 \neq 0$ at $\alpha = .01$. Therefore, the market model is useful for Conoco.

For DuPont:

H_0: $\beta_1 = 0$
H_a: $\beta_1 \neq 0$

The test statistic is t = 18.76.

The rejection region is t < -2.576 or t > 2.576.

Since the observed value of the test statistic falls in the rejection region (t = 18.76 > 2.576), H_0 is rejected. There is sufficient evidence to indicate that $\beta_1 \neq 0$ at $\alpha = .01$. Therefore, the market model is useful for DuPont.

For Mobil:

H_0: $\beta_1 = 0$
H_a: $\beta_1 \neq 0$

The test statistic is t = 16.21.

The rejection region is t < -2.576 or t > 2.576.

Since the observed value of the test statistic falls in the rejection region (t = 16.21 > 2.576), H_0 is rejected. There is sufficient evidence to indicate that $\beta_1 \neq 0$ at $\alpha = .01$. Therefore, the market model is useful for Mobil.

For Seagram:

H_0: $\beta_1 = 0$
H_a: $\beta_1 \neq 0$

The test statistic is t = 6.05.

The rejection region is t < -2.576 or t > 2.576.

Since the observed value of the test statistic falls in the rejection region (t = 6.05 > 2.576), H_0 is rejected. There is sufficient evidence to indicate that $\beta_1 \neq 0$ at $\alpha = .01$. Therefore, the market model is useful for Seagram.

The market model is useful for all 4 firms at $\alpha = .01$.

b. Since x = Rate of Return of Standard and Poor's 500 Composite Index, if x increased by .10, the mean rate of return for Conoco's stock would increase by 1.40(.10) = .14, and the mean rate of return for Seagram's stock would increase by .76(.1) = .076.

c. Conoco's stock is more responsive to changes in the market than Seagram's since the slope is larger.

11.33 From Exercise 11.14, $SS_{xx} = 1,098.5008$, $SS_{xy} = 3,472.6243$, $\sum y = 1257$, $\sum y^2 = 124,459$, $n = 14$, and $\hat{\beta}_1 = 3.1612$

$$SS_{yy} = \sum y^2 - \frac{(\sum y)^2}{n} = 124,459 - \frac{1257^2}{14} = 11,598.3571$$

$$SSE = SS_{yy} - \hat{\beta}_1 SS_{xy} = 11,598.3571 - 3.1612(3,472.6243) = 620.6972$$

$$s^2 = \frac{SSE}{n - 2} = \frac{620.6972}{14 - 2} = 51.7248$$

$$s = \sqrt{s^2} = 7.192$$

For confidence coefficient .90, $\alpha = 1 - .90 = .10$ and $\alpha/2 = .10/2 = .05$. From Table VI, Appendix B, $t_{.05} = 1.833$ with df $= n - 2 = 11 - 2 = 9$. The confidence interval is:

$$\hat{\beta}_1 \pm t_{\alpha/2} s_{\hat{\beta}_1} \quad \text{where} \quad s_{\hat{\beta}_1} = \frac{s}{\sqrt{SS_{xx}}} = \frac{7.192}{\sqrt{1098.5008}} = .217$$

$$\Rightarrow 3.1612 \pm 1.833(.217) \Rightarrow 3.1612 \pm .3978 \Rightarrow (2.7634, 3.5590)$$

11.35 From Exercise 11.23, $n = 20$, $SS_{xx} = 4162.55$, $s = 18.769$, and $\hat{\beta}_1 = -1.28826$.

To determine if the percentage of channels watched for 10 minutes or more decreases as the number of channels available increases, we test:

$$H_0: \quad \beta_1 = 0$$
$$H_a: \quad \beta_1 < 0$$

The test statistic is $t = \dfrac{\hat{\beta}_1 - 0}{s_{\hat{\beta}_1}} = \dfrac{-1.28826 - 0}{\dfrac{18.769}{\sqrt{4162.55}}} = -4.43$

The rejection region requires $\alpha = .10$ in the lower tail of the t distribution with df $= n - 2 = 20 - 2 = 18$. From Table VI, Appendix B, $t_{.10} = 1.330$. The rejection region is $t < -1.330$.

Since the observed value of the test statistic falls in the rejection region ($t = -4.43 < -1.330$), H_0 is rejected. There is sufficient evidence to indicate the percentage of channels watched decreases as the number of channels available increases at $\alpha = .10$.

The necessary assumptions are:

1. The mean of the probability distribution of ε is 0.
2. The variance of the probability distribution of ε is constant for all values of x.
3. The probability distribution of ε is normal
4. The errors associated with any 2 different observations are independent.

11.37   a. If r = 1, there is a perfect positive linear relationship between x and y. As x increases, y increases.

   b. If r = -1, there is a perfect negative linear relationship between x and y. As x increases, y decreases.

   c. If r = 0, there is no linear relationship between x and y.

   d. If r = .90, there is a strong positive linear relationship between x and y. As x increases, y tends to increase.

   e. If r = .10, there is a weak positive linear relationship between x and y. As x increases, y tends to increase.

   f. If r = -.88, there is a strong negative linear relationship between x and y. As x increases, y tends to decrease.

11.39   a.

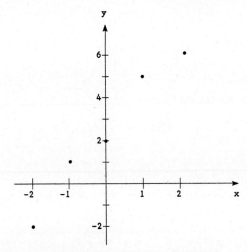

Some preliminary calculations are:

$\sum x_i = 0$ $\sum x_i^2 = 10$ $\sum x_i y_i = 20$

$\sum y_i = 12$ $\sum y_i^2 = 70$

$$SS_{xy} = \sum x_i y_i - \frac{\sum x_i \sum y_i}{n} = 20 - \frac{0(12)}{5} = 20$$

$$SS_{xx} = \sum x_i^2 - \frac{(\sum x_i)^2}{n} = 10 - \frac{0^2}{5} = 10$$

$$SS_{yy} = \sum y_i^2 - \frac{(\sum y_i)^2}{n} = 70 - \frac{12^2}{5} = 41.2$$

$$r = \frac{SS_{xy}}{\sqrt{SS_{xx} SS_{yy}}} = \frac{20}{\sqrt{10(41.2)}} = .985$$

There is a strong positive linear relationship between x and y.

$r^2 = .985^2 = .971$

97.1% of the sample variability around $\bar{y}$ is explained by the linear relationship between x and y.

b.

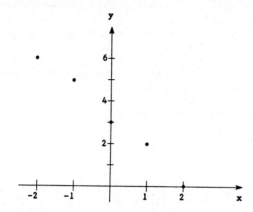

Some preliminary calculations are:

$\sum x_i = 0$ $\sum x_i^2 = 10$ $\sum x_i y_i = -15$

$\sum y_i = 16$ $\sum y_i^2 = 74$

$SS_{xy} = \sum x_i y_i - \dfrac{\sum x_i \sum y_i}{n} = -15 - \dfrac{0(16)}{5} = -15$

$SS_{xx} = \sum x_i^2 - \dfrac{(\sum x_i)^2}{n} = 10 - \dfrac{0^2}{5} = 10$

$SS_{yy} = \sum y_i^2 - \dfrac{(\sum y_i)^2}{n} = 74 - \dfrac{16^2}{5} = 22.8$

$r = \dfrac{SS_{xy}}{\sqrt{SS_{xx} SS_{yy}}} = \dfrac{-15}{\sqrt{10(22.8)}} = -.9934$

There is a strong negative linear relationship between x and y.

$r^2 = (-.993)^2 = .987$

98.7% of the sample variability around $\bar{y}$ is explained by the linear relationship between x and y.

c.

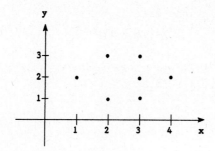

Some preliminary calculations are:

$\sum x_i = 18$ $\sum x_1^2 = 52$ $\sum x_i y_i = 36$

$\sum y_i = 14$ $\sum y_1^2 = 32$

$$SS_{xy} = \sum x_i y_i - \frac{\sum x_i \sum y_i}{n} = 36 - \frac{18(14)}{7} = 0$$

$$SS_{xx} = \sum x_1^2 - \frac{(\sum x_i)^2}{n} = 52 - \frac{18^2}{7} = 5.7143$$

$$SS_{yy} = \sum y_1^2 - \frac{(\sum y_i)^2}{n} = 32 - \frac{14^2}{7} = 4$$

$$r = \frac{SS_{xy}}{\sqrt{SS_{xx} SS_{yy}}} = \frac{0}{\sqrt{5.7143(4)}} = 0$$

There is no linear relationship between x and y.

$r^2 = 0^2 = 0$

None of the sample variability around $\bar{y}$ is explained by the linear relationship between x and y.

d.

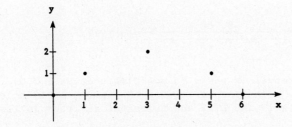

Some preliminary calculations are:

$$\sum x_i = 15 \qquad \sum x_i^2 = 71 \qquad \sum x_i y_i = 12$$

$$\sum y_i = 4 \qquad \sum y_i^2 = 6$$

$$SS_{xy} = \sum x_i y_i - \frac{\sum x_i \sum y_i}{n} = 12 - \frac{15(4)}{5} = 0$$

$$SS_{xx} = \sum x_i^2 - \frac{(\sum x_i)^2}{n} = 71 - \frac{15^2}{5} = 26$$

$$SS_{yy} = \sum y_i^2 - \frac{(\sum y_i)^2}{n} = 6 - \frac{4^2}{5} = 2.8$$

$$r = \frac{SS_{xy}}{\sqrt{SS_{xx} SS_{yy}}} = \frac{0}{\sqrt{26(2.8)}} = 0$$

There is no linear relationship between x and y.

$$r^2 = 0^2 = 0$$

None of the sample variability around $\bar{y}$ is explained by the linear relationship between x and y.

11.41   Some preliminary calculations are:

$$\sum x_i = 72,872 \qquad \sum x_i^2 = 466,515,984 \qquad \sum x_i y_i = 648,132.6$$

$$\sum y_i = 98.7 \qquad \sum y_i^2 = 929.55$$

$$SS_{xy} = \sum x_i y_i - \frac{\sum x_i \sum y_i}{n} = 648,132.6 - \frac{72,872(98.7)}{12} = 48,760.4$$

$$SS_{xx} = \sum x_i^2 - \frac{(\sum x_i)^2}{n} = 466,515,984 - \frac{72,872^2}{12} = 23,988,618.67$$

$$SS_{yy} = \sum y_i^2 - \frac{(\sum y_i)^2}{n} = 929.55 - \frac{98.7^2}{12} = 117.7425$$

$$r = \frac{SS_{xy}}{\sqrt{SS_{xx} SS_{yy}}} = \frac{48,760.4}{\sqrt{23,988,618.67(117.7425)}} = .917$$

The relationship between x and y is positive because r > 0. Since r is close to 1, the relationship between the number of 18-hole and larger golf courses in the U.S. and number of divorces in the U.S. is very strong.

$$r^2 = .917^2 = .841$$

84.1% of the sample variability around the sample mean number of divorces is explained by the linear relationship between the number of golf courses and number of divorces in the U.S.

This does not mean that there is a causal relationship between the number of golf courses and the number of divorces. There are many factors that probably have contributed to both of these variables.

11.43 Some preliminary calculations are

$$\sum x_i = 413.57 \qquad \sum x_i^2 = 4,513.3163 \qquad \sum x_i y_i = 79,556.7049$$

$$\sum y_i = 8,752.59 \qquad \sum y_i^2 = 2,085,261.5855$$

$$SS_{xy} = \sum x_i y_i - \frac{(\sum x_i)(\sum y_i)}{n} = 79,556.7049 - \frac{413.57(8,752.59)}{42}$$
$$= -6629.21525$$

$$SS_{xx} = \sum x_i^2 - \frac{(\sum x_i)^2}{n} = 4,513.3163 - \frac{413.57^2}{42} = 440.931898$$

$$SS_{yy} = \sum y_i^2 - \frac{(\sum y_i)^2}{n} = 2,085,261.5855 - \frac{8,752.59^2}{42} = 261,265.592$$

$$\hat{\beta}_1 = \frac{SS_{xy}}{SS_{xx}} = \frac{-6629.21525}{440.931898} = -15.03455586$$

$$SSE = SS_{yy} - \hat{\beta}_1 SS_{xy} = 261,265.592 - (-15.03455586)(-6629.21525)$$
$$= 161,598.285$$

$$r^2 = 1 - \frac{SSE}{SS_{yy}} = 1 - \frac{161,598.285}{261,265.592} = .381$$

38.1% of the sample variability around the sample mean S&P 500 stock composite average is explained by the linear relationship between the interest rate and the S&P 500 stock composite average.

$$r = -\sqrt{r^2} = -\sqrt{.381} = -.618$$

(r is negative since the slope is negative.)

The relationship between interest rate and S&P stock composite average is negative since $r < 0$. The relationship is not particularly strong because -.618 is not that close to -1.

11.45 Some preliminary calculations are

$$\sum x_i = 230 \qquad \sum x_i^2 = 12150 \qquad \sum x_i y_i = 9850$$

$$\sum y_i = 215 \qquad \sum y_i^2 = 12781$$

$$SS_{xy} = \sum x_i y_i - \frac{\sum x_i \sum y_i}{n} = 9850 - \frac{230(215)}{5} = -40$$

$$SS_{xx} = \sum x_i^2 - \frac{(\sum x_i)^2}{n} = 12150 - \frac{230^2}{5} = 1570$$

$$SS_{yy} = \sum y_i^2 - \frac{(\sum y_i)^2}{n} = 12781 - \frac{215^2}{5} = 3536$$

$$\hat{\beta}_1 = \frac{SS_{xy}}{SS_{xx}} = \frac{-40}{1570} = -.025477707$$

$$\hat{\beta}_0 = \bar{y} - \hat{\beta}_1 \bar{x} = \frac{215}{5} - (-.025477707)\left(\frac{230}{5}\right) = 44.17197452$$

$$SSE = SS_{yy} - \hat{\beta}_1 SS_{xy} = 3536 - (-.025477707)(-40) = 3534.980892$$

$$s^2 = \frac{SSE}{n-2} = \frac{3534.980892}{5-2} = 1178.326964$$

$$s = \sqrt{1178.326964} = 34.3268$$

a. The fitted line is $\hat{y} = 44.17 - .0255x$

b.

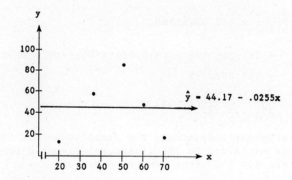

c. H_0: $\beta_1 = 0$
H_a: $\beta_1 \neq 0$

The test statistic is $t = \dfrac{\hat{\beta}_1 - 0}{s_{\hat{\beta}_1}} = \dfrac{-.0255}{\dfrac{34.3268}{\sqrt{1570}}} = -.03$

The rejection region requires $\alpha/2 = .05/2 = .025$ in each tail of the t distribution with df = $n - 2 = 5 - 2 = 3$. From Table VI, Appendix B, $t_{.025} = 3.182$. The rejection region is $t > 3.182$ or $t < -3.182$.

Since the observed value of the test statistic does not fall in the rejection region ($t = -.03 \nless -3.182$), H_0 is not rejected. There is insufficient evidence to indicate the number of tires sold and tire price are linearly related.

d. No. It implies tire price and number of tires sold are not <u>linearly</u> related.

e. $r^2 = 1 - \dfrac{SSE}{SS_{yy}} = 1 - \dfrac{3534.980892}{3536} = .0003$

.03% of the sample variability in the number of tires sold is explained by the linear relationship between number of tires sold and tire price.

11.47 a.

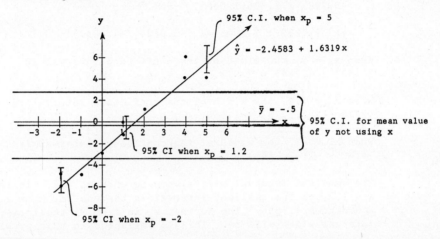

c. The form of the confidence interval is

$$\hat{y} \pm t_{\alpha/2} s \sqrt{\frac{1}{n} + \frac{(x_p - \bar{x})^2}{SS_{xx}}}$$

where $s = \sqrt{\dfrac{SSE}{n-2}} = \sqrt{\dfrac{SS_{yy} - \hat{\beta}_1 SS_{xy}}{n-2}} = \sqrt{\dfrac{162.5 - 1.6319(94)}{10-2}}$

$$= 1.0666$$

$\hat{y} = -2.4583 + 1.6319(5) = 5.7012$ and $\bar{x} = \dfrac{\sum x}{n} = \dfrac{12}{10} = 1.2$

For confidence coefficient .95, $\alpha = 1 - .95 = .05$ and $\alpha/2 = .05/2 = .025$. From Table VI, Appendix β, $t_{.025} = 2.036$ with df = n - 2 = 10 - 2 = 8. The 95% confidence interval is:

$$5.7012 \pm 2.306(1.0666)\sqrt{\frac{1}{10} + \frac{(5 - 1.2)^2}{57.6}}$$

$$\Rightarrow 5.7012 \pm 1.4565 \Rightarrow (4.2447, 7.1577)$$

d. For $x_p = 1.2$, $\hat{y} = -2.4583 + 1.6319(1.2) = -.5000$

The 95% confidence interval is

$$-.5000 \pm 2.306(1.0666)\sqrt{\frac{1}{10} + \frac{(1.2 - 1.2)^2}{57.6}}$$

$$\Rightarrow -.5000 \pm .7778 \Rightarrow (-1.2778, .2778)$$

For $x_p = -2$, $\hat{y} = -2.4583 + 1.6319(-2) = -5.7221$

The 95% confidence interval is

$$-5.7222 \pm 2.306(1.0666)\sqrt{\frac{1}{10} + \frac{(-2 - 1.2)^2}{57.6}}$$

$$\Rightarrow -5.7222 \pm 1.2963 \Rightarrow (-7.0185, -4.4259)$$

e. When $x_p = 5$, the width of the confidence interval is $7.1577 - 4.2447 = 2.913$.

When $x_p = 1.2$, the width of the confidence interval is $.2778 - (-1.2778) = 1.5556$.

When $x_p = -2$, the width of the confidence interval is $-4.4259 - (-7.0185) = 2.5926$.

The smallest interval will always be when $x_p = \bar{x}$. In this case, $\bar{x} = 1.2$, so the smallest interval is the one for $x_p = 1.2$ and has a width of 1.5556. The further x_p is from $\bar{x}$, the larger the interval width will be. This is reflected in this problem.

11.49 a. $\hat{\beta}_1 = \dfrac{SS_{xy}}{SS_{xx}} = \dfrac{20}{25} = .8$

$\hat{\beta}_0 = \bar{y} - \hat{\beta}_1\bar{x} = 3 - .8(2) = 1.4$

The least squares line is $\hat{y} = 1.4 + .8x$

b.

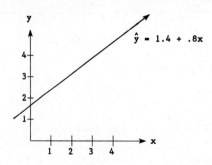

c. $SSE = SS_{yy} - \hat{\beta}_1 SS_{xy} = 17 - .8(20) = 1$

d. $s^2 = \dfrac{SSE}{n - 2} = \dfrac{1}{12 - 2} = .1$

e. The form of the confidence interval is

$$\hat{y} \pm t_{\alpha/2} \; s \sqrt{\frac{1}{n} + \frac{(x_p - \bar{x})^2}{SS_{xx}}}$$

where $\hat{y} = 1.4 + .8(1) = 2.2$

For confidence coefficient .95, $\alpha = 1 - .95 = .05$ and $\alpha/2 = .05/2 = .025$. From Table VI, Appendix B, $t_{.025} = 2.228$ with df $= n - 2 = 10 - 2 = 8$.

The confidence interval is

$$2.2 \pm 2.228 \sqrt{.1} \sqrt{\frac{1}{12} + \frac{(1 - 2)^2}{25}} \; \Rightarrow \; 2.2 \pm .247 \; \Rightarrow \; (1.953, \; 2.447)$$

f. The form of the prediction interval is

$$\hat{y} \pm t_{\alpha/2} \; s \sqrt{1 + \frac{1}{n} + \frac{(x_p - \bar{x})^2}{SS_{xx}}}$$

where $\hat{y} = 1.4 + .8(1.5) = 2.6$

The prediction interval is

$$2.6 \pm 2.228 \sqrt{.1} \sqrt{1 + \frac{1}{12} + \frac{(1.5 - 2)^2}{25}} \; \Rightarrow \; 2.6 \pm .737$$
$$\Rightarrow \; (1.863, \; 3.337)$$

11.51 From Exercise 11.14, the least squares line is $\hat{y} = 36.514 + 3.1612x$

$\bar{x} = 16.8514$

$SS_{xy} = 3472.624 \qquad SS_{xx} = 1098.500771 \qquad SS_{yy} = 11{,}598.3571$

$SSE = SS_{yy} - \hat{\beta}_1 SS_{xy} = 11{,}598.3571 - 3.1612(3472.62429) = 620.6972$

$s^2 = \dfrac{SSE}{n - 2} = \dfrac{620.6972}{14 - 2} = 51.7248 \qquad s = \sqrt{51.7248} = 7.192$

For confidence coefficient .95, $\alpha = 1 - .95 = .05$ and $\alpha/2 = .05/2 = .025$. From Table VI, Appendix B, $t_{.025} = 2.179$ with df $= n - 2 = 14 - 2 = 12$. The confidence interval is

$$\hat{y} \pm t_{\alpha/2} \; s \sqrt{\frac{1}{n} + \frac{(x_p - \bar{x})^2}{SS_{xx}}} \qquad \text{where } \hat{y} = 36.514 + 3.1612(30)$$
$$= 131.35$$

$$\Rightarrow \; 131.35 \pm 2.179(7.192) \sqrt{\frac{1}{14} + \frac{(30 - 16.8514)^2}{1098.500771}}$$

$$\Rightarrow \; 131.35 \pm 7.496 \; \Rightarrow \; (123.854, \; 138.846)$$

11.53 a. From Exercise 11.21,

Brand A $\hat{y} = 6.62 - .0727x$ Brand B $\hat{y} = 9.31 - .1077x$

$s = 1.211$ $s = .610$

$\bar{x} = 50$ $\bar{x} = 50$

$n = 15$ $n = 15$

$SS_{xx} = 3000$ $SS_{xx} = 3000$

For $x_p = 45$ and Brand A,   For $x_p = 45$ and Brand B,

$\hat{y} = 6.62 - .0727(45) = 3.3485$ $\hat{y} = 9.31 - .1077(45) = 4.4635$

The form of the confidence interval is

$$\hat{y} \pm t_{\alpha/2}\, s \sqrt{\frac{1}{n} + \frac{(x_p - \bar{x})^2}{SS_{xx}}}$$

For confidence coefficient .90, $\alpha = 1 - .90 = .10$ and $\alpha/2 = .10/2 = .05$. From Table VI, Appendix B, $t_{.05} = 1.771$ with df $= n - 2 = 15 - 2 = 13$.

For Brand A,

$$3.3485 \pm 1.771(1.211)\sqrt{\frac{1}{15} + \frac{(45 - 50)^2}{3000}}$$

$\Rightarrow 3.3485 \pm .5873 \Rightarrow (2.7612,\ 3.9358)$

For Brand B,

$$4.4635 \pm 1.771(.610)\sqrt{\frac{1}{15} + \frac{(45 - 50)^2}{3000}}$$

$\Rightarrow 4.4635 \pm .2959 \Rightarrow (4.1676,\ 4.7594)$

The width for the confidence interval for Brand B is smaller than that for Brand A because the estimate of the standard deviation ($s = .610$) is smaller.

b. The form of the prediction interval is

$$\hat{y} \pm t_{\alpha/2}\, s \sqrt{1 + \frac{1}{n} + \frac{(x_p - \bar{x})^2}{SS_{xx}}}$$

For Brand A,

$$3.3485 \pm 1.771(1.211)\sqrt{1 + \frac{1}{15} + \frac{(45 - 50)^2}{3000}}$$

$\Rightarrow 3.3485 \pm 2.2237 \Rightarrow (1.1248,\ 5.5722)$

For Brand B,

$$4.4635 \pm 1.771(.610)\sqrt{1 + \frac{1}{15} + \frac{(45 - 50)^2}{3000}}$$

$$\Rightarrow 4.4635 \pm 1.1201 \Rightarrow (3.3434, 5.5836)$$

Again the width of the prediction interval for Brand B is smaller than that for Brand A because the estimate of the standard deviation is smaller. The width of the prediction intervals are always larger than the width of the confidence interval for the mean.

c. For $x_p = 100$ and Brand A,

$$\hat{y} = 6.62 - .0727(100) = -.65$$

For confidence coefficient .95, $\alpha = 1 - .95 = .05$ and $\alpha/2 = .05/2 = .025$. From Table VI, Appendix B, $t_{.025} = 2.160$ with df $= n - 2 = 15 - 2 = 13$.

The prediction interval is

$$-.65 \pm 2.160(1.211)\sqrt{1 + \frac{1}{15} + \frac{(100 - 50)^2}{3000}}$$

$$\Rightarrow -.65 \pm 3.606 \Rightarrow (-4.256, 2.956)$$

We have to assume that the relationship observed between x and y extends to x = 100.

11.55 a. From the printout,

$$\hat{\beta}_0(\text{INTERCEP}) = 575.028672 \approx 575.03$$
$$\hat{\beta}_1(\text{SALARY}) = -0.002186$$

b. SSE = Sum of Squares Error = 293,208.461

s^2 = Mean Square Error = 22,554.497

s = Root MSE = 150.18155

The estimated standard deviation of the retaliation index is 150.18155. We would expect to be able to predict the retaliation index using the salary of the whistle blower to within $\pm 2s$ or $\pm 2(150.18155)$ or ± 300.3631 units.

c. r^2 = R-square = .0664

6.64% of the sample variability in the retaliation index is explained by the linear relationship between the retaliation index and the salary of whistle blowers.

d. To determine if the model is useful, we test:

H_0: $\beta_1 = 0$
H_a: $\beta_1 \neq 0$

The test statistic is t = -0.962.

The observed significance level is .3538.

We would reject H_0 if α is greater than the observed significance level. We wold not reject H_0 at α = .05. There is insufficient evidence to indicate the model is useful for predicting the salary of whistle blowers at α = .05.

e. When the salary is $35,000 (Observation 6),

Lower = 414.7
Upper = 582.3

Therefore, the 95% confidence interval for mean retaliation index of whistle blowers with salaries of $35,000 is

(414.7, 582.3)
=> 498.5 ± 83.8

11.57 a. $\hat{\beta}_0$(INTERCEP) = 506.346   The estimated mean value of y when x_1 = 0 and x_2 = 0 is 506.346.

$\hat{\beta}_1$(X1) = -941.9   The mean value of y is estimated to decrease by 941.9 for each unit increase in x_1, with x_2 held constant.

$\hat{\beta}_2$(X2) = -429.06   The mean value of y is estimated to decrease by 429.06 for each unit increase in x_2, with x_1 held constant.

b. The least squares equation is $\hat{y}$ = 506.34 - 941.9x_1 - 429.06x_2

c. SSE = SUM OF SQUARES for error

SSE = 151,015.72376

$$MSE = \frac{151,015.72376}{17} = 8883.27787$$

$$s = \sqrt{\frac{SSE}{n-3}} = \sqrt{MSE} = ROOT\ MSE = 94.25114$$

About 95% of the observations will fall within 2(94.25114) = 188.50228 of the fitted regression surface.

d. H_0: $\beta_1 = 0$
    H_a: $\beta_1 \neq 0$

The test statistic is t = -3.424 (from printout). The
p-value = .0032. Since p-value < α = .05, we reject H_0 and
conclude β_1 is significantly different from zero.

e. A 95% confidence interval for β_2 is

$$\hat{\beta}_2 \pm t_{\alpha/2} s_{\hat{\beta}_2}$$

$s_{\hat{\beta}_2}$ is the standard error for $\hat{\beta}_2$ which is 379.82567.
For confidence coefficient .95, α = 1 - .95 = .05 and
α/2 = .05/2 = .025. From Table VI, Appendix B, with
df = n - 3 = 20 - 3 = 17, $t_{.025}$ = 2.110. The confidence
interval is:

$$-429.06 \pm 2.11(379.82567)$$

$$\Rightarrow -429.06 \pm 801.432$$

$$\Rightarrow (-1230.492, 372.372)$$

11.59 a. R^2 = R-square = .8911

89.11% of the variability in y is explained by the quadratic
relationship between y and x.

b. H_0: $\beta_1 = \beta_2 = 0$
    H_a: At least one $\beta_i \neq 0$, for i = 1, 2

The test statistic is $F = \dfrac{R^2/k}{(1 - R^2)/[n - (k + 1)]}$

$$= \dfrac{.8911/2}{(1 - .8911)/[19 - (2 + 1)]} = 65.462$$

The rejection region requires α = .05 in the upper tail of the
F distribution with df = ν_1 = k = 1 and ν_2 = n - (k + 1)
= 19 - (2 + 1) = 16. From Table VIII, Appendix B, $F_{.05}$ = 3.63.
The rejection region is F > 3.63.

Since the observed value of the test statistic falls in the
rejection region (F = 65.479 > 3.63), H_0 is rejected. There is
sufficient evidence to indicate the model is useful in predicting
y at α = .05.

c. Prob > F = p-value ≤ .0001

The probability of observing a test statistic of 65.478 or
anything higher is less than .0001. This is very unusual if H_0 is
true. This is very significant.

d. H_0: $\beta_2 = 0$
    H_a: $\beta_2 \neq 0$

The test statistic is t = -6.803 (from printout).

The rejection region requires $\alpha/2 = .05/2 = .025$ in each tail of the t distribution with df = n - (k + 1) = 19 - (2 + 1) = 16. From Table VI, Appendix B, $t_{.025} = 2.12$. The rejection region is t < -2.12 or t > 2.12.

Since the observed value of the test statistic falls in the rejection region (t = -6.803 < -2.12), H_0 is rejected. There is sufficient evidence to indicate $\beta_2 \neq 0$ at $\alpha = .05$. Therefore, the squared term is needed in the model.

The p-value $\leq$ .0001.

The probability of observing a test statistic of -6.803 or anything more unusual is .0001. This is very unusual if H_0 is true. This is very significant.

11.61 a. The least squares prediction equation is:

$$\hat{y} = 1.4326 + .01x_1 + .379x_2$$

b. To determine if the mean food consumption increases with household income, we test:

H_0: $\beta_1 = 0$
H_a: $\beta_1 \neq 0$

The test statistic is t = 3.15.

The rejection region requires $\alpha/2 = .01/2 = .005$ in each tail of the t distribution with df = n - (k + 1) = 25 - (2 + 1) = 22. From Table VI, Appendix B, $t_{.005} = 2.819$. The rejection region is t < -2.819 or t > 2.819.

Since the observed value of the test statistic falls in the rejection region (t = 3.15 > 2.819), H_0 is rejected. There is sufficient evidence to indicate β_1 is not 0 at $\alpha = .01$.

c.

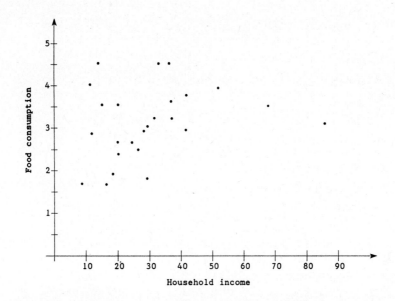

The plot supports the conclusion in part (b) since there is an increasing trend.

11.63 a. To determine if the quadratic term is useful for predicting attitude score, we test:

H_0: $\beta_3 = 0$
H_a: $\beta_3 \neq 0$

The test statistic is $t = \dfrac{\hat{\beta_3}}{s_{\hat{\beta_3}}} = \dfrac{-.1}{.03} = -3.33$.

The rejection region requires $\alpha/2 = .05/2 = .025$ in each tail of the t distribution with df $= n - (k + 1) = 40 - (3 + 1) = 36$. From Table VI, Appendix B, $t_{.025} \approx 1.96$. The rejection region is $t < -1.96$ or $t > 1.96$.

Since the observed value of the test statistic falls in the rejection region ($t = -3.33 < -1.96$), H_0 is rejected. There is sufficient evidence to indicate $\beta_3 \neq 0$ at $\alpha = .05$. Therefore, the quadratic term is useful for predicting attitude score.

b.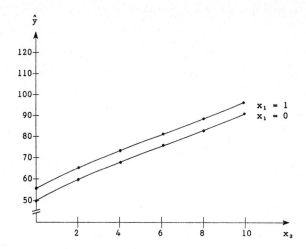

11.65 a. For the model $y_1 = \beta_0 + \beta_1 x + \varepsilon$:

H_0: $\beta_1 = 0$
H_a: $\beta_1 \neq 0$

The test statistic is $F_1 = 1.616$.

The rejection region requires $\alpha = .05$ in the upper tail of the
F distribution with df $= \nu_1 = k = 1$ and $\nu_2 = n - (k + 1)$
$= 264 - (1 + 1) = 262$. From Table VIII, Appendix B, $F_{.05} \approx 3.92$.
The rejection region is $F_1 > 3.92$.

Since the observed value of the test statistic does not fall in
the rejection region ($F_1 = 1.616 \not> 3.92$), H_0 is not rejected.
There is insufficient evidence to indicate the model for
predicting expense per vehicle-mile using the firm's total revenue
is useful at $\alpha = .05$.

For the model $y_2 = \beta_0 + \beta_1 x + \varepsilon$:

H_0: $\beta_1 = 0$
H_a: $\beta_1 \neq 0$

The test statistic is $F_2 = 2.148$.

The rejection region is $F_2 > 3.92$.

Since the observed value of the test statistic does not fall in
the rejection region ($F_2 = 2.148 \not> 3.92$), H_0 is not rejected.
There is insufficient evidence to indicate β_1 is not 0 at $\alpha = .05$.
Therefore, there is insufficient evidence to indicate the model

for predicting expense per ton-mile using the firm's total revenue is useful at $\alpha = .05$.

b. For the model $y_1 = \beta_0 + \beta_1 x + \varepsilon$:

  p-value = $P(F \geq 1.616)$. From Table VII, with $\nu_1 = 1$ and $\nu_2 = 262$,

  p-value $> .10$

For the model $y_2 = \beta_0 + \beta_1 x + \varepsilon$:

  p-value = $P(F \geq 2.148)$. From Table VII, with $\nu_1 = 1$ and $\nu_2 = 262$,

  p-value $> .10$

Therefore, both p-values are greater than .10. Neither one of the tests are significant.

c. The hypotheses tests in part (a) suggest that the economies of scale do not exist in this subsection of the trucking industry.

11.67 To determine if the model is useful, we test:

H_0: $\beta_1 = \beta_2 = \ldots = \beta_{18} = 0$
H_a: At least one $\beta_i \neq 0$, i = 1, 2, ..., 18

The test statistic is $F = \dfrac{R^2/k}{(1 - R^2)/[n - (k + 1)]}$

$= \dfrac{.95/18}{(1 - .95)/[20 - (18 + 1)]} = 1.06$

The rejection region requires $\alpha = .05$ in the upper tail of the F distribution with $\nu_1 = k = 18$ and $\nu_2 = n - (k + 1) = 20 - (18 + 1) = 1$. From Table VIII, Appendix B, $F_{.05} \approx 247$. The rejection region is $F > 247$.

Since the observed value of the test statistic does not fall in the rejection region ($F = 1.06 \not> 247$), H_0 is not rejected. There is insufficient evidence to indicate the model is adequate at $\alpha = .05$.

Note: Although R^2 is large, there are so many variables in the model that ν_2 is small.

11.69 The SAS output is:

```
DEP VARIABLE: TIME
                            ANALYSIS OF VARIANCE

                        SUM OF          MEAN
        SOURCE    DF     SQUARES        SQUARE      F VALUE    PROB>F

        MODEL      2    251.60167     125.80083     54.807     0.0001
        ERROR      7     16.06733367    2.29533338
        C TOTAL    9    267.66900

            ROOT MSE      1.515036     R-SQUARE    0.9400
            DEP MEAN      8.19         ADJ R-SQ    0.9228
            C.V.         18.49861

                            PARAMETER ESTIMATES

                      PARAMETER        STANDARD     T FOR HO:
        VARIABLE   DF   ESTIMATE         ERROR     PARAMETER=0    PROB > |T|

        INTERCEP    1    2.40524442    1.24836624      1.927       0.0954
        MICRO       1    1.42614858    0.14062909     10.141       0.0001
        EXPER       1   -0.36629552    0.13168833     -2.782       0.0272
```

a. Fitting the model to the data, the least squares prediction
    equation is

$$\hat{y} = 2.41 + 1.43x_1 - .366x_2$$

b. To test if the model is useful, we test:

H_0: $\beta_1 = \beta_2 = 0$
H_a: At least 1 $\beta_i \neq 0$ $i = 1, 2$

The test statistic is $F = \dfrac{MS(Model)}{MS(error)} = 54.807$

To see if this is significant, that is, if we can reject H_0, we
compare the p-value to our α level. Since $\alpha = .1$ and the p-value
$\leq .0001 < .1$, we reject H_0. We conclude that at least one
variable is significant in predicting maintenance time at $\alpha = .1$.

c. R^2, which is printed next to R-SQUARE, is .9400. This tells us we
    can explain approximately 94% of the sample variation in
    maintenance time with this model.

d. The SAS output is:

DEP VARIABLE: TIME

ANALYSIS OF VARIANCE

SOURCE	DF	SUM OF SQUARES	MEAN SQUARE	F VALUE	PROB>F
MODEL	3	264.05135	88.01711754	145.980	0.0001
ERROR	6	3.61764738	0.60294123		
C TOTAL	9	267.66900			

ROOT MSE	0.7764929	R-SQUARE	0.9865	
DEP MEAN	8.19	ADJ R-SQ	0.9797	
C.V.	9.480988			

PARAMETER ESTIMATES

VARIABLE	DF	PARAMETER ESTIMATE	STANDARD ERROR	T FOR HO: PARAMETER=0	PROB > |T|
INTERCEP	1	-0.34875688	0.88129883	-0.396	0.7060
MICRO	1	2.06539551	0.15806738	13.067	0.0001
EXPER	1	0.02152454	0.10880943	0.198	0.8497
INTER	1	-0.09187342	0.02021846	-4.544	0.0039

The least squares prediction equation is:

$$\hat{y} = -.349 + 2.07x_1 + .0215x_2 - .0919x_1x_2$$

e. R^2, which is printed next to R-SQUARE, is .9865. This tells us we can explain approximately 98.65% of the sample variation in maintenance time with this model.

f. In comparing R^2, we must realize that additional variables added to the existing model will always increase R^2. We need to determine if the increase is significant.

g. H_0: $\beta_3 = 0$
   H_a: $\beta_3 \neq 0$

The test statistic is $t = -4.544$.

Since the p-value is .0039 < .05, reject H_0. We conclude the interaction is significant in predicting maintenance time at $\alpha = .05$.

h. No. We must test to make sure each term in the model contributes information.

11.71 Plot $\hat{\varepsilon}$ vs x_1.

There is no definite mound or bowl shape to the plot. This implies there is no need for a quadratic term in x_1. From Exercise 12.5, ROOT MSE is .277. Two standard deviations from the mean is ±2(.277) => -.554 to .554. Three standard deviations from the mean is

±3(.277) => −.831 to .831. There are two points more than two standard deviations from the mean, but none beyond three standard deviations. Thus, there is no evidence to indicate outliers are present.

Plot $\hat{\varepsilon}$ vs x_2.

There is a possible mound shape to the plot. We may want to try a model with size^2 added. Again, there are two data points more than 2 standard deviations from the mean, but none more than 3 standard deviations from the mean.

11.73 a. Neither plot, $\hat{\varepsilon}$ vs x_1 nor $\hat{\varepsilon}$ vs x_2, has a mound or bowl shape. This implies there is no need for quadratic terms to be added to the model. The standard deviation is $\sqrt{MSE} = \sqrt{.311} = .558$.

Two standard deviations form the mean is ±2(.558) => −1.116 to 1.116. Three standard deviations form the mean is ± 3(.558) => −1.674 to 1.674.

On both plots, there is one point that is more than three standard deviations above the mean. This point is the 26th household. It appears the additional point is not typical compared to the others or there may be an error.

11.75 a. One would expect the unit price to decrease as the quantity increases.

b. The estimated regression equation is $\hat{y} = 148.055 - 7.57x_1$. Since $x_1 = 0$ is not in the observed range, $\hat{\beta}_0$ does not have an interpretation other than being the y-intercept.

$\hat{\beta}_1 = -7.57$. The change in the mean unit price for each additional thousand tons is estimated to be −7.57.

To determine if the model is useful for predicting unit price, we test:

H_0: $\beta_1 = 0$
H_a: $\beta_1 \neq 0$

The test statistic is $F = \dfrac{MSR}{MSE} = 196.615$.

The rejection region requires $\alpha = .05$ in the upper tail of the F distribution with numerator df = k = 1 and denominator df = n − (k + 1) = 30 − (1 + 1) = 28. From Table VIII, Appendix B, $F_{.05} = 3.34$. The rejection region is F > 3.34.

Since the observed value of the test statistic falls in the rejection region (F = 196.615 > 3.34), H_0 is rejected. There is sufficient evidence to indicate the model is useful for predicting unit price at α = .05.

The estimated standard deviation is Root MSE = 18.74. We would expect about 95% of the observations to lie within ±2(18.74) or ±37.48 units of their mean.

c. Since the plot is in a U-shape, it implies a second-order model may be more appropriate than a first-order model. It is rather difficult to judge, because of the U-shape, whether the spread of the residuals is increasing as $\hat{y}$ is increasing. I would say that there might be a slight trend in that direction, but it probably would not be significant.

11.77 a.

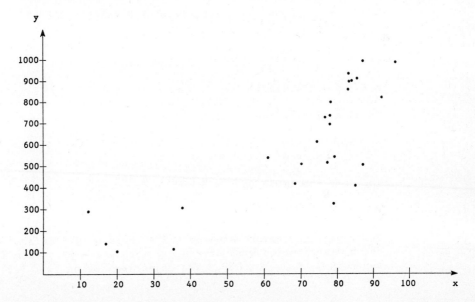

The variables x and y do appear to be related. It appears when x increases, y tends to increase.

b. $r = \dfrac{SS_{xy}}{\sqrt{SS_{xx}SS_{yy}}} = \dfrac{124,348.520}{\sqrt{14,026.16(1,800,417.44)}} = .7825$

The correlation between concentration and exhaustion index is .7825. This relationship is positive since r > 0. The relationship is fairly strong.

c. $\hat{\beta}_1 = \dfrac{SS_{xy}}{SS_{xx}} = \dfrac{124,348.520}{14,026.16} = 8.865$

$\hat{\beta}_0 = \bar{y} - \hat{\beta}_1\bar{x} = 578.32 - (8.865)68.560 = -29.464$

The least squares line is $\hat{y} = -29.464 + 8.865x$.

d. $r^2 = .7825^2 = .6123$

61.23% of the sample variation of exhaustion index is explained by the linear relationship between the exhaustion index and concentration.

e. Some preliminary calculations are:

$SSE = SS_{yy} - \hat{\beta}_1 SS_{xy} = 1,800,417.44 - 8.865(124,348.52)$
$$= 698,067.8102$$

$s^2 = \dfrac{SSE}{n-2} = \dfrac{698,067.8102}{25-2} = 30,350.77436$

$s = \sqrt{s^2} = 174.21474$

To determine if the straight-line relationship is useful, we test:

$H_0:\ \beta_1 = 0$
$H_a:\ \beta_1 \neq 0$

The test statistic is $t = \dfrac{\hat{\beta}_1 - 0}{s_{\hat{\beta}_1}} = \dfrac{8.865 - 0}{\dfrac{174.2147}{\sqrt{14.026.16}}} = 6.03$

The rejection region requires $\alpha/2 = .05/2 = .025$ in each tail of the t distribution with df = $n - 2 = 25 - 2 = 23$. From Table VI, Appendix B, $t_{.025} = 2.069$. The rejection region is $t > 2.069$ or $t < -2.069$.

Since the observed value of the test statistic falls in the rejection region ($t = 6.03 > 2.069$), H_0 is rejected. There is sufficient evidence to indicate the model is useful for predicting burnout at $\alpha = .05$.

f. In part (e), we tested $H_0: \beta_1 = 0$ against $H_a: \beta_1 \neq 0$. This is equivalent to testing $H_0: \rho = 0$ against $H_a: \rho \neq 0$. Since we rejected H_0 in part (e) and decided $\beta_1 \neq 0$, then $\rho \neq 0$. Therefore, there is evidence that the correlation between emotional exhaustion and concentration differs from 0 at $\alpha = .05$.

This does not infer that concentration causes emotional exhaustion.

g. For confidence coefficient .95, $\alpha = 1 - .95 = .05$ and $\alpha/2 = .05/2$ = .025. From Table VI, Appendix B, $t_{.025} = 2.069$ with df = 23.

The prediction interval is

$$\hat{y} \pm t_{\alpha/2}\ s\sqrt{1 + \frac{1}{n} + \frac{(x_p - \bar{x})^2}{SS_{xx}}}$$

where $\hat{y} = -29.464 + 8.865(80) = 679.736$

$\Rightarrow 679.736 \pm 2.069(174.21474)\sqrt{1 + \frac{1}{25} + \frac{(80 - 68.56)^2}{14,026.16}}$

$\Rightarrow 679.736 \pm 369.234 \Rightarrow (310.502, 1,048.97)$

We are 95% confident that the level of emotional exhaustion when the human services professional has 80% of her social contacts within her work group will fall in the interval from 310.502 to 1,048.97.

h. The confidence interval is

$$\hat{y} \pm t_{\alpha/2}\ s\sqrt{\frac{1}{n} + \frac{(x_p - \bar{x})^2}{SS_{xx}}}$$

$\Rightarrow 679.736 \pm 2.069(174.21474)\sqrt{\frac{1}{25} + \frac{(80 - 68.56)^2}{14,026.16}}$

$\Rightarrow 679.736 \pm 80.058 \Rightarrow (599.678, 759.794)$

We are 95% confident that the interval from 599.678 to 759.794 encloses the mean exhaustion level for all professionals who have 80% of their social contacts within their work groups.

11.79 From Exercise 11.29, $\hat{y} = 44.1311 + .2366x$, $s = 19.4038$, and $n = 19$.

a. For confidence coefficient .90, $\alpha = 1 - .90 = .10$ and $\alpha/2 = .10/2$ = .05. From Table VI, Appendix B, $t_{.05} = 1.740$ with df = n - 2 = 19 - 2 = 17.

The prediction interval is

$$\hat{y} \pm t_{\alpha/2}\ s\sqrt{1 + \frac{1}{n} + \frac{(x_p - \bar{x})^2}{SS_{xx}}}$$

where $\hat{y} = 44.1311 + .2366(55) = 57.1441$

$\Rightarrow 57.1441 \pm 1.74(19.4038)\sqrt{1 + \frac{1}{19} + \frac{(55 - 44.1579)^2}{10,824.5263}}$

$\Rightarrow 57.144 \pm 34.818 \Rightarrow (22.326, 91.962)$

b.   The number of interactions with outsiders in the study went from 10 to 82. The value 110 is not within this interval. We do not know if the relationship between x and y is the same outside the observed range. Also, the farther x_p lies from $\bar{x}$, the larger will be the error of prediction. The prediction interval for a particular value of y will be very wide when x_p = 110.

c.   The prediction interval for a manager's success index will be narrowest when the number of contacts with people outside her work unit is $\bar{x}$ = 44.1579 (44).

11.81   a.

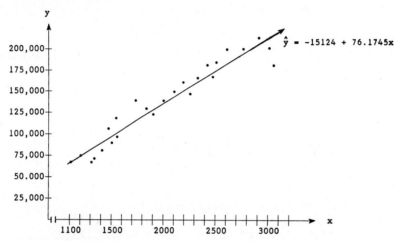

b.   From the printout:

$\hat{\beta}_0$(INTERCEP) = -15124

$\hat{\beta}_1$(AREA) = 76.174547

The least squares line is $\hat{y}$ = -15124 + 76.1745x.

c. r^2 = R-SQUARE = .9185

91.85% of the sample variability in price is explained by the linear relationship between price and area.

d.   To determine if living area contributes information for predicting the price of a home, we test:

H_0: β_1 = 0
H_a: $\beta_1 \neq 0$

The test statistic is t = 15.743 (from printout)

The p-value is .0001.

Since the p-value is less than α = .05, H_0 is rejected. There is sufficient evidence to indicate living area contributes information for predicting the price of a home at α = .05.

e. For confidence coefficient .95, $\alpha = 1 - .95 = .05$ and
$\alpha/2 = .05/2 = .025$. From Table VI, Appendix B, $t_{.025} = 2.074$
with df $= n - 2 = 24 - 2 = 22$. The confidence interval is

$$\hat{\beta}_1 \pm t_{\alpha/2}s_{\hat{\beta}_1} \Rightarrow 76.1745 \pm 2.074(4.8385)$$

$$\Rightarrow 76.1745 \pm 10.0350 \Rightarrow (66.1395, 86.2095)$$

Since 0 is not in the confidence interval, it is not a likely
value for $\beta_1 \Rightarrow$ reject H_0. This corresponds to the conclusion in
(d).

f. The observed significance level is .0001. Since this is less than
$\alpha = .05$, H_0 is rejected in part (d).

g. From the 25 observations on the printout, the point estimate for
price when $x_p = 2200$ is $\hat{y} = 152,460$. The 95% confidence interval
is $(146,713, 158,206)$.

11.83 Some preliminary calculations are:

$$\sum x_i = 254.75 \qquad \sum x_i^2 = 2860.6875 \qquad \sum x_i y_i = 174.2575$$

$$\sum y_i = 16.52 \qquad \sum y_i^2 = 19.553$$

$$SS_{xy} = \sum x_i y_i - \frac{\sum x_i \sum y_i}{n} = 174.2575 - \frac{254.75(16.52)}{23} = -8.7194565$$

$$SS_{xx} = \sum x_i^2 - \frac{(\sum x_i)^2}{n} = 2860.6875 - \frac{254.75^2}{23} = 39.054348$$

$$SS_{yy} = \sum y_i^2 - \frac{(\sum y_i)^2}{n} = 19.553 - \frac{16.52^2}{23} = 7.68733043$$

$$r = \frac{SS_{xy}}{\sqrt{SS_{xx}SS_{yy}}} = \frac{-8.7194565}{\sqrt{39.054348(7.68733043)}} = -.503$$

This correlation coefficient is not very close to 0, so it probably is
not spurious. To check for sure, we could run a test of hypothesis.

11.85 a. H_0: $\beta_1 = \beta_2 = \beta_3 = \beta_4 = \beta_5 = \beta_6 = \beta_7 = 0$
H_a: At least one $\beta_i \neq 0$, for $i = 1, 2, \ldots, 7$

The test statistic is $F = \dfrac{R^2/k}{(1 - R^2)/[n - (k + 1)]}$

$$= \frac{.8979/7}{(1 - .8979)/[140 - (7 + 1)]} = 165.84$$

The rejection region requires $\alpha = .01$ in the upper tail of the F distribution with $v_1 = k = 7$ and $v_2 = n - (k + 1) = 140 - (7 + 1)$ = 132. From Table X, Appendix B, $F_{.01} \approx 2.79$. The rejection region is $F > 2.79$.

Since the observed value of the test statistic falls in the rejection region ($F = 165.84 > 2.79$), H_0 is rejected. There is sufficient evidence to indicate the model is useful at $\alpha = .01$. There is a relationship between rates per long ton and at least one of the independent variables.

b. The closer R^2 is to 1, the more variability in y is explained by the model. Therefore, since the Brinkley and Harrer model only had an $R^2 = .46$, Martin and Clement's model with an $R^2 = .8979$ explains more of the variation in rates per long ton.

c. To determine if the transport rates increase with distance, we test:

H_0: $\beta_2 = 0$
H_a: $\beta_2 > 0$

The test statistic is $t = 3.64$.

The rejection region requires $\alpha = .05$ in the upper tail of the t distribution with df $= n - (k + 1) = 140 - (7 + 1) = 132$. From Table VI, Appendix B, $t_{.05} \approx 1.645$. The rejection region is $t > 1.645$.

Since the observed value of the test statistic falls in the rejection region ($t = 3.64 > 1.645$), H_0 is rejected. There is sufficient evidence to indicate that the transport rates increase with distance at $\alpha = .05$.

To determine if the transport rates increase with distance at an increasing rate (the coefficient of x_2^2 is positive), we test:

H_0: $\beta_3 = 0$
H_a: $\beta_3 > 0$

The test statistic is $t = -2.25$.

The rejection region is $t > 1.645$.

Since the observed value of the test statistic does not fall in the rejection region ($t = -2.25 \not> 1.645$), H_0 is not rejected. There is insufficient evidence to indicate the transport rates increase with distance at an increasing rate at $\alpha = .05$.

Note: $\hat{\beta}_3 < 0$

11.87 a. The least squares prediction equation is

$$\hat{y} = .0562 + .273x_1 + .0006x_2$$

b. To determine if the model contributes information for predicting the number of positions filled, we test:

H_0: $\beta_1 = \beta_2 = 0$
H_a: At least one $\beta_i \neq 0$ i = 1, 2

The test statistic is $F = \dfrac{MSR}{MSE} = \dfrac{291.59}{1.77} = 164.74$.

The rejection region requires $\alpha = .05$ in the upper tail of the F distribution with $\nu_1 = k = 2$ and $\nu_2 = n - (k + 1) = 10 - (2 + 1) = 7$. From Table VIII, Appendix B, $F_{.05} = 4.74$. The rejection region is $F > 4.74$.

Since the observed value of the test statistic falls in the rejection region (F = 164.74 > 4.74), H_0 is rejected. There is sufficient evidence to indicate the model is useful for predicting the number of positions filled at $\alpha = .05$.

c. H_0: $\beta_2 = 0$
   H_a: $\beta_2 \neq 0$

The test statistic is t = 4.34 (from printout).

The rejection region requires $\alpha/2 = .05/2 = .025$ in the each tail of the t distribution with df = n - (k + 1) = 10 - (2 + 1) = 7. From Table VI, Appendix B, $t_{.025} = 2.365$. The rejection region is t < -2.365 or t > 2.365.

Since the observed value of the test statistic falls in the rejection region (t = 4.34 > 2.365), H_0 is rejected. There is sufficient evidence to indicate the recruiting budget contributes information for predicting the number of positions that are filled at $\alpha = .05$.

d. If $x_1 = 30$ and $x_2 = 10,000$,

$$\hat{y} = .0562 + .273(30) + .0006(10,000)$$
$$= 14.25$$

e. Since the dependent variable is discrete (number of positions filled), it is unlikely that ε is normally distributed.

11.89 a. For x = 1, $\hat{y} = 51.3 - 10.1(1) + .15(1)^2 = 41.35$
       For x = 2, $\hat{y} = 51.3 - 10.1(2) + .15(2)^2 = 31.7$
       For x = 3, $\hat{y} = 51.3 - 10.1(3) + .15(3)^2 = 22.35$
       For x = 4, $\hat{y} = 51.3 - 10.1(4) + .15(4)^2 = 13.3$

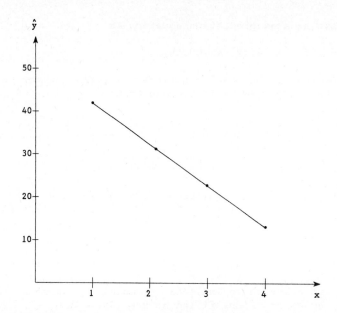

b. To determine if the quadratic term contributes information for
    predicting the miles per gallon rating, we test:

H_0: $\beta_2 = 0$
H_a: $\beta_2 \neq 0$

The test statistic is $t = \dfrac{\hat{\beta}_2 - 0}{s_{\hat{\beta}_2}} = \dfrac{.15 - 0}{.0037} = 40.54$

The rejection region requires $\alpha/2 = .05/2 = .025$ in each tail of
the t distribution with df $= n - (k + 1) = 50 - (2 + 1) = 47$.
From Table VI, Appendix B, $t_{.025} \approx 1.96$. The rejection region is
$t < -1.96$ or $t > 1.96$.

Since the observed value of the test statistic falls in the
rejection region ($t = 40.54 > 1.96$), H_0 is rejected. There is
sufficient evidence to indicate the addition of the quadratic term
contributes significant information for the prediction of the
miles per gallon rating at $\alpha = .05$.

c. For $x = 3.5$, $\hat{y} = 51.3 - 10.1(3.5) + .15(3.5)^2 = 17.7875$

d. I am 95% confident the mean miles per gallon rating for all cars
    with 350-cubic-inch engines is between 17.2 and 18.4.

e. The confidence interval given in part (d) is for the mean miles
    per gallon rating for all cars with 350-cubic-inch engines, not
    for one particular car. Therefore, it is not surprising that the
    value is not within the interval.

11.91 a. $\hat{\beta}_1$ = .02573. The mean GPA is estimated to increase by .02573 for each 1 point increase in verbal score, mathematics score held constant.

$\hat{\beta}_2$ = .03361. The mean GPA is estimated to increase by .03361 for each 1 point increase in mathematics score, verbal score held constant.

b. The standard deviation is $\sqrt{MSE} = \sqrt{.16183}$ = .40228. We would expect about 95% of the observations to fall within 2(.40228) = .80456 of the predicted value.

R^2 = .68106. About 68% of the sample variability in GPA's is explained by the model containing verbal and mathematics scores.

c. To determine if the model is useful for predicting GPA, we test:

H_0: $\beta_1 = \beta_2 = 0$
H_a: At least 1 $\beta_i \neq 0$ i = 1, 2.

The test statistic is $F = \dfrac{MSR}{MSE} = \dfrac{6.39297}{.16183}$ = 39.505

The p-value is .0000. Since .0000 < α = .05, H_0 is rejected. There is sufficient evidence to indicate the model is useful for predicting GPA at α = .05.

d. For x_2 = 60, $\hat{y}$ = -1.57 + .026x_1 + .034(60) = .47 + .026x_1

For x_2 = 75, $\hat{y}$ = -1.57 + .026x_1 + .034(75) = .98 + .026x_1

For x_2 = 90, $\hat{y}$ = -1.57 + .026x_1 + .034(90) = 1.49 + .026x_1

The plot is:

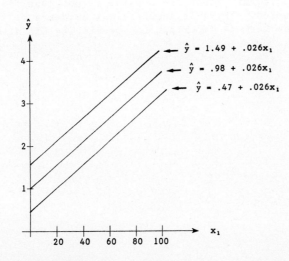

11.93 a. The standard deviation for the first-order model is

$$\sqrt{MSE} = \sqrt{.16183} = .4023$$

The standard deviation for the second-order model is

$$\sqrt{MSE} = \sqrt{.03502} = .1871$$

The relative precision for the first-order model is $\pm 2(.4023) \Rightarrow \pm .8046$.

The relative precision for the second-order model is $\pm 2(.1871 \Rightarrow \pm .3742$.

b. To determine if the model is useful, we test:

$$H_0: \quad \beta_1 = \beta_2 = \beta_3 = \beta_4 = \beta_5 = 0$$
$$H_a: \quad \text{At least 1 } \beta_i \neq 0 \quad i = 1, 2, \ldots, 5$$

The test statistic is $F = \dfrac{MSR}{MSE} = \dfrac{3.51655}{.03502} = 100.409$

The p-value is .0000. Since the p-value is less than $\alpha = .05$, H_0 is rejected. There is sufficient evidence to indicate the model is useful for predicting GPA at $\alpha = .05$.

c. To determine if the interaction term is important, we test:

$$H_0: \quad \beta_5 = 0$$
$$H_a: \quad \beta_5 \neq 0$$

The test statistic is $t = 1.675$.

The p-value is .1032. Since the p-value is not less than $\alpha = .10$, H_0 is not rejected. There is insufficient evidence to indicate the interaction term is important for predicting GPA at $\alpha = .10$.

CHAPTER 12

METHODS FOR QUALITY IMPROVEMENT

12.1 A control chart is a time series plot of individual measurements or means of a quality variable to which a centerline and two other horizontal lines called control limits have been added. The center line represents the mean of the process when the process is in a state of statistical control. The upper control limit and the lower control limit are positioned so that when the process is in control the probability of an individual measurement or mean falling outside the limits is very small. A control chart is used to determine if a process is in control (only common causes of variation present) or not (both common and special causes of variation present). This information helps us to determine when to take action to find and remove special causes of variation and when to leave the process alone.

12.3 When a control chart is first constructed, it is not known whether the process is in control or not. If the process is found not to be in control, then the centerline and control limits should not be used to monitor the process in the future.

12.5 Even if all the points of an $\bar{x}$-chart fall within the control limits, the process may be out of control. Nonrandom patterns may exist among the plotted points that are within the control limits, but are very unlikely if the process is in control. Examples include six points in a row steadily increasing or decreasing and fourteen points in a row alternating up and down.

12.7 Rule 1: One point beyond Zone A: No points are beyond Zone A.

Rule 2: Nine points in a row in Zone C or beyond: No sequence of 9 points are in Zone C (on one side of the centerline) or beyond.

Rule 3: Six points in a row steadily increasing or decreasing: No sequence of 6 points steadily increase or decrease.

Rule 4: Fourteen points in a row alternating up and down: This pattern does not exist.

Rule 5: Two out of three points in Zone A or beyond: There are no groups of three consecutive points that have two or more in Zone A or beyond.

Rule 6: Four out of five points in a row in Zone B or beyond: Points 18 thru 21 are all in Zone B or beyond. This indicates the process is out of control.

Thus, Rule 6 indicates this process is out of control.

12.9   Using Table XIV, Appendix B:

a. With $n = 3$, $A_2 = 1.023$

b. With $n = 10$, $A_2 = 0.308$

c. With $n = 22$, $A_2 = 0.167$

12.11   a. For each sample, we compute $\bar{x} = \frac{\sum \bar{x}}{n}$ and R = range = largest measurement - smallest measurement. The results are listed in the table:

Sample No.	$\bar{x}$	R	Sample No.	$\bar{x}$	R
1	20.225	1.8	11	21.225	3.2
2	19.750	2.8	12	20.475	0.9
3	20.425	3.8	13	19.650	2.6
4	19.725	2.5	14	19.075	4.0
5	20.550	3.7	15	19.400	2.2
6	19.900	5.0	16	20.700	4.3
7	21.325	5.5	17	19.850	3.6
8	19.625	3.5	18	20.200	2.5
9	19.350	2.5	19	20.425	2.2
10	20.550	4.1	20	19.900	5.5

b. $\bar{\bar{x}} = \frac{\bar{x}_1 + \bar{x}_2 + \ldots + \bar{x}_{20}}{n} = \frac{402.325}{20} = 20.11625$

$\bar{R} = \frac{R_1 + R_2 + \ldots + R_{20}}{n} = \frac{66.2}{20} = 3.31$

c. Centerline = $\bar{\bar{x}} = 20.116$

From Table XIV, Appendix B, with $n = 4$, $A_2 = .729$.

Upper control limit = $\bar{\bar{x}} + A_2 \bar{R} = 20.116 + .729(3.31) = 22.529$

Lower control limit = $\bar{\bar{x}} - A_2 \bar{R} = 20.116 - .729(3.31) = 17.703$

d. Upper A-B Boundary = $\bar{x} + \frac{2}{3}(A_2\bar{R})$ = 20.116 + $\frac{2}{3}$(.729)(3.31) = 21.725

Lower A-B Boundary = $\bar{x} - \frac{2}{3}(A_2\bar{R})$ = 20.116 − $\frac{2}{3}$(.729)(3.31) = 18.507

Upper B-C Boundary = $\bar{x} + \frac{1}{3}(A_2\bar{R})$ = 20.116 + $\frac{1}{3}$(.729)(3.31) = 20.920

Lower B-C Boundary = $\bar{x} - \frac{1}{3}(A_2\bar{R})$ = 20.116 − $\frac{1}{3}$(.729)(3.31) = 19.312

e. The $\bar{x}$-chart is:

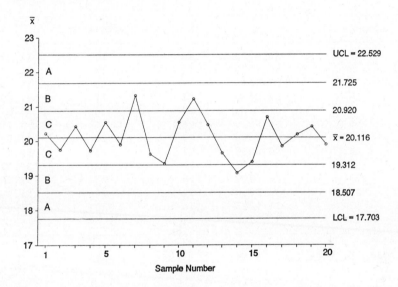

Rule 1: One point beyond Zone A: No points are beyond Zone A.

Rule 2: Nine points in a row in Zone C or beyond: No sequence of 9 points are in Zone C (on one side of the centerline) or beyond.

Rule 3: Six points in a row steadily increasing or decreasing: No sequence of 6 points steadily increase or decrease.

Rule 4: Fourteen points in a row alternating up and down: This pattern does not exist.

Rule 5: Two out of three points in Zone A or beyond: There are no groups of three consecutive points that have two or more in Zone A or beyond.

Rule 6: Four out of five points in a row in Zone B or beyond: No sequence of 5 points has 4 or more in Zone B or beyond.

The process appears to be in control.

12.13 a. The process of interest is the production of bolts used in military aircraft.

b. For each sample, we compute $\bar{x} = \dfrac{\sum \bar{x}}{n}$ and R = range = largest measurement - smallest measurement. The results are listed in the table:

Sample No.	$\bar{x}$	R	Sample No.	$\bar{x}$	R
1	36.9725	.20	14	37.0725	.06
2	36.9575	.19	15	36.9925	.15
3	37.0675	.17	16	36.9550	.09
4	37.0650	.22	17	37.0375	.20
5	36.9475	.29	18	37.0100	.20
6	36.9975	.24	19	36.9550	.13
7	37.0000	.13	20	37.0350	.25
8	37.0050	.21	21	36.9950	.09
9	37.0275	.27	22	37.0225	.19
10	36.9700	.24	23	37.0025	.09
11	37.0200	.22	24	36.9950	.17
12	36.9825	.16	25	37.0100	.20
13	37.0700	.31			

$$\bar{\bar{x}} = \frac{\bar{x}_1 + \bar{x}_2 + \ldots + \bar{x}_{25}}{n} = \frac{925.1650}{25} = 37.0066$$

$$\bar{R} = \frac{R_1 + R_2 + \ldots + R_{25}}{n} = \frac{4.67}{25} = .1868$$

Centerline = $\bar{\bar{x}}$ = 37.007

From Table XIV, Appendix B, with n = 4, A_2 = .729.

Upper control limit = $\bar{\bar{x}} + A_2\bar{R}$ = 37.007 + .729(.1868) = 37.143

Lower control limit = $\bar{\bar{x}} - A_2\bar{R}$ = 37.007 - .729(.1868) = 36.871

Upper A-B Boundary = $\bar{\bar{x}} + \frac{2}{3}(A_2\bar{R})$ = 37.007 + $\frac{2}{3}$(.729)(.1868) = 37.098

Lower A-B Boundary = $\bar{\bar{x}} - \frac{2}{3}(A_2\bar{R})$ = 37.007 - $\frac{2}{3}$(.729)(.1868) = 36.916

Upper B-C Boundary = $\bar{\bar{x}} + \frac{1}{3}(A_2\bar{R})$ = 37.007 + $\frac{1}{3}$(.729)(.1868) = 37.052

Lower B-C Boundary = $\bar{\bar{x}} - \frac{1}{3}(A_2\bar{R})$ = 37.007 - $\frac{1}{3}$(.729)(.1868) = 36.962

The $\bar{x}$-chart is:

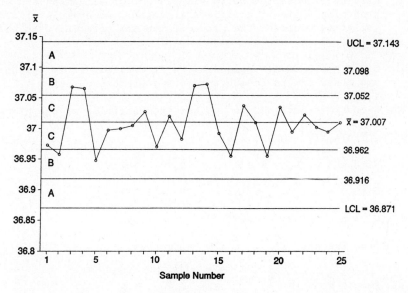

c. To determine if the process is in or out of control, we check the 6 rules:

Rule 1: One point beyond Zone A: No points are beyond Zone A.

Rule 2: Nine points in a row in Zone C or beyond: No sequence of 9 points are in Zone C (on one side of the centerline) or beyond.

Rule 3: Six points in a row steadily increasing or decreasing: No sequence of 6 points steadily increase or decrease.

Rule 4: Fourteen points in a row alternating up and down: This pattern does not exist.

Rule 5: Two out of three points in Zone A or beyond: There are no groups of three consecutive points that have two or more in Zone A or beyond.

Rule 6: Four out of five points in a row in Zone B or beyond: No sequence of 5 points has 4 or more in Zone B or beyond.

The process appears to be in control. No special causes of variation appear to be present.

d. An example of a special cause of variation would be if the machine used to produce the bolts slipped out of alignment and started producing bolts of a different length. An example of common cause variation would be the grade of the raw material used to make the bolts.

e. Since the process appears to be in control, it is appropriate to use these limits to monitor future process output.

12.15 The R-chart is designed to monitor the variation of the process.

12.17 Using Table XIV, Appendix B:

a. With $n = 4$, $D_3 = 0.000$ $D_4 = 2.282$

b. With $n = 12$, $D_3 = 0.283$ $D_4 = 1.717$

c. With $n = 24$, $D_3 = 0.451$ $D_4 = 1.548$

12.19 a. From Exercise 12.11, the R values are:

Sample No.	R	Sample No.	R
1	1.8	11	3.2
2	2.8	12	0.9
3	3.8	13	2.6
4	2.5	14	4.0
5	3.7	15	2.2
6	5.0	16	4.3
7	5.5	17	3.6
8	3.5	18	2.5
9	2.5	19	2.2
10	4.1	20	5.5

$$\bar{R} = \frac{R_1 + R_2 + \ldots + R_{20}}{n} = \frac{66.2}{20} = 3.31$$

Centerline = $\bar{R}$ = 3.31

From Table XIV, Appendix B, with $n = 4$, $D_4 = 2.282$ and $D_3 = 0$.

Upper control limit = $\bar{R}D_4$ = 3.31(2.282) = 7.553

Since $D_3 = 0$, the lower control limit is negative and is not included on the chart.

b. From Table XIV, Appendix B, with n = 4, d_2 = 2.059 and d_3 = .880.

Upper A–B Boundary = $\bar{R} + 2d_3 \dfrac{\bar{R}}{d_2}$ = 3.31 + 2(.880)$\dfrac{3.31}{2.059}$ = 6.139

Lower A–B Boundary = $\bar{R} - 2d_3 \dfrac{\bar{R}}{d_2}$ = 3.31 − 2(.880)$\dfrac{3.31}{2.059}$ = 0.481

Upper B–C Boundary = $\bar{R} + d_3 \dfrac{\bar{R}}{d_2}$ = 3.31 + (.880) $\dfrac{3.31}{2.059}$ = 4.725

Lower B–C Boundary = $\bar{R} - d_3 \dfrac{\bar{R}}{d_2}$ = 3.31 − (.880) $\dfrac{3.31}{2.059}$ = 1.895

c. The R-chart is:

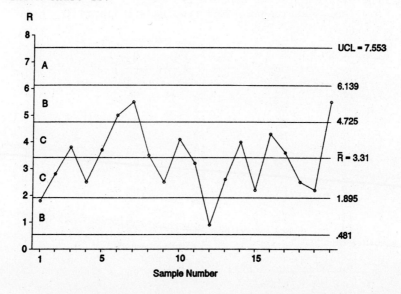

To determine if the process is in or out of control, we check the 6 rules:

Rule 1: One point beyond Zone A: No points are beyond Zone A.

Rule 2: Nine points in a row in Zone C or beyond: No sequence of 9 points are in Zone C (on one side of the centerline) or beyond.

Rule 3: Six points in a row steadily increasing or decreasing: No sequence of 6 points steadily increase or decrease.

Rule 4: Fourteen points in a row alternating up and down: This pattern does not exist.

Rule 5: Two out of three points in Zone A or beyond: There are no groups of three consecutive points that have two or more in Zone A or beyond.

Rule 6: Four out of five points in a row in Zone B or beyond: No sequence of 5 points has 4 or more in zone B or beyond.

The process appears to be in control.

12.21 a. Yes. Because all five observations in each sample were selected from the same dispenser, the rational subgrouping will enable the company to detect variation in fill caused by differences in the carbon dioxide dispensers.

b. For each sample, we compute the range = R = largest measurement - smallest measurement. The results are listed in the table:

Sample No.	R	Sample No.	R
1	.05	13	.05
2	.06	14	.04
3	.06	15	.05
4	.05	16	.05
5	.07	17	.06
6	.07	18	.06
7	.09	19	.05
8	.08	20	.08
9	.08	21	.08
10	.11	22	.12
11	.14	23	.12
12	.14	24	.15

$$\bar{R} = \frac{R_1 + R_2 + \ldots + R_{24}}{n} = \frac{1.91}{24} = .0796$$

Centerline = $\bar{R}$ = .0796

From Table XIV, Appendix B, with n = 5, D_4 = 2.114 and D_3 = 0.

Upper control limit = $\bar{R}D_4$ = .0796(2.114) = .168

Since D_3 = 0, the lower control limit is negative and is not included on the chart.

From Table XIV, Appendix B, with n = 5, d_2 = 2.326 and d_3 = .864.

$$\text{Upper A-B Boundary} = \bar{R} + 2d_3 \frac{\bar{R}}{d_2} = .0796 + 2(.864)\frac{.0796}{2.326} = .139$$

$$\text{Lower A-B Boundary} = \bar{R} - 2d_3 \frac{\bar{R}}{d_2} = .0796 - 2(.864)\frac{.0796}{2.326} = .020$$

$$\text{Upper B-C Boundary} = \bar{R} + d_3 \frac{\bar{R}}{d_2} = .0796 + (.864) \frac{.0796}{2.326} = .109$$

$$\text{Lower B-C Boundary} = \bar{R} - d_3 \frac{\bar{R}}{d_2} = .0796 - (.864) \frac{.0796}{2.326} = .050$$

The R-chart is:

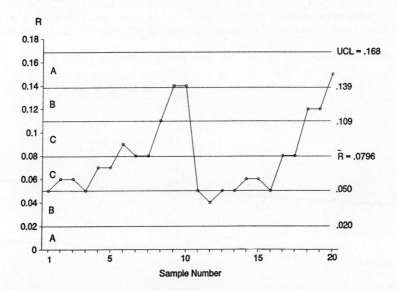

c. To determine if the process is in or out of control, we check the 6 rules:

Rule 1: One point beyond Zone A: No points are beyond Zone A.

Rule 2: Nine points in a row in Zone C or beyond: No sequence of 9 points are in Zone C (on one side of the centerline) or beyond.

Rule 3: Six points in a row steadily increasing or decreasing: No sequence of 6 points steadily increase or decrease.

Rule 4: Fourteen points in a row alternating up and down: This pattern does not exist.

Rule 5: Two out of three points in Zone A or beyond: Points 11 and 12 are in Zone A or beyond. This indicates the process is out of control.

Rule 6: Four out of five points in a row in Zone B or beyond: No sequence of 5 points has 4 or more in Zone B or beyond.

Rule 5 indicates that the process is out of control. The process is unstable.

d. Since the process variation is out of control, the R-chart should not be used to monitor future process output.

e. The $\bar{x}$-chart should not be constructed. The control limits of the $\bar{x}$-chart depend on the variation of the process. (In particular, they are constructed using $\bar{R}$.) If the variation of the process is out of control, the control limits of the $\bar{x}$-chart are meaningless.

12.23. a. From Exercise 12.13, we get the following data:

Sample No.	R	Sample No.	R
1	.20	14	.06
2	.19	15	.15
3	.17	16	.09
4	.22	17	.20
5	.29	18	.20
6	.24	19	.13
7	.13	20	.25
8	.21	21	.09
9	.27	22	.19
10	.24	23	.09
11	.22	24	.17
12	.16	25	.20
13	.31		

$$\bar{R} = \frac{R_1 + R_2 + \ldots + R_{25}}{n} = \frac{4.67}{25} = .1868$$

Centerline = $\bar{R}$ = .1868

From Table XIV, Appendix B, with n = 4, D_4 = 2.282 and D_3 = 0.

Upper control limit = $\bar{R}D_4$ = .1868(2.282) = .426

Since D_3 = 0, the lower control limit is negative and is not included on the chart.

From Table XIV, Appendix B, with n = 4, d_2 = 2.059 and d_3 = .880.

$$\text{Upper A-B Boundary} = \overline{R} + 2d_3\frac{\overline{R}}{d_2} = .1868 + 2(.880)\frac{.1868}{2.059} = .346$$

$$\text{Lower A-B Boundary} = \overline{R} - 2d_3\frac{\overline{R}}{d_2} = .1868 - 2(.880)\frac{.1868}{2.059} = .027$$

$$\text{Upper B-C Boundary} = \overline{R} + d_3\frac{\overline{R}}{d_2} = .1868 + (.880)\frac{.1868}{2.059} = .267$$

$$\text{Lower B-C Boundary} = \overline{R} - d_3\frac{\overline{R}}{d_2} = .1868 - (.880)\frac{.1868}{2.059} = .107$$

The R-chart is:

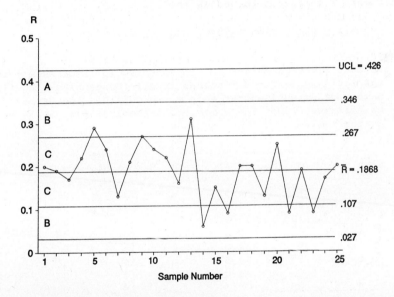

b. To determine if the process is in or out of control, we check the 6 rules:

Rule 1: One point beyond Zone A: No points are beyond Zone A.

Rule 2: Nine points in a row in Zone C or beyond: No sequence of 9 points are in Zone C (on one side of the centerline) or beyond.

Rule 3: Six points in a row steadily increasing or decreasing: No sequence of 6 points steadily increase or decrease.

Rule 4: Fourteen points in a row alternating up and down: This pattern does not exist.

Rule 5: Two out of three points in Zone A or beyond: No group of three consecutive points have two or more in Zone A or beyond.

Rule 6: Four out of five points in a row in Zone B or beyond: No sequence of 5 points has 4 or more in zone B or beyond.

The process appears to be in control. There do not appear to be any special causes of variation during the time the data were collected.

c. Since the process appears to be in control, it is appropriate to use these limits to monitor future process output.

12.25. The sample size is determined as follows:

$$n > \frac{9(1 - p_0)}{p_0} = \frac{9(1 - .08)}{.08} = 103.5 \approx 104$$

12.27 a. We must first calculate $\bar{p}$. To do this, it is necessary to find the total number of defectives in all the samples. To find the number of defectives per sample, we multiple the proportion by the sample size, 150. The number of defectives per sample are shown in the table:

Sample No.	p	No. defectives	Sample No.	p	No. defectives
1	.03	4.5	11	.07	10.5
2	.05	7.5	12	.04	6.0
3	.10	15.0	13	.06	9.0
4	.02	3.0	14	.05	7.5
5	.08	12.0	15	.07	10.5
6	.09	13.5	16	.06	9.0
7	.08	12.0	17	.07	10.5
8	.05	7.5	18	.02	3.0
9	.07	10.5	19	.05	7.5
10	.06	9.0	20	.03	4.5

Note: There cannot be a fraction of a defective. The proportions presented in the exercise have been rounded off. I have used the fractions to minimize the roundoff error.

To get the total number of defectives, sum the number of defectives for all 20 samples. The sum is 172.5. To get the total number of units sampled, multiply the sample size by the number of samples:

$$150(20) = 3000$$

$$\bar{p} = \frac{\text{Total defective in all samples}}{\text{Total units sampled}} = \frac{172.5}{3000} = .0575$$

Centerline = $\bar{p}$ = .0575

$$\text{Upper control limit} = \bar{p} + 3\sqrt{\frac{\bar{p}(1 - \bar{p})}{n}} = .0575 + 3\sqrt{\frac{.0575(.9425)}{150}}$$
$$= .1145$$

$$\text{Lower control limit} = \bar{p} - 3\sqrt{\frac{\bar{p}(1 - \bar{p})}{n}} = .0575 - 3\sqrt{\frac{.0575(.9425)}{150}}$$
$$= .0005$$

b. $$\text{Upper A-B boundary} = \bar{p} + 2\sqrt{\frac{\bar{p}(1 - \bar{p})}{n}} = .0575 + 2\sqrt{\frac{.0575(.9425)}{150}}$$
$$= .0955$$

$$\text{Lower A-B boundary} = \bar{p} - 2\sqrt{\frac{\bar{p}(1 - \bar{p})}{n}} = .0575 - 2\sqrt{\frac{.0575(.9425)}{150}}$$
$$= .0195$$

$$\text{Upper B-C boundary} = \bar{p} + \sqrt{\frac{\bar{p}(1 - \bar{p})}{n}} = .0575 + \sqrt{\frac{.0575(.9425)}{150}}$$
$$= .0765$$

$$\text{Lower B-C boundary} = \bar{p} - \sqrt{\frac{\bar{p}(1 - \bar{p})}{n}} = .0575 - \sqrt{\frac{.0575(.9425)}{150}}$$
$$= .0385$$

c. The p-chart is:

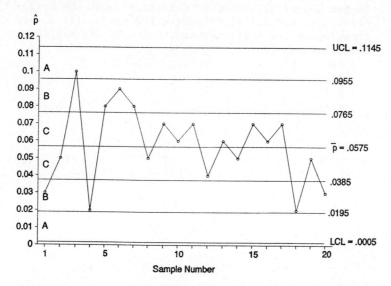

d. To determine if the process is in or out of control, we check the 6 rules:

Rule 1: One point beyond Zone A: No points are beyond Zone A.

Rule 2: Nine points in a row in Zone C or beyond: No sequence of 9 points are in Zone C (on one side of the centerline) or beyond.

Rule 3: Six points in a row steadily increasing or decreasing: No sequence of 6 points steadily increase or decrease.

Rule 4: Fourteen points in a row alternating up and down: Points 7 thru 20 alternate up and down. This indicates the process is out of control.

Rule 5: Two out of three points in Zone A or beyond: No group of three consecutive points have two or more in Zone A or beyond.

Rule 6: Four out of five points in a row in Zone B or beyond: Points 3, 5, 6, and 7 are in Zone B or beyond. This indicates the process is out of control.

Rules 4 and 6 indicate that the process is out of control.

e. Since the process is out of control, the centerline and control limits should not be used to monitor future process output. The centerline and control limits are intended to represent the behavior of the process when it is under control.

12.29 a. The sample size is determined as follows:

$$n > \frac{9(1 - p_0)}{p_0} = \frac{9(1 - .07)}{.07} = 119.6 \approx 120$$

The minimum sample size is 120.

b. To compute the proportion of defectives in each sample, divide the number of defectives by the number in the sample, 120:

$$\hat{p} = \frac{\text{No. defectives}}{\text{No. in sample}}$$

The sample proportions are listed in the table:

Sample No.	$\hat{p}$	Sample No.	$\hat{p}$
1	.092	11	.083
2	.042	12	.100
3	.033	13	.067
4	.067	14	.050
5	.083	15	.083
6	.108	16	.042
7	.075	17	.083
8	.067	18	.083
9	.083	19	.025
10	.092	20	.067

To get the total number of defectives, sum the number of defectives for all 20 samples. The sum is 171. To get the total number of units sampled, multiply the sample size by the number of samples:

$$120(20) = 2400.$$

$$\bar{p} = \frac{\text{Total defective in all samples}}{\text{Total units sampled}} = \frac{171}{2400} = .071$$

Centerline $= \bar{p} = .071$

$$\text{Upper control limit} = \bar{p} + 3\sqrt{\frac{\bar{p}(1 - \bar{p})}{n}} = .071 + 3\sqrt{\frac{.071(.929)}{120}}$$
$$= .141$$

Lower control limit $= \bar{p} - 3\sqrt{\dfrac{\bar{p}(1 - \bar{p})}{n}} = .071 - 3\sqrt{\dfrac{.071(.929)}{120}}$
$$= .001$$

Upper A–B boundary $= \bar{p} + 2\sqrt{\dfrac{\bar{p}(1 - \bar{p})}{n}} = .071 + 2\sqrt{\dfrac{.071(.929)}{120}} = .118$

Lower A–B boundary $= \bar{p} - 2\sqrt{\dfrac{\bar{p}(1 - \bar{p})}{n}} = .071 - 2\sqrt{\dfrac{.071(.929)}{120}} = .024$

Upper B–C boundary $= \bar{p} + \sqrt{\dfrac{\bar{p}(1 - \bar{p})}{n}} = .071 + \sqrt{\dfrac{.071(.929)}{120}} = .094$

Lower B–C boundary $= \bar{p} - \sqrt{\dfrac{\bar{p}(1 - \bar{p})}{n}} = .071 - \sqrt{\dfrac{.071(.929)}{120}} = .048$

The p-chart is:

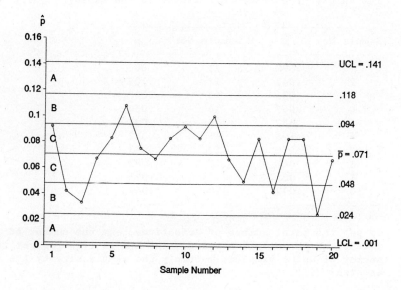

c. To determine if the process is in or out of control, we check the 6 rules:

Rule 1: One point beyond Zone A: No points are beyond Zone A.

Rule 2: Nine points in a row in Zone C or beyond: No sequence of 9 points are in Zone C (on one side of the centerline) or beyond.

Rule 3: Six points in a row steadily increasing or decreasing: No sequence of 6 points steadily increase or decrease.

Rule 4:   Fourteen points in a row alternating up and down: This
           pattern does not exist.

Rule 5:   Two out of three points in Zone A or beyond: No group of
           three consecutive points have two or more in Zone A or
           beyond.

Rule 6:   Four out of five points in a row in Zone B or beyond: No
           sequence of 5 points has 4 or more in Zone B or beyond.

The process appears to be in control.

d. Since the process is in control, it is appropriate to use the
control limits to monitor future process output.

e. No. The number of defectives recorded was per day, not per hour.
Therefore, the p-chart is not capable of signaling hour-to-hour
changes in p.

12.31 a. The sample size is determined as follows:

$$n > \frac{9(1 - p_0)}{p_0} = \frac{9(1 - .03)}{.03} = 291$$

The minimum sample size needed is 291. The sample size of 300 is
large enough.

b. To compute the proportion of defectives in each sample, divide the
number of defectives by the number in the sample, 300:

$$\hat{p} = \frac{\text{No. of defectives}}{\text{No. in sample}}$$

The sample proportions are listed in the table:

Sample No.	$\hat{p}$	Sample No.	$\hat{p}$
1	.027	11	.040
2	.020	12	.037
3	.037	13	.047
4	.050	14	.027
5	.040	15	.023
6	.037	16	.010
7	.030	17	.030
8	.020	18	.037
9	.017	19	.033
10	.013	20	.020

To get the total number of defectives, sum the number of
defectives for all 20 samples. The sum is 178. To get the total
number of units sampled, multiply the sample size by the number of
samples:

$$300(20) = 6000$$

$$\bar{p} = \frac{\text{Total defective in all samples}}{\text{Total units sampled}} = \frac{178}{6000} = .0297$$

Centerline = $\bar{p}$ = .0297

$$\text{Upper control limit} = \bar{p} + 3\sqrt{\frac{\bar{p}(1 - \bar{p})}{n}} = .0297 + 3\sqrt{\frac{.0297(.9703)}{300}}$$
$$= .0591$$

$$\text{Lower control limit} = \bar{p} - 3\sqrt{\frac{\bar{p}(1 - \bar{p})}{n}} = .0297 - 3\sqrt{\frac{.0297(.9703)}{300}}$$
$$= .0003$$

b. $$\text{Upper A-B boundary} = \bar{p} + 2\sqrt{\frac{\bar{p}(1 - \bar{p})}{n}} = .0297 + 2\sqrt{\frac{.0297(.9703)}{300}}$$
$$= .0493$$

$$\text{Lower A-B boundary} = \bar{p} - 2\sqrt{\frac{\bar{p}(1 - \bar{p})}{n}} = .0297 - 2\sqrt{\frac{.0297(.9703)}{300}}$$
$$= .0101$$

$$\text{Upper B-C boundary} = \bar{p} + \sqrt{\frac{\bar{p}(1 - \bar{p})}{n}} = .0297 + \sqrt{\frac{.0297(.9703)}{300}}$$
$$= .0395$$

$$\text{Lower B-C boundary} = \bar{p} - \sqrt{\frac{\bar{p}(1 - \bar{p})}{n}} = .0297 - \sqrt{\frac{.0297(.9703)}{300}}$$
$$= .0199$$

The p-chart is:

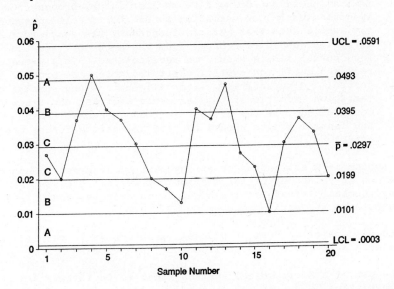

c. To determine if the process is in or out of control, we check the 6 rules:

Rule 1: One point beyond Zone A: No points are beyond Zone A.

Rule 2: Nine points in a row in Zone C or beyond: No sequence of 9 points are in Zone C (on one side of the centerline) or beyond.

Rule 3: Six points in a row steadily increasing or decreasing: Points 4 thru 10 are steadily decreasing. This indicates the process is out of control.

Rule 4: Fourteen points in a row alternating up and down: This pattern does not exist.

Rule 5: Two out of three points in Zone A or beyond: No group of three consecutive points have two or more in Zone A or beyond.

Rule 6: Four out of five points in a row in Zone B or beyond: No sequence of 5 points has 4 or more in Zone B or beyond.

Rule 3 indicates that the process is out of control. A special cause of variation appears to be present.

e. Since the process is out of control, the centerline and control
    limits should not be used to monitor future process output. The
    special cause(s) of variation should be identified and eliminated.
    Any sample data that were influenced by the special cause(s) of
    variation should be dropped from the data set, and the centerline
    and control limits should be recalculated. This process should be
    repeated until the control chart indicates the process is in
    control. Alternatively, after eliminating the special cause(s) of
    variation, additional samples could be taken and a new p-chart
    constructed. If the process is then judged to be in control, the
    new control limits should be used to monitor future process
    output.

12.33 A system is a collection or arrangement of interacting components that
       has an on-going purpose or mission. A system receives inputs from its
       environment, transforms those inputs to outputs, and delivers those
       outputs to its environment.

12.35 The five major sources of process variation are: people, machines,
       materials, methods, and environment.

12.37 The use of a hierarchical systems model to facilitate and guide the
       description, exploration, analysis, and/or understanding of
       organizations and their problems is called systems thinking. It has
       many benefits, but one of the most important is that it focuses
       attention on the processes through which things get done rather than
       on final outcomes. Thus, it facilitates the prevention of problems
       rather than after-the-fact correction of problems.

12.39 If a process is in control and remains in control, its future will be
       like its past. It is predictable in that its output will stay within
       certain limits. If a process is out of control, there is no way of
       knowing what the future pattern of output from the process may look
       like.

12.41 The upper control limit and the lower control limit are positioned so
       that when the process is in control, the probability of an individual
       value falling outside the control limits is very small. Most
       practitioners position the control limits a distance of three standard
       deviations from the centerline. If the process is in control and
       follows a normal distribution, the probability of an individual
       measurement falling outside the control limits is .0026.

12.43 The probability of observing a value of $\bar{x}$ more than 3 standard
       deviations from its mean is:

$$P(\bar{x} > \mu + 3\sigma_{\bar{x}}) + P(\bar{x} < \mu - 3\sigma_{\bar{x}}) = P(z > 3) + P(z < 3)$$
$$= .5000 - .4987 + .5000 - .4987 = .0026$$

If we want to find the number of standard deviations from the mean the control limits should be set so the probability of the chart falsely indicating the presence of a special cause of variation is .10, we must find the z score such that:

$$P(z > z_0) + P(z < -z_0) = .1000 \text{ or } P(z > z_0) = .0500.$$

Using Table IV, Appendix B, $z_0 = 1.645$. Thus the control limits should be set 1.645 standard deviations from the mean.

12.45 a. The centerline $= \bar{x} = \dfrac{\sum x}{n} = \dfrac{150.58}{20} = 7.529$

The time series plot is:

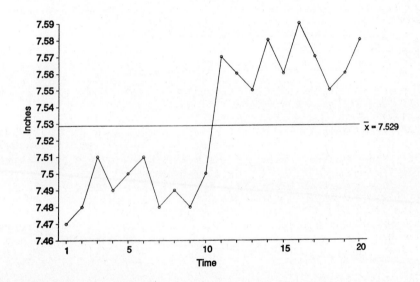

b. The variation pattern that best describes the pattern in this time series is the level shift. Points 1 through 10 all have fairly low values, while points 11 through 20 all have fairly high values.

12.47 a. In order for the $\bar{x}$-chart to be meaningful, we must assume the variation in the process is constant (i.e., stable).

For each sample, we compute $\bar{x} = \dfrac{\sum x}{n}$ and R = range = largest measurement - smallest measurement. The results are listed in the table:

Sample No.	$\bar{x}$	R	Sample No.	$\bar{x}$	R
1	32.325	11.6	13	31.050	13.3
2	30.825	12.4	14	34.400	9.6
3	30.450	7.8	15	31.350	7.3
4	34.525	10.2	16	28.150	8.6
5	31.725	9.1	17	30.950	7.6
6	33.850	10.4	18	32.225	5.6
7	32.100	10.1	19	29.050	10.0
8	28.250	6.8	20	31.400	8.7
9	32.375	8.7	21	30.350	8.9
10	30.125	6.3	22	34.175	10.5
11	32.200	7.1	23	33.275	13.0
12	29.150	9.3	24	30.950	8.9

$$\bar{x} = \frac{\bar{x}_1 + \bar{x}_2 + \ldots + \bar{x}_{24}}{n} = \frac{755.225}{24} = 31.4677$$

$$\bar{R} = \frac{R_1 + R_2 + \ldots + R_{24}}{n} = \frac{221.8}{24} = 9.242$$

Centerline = $\bar{x}$ = 31.468

From Table XIV, Appendix B, with n = 4, A_2 = .729.

Upper control limit = $\bar{x} + A_2\bar{R}$ = 31.468 + .729(9.242) = 38.205

Lower control limit = $\bar{x} - A_2\bar{R}$ = 31.468 - .729(9.242) = 24.731

Upper A-B Boundary = $\bar{x} + \frac{2}{3}(A_2\bar{R})$ = 31.468 + $\frac{2}{3}$(.729)(9.242) = 35.960

Lower A-B Boundary = $\bar{x} - \frac{2}{3}(A_2\bar{R})$ = 31.468 - $\frac{2}{3}$(.729)(9.242) = 26.976

Upper B-C Boundary = $\bar{x} + \frac{1}{3}(A_2\bar{R})$ = 31.468 + $\frac{1}{3}$(.729)(9.242) = 33.714

Lower B-C Boundary = $\bar{x} - \frac{1}{3}(A_2\bar{R})$ = 31.468 - $\frac{1}{3}$(.729)(9.242) = 29.222

The $\bar{x}$-chart is:

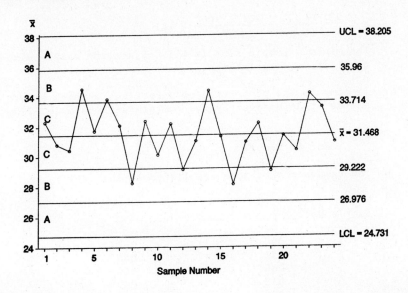

b. To determine if the process is in or out of control, we check the 6 rules:

Rule 1: One point beyond Zone A: No points are beyond Zone A.

Rule 2: Nine points in a row in Zone C or beyond: No sequence of 9 points are in Zone C (on one side of the centerline) or beyond.

Rule 3: Six points in a row steadily increasing or decreasing: No sequence of 6 points steadily increase or decrease.

Rule 4: Fourteen points in a row alternating up and down: This pattern does not exist.

Rule 5: Two out of three points in Zone A or beyond: There are no groups of three consecutive points that have two or more in Zone A or beyond.

Rule 6: Four out of five points in a row in Zone B or beyond: No sequence of 5 points has 4 or more in Zone B or beyond.

The process appears to be in control. There are no indications that special causes of variation are affecting the process.

c. Since the process appears to be in control, these limits should be used to monitor future process output.

12.49 a. The sample size is determined by the following:

$$n > \frac{9(1 - p_0)}{p_0} = \frac{9(1 - .06)}{.06} = 141$$

The minimum sample size is 141. Since the sample size of 150 was used, it is large enough.

b. To compute the proportion of defectives in each sample, divide the number of defectives by the number in the sample, 150:

$$\hat{p} = \frac{No. \ of \ defectives}{No. \ in \ sample}$$

The sample proportions are listed in the table:

Sample No.	$\hat{p}$	Sample No.	$\hat{p}$
1	.060	11	.047
2	.073	12	.040
3	.080	13	.080
4	.053	14	.067
5	.067	15	.073
6	.040	16	.047
7	.087	17	.040
8	.060	18	.080
9	.073	19	.093
10	.033	20	.067

To get the total number of defectives, sum the number of defectives for all 20 samples. The sum is 189. To get the total number of units sampled, multiply the sample size by the number of samples:

$$150(20) = 3000.$$

$$\bar{p} = \frac{Total \ defective \ in \ all \ samples}{Total \ units \ sampled} = \frac{189}{3000} = .063$$

Centerline = $\bar{p}$ = .063

$$Upper \ control \ limit = \bar{p} + 3\sqrt{\frac{\bar{p}(1 - \bar{p})}{n}} = .063 + 3\sqrt{\frac{.063(.937)}{150}}$$
$$= .123$$

$$Lower \ control \ limit = \bar{p} - 3\sqrt{\frac{\bar{p}(1 - \bar{p})}{n}} = .063 - 3\sqrt{\frac{.063(.937)}{150}}$$
$$= .003$$

$$\text{Upper A-B boundary} = \bar{p} + 2\sqrt{\frac{\bar{p}(1-\bar{p})}{n}} = .063 + 2\sqrt{\frac{.063(.937)}{150}} = .103$$

$$\text{Lower A-B boundary} = \bar{p} - 2\sqrt{\frac{\bar{p}(1-\bar{p})}{n}} = .063 - 2\sqrt{\frac{.063(.937)}{150}} = .023$$

$$\text{Upper B-C boundary} = \bar{p} + \sqrt{\frac{\bar{p}(1-\bar{p})}{n}} = .063 + \sqrt{\frac{.063(.937)}{150}} = .083$$

$$\text{Lower B-C boundary} = \bar{p} - \sqrt{\frac{\bar{p}(1-\bar{p})}{n}} = .063 - \sqrt{\frac{.063(.937)}{150}} = .043$$

The p-chart is:

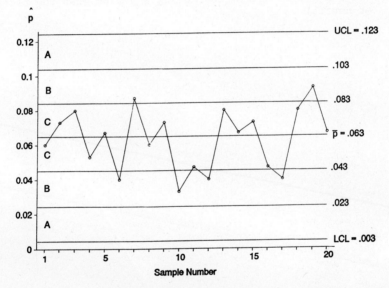

c. To determine if the process is in or out of control, we check the 6 rules:

Rule 1:   One point beyond Zone A: No points are beyond Zone A.

Rule 2:   Nine points in a row in Zone C or beyond: No sequence of 9 points are in Zone C (on one side of the centerline) or beyond.

Rule 3:   Six points in a row steadily increasing or decreasing: No sequence of 6 points steadily increase or decrease.

Rule 4:   Fourteen points in a row alternating up and down: Points 2 thru 16 alternate up and down. This indicates the process is out of control.

Rule 5: Two out of three points in Zone A or beyond: No group of three consecutive points have two or more in Zone A or beyond.

Rule 6: Four out of five points in a row in Zone B or beyond: No sequence of 5 points has 4 or more in Zone B or beyond.

Rule 4 indicates that the process is out of control. Special causes of variation appear to be present.

e. Since the process is out of control, the control limits should not be used to monitor future process output. It would not be appropriate to evaluate whether the process is in control using control limits determined during a period when the process was out of control.